DEEP (Development Experience Exchange Partnership)
for the Vision of Vietnam

Vol. 3

Establishment and Improvement of Market Economy System (EIMES) for State Capacity and Sustainable Development in Vietnam

Written by Doowon Lee, Jin Park, Ki Young Park,
Yun Jeong Choi, Ji Young Park

YONSEI UNIVERSITY PRESS

DEEP (Development Experience Exchange Partnership)
for the Vision of Vietnam
Volume 3

Establishment and Improvement of Market Economy System (EIMES) for State Capacity and Sustainable Development in Vietnam

Written by Doowon Lee, Jin Park, Ki Young Park, Yun Jeong Choi, Ji Young Park

Published and Printed in the Republic of Korea
by Yonsei University Press.
50 Yonsei-ro, Seodemun-gu, Seoul, 03722, Republic of Korea
Tel: (+82-2) 2123-3380~2 Fax: (+82-2) 2123-8673 E-mail: ysup@yonsei.ac.kr
ISBN 978-89-6850-379-5 (94300)
978-89-6850-371-9 (Set)

The National Library of Korea cataloging in Publication (CIP) data for this volume can be found at the library's e-CIP homepage(http://seoji.nl.go.kr). and in the Korean Library Information System Network(http://kolis-net.nl.go.kr).
CIP Control Number: 2019053632

Table of Contents

CHAPTER THREE:

Indentifying and Promoting Sound Economic Policies for Growth and Financial Market Development

Author : Ki Young Park

CHAPTER FOUR:

Enhancing the Industry Ecosystem in Vietnam

Author : Yun Jeong Choi

CHAPTER FIVE:
Sustainable Welfare for Labor Market: Labor Flexibility and Employment Protection

Author : Ji Young Park

List of Figures and Tables

Figures

Tables

Abbreviations

General

AHRD	Advanced Human Resource Development
DEEP	Development Experience Exchange Partnership
EIMES	Establishment and Improvement of Market Economy System
EITC	Earned Income Tax Credit
FDI	Foreign Direct Investments
GDP	Gross Domestic Product
HCI	Heavy and Chemical Industry
HCMA	Ho Chi Minh National Academy of Politics
ICOR	Incremental Capital Output Ratio
IMF	International Monetary Fund
MOF	Ministry of Finance
KDI	Korea Development Institute
KOICA	Korea International Cooperation Agency
PAR	Public Administration Reform
R&D	Research and Development
SCIC	State Capital Investment Corporation
SEDP	Socio-Economic Development Plan
SEDS	Socio-Economic Development Strategy
SMEs	Small and Medium-sized Enterprises
SOEs	State-Owned Enterprises
TFP	Total Factor Productivity
WTO	World Trade Organization

Chapter One:

Developmental Gap between Vietnam and Korea

CPI	Consumer Price Index
ESDP	Economic Social Development Plan
ESI	Export Similarity Index
MIT	Middle-Income Trap
PPP	Purchasing Power Parity

Chapter Two:

Economic System for Vietnam: Social Welfare System

BHXH-THU	Social Insurance Income
CHWs/com	Community Health Workers per Communes
CT/TW	Directive of the Central Communist Party
DOH	Department of Health
FAO	Food and Agriculture Organization
GHI	Global Hunger Index
GSO	Government Statistical Office
GoV	Government of Vietnam
HDI	Human Development Index
HI	Health Insurance
MDG	Millennium Development Goal
MOLISA	Ministry of Labor, Invalids and Social Affairs
MP	Multidimensional Poverty
NPO	Nonprofit Organization
NHIS	National Health Insurance Service
NQ-CP	Decree of the Government
QD-TTg	Decision of the Prime Minister

UI	Unemployment Insurance
SI	Social Insurance
VASS	Vietnamese Academy of Social Science
VCP	Vietnam's Communist Party
VHWs	Vietnamese Health Workers
VND	Vietnamese Dong
VSS	Vietnamese Social Security

Chapter Three:

Identifying and Promoting Sound Economic Policies for Growth and Financial Market Development

BIDV	Bank for Investment and Development of Vietnam
BOCHK	Bank of China Hong Kong
CA	Capital Account
CMT	Capital Management Technique
CML	Capital Market Liberalization
CBA	Commonwealth Bank of Australia
CPTPP	Comprehensive Progressive Agreement for Trans-Pacific Partnership
DSR	Debt Service Ratio
DTI	Debt-to-Income
FX	Foreign Exchange or Foreign Currency
FII	Foreign Indirect Investment
FTA	Free Trade Agreement
GFC	Global Financial Crisis
HASTC	Hanoi Securities Trading Center
HNX	Hanoi Stock Exchange
HOSTC	Ho Chi Minh City Securities Trading Center
HOSE	Ho Chi Minh City Stock Exchange

HCMC	Ho Chi Minh Stock Exchange
IPO	Initial Public Offering
JSCB	Joint Stock Commercial Bank
JVB	Joint Venture Bank
LTV	Loan-to-Value
NFMPAC	National Financial and Monetary Policy Advisory Council
NFSC	National Financial Supervisory Commission
NCG	Net Capital Gain
NIIP	Net International Investment Position
NPL	Non-Performing Loan
OMO	Open Market Operation
REIT	Real Estate Investment Trust
REE	Refrigeration Electrical Engineering Joint Stock Corporation
ROSCA	Rotating Savings and Credit Association
SACOM	Saigon Cable and Telecommunication Material Joint Stock Company
SBV	The State Bank of Vietnam
SIP	Share-Issue Privatization
SOCB	State-Owned Commercial Bank
SOE	State-Owned Enterprise
UPCoM	Unlisted Public Company Market
VAMC	Vietnam Asset Management Company
VBSP	Vietnam Bank for Social Policy
VBP	Vietnam Bank for the Poor

Chapter Four:

Enhancing the Industry Ecosystem in Vietnam

ALIO	All Public Information In-One
AMPI	Act on the Management of Public Institutions
ASEAN	Association of Southeast Asian Nations

BOK	Bank of Korea
CMSC	Commission on Management of State Capital in enterprises
CEO	Chief Executive Officer
CIEM	Central Institute for Economic Management
CMP	Clean Market Project
DATC	Debt Asset Trading Company
EPB	Economic Planning Board
EPC	Economic Policy Council
EPM	Export promotion meeting
e-IPSES	electronic-Integrated Public Service Evaluation System
FIPA	Foreign Investment Promotion Act
GIIs	Government Invested Institutions
IBK	Industrial Bank of Korea
IT	Information Technology
KB	Kookmin Bank
KBIZ	Korea Federation of SMEs
KCCP	Korea Commission for Corporate Partnership
KDB	Korea Development Bank
KEB	Korea Exchange Bank
KEPCO	Korea Electric Power Corporation
KFTC	Korea Fair Trade Commission
KGC	Korea Ginseng Corporation
KHIC	Korea Heavy Industry Construction Co.
KVIC	Korea Venture Investment Corporation
KODIT	Korea Credit Guarantee Fund
KOREG	Korea Federation of Credit Guarantee Foundations
KOTRA	Korea Trade-Investment Promotion Agency
KOTEC	Korea Technology Finance Corporation
KPX	Korea Power Exchange
KT	Korea Telecom
KT&G	Korea Tobacco & Ginseng Corporation
K-SURE	Korea Trade Insurance Corporation

LEs	Large Enterprises
M&A	Merger and Acquisition
MCIE	Ministry of Commerce, Industry, and Energy
MOIT	Minister of Industry and Trade
MOSF	Ministry of Strategy and Finance
MPI	Ministry of Planning and Investment
MRFTA	Monopoly Regulation and Fair Trade Act of Korea
MSS	Minister Ministry of SMEs and Startups
OECD	Organization for Economic Co-operation and Development
PIMC	Public Institutions Management Committee
POSCO	Pohang Iron and Steel
RIA	Regulatory Impact Analysis
ROA	Return on Assets
ROE	Return on Equity
SBC	Small and Medium Business Corporation
SMBA	Small and Medium Business Administration
VCA	Vietnam Competition Authority
VCC	Vietnam Competition Council

Chapter Five:

Sustainable Welfare for Labor Market: Labor Flexibility and Employment Protection

ALMP	Active Labor Market Policy
CMEs	Coordinated Market Economies
MPSIR	Master Plan for the Social Insurance Reform
TVET	Technical and Vocational Education and Training
VGCL	Vietnam General Confederation of Labor
VLFS	Vietnam Labor Force Survey

EXECUTIVE SUMMARY:

ESTABLISHMENT AND IMPROVEMENT OF MARKET ECONOMY SYSTEM FOR STATE CAPACITY AND SUSTAINABLE DEVELOPMENT IN VIETNAM

Doowon Lee

Professor, School of Economics, Yonsei University

EXECUTIVE SUMMARY:

ESTABLISHMENT AND IMPROVEMENT OF MARKET ECONOMY SYSTEM FOR STATE CAPACITY AND SUSTAINABLE DEVELOPMENT IN VIETNAM

This publication is the result of three-year long KOICA-funded joint research project by both HCMA and University Industry Foundation of Yonsei University called "DEEP (Development Experience Exchange Partnership) for the Vision of Vietnam". Professor Doowon Lee of Yonsei University served as the project leader (PL) of this three-year project along with a project manager (PM) assigned for each year's project. Dr. Kwang Woo Jun, the former Chairman of the Financial Services Commission of the Korean government also served as the Chairman of the Coordination Committee of this project. We appreciate Dr. Jun a lot for his valuable advices and considerate supervision. Also, we appreciate Dr. Nguyen Xuan Thang, President of HCMA, for his devoted cooperation and support.

As the third year part of this project, this report aims to analyze the current state of the Vietnamese economic system and compare it to the past experience of Korea. This report starts with estimating developmental time gap between the Vietnamese economy and the Korean economy, and concludes that today's Vietnam is similar to the mid-1980s Korea in terms of real income per capita and economic structure. Then, this report analyzes Vietnam and compares it to Korea in four key areas of social welfare system, financial market, industry ecosystem, and labor market. These four areas are chosen because they are the most important economic aspect with regard to economic system. In each chapter, authors try to compare the current situation of Vietnam to the past experience of Korea, and try to draw policy implications.

The research team is comprised of five Korean researchers and seventeen Vietnamese researchers. Korean researchers include Professor Doowon Lee (Yonsei University), Dr. Jin Park (President of National Assembly Futures Institute, Former Professor at KDI School of Public Policy and Management), Professor Ki Young Park (Yonsei University), Professor Yun Jeong Choi (Yonsei University), and Dr. Ji Young Park (Yonsei University). The Vietnamese research team led by team leader Nguyen Viet Thao (HCMA) and deputy team leader Hoang Van Nghia (HCMA) is comprised of both HCMA researchers and external experts. Bui Van Huyen, Nguyen Ngoc Toan, Nguyen Manh Hung, De Van Chien, Ngo Tuan Nghia, Do Tat Cuong, Ngo Huy Duc, and Nguyen Tri Tung are HCMA researchers. There are seven external experts including Phan Thi Song Thuong (Ministry of Planning and Investment), Nguyen Dinh Chuc (Vietnam Academy of Social Sciences), Nguyen Thang (Vietnam Academy of Social Sciences), Bui Duy Hung (Banking Academy of Vietnam), Nguyen Manh Hung (National Financial Supervisory Commission), Truong Thi Chi Binh (Ministry of Industry and Trade), and Nguyen Thi Quynh Giang (Ministry of Home Affairs). The research team is organized as summarized below.

This study is composed of five chapters. The first chapter tries to estimate the developmental time gap between Vietnam and Korea in terms of real income per capita and economic structure. This chapter is added to the final report of the original project for the sake of this publication. Chapter two introduces concept of economic system, and analyze social welfare system of Vietnam. Chapter three introduces financial market development of Korea including Korea's experience of financial crisis, and tries to provide policy

Table P-1 Participants of EIMES Research Team

		Korea	Vietnam
Project Leader		Prof. Doowon Lee (Yonsei University)	Prof. Dr. Nguyen Xuan Thang, member of the CPV Central Committee, member of the Prime Minister's Economic Advisory Board, President (HCMA)
EIMES Team Leader		Prof. Doowon Lee (Yonsei University)	Assoc. Prof. Dr. Nguyen Viet Thao,Vice-President (HCMA)
Research Theme	**Economic System for Vietnam: Social Welfare System**	Prof. Jin Park (KDI School of Public Policy and Management)	Assoc. Prof. Dr. Bui Van Huyen (HCMA) Dr. Nguyen Ngoc Toan (HCMA) Assoc. Prof. Dr. Nguyen Manh Hung (HCMA) Dr. Phan Thi Song Thuong (Ministry of Planning and Investment)
	Identifying and Promoting Sound Economic Policies for Growth and Financial Market Development	Prof. Ki Young Park (Yonsei University)	Dr. Le Van Chien (HCMA) Dr. Nguyen Dinh Chuc (Vietnam Academy of Social Sciences) Dr. Nguyen Thang (Vietnam Academy of Social Sciences) Dr. Bui Duy Hung (Banking Academy of Vietnam)
	Enhancing the Industry Ecosystem in Vietnam	Prof. Yun Jeong Choi (Yonsei University)	Assoc. Prof. Dr. Ngo Tuan Nghia (HCMA) Dr. Do Tat Cuong (HCMA) Dr. Nguyen Manh Hung (National Financial Supervisory Commission) Dr. Truong Thi Chi Binh (Ministry of Industry and Trade)
	Sustainable Welfare for Labor Market: Labor Flexibility and Employment Protection	Dr. Ji Young Park (Yonsei University)	Dr. Ngo Huy Duc (HCMA) Dr. Nguyen Tri Tung (HCMA) Ms. Nguyen Thi Quynh Giang (Ministry of Home Affairs)

implications for Vietnam. Chapter four also introduces evolution of Korea's competition policies and experiences of industrial policies. Chapter five analyzes labor market of Vietnam, and provides policy suggestions based on Korea's experience.

Summary of Research

Chapter 1. Developmental Gap between Vietnam and Korea

This chapter is written by Professor Doowon Lee, the project leader of three-year long project and the team leader of the third year research team. The author tries to estimate developmental time gap between Vietnam and Korea in terms of real income per capita and export structure. According to this estimation, today's Vietnamese economy is similar to the mid-1980s Korean economy in many aspects. In the mid-1980s, the Korean economy was implementing the 5th Five Year Economic and Social Development Plan (19082-1986) just like the Vietnamese economy is carrying out SEDP 2016-2020 today. There are many similarities in terms of policy targets between these two development plans. More than anything else, both economies were trying to upgrade its industrial structure and improve its technological level. After reviewing and comparing Korea's past and Vietnam's presence, this chapter provides the following policy suggestions to Vietnam. First, maintaining macroeconomic stability such as stable inflation and balanced budget is essential for any reform to succeed. In this regard, Vietnam needs to pay more attention to its budget imbalance problem. Second, sensible and comprehensive industrial policy is needed to create high value-added industries. Third, even though it is the government who sets up industrial policy, the real action has to be taken by private sector. It has to be private sector who makes real investment and explore overseas market just like Korea did in the mid-1980s. Fourth, qualified human capital is critical to achieve policy goals mentioned above. The last part of Chapter 1 discusses about MIT (middle-income trap) and the possibility of the Vietnamese economy trapped in MIT. Now that the Vietnamese economy has become a middle-income country according to the World Bank, Vietnam needs to grow continuously in order to escape MIT and join the high-income country group. In order to do this, innovative capability is needed more than anything else. Even though Vietnam is on the right track in terms of improving its human capital and research capabilities, the Vietnamese government needs to accelerate this effort.

Chapter 2. Economic System for Vietnam: Social Welfare System

This chapter is written by Dr. Jin Park. Dr. Park is currently the President of National Assembly Research Institute, and he was a former professor at the KDI School of Public Policy and Management. There are things that Korean government did well. First, Korea started focusing on the social welfare after 1980s, and it was a right timing. Second, it expands the social welfare gradually so that it can maintain fiscal balance. Third, in terms of financing, the social insurance which mandates contribution of both employees and employers has been the dominant form of social welfare before 2000. Fourth, universal and mandatory health insurance system was a good choice to avoid adverse selection. However, there were mistakes that Korea has committed. First, when it first introduced the national pension system, it did not carefully predict the future trend of aging society. To attract people's support, the government created too generous pension scheme. Second, due to many tax exemptions, 48% of workers are not paying income tax compared to OECD average of 16%. When tax is financed by only 52% of the population, 48% will consider the social welfare a free lunch. Third, there are too many subsidized in-kind service which is not considered a social welfare by the beneficiaries. Based on the Korean experiences, let us suggest the following policies for general social welfare. First, build a multi-layered and flexible social welfare system. Although the social welfare system should be flexible, its implementation should be very strict. Second, gradually expand both coverage and level of assistance, while increasing contribution rates. Social insurance should maintain self-sufficient financing without fiscal support from government's general account. As we have seen in Korea's experience, gradual expansion of social insurance is very important to maintain fiscal soundness. Third, diversify sources of the social insurance fund. The managing organization of the fund should be separated to an independent agency whose CEO should be recruited from among private sector experts. Fourth, effectively implement social welfare policies to encourage participation of the whole society. Although the supplementary pension can be open to people's voluntary choice, the basic national pension should be compulsory to all people in the long run with an exception of those who cannot afford it. Fifth, encourage people to work rather than providing unconditional benefits. In this respect, EITC (Earned Income Tax Credit) is a very useful tool to support people's work incentive. With respect to pension system, the following suggestions are made. First, the Vietnam government has a plan to postpone the retirement age from 60 to 62 for male, from 55 to 60 for female after 2021. Although it does not attract people's support, the plan should be implemented for fiscal soundness. The gender difference in retirement age and pension scheme should be abolished in the long run. Second, pension insurance regime should be built more multi-layered and flexible. The government should reduce the rate of retirement pension for people who want to receive one-time social insurance pension. Third, adjust formula of retirement pension rate in line with international standard. Fourth, expand coverage of the pension scheme. We may have to consider non-contributory pensions for elderly as Korea does. This should be, however, paid to those who are in the lower income bracket. Fifth, promoting socialization for old-age people in terms of provision of health care services and old-age assistants which are to ensure minimum standard of living them. Also, the following suggestions are made for health. First, the reform progress towards developing the benchmarks of fairness. A more standardized fee-for-service payment scheme should be introduced. Second, the reform focuses on gradually expending both coverage and the level of assistance, while lessening requirements for receiving benefits. The health insurance should fully cover serious diseases whereas impose relatively high copayment rate for less serious diseases such as cold, stomachache. Third, strengthen awareness of health insurance and health care to the people. Health insurance should be mandatory, and it should be implemented without exception. If it is open to people's choice, it will create adverse selection as we have seen in the case of U.S.A. Fourth, improving the quality and effectiveness of the health system. In order to achieve this goal, competition among public hospitals should be introduced. At the same time, medical hospitals should be expanded to overcome the current lack of labor supply in the health market. In conclusion, the social welfare system is a very important part of the economic system. In the level of the social welfare, Vietnam should gradually expand its coverage and benefits so that it can maintain the fiscal balance. Korea has respected this principle until 1990s, but speeded up too much after 2000 causing a fiscal imbalance now. Social welfare should be expanded, but at a pace that the public finance can handle.

Chapter 3. Identifying and Promoting Sound Economic Policies for Growth and Financial Market Development

In this chapter, we focus on the issues related to financial markets. Our criteria of choosing the topics are as follows: (1) it is relevant to the main challenges the Vietnamese economy faces, (2) it is not much discussed by other programs such as Vietnam 2035 and KSP (Knowledge Sharing Program), (3) South Korea has experienced similar situations. More specifically, we attempt to provide "bad" examples where South Korea should not have done or would have avoided. By examining those "bad" examples, we identify what policy options South Korea should have used in the past and make policy recommendations by combining South Korea's precedents with the current situation of Vietnamese economy.

Based on these criteria, we choose two main topics. The first topic we discuss is on capital market liberalization (CML). The second is on financial resource allocation during the transition toward more market-oriented economy.

Let us discuss on CML first. There were two major economic crises on the solid growth path of Korean economy. One is 1997 Asian financial crisis and the other is a liquidity crisis resulting from the 2008 global financial crisis (GFC). There were two huge drops in real GDP growth rate around 1997 and 2008. There exists a common cause at the heart of the two crises. It is maturity mismatch (along with currency mismatch), which took place in the process of CML. Unfortunately, South Korea has experienced the same liquidity crisis in

2008 following the experience of 1997. This time, it was brought by factors that are seemingly innocuous by themselves: outstanding performance of South Korea's shipping industry in 2000s and high demand for hedging FX risk through FX forward, twin surpluses of trade and capital accounts and allowance of capital outflows through FDI and portfolio investment in order to alleviate pressure on the appreciation of Korean won, regulation that urge to use FX forward for overseas portfolio investment and a change in regulation related to FX forward, and domestic banks' drive to increase their sizes and reliance on foreign borrowing. The combined effect of all these factors led South Korea to the other crisis in 2008.

Then, what can we learn from the experience of South Korea prior to the GFC? There are several things to learn: (1) most of all, managing currency/maturity mismatches matters, (2) consolidated prudential supervision is necessary and important, and (3) managing capital outflows is important not only in bad times but also in good times

In this regard, policy options should include at least measures of curbing volatility of capital flows, managing the structures of maturity and currency, and promoting long-term investment.

Macroprudential Measures for Capital Flows

There are several macroprudential policy options related to capital flows: leverage caps on FX derivatives, macroprudential stability levy, taxation on foreign bond investment, and so on. These policies have been proven very effective in South Korea.

Macroprudential Policy for Household Debt

It is reckoned that South Korea's household debt problem was largely originated from banks' switching to loans to households around 1997. Since then, rising housing prices and household debts are often cited as the major threat to the economy. In response, the government has implemented various macroprudential polices and South Korea is at the forefront of countries using macroprudential policy. In South Korea, both LTV (loan-to-value)/DTI (debt-to-income) regulations have put brakes on housing prices and mortgage loans and are successful in reducing systemic risks.

Making the Most Effective Use of Foreign Capital

While foreign capital is essential for economic growth of emerging economies that lack sufficient capital, it exerts both positive and negative influences on the economy as we have observed in case of South Korea. As a way to minimize the negative effects of foreign capital, promoting FDI is desirable since it is not volatile like portfolio investment and it helps accumulate domestic capital stock. To entice FDI, it is important to make favorable market conditions to potential investors.

Chapter 4. Enhancing the Industry Ecosystem in Vietnam

Vietnam has made remarkable achievements during nearly 30 years of Doi Moi and became an attractive investment destination with great potential, bringing foreign direct investment of US$ 35.88 billion in 2017. However, Vietnam 2035 pointed out Vietnam needs further improvements in productivity and efficiency of the private sector and the public sector.

The major reasons behind prevalent inefficiency are lack of competition and failure of market principle. Insufficient competition is rooted in the preferential treatments of the state-owned enterprises (SOEs), which hampered not only the competitiveness and growth of private firms, but also the efficiency of SOEs itself.

To overcome challenges and advance the industry ecosystem into the next level, fostering competition and ensuring a level-playing field is necessary since pressure from competition improves the efficiency of enterprises and makes policies work. This gives us the highest priority in the following policy suggestions.

First, the Vietnam government should strengthen the institutions and systems to support competitive neutrality and level-playing field. In fostering a level-playing field and fair competition, the active role of the Korea Fair Trade Commission (KFTC) and the supports from the government have been critical. The Vietnam government needs to make sure that every player including the government itself has full acknowledgement of competitive neutrality and by changing the culture of preferential treatment. This will pull up the motivation of players on the field to maximum for the best.

Second, to improve the competitiveness and efficiency of SOEs, either the privatization of SOEs or the internal reform of SOEs can be carried out. From the Korea's experience, the most key success factor of the SOE internal reform was the effective monitoring while providing appropriate incentives through the performance evaluation and the information public disclosure system. The key success factors in the privatization were the government's strong drive, the active role of the independent committee, and the creation of a competitive environment. Therefore, the Vietnam government should make sure that the independent authority can carry out well-prepared and detailed action plans with the full supports of the country leader and people. Moreover, incentives should be allocated by competition and performance following market principle under the transparent system. So the current performance evaluation system and information public disclosure system that exist in paper should be linked with incentives and penalties.

Third, in enhancing the international competitiveness of the private sector, Korea's industrial policy and Chaebols played a big role. The key success factors include the comprehensive export-oriented industrial policy under the strong control tower and the synchronized support of political leaders, private sectors, and people. Most importantly, it was not state-owned enterprises, but private firms that developed and upgraded the industrial competitiveness. Therefore, the Vietnam government should coordinate the industrial policy and the competition policy well, so that they should not contradict each other. Government's intervention and industry policy should be used to overcome market failure and enhance the nation's industrial competitiveness, not for some favored groups. Getting industrial policy right at the right timing is important. So the synchronization of public-private interest and collaboration should be facilitated to utilize expertise from the formation of the policy. It would also bring the active participation of the private sector in achieving the nation's goal. But, most of all, detailed action plans should be prepared under the strong leadership.

Chapter 5. Sustainable Welfare for Labor Market: Labor Flexibility and Employment Protection

According to a report named *Vietnam 2035: Toward Prosperity, Creativity, Equity, and Democracy,* the concept of *labor flexibility* can show us a future vision and strategy to Vietnam's sustainable prosperity. To increase labor market flexibility and to achieve long-term growth, rationalization of existing regulations is needed; a gradual expansion of social insurance coverage, an enhancement of labor market efficiency and labor welfare with active labor market policy, and an accurate examination of the actual influences of government's intervention on labor environment and taxation.

The characteristics of the labor market structure in Vietnam can be pointed out as follows. First, there is a vacancy of the middle management in Vietnamese employment structure with the overwhelming number of unskilled workers. Second, its level of employment protection in the public sector is already strong, while there is still a need to widen social insurance coverage. Third, the government tries to promote the loans from the National Fund for encouraging employment. Fourth, labor flexibility is not well guaranteed in some areas; a lack of a range of skills among companies, the dissatisfaction of merit system in recruitment and promotion system. Above all, however, the most severe problem in Vietnam's labor market is related to the enormous size of its underground economy.

In Korea, whenever the regime changes, the government's labor relations policy has changed and the policy consistency has not been maintained, which hinders the development of industrial relations. In the process of seeking a model for the Korean version of the flexicurity model, however, the evolution of the tripartite structure from the current 'Flexibility-Safety-ALMP (active labor market policy)' to the future 'labor relations-welfare-employment.'

Based on the Korean experience, the following policy recommendations can be made. There is a need for an effective tripartite commission between the government, labor, and management to improve the labor relations policies necessary for crystalizing the legal system based on the Labor Standards Act, the Labor Union Act, the Labor Disputes Adjustment Act, and Labor Relations Commission Law. Dialogues in a trilateral consultation plays an important role in promoting socially responsible business and labor practices.

Improve the re-training policies such as the obligation of in-house vocational training. It is necessary to change from the manpower supply policy that supports economic growth to the employment policy to promote disparity in supply and demand and job creation.

Labor policy should take into account various factors such as economic growth, price stability, dispelling social unrest, and power relations between labor and management. Labor policy has been changed and influenced by economic conditions, political situation, and terrain of labor relations by economic growth stage. These influencing factors should be considered in policy cooperation between ministries.

An underground economy does not pay taxes and leads to a decrease in tax revenue. It also increases the burden on the public and deteriorates income distribution. In terms of securing welfare resources, improving tax equality, and countering corruption, legalization of the underground economy is a necessary policy task.

In order to legalize the underground economy, it is necessary to prepare tailored countermeasures appropriate to domestic circumstances. Institutional incentives for securing tax revenue while minimizing the tax resistance of small scale self-employed persons and side effects towards people on low incomes.

CHAPTER ONE:

DEVELOPMENTAL GAP BETWEEN VIETNAM AND KOREA

Doowon Lee
Professor, School of Economics, Yonsei University

CHAPTER ONE:

Developmental Gap between Vietnam and Korea

I. Introduction

Since Vietnam has initiated the Doi Moi reform in 1986, the Vietnamese economy has achieved remarkable growth and structural changes despite the initial difficulties. According to Lee (2000, in Korean), the Vietnamese economy has implemented three major reforms of 'price liberalization', 'privatization', and 'trade liberalization' successfully. In particular, the pace of the Vietnamese economic reform was faster than the Chinese way of gradual reform. Thanks to these successful reform and growth, Vietnam has joined the lower middle-income country group in 2009 according to the World Bank classification[1].

In the process of rapid economic growth, the Vietnamese economy has followed the development path of the other East Asian economies which were industrialized earlier than Vietnam. According to the flying geese hypothesis of Akamatsu (1962), developing countries in Asia is supposed to go through several development stages as Japan had experienced in the 20th century. Also, Fei, Ranis, and Ohkawa (1985) has summarized these development stages into four distinctive stages, and compared Japan, Taiwan, and Korea according to time period each country entered into each stage. As countries enter into a certain stage at different time, there exists a certain time gap between countries

1 Refer to https://datahelpdesk.worldbank.org/knowledgebase/articles/378834-how-does-the-world-bank-classify-countries.

in terms of economic development. For example, the Korean economy in the 1960s had faced similar policy challenges as the Japanese economy had experienced in the early 20th century. Both economies tried to promote export industries, and adopted similar policies even though there existed almost half a century time gap. When there exists a certain time gap between two countries, backward country can learn from the experience of advanced country and avoid trial and error. This learning experience can enable the backward country to catch-up rapidly with advanced countries. As World Bank (2015, pp. 31-33) emphasized, it is important for the Vietnam economy to catch-up with other successful economies. Likewise, the Vietnamese economy has been following the development path of the other East Asian economies with a certain time gap. The goal of this paper is to examine this time gap between Korea and Vietnam, and draw policy implications for the Vietnamese economy.

In measuring developmental time gap between Vietnam and Korea, this paper relies on two aspects; real income per capita and export structure. As real income per capita is the best proxy for living standard, it would be meaningful to compare real income per capita of both countries to measure time gap. Also, in terms of economic structure, this paper compares export structure of manufacturing industry of both countries. As both countries has relied on outward-oriented industrialization strategy, export has been the engine of growth for both countries. Therefore, export structure, especially manufacturing industry's export structure, would be the best variable to compare both countries' economic structure. After measuring the time gap between two economies, this paper tries to draw policy implications for the Vietnamese economy based on the past experience of the Korean economy.

This paper will also introduce MIT (middle-income-trap) argument, and its relevance to Vietnam. As the Vietnamese economy has joined the middle-income country group in 2009, it would be important for the Vietnamese economy to maintain decent growth and eventually become a high income country in the future. However, many middle-income countries failed to join the high-income country group for a long period of time. This phenomenon is called as MIT, and policy makers in Vietnam should be aware of this problem.

II. Measuring the Developmental Gap

1. Developmental Gap in Terms of Income

As we compare per capita income of two countries across time, we face two problems. One is the inflation between the past and the present, and this problem can be adjusted by measuring real GDP. The other is the price level difference across countries. That is to say, price level in a developing country can be lower than the price level in a developed country. This problem can be resolved when we apply ppp (purchasing power parity) exchange rate. Therefore, we need to compare real GDP per capita at ppp between Vietnam's recent years and Korea's past years in order to measure the time gap in terms of income. The Vietnamese income data this paper has used is 'GDP per capita at 2011 international price, ppp' obtained from IMF World Economic Outlook Database (October, 2018). Also, the Korean income data is obtained from Penn World Table (Version 9.0). Both data sources use 2011 as the base year. According to these database, the 2018 real GDP per capita at ppp of Vietnam is $6,646. This is similar to the 1984 real GDP per capita at ppp of Korea, which was $6,589. Also, the real GDP per capita of Vietnam between 2009 and 2018 follows the real GDP per capita trajectory of Korea between 1975 and 1984 as it is shown in Figure 1-1. Therefore, it can be concluded that there exists 34 years' time gap between Vietnam and Korea in terms of real income. It means that the living standard of Vietnam in 2018 would be similar to the living standard of Korea in 1984. Therefore, we can presume that Vietnam policy makers in 2018 would have similar challenges as those Korean policy makers would have faced in 1984 to improve the living standard of their people.

2. Developmental Gap in terms of Export Structure

Next, let us compare economic structures of Korea and Vietnam. In terms of economic structure, there can be many kinds of economic structures to be compared between two countries. For example, there are industrial structure, trade structure, investment structure, consumption structure, and so on. In this

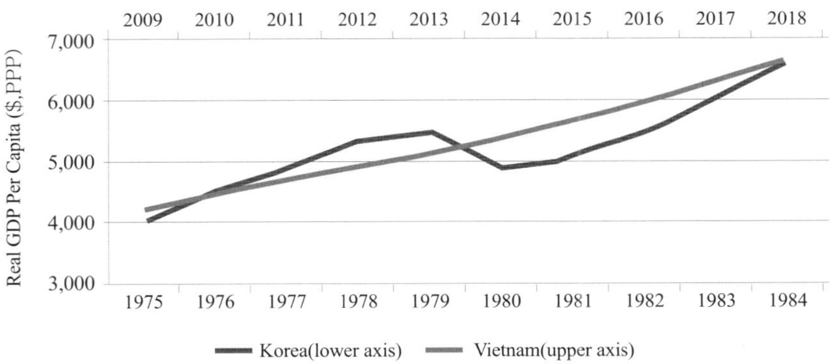

Figure 1-1 Real GDP per capita at ppp of Korea (1975-1984) and Vietnam (2009-2018)

paper, however, we will compare export structures of manufacturing sector between two countries as they can represent comparative advantage of each country. Also, we have narrowed our analysis on manufacturing sector's export because export of primary products does not reflect international competitiveness of country's industrial sector. One of the best way to compare is to measure ESI (export similarity index) between today's Vietnam and Korea's past to find out which year of Korean export structure resembles most to today's Vietnam export structure. The equation to calculate ESI is the following, and we have computed ESI between 2017 export of Vietnam and various past years' export of Korea. The export data are obtained from SITC 2-digit, Rev. 2 of UN Comtrade database. When you define ESI like the following equation, ESI will become '1' if two country's export structure is identical with each other, and it will approach to '0' if two country's export structure is different from each other. We have calculated ESI between Vietnam (2017) and Korea (1981-1993), and the result is shown in Figure 1-2 The horizontal axis represents each year of Korea's export structure, which was compared to 2017 export structure of Vietnam.

$$\textbf{ESI between Korea (1981} - \textbf{1993) and Vietnam (2017)} = \sum_{i=1}^{n} \min\{XK(i), XV(i)\}$$

Where XK(i) is the ratio of commodity i's export out of Korea's total manufacture export, and XV(i) is the ratio of commodity i's export out of Vietnam's total manufacture export

As it is shown in Figure 1-2, ESI reaches its highest level when it is calculated between Vietnam (2017) and Korea (1988). Therefore, we can conclude that there exists roughly 30 years' time gap in terms of export structure between

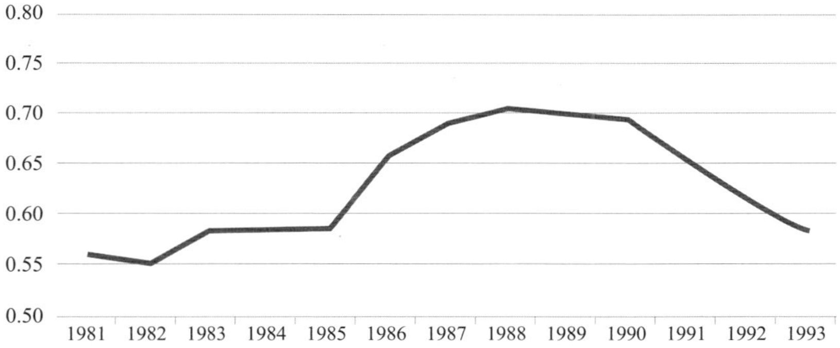

Figure 1-2 ESI between Vietnam (2017) and Korea (1981-1993)

today's Vietnam and Korea's past. This time gap is not that different from the time gap we have estimated in terms of real income. In order to examine how similar export structure is between Vietnam (2017) and Korea (1988), Table 1-1 shows top 10 export items between Vietnam (2017) and Korea (1988). As it is shown in Table 1-1, 8 items out of 10 items are overlapped between Vietnam (2017) and Korea (1988) even though the proportion each item occupies in the total export may be different from each other.

Table 1-1 Top 10 Export Items of Korea (1988) and Vietnam (2017)

Rank	Korea (1988)	Vietnam (2017)
1	Articles of apparel and clothing accessories	Telecommunications, sound recording and reproducing equipment
2	Electric machinery, apparatus and appliances, nes, and parts, nes	Articles of apparel and clothing accessories
3	Telecommunications, sound recording and reproducing equipment	Electric machinery, apparatus and appliances, nes, and parts, nes
4	Textile yarn, fabrics, made-up articles, nes, and related products	Footwear
5	Road vehicles	Office machines and automatic data processing equipment
6	Miscellaneous manufactured articles, nes	Textile yarn, fabrics, made-up articles, nes, and related products
7	Footwear	Furniture and parts thereof
8	Iron and steel	Miscellaneous manufactured articles, nes
9	Office machines and automatic data processing equipment	Professional, scientific, controlling instruments, apparatus, nes
10	Other transport equipment	Iron and steel

Even though Table 1-1 verifies how similar today's Vietnam is to Korea's past, there are some differences as well. There are two items which are not overlapped between Korea (1988) and Vietnam (2017); road vehicles and other transport equipment. It means that Korea in 1988 could export capital-intensive products such as automobiles and ships to the world when export structure of today's Vietnam is still largely dominated by labor-intensive products. In particular, today's Vietnamese export structure is heavily biased by number 1 export item of 'telecommunications, sound recording and reproducing equipment', which is accounting for 31% of the total manufacturing export in Vietnam. We believe that it is the result of Vietnam's heavy reliance on FDI in this sector.

3. Policy Implications for Vietnam

3.1. Comparison between Korea's Past and Vietnam's Today

As we have measured the developmental time gap between today's Vietnam and Korea's past both in terms of real income and export structure, we can conclude that today's Vietnamese economy resembles most to the Korean economy in the mid-1980s. Therefore, we can assume that policy makers in Vietnam today would have similar challenges as policy makers in Korea had in the mid-1980s. Let us now examine policy goals and challenges both countries have in these periods.

First, let us examine recent effort of the Vietnamese government. A few years ago, the Vietnamese government has finished the Five Year SEDP (socio-economic development plan) 2011-2015. The main targets and actual results of SEDP 2011-2015 are summarized in Table 1-2.

Table 1-2 The Results of Main Targets in SEDP 2011-2015

	Target	Actual Outcome
Average annual GDP growth rate	7%	5.9%
Ratio of real personal income in the final year compared to 2010	2-2.5 times	2.02 times
Share of high-tech products in total industrial production value	30%	18.4%
Average proportion of social investment in GDP	35%	31.7%
Ratio of trade surplus over total import-export volume till the final year	Less than 10%	2%
Increase in social labor productivity till the final year compared to 2010	29-32%	23.6%
Budget deficit in GDP in the final year	4.5%	6.1%
Public debt, Government debt, Nation's debt in GDP in the final year (respectively)	65%, 50%, 50%	62.2%, 50.3%, 43.1%
CPI in the final year	5-7%	0.6%
Unemployment rate in urban area in the final year	4%	3.29%

Source: Socialist Republic of Vietnam (2016), pp. 56-58. IMF World Economic Outlook Database 2019 April

Table 1-2 shows mixed results of success and failure in terms of achieving targets. For example, targets were under-achieved in terms of income, growth, investment, labor productivity, and budget deficit. In particular, percentage share of high-tech products was substantially lower than the target. It implies that the effort of the Vietnamese government to upgrade its industrial structure did not fully achieved under SEDP 2011-2015. However, targets in terms of debt, CPI, and unemployment were achieved. Even though some targets were not fully achieved, we can conclude that the Vietnamese economy has maintained decent growth of income with relatively stable macroeconomic variables.

Currently, Vietnam is implementing SEDP 2016-2020. According to the publication of Socialist Republic of Vietnam (2016, pp. 8-16), the top 10 primary objectives of SEDP 2016-2020 are the followings:

1. Develop a market-based socialism-oriented economy, stabilize the macroeconomy, create the environment and drive for socio-economic development.
2. Continue pushing economic restructure with new growth model; improve productivity, efficiency and competitiveness of the economy
3. Continue to push for the strategic breakthrough of building the infrastructure system in sync with modern buildings
4. Improve the quality of human resource and scientific and technological capability
5. Sustainably develop culture, society, health care base on close and harmonious connection between economic development and cultural development, strive for social advancement and equality, and improve people's living standards
6. Actively cope with climate change, prevent and cope with natural disasters, enhance the management of natural resources and environment protection
7. Focus on anti-corruption, practice saving and anti-wastefulness
8. Enhance the effectiveness of public administration and ensure the freedom and democracy of the people in socio-economic development
9. Enhance national defense and security; ensure the independence, sovereignty and territorial integrity, maintain socio-political stability and peace for the development of our nation
10. Improve the effectiveness of foreign relation activities, proactively integrate into the globe, and create a peaceful environment and favorable conditions for national development

Also, key objectives of SEDP 2016-2020 and their results as of the end of 2018 are summarized in Table 1-3.

Table 1-3 Key Objective of SEDP 2016-2020 and Its Results

	Objectives	Result (as of 2018)
Average annual GDP Growth rate	6.5-7%	7.08% (2016-2018 average: 6.7%)
GDP per capita	3,200-3,500 USD	2,551 USD
Total social invested capital comparing to GDP	31.8-33.9%	26.6% (total investment)
State budget deficit comparing to GDP	<4% in 2020	4.6% (General government budget deficit)
Public debts, Government debts, National foreign debts comparing to GDP (respectively)	<65%, <55%, <50%	63.9% (estimated), 52.5% (estimated), N/A
Unemployment in urban areas	<4%	2.2%

Source: Socialist Republic of Vietnam (2016, pp. 134-136), IMF World Economic Outlook Database 2019 April, Estimation of debts: https://e.vnexpress.net/news/business/data-speaks/vietnam-s-public-debt-rises-to-1-500-per-citizen-3793295.html

As it is shown in Table 1-3, it seems like many targets of SEDP 2016-2020 would be achieved by 2020. Especially, the growth rate and income level targets would be achieved if the current rate of economic growth is maintained until 2020. However, one of the key objectives of SEDP 2016-2020 is to improve its growth model by increasing productivity. More specifically, according to Socialist Republic of Vietnam (2016, p. 68), the TFP contribution to growth is supposed to be 30-35% of GDP growth by the end of 2020. However, it is doubtful whether this goal would be achieved on time.

Now, let us examine main policy goals and challenges of Korea in the mid-1980s. In the mid-1980s, the Korean government was implementing the 5th Five Year Economic and Social Development Plan (1982-1986). And, according to KDI (1995, in Korean, p. 408), its main objectives are summarized in the following:

1. Strengthen economic stability and building foundation for self-sustaining growth
2. Narrow technological gap with advanced countries by technology-led industrialization
3. Expand social overhead capital and improve quality of people's living standard by social development
4. Improve government function, and build credible administrative culture

According to KDI (1997, p. 272), the fundamentals of the plan were to achieve stability, efficiency, and balance. Many believe that the 5th Five Year Economic and Social Development Plan was the most successful plan ever implemented in Korea, which had achieved three main goals of stability, efficiency, and balance. During this period, the Korean economy had stabilized inflation, which was caused by the 2nd oil shock and the aggressive pursuit of HCI (heavy and chemical industry) promotion policies of the late 1970s. Also, the Korean economy had undergone painful reform of restructuring, and it had transformed its economic structure from low value-added economy into high value-added economy. Furthermore, the Korean economy could escape from the chronic problem of current account imbalance by the mid-1980s. Also, it was during this period that the Korean economy had initiated trade liberalization policies and remove/reduce trade barriers in terms of manufacturing sector's import. These policies were implemented with comprehensive and practical planning and proper allocation of necessary resources by the government. However, it would have not been successful without cooperation and effort of the private sector. The private sector, especially large conglomerates, had engaged in restructuring effort actively and voluntarily. Also, it was during this period that private sector began to lead R&D effort to improve the quality of their productions. Thanks to these efforts, the Korean economy could regain international competitiveness of shipbuilding industry, begin to export automobiles to USA, and lay the foundation of semi-conductor industry during this period.

As it was stated in KDI (2010, p. 40), it was truly a private sector-led growth, which was advocated by President Doo-hwan Chun in the mid-1980s.

3.2. Lessons from Korea's Past Experience for Vietnam

From the experiences of the Korean economy in the mid-1980s, we can draw some policy implications and lessons for the Vietnamese economy of today. First, macroeconomic stability has to be preceded before any other meaningful policy would be implemented. In order to have a sustainable macroeconomic stability, not only stable inflation but also balance in government budget account and current account has to be achieved. In this regard, it was very timely and appropriate to emphasize macroeconomic stability as the first objective of SEDP 2016-2020. Unfortunately, however, the Vietnamese government has been running chronic budget deficit problem in recent years, and this can impede macroeconomic stability in the future. Second, sensible and comprehensive industrial policy is needed to upgrade industrial structure and create high value-added industries. This aspect is emphasized in the second and third objectives of SEDP 2016-2020. Also, Chapter 4 of this research will touch upon this issue in more detail. Third, these changes have be led by private sector. Many existing literatures have already analyzed problems of SOE (state-owned enterprise) in the Vietnamese economy. As we have observed in the mid-1980s Korean economy, private sector-led growth is essential in order to have a sustainable and efficient long-term growth. Even though major policy goals were set by the government, it was private companies who implemented investment and export in Korea. This would be one of key differences between Korea and the other developing countries where major industrial policies were carried out by SOE. The importance of private sector-led growth will be analyzed in more detail in Chapter 4. Fourth, in order to carry out these reforms, qualified human capital in every area is needed. This aspect is emphasized in objective 4 of SEDP 2016-2020, and it was the main theme of the 1st year project of DEEP.

Even though the Vietnamese economy has problems of budget deficit and inefficient SOE sector, there are many areas where the Vietnamese economy has advantage over other developing countries. First, Vietnam has highly qualified human capital today, which can be as good as those Korea had in the mid-1980s. Also, in terms of labor market efficiency and financial market development, Vietnam's global ranking is even higher than that of Korea. According to WEF (World Economic Forum)'s GCR (Global Competitiveness Report) 2017-2018, Vietnam is ranked as number 57 and 71 respectively while Korea is ranked as number 73 and 74 out of 137 countries[2]. Moreover, Vietnam today has more open economic system in terms of international trade and investment than Korea had in the mid-1980s. If the Vietnamese economy could promote dynamic and competitive private sector using these advantages, it would be possible for Vietnam to follow the development path of Korea.

---

2 Refer to http://gcr.weforum.org for more details.

III. The Vietnam Economy and the MIT

Unless the Vietnamese economy overcome current hurdles, there is a danger that the Vietnamese economy will fall into the so-called 'MIT (middle-income trap)' like many other middle-income countries had experienced. Many middle-income countries in Latin America and Southeast Asia could transform their economies from low-income country to middle-income country. They could do so by exploiting 'advantage of backwardness' as mentioned by Gerschenkron (1962). However, once they joined the middle-income country group, this advantage of backwardness disappeared and they failed to become high-income country for a long time. Now that the Vietnamese economy has become a middle-income country, the main concern of the Vietnamese government should be how not to fall in MIT and eventually become a high-income country. In order to do that, they most critical factor according to Lee & Han (2014) is to improve its innovative capability just like Korea did in the mid-1980s. Lee & Han (2014) found that only a few countries such as Japan, Korea, Taiwan, Hong Kong, and Singapore could escape MIT in the 20th century, and countries such as Chile and Malaysia are showing a good chance of escaping MIT nowadays. On the other hands, countries such as Thailand, Turkey, Botswana, South Africa, Mexico, and Brazil remain as middle-income country for an extended period of time. As it is shown in Figure 1.3, these countries' real GDP per capita measured at ppp remains somewhere between 20% and 40% of that of USA for a long period of time.

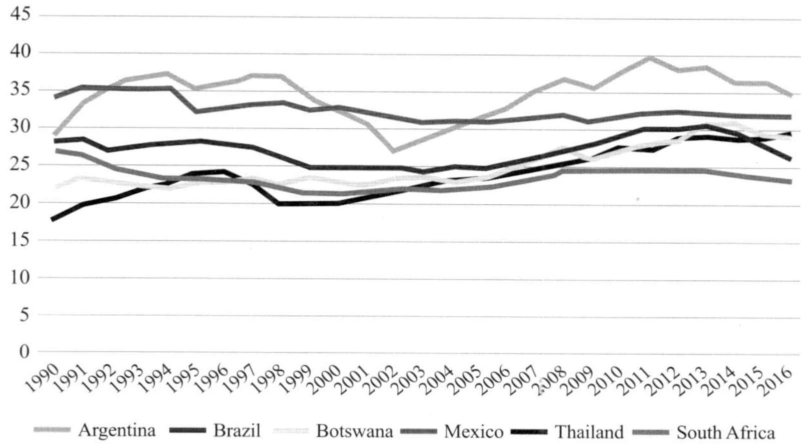

Source: World Bank (http://data.worldbank.org)

Figure 1-3 Real GDP per capita at ppp (2011 constant price) relative to that of USA

As it was emphasized in Lee & Han (2014), the most critical factor that can enable a country to escape MIT would be innovative capability. As it is shown in the following table, countries that are still in MIT rely heavily on labor and capital rather than on TFP. In Table 1.4, Korea, Turkey, Chile, Malaysia, and Thailand have experienced similar rate of annual growth during the period of 1990-2018. However, TFP estimated by the Conference Board using the growth accounting technique are substantially different across countries While Korea has relied heavily on TFP for the source of growth, contribution of TFP to economic growth in the other four countries is negligible. What is worrisome about the Vietnamese economy is that contribution of TFP to economic growth in Vietnam is negative in recent years. It implies that Vietnam could have grown even faster if only it had used its labor and capital more efficiently. Moreover, even though the Vietnamese economy has maintained relatively high growth rate recently, it would not be maintained in the near future unless it improves its TFP contribution.

Table 1-4 Average Growth Rates of GDP & TFP (1990-2018)

Country	GDP	TFP
Korea	4.9	0.9
Turkey	4.5	-0.3
Chile	4.5	-0.8
Argentine	2.8	0.7
Mexico	2.6	0.0
Malaysia	5.6	-0.2
Thailand	4.3	0.3
Vietnam	6.6	-1.8

Source: The Conference Board TED2, April 2019.

Even though the growth of TFP in Vietnam is disappointing, Vietnam still has a potential to improve it in terms of its human capital level and R&D investment. As it is shown in Table 1.5, in terms of tertiary education enrollment ratio and R&D/GDP ratio, today's Vietnam looks very similar to the early- and mid-1980s of Korea. Just like today's Vietnam, Korea's R&D/GDP ratio remained below 5% until the early 1980s. Since then, however, this ratio started to increase rapidly from the early-1980s, and it has been almost tripled within a decade. Also, it is encouraging to find that the current level of tertiary education in Vietnam is similar to that of Korea in the mid-1980s. Therefore, if Vietnam can increase its human capital level and R&D investment rapidly from now on, it would be possible for Vietnam to follow the path of Korea in the near future.

Table 1-5 Tertiary Education Enrollment Ratio and R&D/GDP Ratio in Vietnam and Korea

	Years	2000	2005	2010	2011	2013	2015	2016	2017
Vietnam	Tertiary Education Enrollment Ratio (%)	9	16	23	25	25	29	29	
	R&D/GDP (%)				0.19	0.37	0.44		0.53
Korea	Years	1980	1982	1983	1985	1987	1989	1990	1992
	Tertiary Education Enrollment Ratio (%)	12.4	19.1	23.7	30.9	34.6	35.5	36.5	39.2
	R&D/GDP (%)	0.54					1.56		1.89

Source: The World Bank, World Development Indicators, http://data.worldbank.org/indicators
R&D data on Korea comes from Korea-National Science and Technology Information Service, Ministry of Science, ICT and Future Planning (http://sts.ntis.go.kr).

However, according to Ch. 4 of the first volume of this research on AHRD (advanced human resource development), the innovation environment of Vietnam today has the following problems: fragmented innovation system, weak research capacity and weak link between R&D institutes and business, weak technology transfer from FDI, ineffective implementation and evaluation of R&D basic plans, and so on. Based on this analysis, they have made the following policy recommendations: Restructure the role and capacity of government-affiliated R&D organizations (select and concentrate strategy needed), renovate growth model based on innovation, invest more in GRI and universities R&D, strengthen collaboration among GRI, universities, and business, introduce more competition to domestic market, promote brain circulation and use strategic FDI policy, strengthen its implementation and evaluation capacity by creating a new R&D governing system including human resource department, and facilitate entrepreneurship at government research institutions and universities.

IV. Conclusion

This chapter has estimated developmental time gap between Vietnam and Korea in terms of real income per capita and export structure. According to this estimation, today's Vietnamese economy is similar to the mid-1980s Korean economy in many aspects. In the mid-1980s, the Korean economy was implementing the 5th Five Year Economic and Social Development Plan (19082-1986) just like the Vietnamese economy is carrying out SEDP 2016-2020 today. There are many similarities in terms of policy targets between these two development plans. More than anything else, both economies were trying to upgrade its industrial structure and improve its technological level. After reviewing and comparing Korea's past and Vietnam's presence, this chapter provides the following policy suggestions to Vietnam. First, maintaining macroeconomic stability such as stable inflation and balanced budget is essential for any reform to succeed. In this regard, Vietnam needs to pay more attention to its budget imbalance problem. Second, sensible and comprehensive industrial policy is needed to create high value-added industries. Third, even though it is the government who sets up industrial policy, the real action has to be taken by private sector. It has to be private sector who makes real investment and explore overseas market just like Korea did in the mid-1980s. Fourth, qualified human capital is critical to achieve policy goals mentioned above. The last part of this chapter discusses about MIT (middle-income trap) and the possibility of the Vietnamese economy trapped in MIT. Now that the Vietnamese economy has become a middle-income country according to the World Bank, Vietnam needs to grow continuously in order to escape MIT and join the high-income country group. In order to do this, innovative capability is needed more than anything else. Even though Vietnam is on the right track in terms of improving its human capital and research capabilities, the Vietnamese government needs to accelerate this effort. In particular, policy suggestions made by the first volume of this research on AHRD (advanced human resource department) are essential to improve innovation capacity of Vietnam.

CHAPTER TWO:

ECONOMIC SYSTEM FOR VIETNAM: SOCIAL WELFARE SYSTEM

Jin Park
Professor, KDI School of Public Policy and Management

CHAPTER TWO:

Economic System for Vietnam: Social Welfare System

I. Introduction

1. Background

In general, the economic system is a relation between three major economic players: The government, a firm, and an individual. The government - individual relation is about providing social welfare and services in return for tax paid by the individual. The government - firm relation is found in two markets: the real and the financial sector. The government also taxes, subsidizes and regulates the firm in the real sector. In the financial sector, the government and the firm have a middle man called a bank. The firm - individual relation is mostly realized in the labor market. Based on this framework, the 3rd year research has the following four topics: Social welfare system, Industrial policy, Financial policy, and Labor market policy. Many European countries guarantees minimum standard of living of the public from cradle to grave through universal service. On the other hand, USA emphasizes the responsibility of each individual by providing minimum social security for the needy. Determination on the scope of the government service and its optimal mix among diverse services depends on two factors: demand for universal service for equality and willingness to pay. The first issue is how much value the Vietnamese people put on the equality. The more social welfare is provided by the government in a universal way, the higher equality is guaranteed. With a more social welfare, however, Vietnamese people will have to pay a higher tax. The social welfare system determines the size of the government expenditure and the tax burden of the citizen. Therefore, the level of the social welfare system is up to Vietnam's decision. This research will focus on the scope of the social welfare, and will show how much the government should support the daily life of an individual, and how much tax the government should levy to finance such expenditure. The social welfare system in this paper includes social insurance including old-age pension, health, unemployment, and worker's compensation, and public assistance such as minimum standard of living, old-age assistance, youth assistance. This paper will answer the following questions. What is the current status of Vietnam's social welfare system? What was historical development path of Korea's social welfare system? What is the mid- and long-term vision of Vietnam in the scope of social welfare considering the stage of economic development? What are the directions of reform in Vietnam regarding the social welfare system towards the long-term goal?

To derive the optimal future development path of Vietnam's social welfare system, two pillars of investigations will be made. First, the historical overview of Korea's social welfare will be referred to in Ch. III. Second, the current status (Ch. II) and plan of Vietnam (Ch. IV) will be studied. Based on these two pillars, this paper will suggest a desirable form of social welfare system for Vietnam and the current policy reform to be taken in Ch. V.

2. Conceptual Framework

According to Gilbert & Terrell (2002), the social welfare system is composed of four components: Allocation, provision, delivery, and finance. Allocation is about who will be the beneficiaries of the welfare system, and it includes financial condition like means-test in public assistance, personal status such as handicap, behavioral condition as the job search in the case of unemployment insurance. Provision indicates the type and level of the benefits that the beneficiaries will receive. Delivery means who will provide the benefits to the beneficiaries. And finally finance is about who finances the welfare system. Based on the framework, this paper will explain the social welfare system of Korea and Vietnam, but the focus of the analysis will be the financing component.

Table 2-1 Dimension of Social Welfare

Categories		
Allocation (Entitlement)	Financial condition	universal eligibility, means-test, contribution-based (like pension), obligator of support
	Personal status	occupation, with children, ability to work, health, handicapped, veteran ...
	Behavioral condition	willingness to work
Provision (Benefit)	Type	cash, in-kind, vouchers, power, opportunity
	Level	amount of cash transfer, quality of the service
Delivery (Provider)	Horizontal	government, nonprofit organization (NPO), private sector
	Vertical	central government/NPO or local government/NPO
Finance	Sources	tax, social insurance, voluntary contribution, private spending
	Transfer	100% free, subsidized*, market-based

Source: Modified from Gilbert, N., & Terrell, P. (2002). Dimensions of social welfare policy (5thEd.) Boston: Allyn & Bacon. Note: 'Subsidized' means that the govt subsidizes the provider to maintain the price lower than the market level.

Depending on the total tax revenue ratio [(tax + social insurance compensation)/GDP] and the ratio of social expenditure to the total budget, the social welfare system in the world can be divided into five groups. First, the Nordic model has high ratio in both revenue and expenditure side as we can see in the Scandinavian countries who shows around 50% of total tax revenue ratio. Social services are very well developed in these countries. Second, the continental model as we can see in France and Germany exhibits both mid-level revenue and expenditure ratio. Their total tax revenue ratio is around 40% which is mostly financed by the social insurance contribution. Three, the Anglo-Saxon model in the USA and the UK shows relatively lower revenue and expenditure ratio around 30%. This model intends to provide a focused social welfare system for the needy rather than a universal service to the public in general. Four, East Asian model has even lower ratio in both revenue and expenditure at around 25%. Korea and Vietnam fall onto into this category. Fifth, South European model as found in Italy, Spain and Greece shows unbalanced fiscal structure in the social welfare system by enjoying higher expenditure than the continental model financed by the total tax revenue ratio of the Anglo-Saxon model. Financial crisis is unavoidable consequence of this imbalance. Vietnam is in the trend of expanding the social welfare expenditure. What will be the social welfare model of Vietnam when its per capital GDP reaches that of Korea? The decision is at the hands of the Vietnamese people, but this paper tries to suggest tentative answer in the conclusion.

II. Current Standing in Vietnam

1. Aggregate Dimension (Assoc. Prof. Dr. Bui Van Huyen)

1.1. Tax Revenue: Trend and Composition

Through quite high economic growth, tax revenue keeps rising in the last five years. Total tax revenue as of 2016 is estimated at 1,101 thousand billion VND (figure 2-1). However, tax revenue to GDP ratio has been consistently declining, from 26,4% in the period 2006-2010 to 23,4% in the period 2011-2015 and is expected to be around 21% in 2020. That is due in part to tariff cut but largely to decreasing share of corporate tax revenue (figure 2-2). Only around a third of registered companies in Vietnam paid corporate tax in the period 2010- 2015 compared to two thirds in the period 2006-2010.

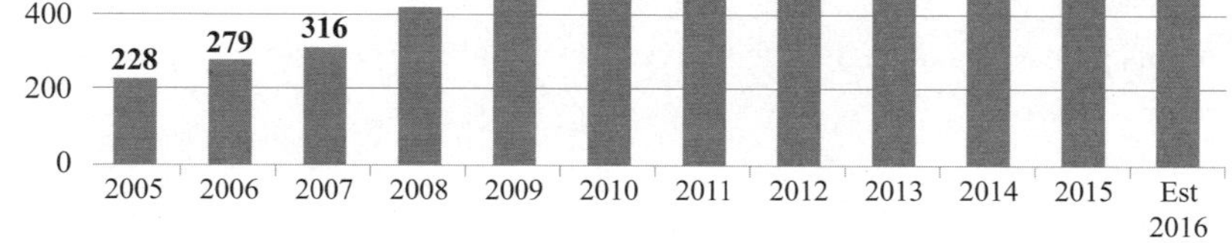

Source: Data from website of GSO of Vietnam

Figure 2-1 Vietnam's Tax Revenue from 2005 to 2016 (unit: thousand billion VND)

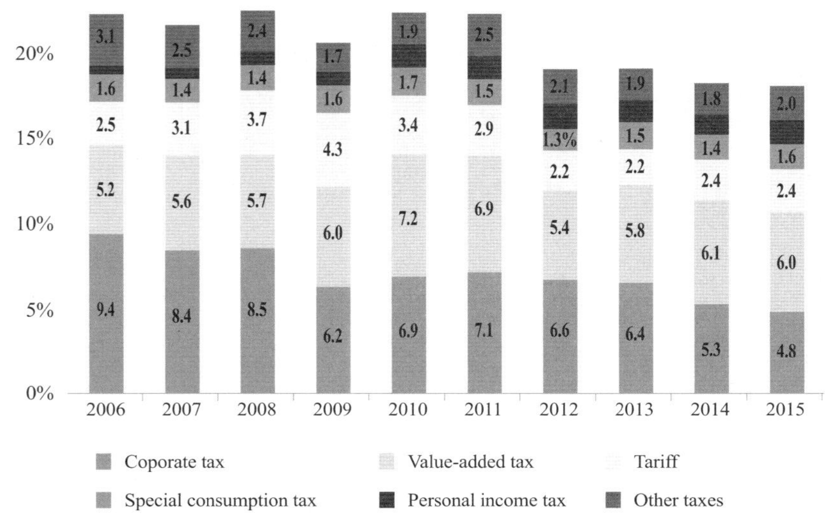

Source: World Bank and GoV(2017) "Vietnam Public Expenditure Review: Fiscal Policies towards Sustainability, Efficiency and Equity Overview, A joint review by the Government of Vietnam and the World Bank.

Figure 2-2 Declining Tax Revenue to GDP Ratio (%)

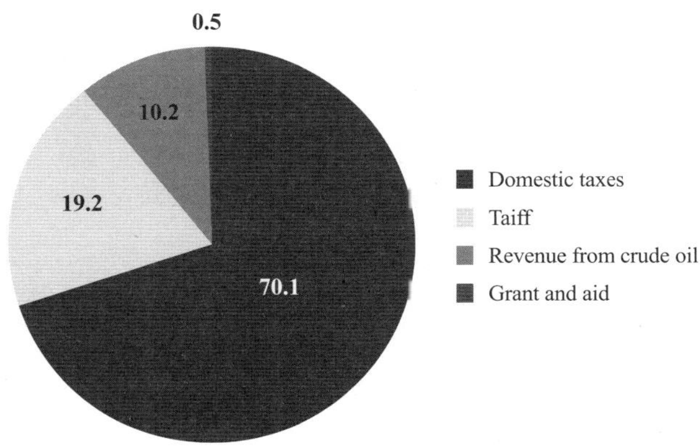

Source: GSO Website

Figure 2-3 Composition of Tax Revenue in 2015 (%)

In 2015, domestic taxes and tariff accounted for 70.1% and 19.2% of total state budget, respectively. Since 2018 onward, tariff is expected to decline sharply due to the implementation of free trade agreements.

1.2. Budget Expenditure: Trend and Composition

While revenue has been increasing consistently, the growth rate of budget expenditure has often outpaced that of revenue, leading to chronic budget deficit. The share of recurrent expenditure is rising up to 70% of total expenditure, giving smaller space for capital expenditure. Budget expenditure to GDP has been around 30%. Debt payment has been rising in the last few years and will be rising in the future.

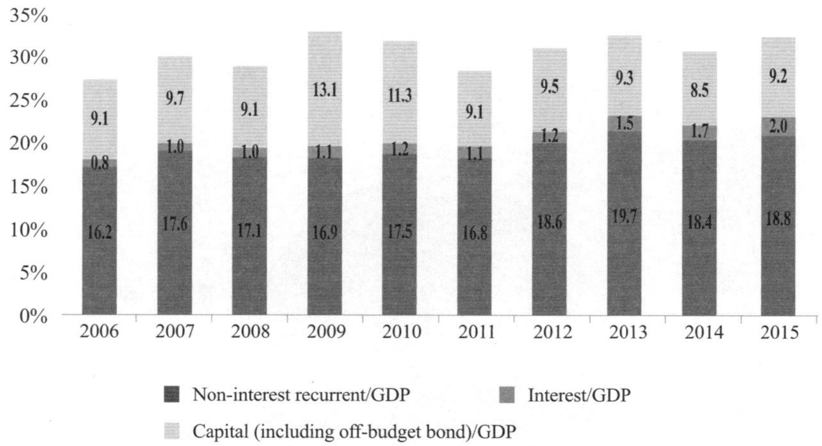

Source: GoV and the World Bank (2017)

Figure 2-4 Expenditure to GDP ratio and composition from 2006 to 2015 (%)

1.3. Social Welfare Expenditure: Trend and detailed Composition

Recently, the budget expenditure for health care, pension and social relief has been slightly increasing, accounted for 14% of GDP. Particularly, the budget expenditure to GDP ratio for health care services increased from 3.87% in 2010 to 4.51% in 2014 (figure 2-5). Total expenditures are gradually catching up with total revenue and is expected to exceed the total revenues in the coming years (Table 2-1). Vietnam has to face with the rupture risk of social insurance funds in near future if the government doesn't have significant policies to balance its revenues and expenditures.

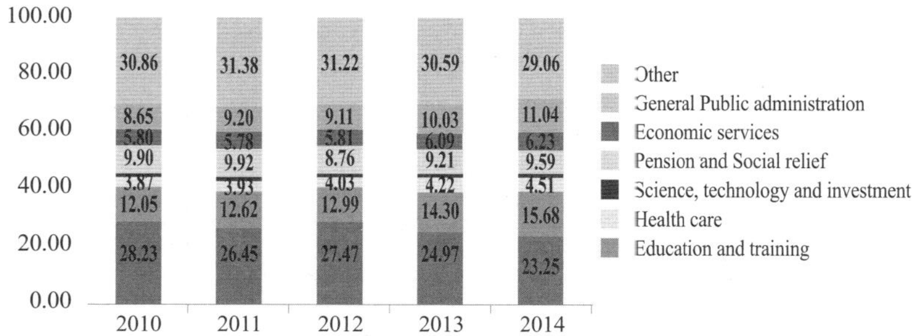

Source: GSO of Vietnam

Figure 2-5 Budget Expenditure Composition by Sectors

Table 2-2 Revenue and Expenditures of Social Insurance Fund (2009 -2015)

	2009	2010	2011	2012	2013	2014	2015
Revenue	37557	49914	62509	89992	106861	130770	145880
- Compulsory SI	37488	49740	62258	89613	106305	130059	145053
- Voluntary SI	69	174	251	379	556	711	827
Expenditure	28420	35188	44261	59097	75690	86266	101201
- Compulsory SI	28419	35163	44237	59043	75590	86106	100891
- Voluntary SI	0.67	25	24	54	100	160	310

(Unit: VND Bil)

Source: Vietnam Social Security

Vietnam is one of the countries having high current health expenditure to GDP ratio compared to other East Asian countries. In 2015, the current health expenditure accounted for 5.7% of GDP, 2.4% of which came from public sectors and the rest came from private ones. The Vietnamese government takes care of social welfare, especially for the poor, the disabled, children, and old people. However, the social welfare system in Vietnam is rather complex with overlapping policies and programs.

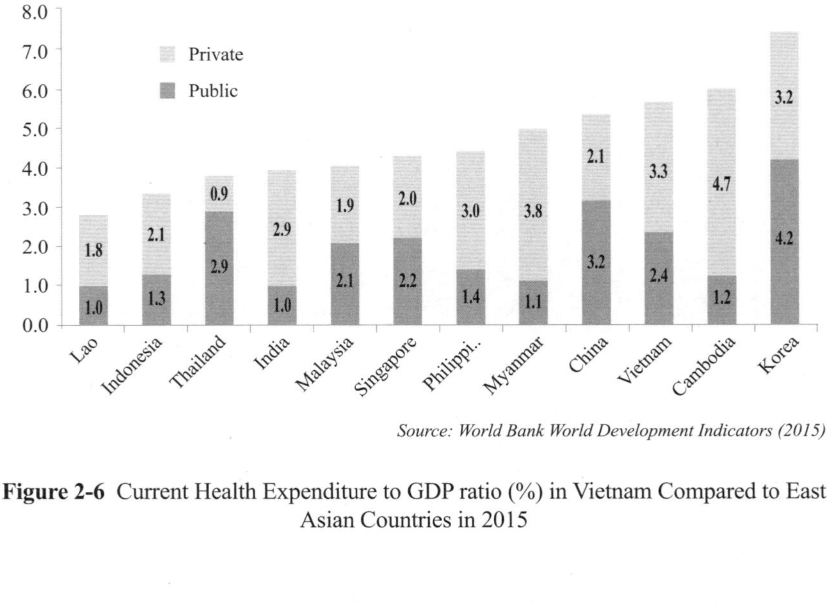

Source: World Bank World Development Indicators (2015)

Figure 2-6 Current Health Expenditure to GDP ratio (%) in Vietnam Compared to East Asian Countries in 2015

2. Institutional Dimension: Social Welfare System in Vietnam (Dr. Nguyen Ngoc Toan)

2.1. Poverty Alleviation: The Level of Poverty and Social Welfare System for the Poor

Along with economic growth, Vietnam has achieved remarkable poverty reduction. In 2016, the poverty rate is 8.238%, down about 1.67% point compared to that of 2015. Geographically, the poverty rate in the mountainous North East is about 18.24% (down 2.5% point); in North West is 31.82% (down 2.7% point), the Hong river delta is 4.06% (down 0.71 % point), Northern Central is 10.2% (down 2.3% point), Central Coast is 9.6% (down 1.8% point), Central Highlands is 15.14% (down 2% point), South East is 1.13% (down 0.1% point), and Mekong river delta is 8.46% (down 1.2% point). The poverty rate reduced from 22% in 2005 to 6.72% in 2017.The Government of Vietnam. has been consistently supporting the poor so as to fight against poverty. In 2014, Resolution 76/2014 /QH13 of the National Assembly was issued to promote the implementation of sustainable poverty reduction goals up to 2020. In addition, the government issued Resolution 80/NQ-CP dated 19th May, 2016 on directions of sustainable poverty reduction for the period 2011-2020 and the national target program on sustainable poverty reduction for the period 2012- 2016. The national target program was extended for period 20162020 by issuing Decision 1722/QĐ-TTg dated 2nd on September 2016. The targets of the program are the poor and poor districts and communes. The total fund for the 2016- 2020 period is VND 41,449 billion from central budget, VND 4,848 billion from provincial budget and VND 2100 billion from non-pubic funds. The program consists of several projects:

- Project 30A (VND 48,397 billion) to support poor districts and communes:
  · Investing in infrastructure for production and livings
  · Supporting production and diversifying livelihoods of the poor in poor districts and communes
  · Improving quality of labors from poor communes and districts to work abroad as new livelihoods to increase income and reduce poverty.
- Project 135: Supporting poor mountainous, bordering communes
  · Investing in infrastructure
  · Supporting production, diversifying livelihoods
  · Enhancing community and grass-root official capacity
- Project 3: Supporting production, diversifying livelihoods in communes not included in the Project 30A and Project 135.
- Project 4: Communication on poverty reduction and information access of the poor.
- Project 5: Enhancing government capacity and monitoring the program.

Furthermore, the government issued Decision 1557/QĐ-TTg dated 10/09/2015 on approving some indicators of implementation of MDGs for ethnic minority communities in line with SDGs after 2015". The Decision documents a number of targeted indicators for ethnic minority communities as a basis for sustainable development. Over the past few years, the Vietnamese government has conducted many policies to improve life of ethnic minority people. Vietnam has more than 14 million ethnic minority people living in 52 cities and provinces of the country. The rate of poor households in ethnic minority communities is quite high, about …With the aim of reducing this rate, the Prime Minister signed Decision 2085/QĐ-TTg dated 31st October, 2016 on approving specific policies on supporting for socio-economic development of ethnic minority and mountainous areas in the 2017-2020 period. In general, there are four groups of policies on poverty reduction for ethnic minority which are:

(1) Policies for Comprehensive poverty reduction such as Program 135, Program 30A, National target programs on poverty reduction. These policies aim to comprehensively improve livelihoods of poor households, for instance increasing access to infrastructure and services; supporting production, access commodity markets, vocational training; and facilitating development of economic, cultural and social life for people.
(2) Policies that have direct or indirect impacts on improving livelihoods of poor households at national level. These policies focus on a number of specific areas such as national target programs on clean water, health care for the poor, vocational training and education, job creation, family planning, forest plantations, and new rural development.
(3) Regional policies are targeted to support specific areas such as cultivated land and residential land settling for ethnic minority people living in the South West, the socio-economic development program for Vietnam-Laos-Cambodia in border communes, and forest protection for ethnic minority communes in the Central Highlands, etc.
(4) Policies for supporting specific poor facing special difficulties and specific ethnic minorities. In fact, supporting for the poor is blended in various national and local programs; and by different agencies and organization, including social, political organizations and NGOs. Supports come to the poor in various forms: direct subsidy, support on education, training and healthcare, support on accessing to resources such as land, credit, information, etc.

2.2. Old Age: Pension and other Old Age Assistance

According to the 2014 Social Insurance Law, social insurance is compulsory for employees with contracts of 3 months or more and for officials in the public sector. Social insurance compensation includes payments for sickness, pregnancy, work accident and diseases, pension and death gratuity. Employees with 20 years or more of participation in social insurance are entitled to pension in the following cases:

- Male who are 60 years old or above; female who are 55 years old or above.
- Male who are 55 or above; female who are 50 or above having 15 years working in heavy duty or dangerous jobs.

For old-aged people who are poor and without support from family members or those are from 80 years old or above are entitled to monthly subsidy of at least VND 270,000. Figure 2-7 illustrates the current coverage of the pension system in Vietnam. The pension schemes include contributory and non-contributory. The horizontal axis shows individual/households at different income levels who are covered by the pension system. The vertical axis represents level of income protection, which shows benefit levels to beneficiaries. Social insurance coverage in labor force has been gradually increasing. The percent of total workforce contributing to pension scheme rose up from 20% in 2012 to over 25% in 2017 (figure 2-8). As of the end of 2017, there are 13.9 million people participated in social insurance, increasing by 2.3 times compared to the year of 2007. 13.6 million of which were contributing to compulsory program and the rest (0.3 million people) were contributing to the voluntary program. However, social insurance policies have not attracted people to participate in contributory and non-contributory schemes, especially people who work informal sectors. As a result, the number of participants in social insurance is low.

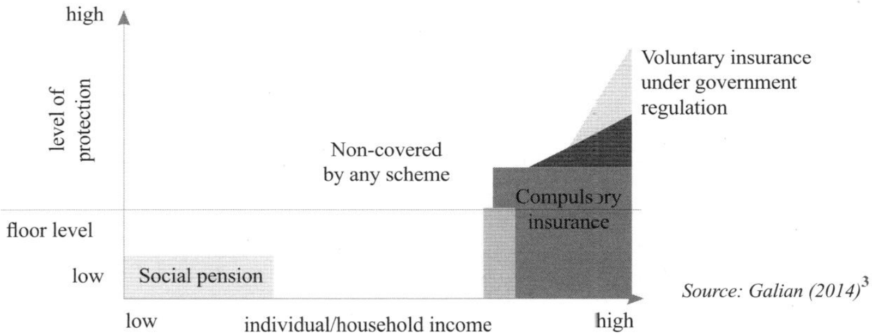

Figure 2-7 Current Coverage of the Pension System in Vietnam

3 Galian, C. (2014). 'Development of the voluntary social insurance system-International experience'. Presentation prepared for the meeting at National Assembly's Committee for Social Affairs in June, 2014.

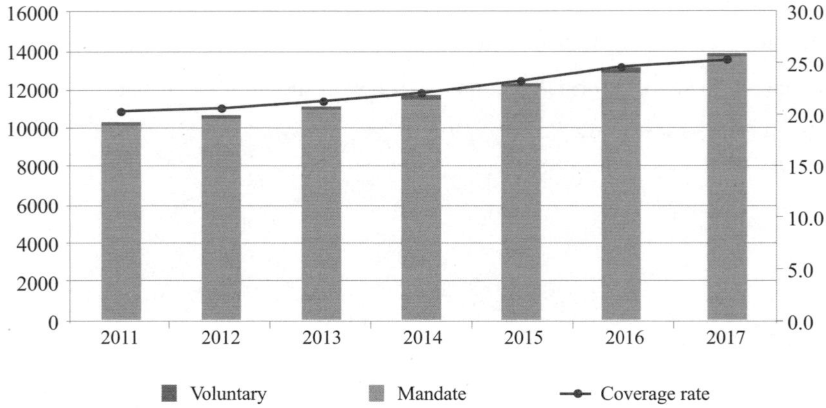

Source: Website of GSO and VSS

Figure 2-8 Social Insurance Coverage in Labor Force (# of people, %)

2.3. Health: Insurance, Health Care

In Vietnam, health insurance was originally provided in two forms: compulsory and voluntary schemes. Compulsory health insurance was provided to employees in the public sector, SOEs, and private companies. Others participate in health insurance on a voluntary basis. Since 2015 with the enforcement of law on health insurance, health insurance is compulsory for all people towards total population coverage. Households can buy health insurance as a whole. For special groups such as invalid people and poor people, the Vietnamese government provides them with health insurance using state budget. Figure 2-9 and 2-10 give an illustrative representation of the national health system in Vietnam.

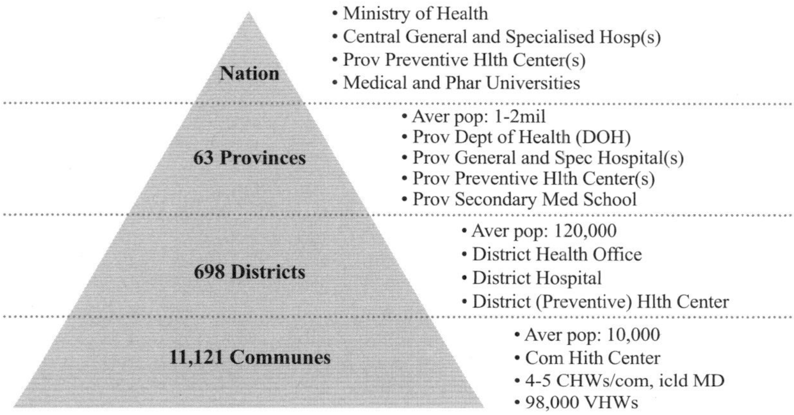

Source: Department of Planning and Finance and Health Insurance, MoH of Vietnam, Tokyo, 06 June 2016[4]

Figure 2-9 Structure of Health System in Vietnam

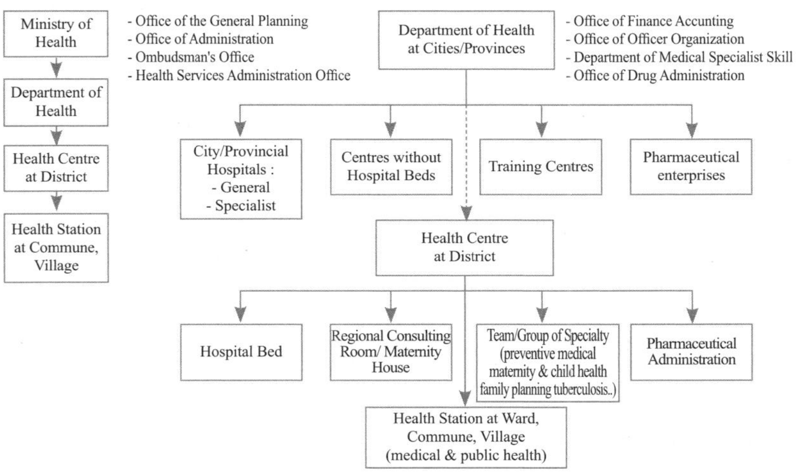

Source: https://www.khidi.or.kr/board/view?linkId=157175&menuId=MENU01144

Figure 2-10 National Health System in Vietnam

4 https://www.mof.go.jp/pri/research/seminar/fy2016/tff2016_s1_04.pdf

Health care of citizens in Vietnam has been stipulated in many policies and legal documents. The government strives for equitable coverage by improving and developing pro poor health programs. The government issued three decrees (Decree 299 in 1992, Decree 58 in 1998, and Decree 63 in 2005) to expand health insurance coverage (figure 2-11). The Law on Health Insurance in 2008 makes universal health coverage as a national goal, and revised HI Law in 2014.

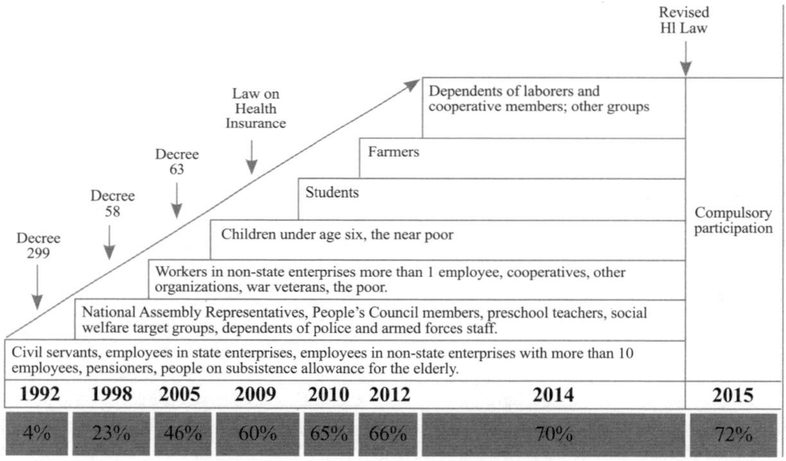

Source: Department of Planning and Finance and Health Insurance, MoH of Vietnam, Tokyo, 06 June 2016

Figure 2-11 Health Insurance Coverage Expansion Policies

The figure 2-12 reports the trend in health insurance coverage in Vietnam. As of 2016, about 82% of Vietnamese population is entitled to health insurance. Interestingly, many relatively poor er provinces have higher coverage rates than richer one, thanks to the fact that the government offers free health insurance to the poor.

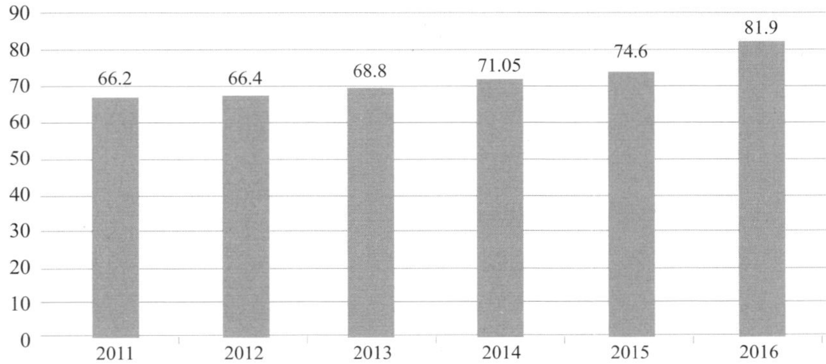

Source: VSS Reports on the implementation of social and healthcare insurance policies in 2011, 2012, 2013, 2014, 2015, 2016.

Figure 2-12 Healthcare Insurance Coverage in Vietnam (%)

2.4. Work: Unemployment Insurance and Worker's Compensation

Unemployment insurance (UI) has just been implemented in Vietnam since 2006. The Vietnamese government applies UI with the aim of providing security for the laid-off workers and facilitating the adjustment of the labor market. Employment retention in Vietnam includes unemployment allowance and employment services such as vocational training, job research, job creation, etc. The first UI legal provision is mentioned in the Social Insurance Law 2006. According to the 2006 Law, the first UI contributions are collected in January 2009 and the first UI payments are conducted in one year later. After first few years of operation, UI implementation faced two key challenges. First, the UI scheme does not coverage seasonal workers having labor contract less than 1 year and labors working for small enterprises (with less than 10 workers). Second, UI monthly allowance is relatively low compared to the base salary on which UI participants contribute. Therefore, the government has revised UI legal provisions in Employment Law endorsed in 2013, effective from 1/1/2015 (Table 2-3). The Social Insurance Law was revised in 2014. UI monthly allowance in this revised law are adjusted, equivalent to 60% of average salary of consecutive 6 months before workers are unemployed. In fact, evasions in remitting UI contribution has been remained due to the weakness of administrative procedures. Total late UI contribution payments caused by employers in 2010 remarkably increased from VND 76.47 billion to VND 273.84 billion in 2015.

Table 2-3 Social Insurance, Health Insurance and Unemployment Insurance Contributions by Law

Insurance contributions	By employers (%)	By employees (%)	Total (%)
Social insurance	18	8	26
Health insurance	3	1.5	4.5
Unemployment insurance	1	1	2
Total	22	10.5	32.5

(Unit: VND Bil) Source: Vietnam Social Security

Number of UI participants have been gradually increasing after more than 10 year history of UI in Vietnam. According to Vietnam Social Security (VSS), as of June 2017, 11.28 million people participate in unemployment insurance. In addition, total UI contribution raised from VND 3,510 billion at the first year of its implementation 2009 to VND 9,939 billion in 2015. The total UI contribution has been over the total UI payment since 2010. As a result, the amount of cumulative balance between UI contribution and payment has been increasingly (Table 2-4). The number of cases received UI allowance raised above 3.3 times from 2010 to 2015. However, the number of UI participants is quite small. UI participants accounted for about 10.3% of total labor force in

2015, increasing 3.1% point compared to that of 2010.

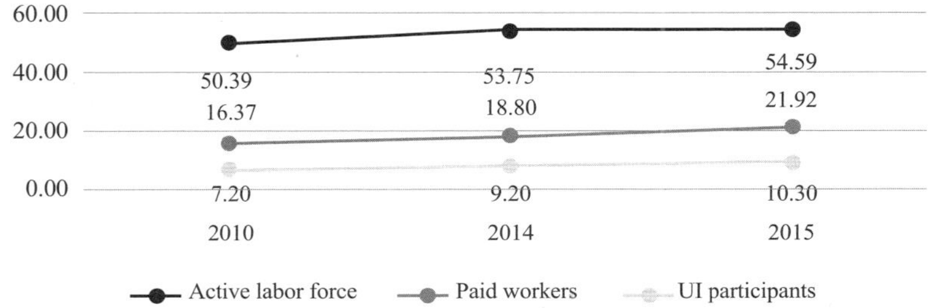

Source: Reports on UI implementation by Bureau of Employment, MOLISA

Figure 2-13 Percentage of UI Participants in Labor Force

Table 2-4 Unemployment Insurance Contribution and Payments in Vietnam

Indictors	Unit	2009	2010	2011	2012	2013	2014	2015
Total UI contribution	VND Billion	3,510.6	5,400.3	6,747.1	8,664.8	10,094.7	11,812.7	9,939.5
Total UI payments	VND Billion		145.2	1,120.7	2,428.2	3,553.9	4,528.0	4,833.3
Balance	VND Billion		5,255.1	10,881.5	17,118.1	23,658.9	30,943.6	36,049.8
Number of cases received UI allowance	Case		156,765	289,181	421,048	454,839	514,853	526,309

Source: Reports on UI implementation by Bureau of Employment, MOLISA

3. Current Issues for Vietnam's Social Welfare System

3.1. Institutional Dimension of Vietnam's Social Welfare System

There is no ideal and one-size-fit-all social welfare system. Developed countries tailored the provision and management of social welfare in line with the free-market or welfare style. Developing countries designs and develops different systems, accommodating their historical and demographic trend as well as socio-economic conditions. Social welfare reforms have been always on top of liberalization in those countries as required by the WB's and IMF's structural adjustment programs to ease financial burden on the government. Liberalization was also considered as the key welfare reform strategy in the countries transitioning from central planning to market mechanism. Long-term vision that takes into account the factors of labor market, demographic trend, financing and economic growth is crucial for the success of social welfare reforms, particularly the reforms of the social insurance system such as pension. "Best practices" of social welfare policy around the world converge on three key principles: equality and expansion of coverage; financial sustainability; and sharing. In general, the government is reluctant to increase benefit of social welfare at the expense of its coverage provision. Financial sustainability requires the contribution of the future recipients of social care whereas sharing would mean the different levels of contribution. Formal social welfare policy of Vietnam was dated back in the early 1960s in the form of social insurance that initially focused on the pension, maternity, sickness, death, and injury for the government officials. The services were provided and financed by the government. With socialist orientation, the Communist Party and the Government of Vietnam pay special attention to the development of social welfare system and welfare policy. The Political Program of VCP in 1991 set an objective of "establishing a synchronized and diverse system of social insurance and social subsidies". In 1995, for the first time Vietnam had Regulation on Social Insurance (as stipulated in Decree 12/CP) which laid out the social insurance scheme based on the contribution of employees and employers with the support from the government. This new policy which was in line with the transition to the market economy then altered the views that social benefits would come only from the government's funding. In 1997, the Politburo issued Decree 15-CT/TW on strengthening the leadership on the implementation of social insurance that highlight: *"social insurance is the major policy of the Party and State to contribute to ensuring stable livelihood of the employees, political stability, social order..."*. In 2007, the first-ever Law on Social Insurance became effective. In 2012, the Politburo issued Resolution 21-NQ/TW on strengthening the leadership on social insurance and health insurance in the 2012-2020 period that emphasizes: *"social insurance and health insurance are two important social policies, representing two main pillars of social welfare system – contributing to realizing social progress and equity, ensuring social-political stability and socio-economic development..."*

Resolution 21-NQ/TW in 2012 also set several specific targets, for example: by 2020, 50 percent of total workforce to have social insurance; 35 percent of total workforce have unemployment insurance; 80 percent of total population to have health insurance. Using with care and balance Social Insurance Fund in the long term; managing and using with efficiency and balance Health Insurance Fund. Developing modern, professional and efficient social insurance and health insurance systems...

Developing social welfare system is considered an important part of building the institutions of the market economy with socialist orientation.

Resolution 21-NQ/TW in 2008 states: *"building a diverse and flexible system of social insurance in line with the requirement of the market economy with socialist orientation"*. In 2017, Resolution 11-NQ/TW on perfecting institution of market economy with socialist orientation highlights the need to: *"provide all members of the society with the opportunities to participate equally and receive the benefits of the development process"*. Resolution 11-NQ/TW also emphasizes two key tasks: i) *"mobilizing the participation of the social strata and social communities to implement social-welfare policy; encouraging the people to voluntarily participate into social insurance scheme"; and ii) "developing a diverse, multi-layer and connected social welfare system"*.

In practice, since the beginning of Doi moi (renovation), the Vietnamese social welfare system has been gradually transforming from traditional-familial and state-control model to a mixed model. This process is occurring together with three waves of transition in the workforce: from agricultural work to [informal] non-agricultural works; from informal sector (mostly industries and services) to formal sector where workers are ensured to participate into social welfare programs (e.g. pension, maternity, sickness, health insurance…); and from low-pay formal sector to high-pay formal sector where social welfare services are higher and better provided.

Given a large proportion of Vietnamese workforce are still in the informal sector, agricultural work and family economy, many social needs are still provided by the family instead of the government. However, the government is playing a significant role in the management and provision of social welfare services (e.g. policy-making, resources distribution and service monitoring). The government provides public assistance to the poor, needy, old age and other "policy beneficiaries" (e.g. veteran, ethnic minority groups…). Due to increasing reliance on government funding, most of the non-governmental organizations choose to be in line with government social welfare policy. Private sector is nowadays playing increasingly important role.

At present, the social welfare system, especially the system of social insurance, represents major shortcomings: First, the current policies of social welfare have less efficiency and effectiveness to attract or coverage whole population. Many people are still outside the social welfare scheme, especially those in the informal sector. By 2017, only 29 percent of total workforce (approximately 14 million people) participate in social insurance. The number of workers who join voluntary social insurance program is insignificant (approximately 0.62% of total workforce). Second, the linkages of social welfare system have still been weakness. There is lack of collaboration and corporation among ministries/line ministries in implementation of social welfare policies. Some policies are less reasonable, especially for people who live in rural and remote areas. *Third,* the social welfare administration has less developed, such as less capacity of management and organization capacity to meet the rapidly changing needs of socio-economic development and an aging population. As a result, the quality of social welfare services has still remained poor, especially healthcare services.

3.2. Significant Issues of Social Welfare System in Vietnam[5]

3.2.1 Poverty Alleviation

Vietnam has met a majority of MDG targets with greatest success in the areas of poverty reduction and primary education. It has reached to a status of

5 By Nguyen Manh Hung, Nguyen Hong Nga, Tran Thi Minh Thi, Vo Minh Le, Nguyen Hong Nhung. Other issues in the social welfare will be explained in the annex.

lower-middle-income country in 2009 and set the ambitious target of becoming the upper-middle income country by the 2030-2035 period. Despite economic slowdown compared to the previous period, Vietnam maintained its position among the fastest-growing economies in East Asia with annual GDP growth at approximately 6.5-7% during the past decade. Vietnam's economic growth bounces back in 2017 while the prospect is positive in 2018. The momentum has been fueled by rising tide of FDI inflows, increasing domestic and external demand thanks to the global cyclical economic recovery. The success also underlined the first ever determination of the new leadership to build "a transparent and constructive government in service of the business" and reach the average level of ASEAN top 4 (i.e. Singapore, Thailand, Malaysia and Indonesia) in terms of business environment. Through stable economic growth, poverty continues to fall in Vietnam, albeit more slowly than in the past. Although Vietnam is still far behind the more developed ASEAN members in terms of GDP per capita, the gap has been considerably narrowed. By the end of 2016, GDP per capita of Vietnam reached \$2,185.7;[6] by the measure of 2011 PPP \$, it was \$5,955.3.[7] Compared to other countries in the process of market transition, Vietnam has been successfully in sustaining both high economic growth rate and income equality. The GINI index has dropped from 38.7 in 2012 to 37.6 in 2014.[8] Human Development Index (HDI) values of Vietnam have been gradually increasing since 1990 and now belong to group of countries with medium human development. Vietnam ranks in terms of human

---

6 The World Bank (2017), World Development Indicator, GDP per capita (current US$)https://data.worldbank.org/indicator/NY.GDP.PCAP.CD?locations=VN

7 The World Bank (2017), World Development Indicator, GDP per capita (2011 PPP $) https://data.worldbank.org/indicator/NY.GDP.PCAP.PP.KD?locations=VN

8 The World Bank, World Development Indicator 2017, the GINI index

development 115 out of 188 countries and territories in 2015.[9]

Vietnam has made substantial progress towards ensuring food security since the early 1990s with significant improvements across four dimensions of FAO food security: food availability, food accessibility, food utilization and food stability. These achievements are thanks to rapid economic growth, a significant increase in agricultural productivity and output, and strong growth in agricultural incomes. The prevalence of undernourishment has also followed a decline trend since 1992. The Global Hunger Index (GHI) scores of Vietnam decreased by 65% during period 1992-2016 and listed in the "moderate" range.

The expansion of the middle class, especially those at the lower rung, in Vietnam is noticeable.[10] The proportion of the lower middle class (with the income from $4 to $10 per day in 2005 PPP) increased from 28.4% in 2004 to 47.8% in 2012.[11] Including the floating class ($2 - $4 per day in 2005 PPP) or those who have income above $3.1 per day in 2011 PPP, the size of the lower middle class is significant (88% in 2013/2014). The emerging middle class is a positive sign in the development course. It is not only the drive of the economic growth due to their large consumption but also a force for changes toward a political system that promotes fair competition, accountability in the government and are less vulnerable toward patronage networks.[12] However, much attention needs to be paid to the near poor segment of the population

---

9 UNDP (2017), Human Development Indicator (data released on 21/03/2017), http://hdr.undp.org/en/countries/profiles/

10 the middle class can comprise: 1) the floating class (US$2 - US$4) comprises no longer poor but still vulnerable households; 2) the lower middle-class (US$4-US$10); 3) the upper middle-class (US$10-US$20); and 4) the higher middle-class (US$20-US$100) [Riana Razafimandimby Andrianjaka (2017). Middle Class Composition and Growth in Middle-Income Countries, No. 753 June 2017, Asian Development Bank Institute]

11 Vietnam Academy of Social Science (2016), Policy Brief December 2016, Hanoi

12 Birdsall, Nancy. 2016."Middle-class Heroes: the Best Guarantee of Good Governance."Foreign Affairs, March/April 2016 Issue.

who still have low income level and are deprived of education, health and other aspects of living conditions, but no longer receive the government's benefits.

In terms of multidimensional poverty (MP), which complements monetary measures by considering other deprivations (i.e. education, health and living standards such as cooking fuel, water, electricity, toilet, floor, and assets), considerable population of Vietnam remain poor (7.1% of the population are living in multidimensional poverty, 3.3% near poverty and 1.2% in severe poverty condition in 2013/2014).[13] However, Vietnam still performs better than the Philippines and Indonesia.

Cooking fuel and sanitation stand out among the deprivation aspects of the MP poor. Vietnam faces alarmingly high rate of child mortality, underlining the serious flaws of the child care system, especially the vaccination service. Expenditure on education and health occupies a large share of total household spending in Vietnam and it is expected to rise because of the "socialization" policy that encourages the market-based provision of educational and medical services.

A considerable population remains at significant risks of undernourishment as a result of temporary shocks (e.g. natural disasters) that alter the food prices or their income. There is no hedging measure against the increasing frequency and severity of extreme weather that pose risks of food insecurity. Changes in precipitation or rainfall patterns, either drought or flood, added significant uncertainty to the availability of freshwater for agriculture. For example, over the last two years, Vietnam has experienced severe droughts that caused serious

13 Oxford Poverty and Human Development Initiative (2017). MPI Countries Briefing 2017. [http://www.dataforall.org/dashboard/ophi/index.php/mpi/country_briefings]

water shortages for consumption and domestic use.[14] A drop in water in the Mekong River Delta levels also triggered salt intrusion that posed risks to areas of paddy rice.[15] Currently, Vietnam continues to rely on the Mekong river to enhance the livelihoods and food production of millions of people. Heavy torrential rains and tropical storms also seriously affected Vietnam in 2017. These extreme phenomena not only lead to temporary disruption in agricultural production, but also affect household incomes and prices of food in the long term. Higher food price is limiting food accessibility, especially of low-income households, depriving their child of nutrition, and is one of the main culprits to their multidimensional poverty condition. Social safety net and social protection programs should be enhanced to relieve vulnerable groups from distress and disruption of their livelihood

The current policy is stuck on the outdated concept of food security that heavily emphasizes the availability of food and quantity of the agricultural output. Vietnam's agricultural production has become famous under the notion of "rescue", meaning whenever there is an excessive of outputs, farmers will not be able to sell their products in the market because of the falling price. Vietnam's approach to food security should therefore focus on the supply management to reduce the price vulnerability and overcome the distribution barriers, especially in the food shortage areas. However, Vietnam's recent pilot policy to concentrate household farm lands with an aim to increase agricultural productivity raises concern over the issues of inadequate compensation, misuse of agricultural land for industrial purpose and job loss of agricultural workers.

---

14 In Vietnam, all supplies of rice – the main staple crop are in jeopardy. It is estimated that during the peak of drought (February – May 2016), there are 2 million people did not have access to water, 1.1 million were food insecure and more than 2 million people lost incomes due to damaged or lost livelihoods.

15 Saltwater intrusion in the Mekong delta (Vietnam) has destroyed at least 159,000 hectares of paddy rice in 2016, and a further 500,000 hectares is expected at risk.

3.2.3 Old Age Pension and Healthcare

Vietnam is in a growing process of urbanization,[16] leading to dynamic flow of rural-urban migration. Children live apart from their parents for reasons such as moving to attend schools, economic problems and work. Rural-urban migration and changing family structures lead to increasing number of the left-behind elderly in rural villages. The context places the left-behind elderly in rural villages under double burdens. They have to manage and restructure their lives to take care of themselves if living alone and/or helping migrating couples with taking care of grandchildren. Care work includes daily activities, domestic work, care and educational work in the families and social services, which are really challenges for the left-behind elderly. The challenges are more serious for the left-behind elderly in rural villages with poor public social services.

Asian traditional norms of filial piety emphasize care roles of children upward their elderly parents, responsible for providing instrumental care as well as affective and emotional support to old parents. Caregiving is often responsibility of women, who are increasingly migrating and participating in the labor market. Subsequently, there is an increasing withdrawal of family caregivers from caregiving upward their parents, especially in rural villages near big cities and industrial zones. With limit of institutional care for the elderly, care provision is often given to family and community. Community is the main care provider of emotional support to the elderly traditionally and currently as majority of people are living in the rural areas with strong community network and solidarity. In Vietnam, the government plans to use local mass organizations and other stakeholders to propose the proper

16 The share of urban population in the total population of Vietnam constitutes about 33%.

alternative of care to the elderly in communities, especially those who are living alone and/or have to take care of the grandchildren.

Although Vietnam has the young population in the working age, these countries are all facing the ageing process, which is faster than in most of more developed ASEAN countries. Vietnam is observing a decline in young dependency ratio, increase in old-aged dependency ratio and hence a gradual and faster increase in total dependency ratio. The tendency is faster in Vietnam and the country is passing through the "population golden structure".[17]

The governments provide social support to the elders via social insurance, health insurance, and social allowances. In addition, family provides care to family members as one important channel of security net. However, the level of social support is low and not effective because the costs of living and healthcare are much higher than capacity of support. For instance, the starting age to be categorized as elderly in Vietnam is now 60. but the elderly have to wait until they are 80 year old to receive this social allowance, unless they have the document saying they are from a poor household and/or have disabilities. Therefore, many elderly people in the informal sector, who have no pension, may not have the opportunity to receive the social allowance if they die by the age of 80.

Government's health expenditure as a percentage of GDP in Vietnam always remained on par with some countries at the rank of high human development for the last decade, even higher than the level of Thailand and Malaysia. Major successes are recorded in the improvement of child and mother health. During the 2002-2015 period, the infant mortality rate in Vietnam decreased

17 When the total dependency ratio of the population aged from 15-64 reaches to 50, which means every two working person will carry one non-working person, the population then enter the period of "population golden structure".

dramatically thanks to the effective implementation of the national programs on immunization for the last two decades with the assistance of the UNICEF and WHO. The combat against tuberculosis – represented by two indicators of the MDGs also proves to be extremely successful. However, the progress in reducing the HIV prevalence among the adults is slow, even with some regression mostly due to continued high infection rate among indigenous groups in the border areas. Vietnam maintains a mixed healthcare system, comprising both private and public actors and various sources of funding under the monitoring of the Ministry of Health (MOH). While the private sector has participated actively in the provision of medical service, it is far from sufficient in terms of quantity and quality. Accessibility to medical treatment is still very limited for people in the mountainous areas. High out-of-pocket expenditures remain an important concern. The coverage of health insurance is still limited.

In addition, pension benefits are less fairness between public and private sector employees because of applying different rules in calculating pensions. Pension benefits are calculated based on the average of the last ten years of wages for public sector while private sector workers based on the average of lifetime wages. In addition, coverage of the voluntary insurance has remained very low, mainly because of less attractive to new participants.

III. Korea's Social Welfare System (Prof. Jin Park, Daemyeong Kwon)

1. Aggregate Aspect

In this section, we are going to discuss various social insurance services and a public assistance program in Korea from the point of the aggregate level, especially focusing on the ratio of composition and expenditure compared to Nominal GDP. To understand this ratio is important because Vietnam can derive some lessons on how much budget they should distribute to each program in a specific period by referring to the historical development path of social welfare programs in Korea. Specific explanation on the social welfare system will be dealt with in the Institutional Aspect section.

1.1. National Basic Livelihood Security Act

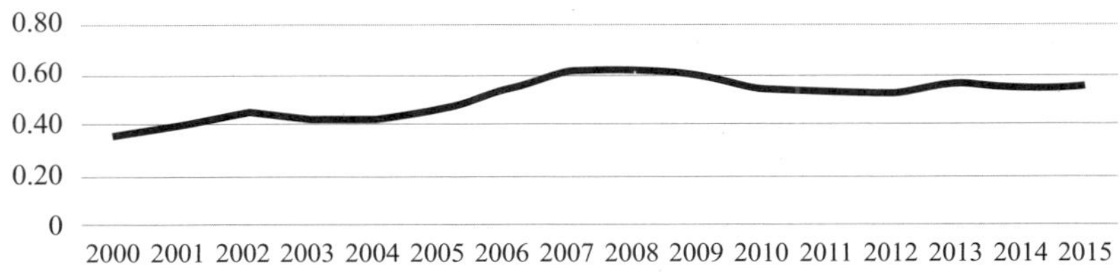

Source: The author created the figure based on the following references: The internal source of the Ministry of Health and Welfare (n.d.); e-Country Index (n.d.).

Figure 2-14 Budget of National Basic Livelihood Security System / Nominal GDP(%)

This figure shows the changing ratio of the National Basic Livelihood Security system compared to Nominal GDP. The National Basic Livelihood Security Act was implemented in 1962 as the public assistance program in Korea. Because of the limitation of data access, we cannot graph the overall trend of the National Basic Livelihood Security Act from the beginning, but as can be seen from the above, the overall trend is gradually on the rise. Especially, from 2004 to 2008, the ratio has increased abruptly. This is because the government has changed some requirements of receiving benefit such as relaxing family support obligation However, there are still many poor people living in blind spots in Korea.

1.2. National Health Insurance

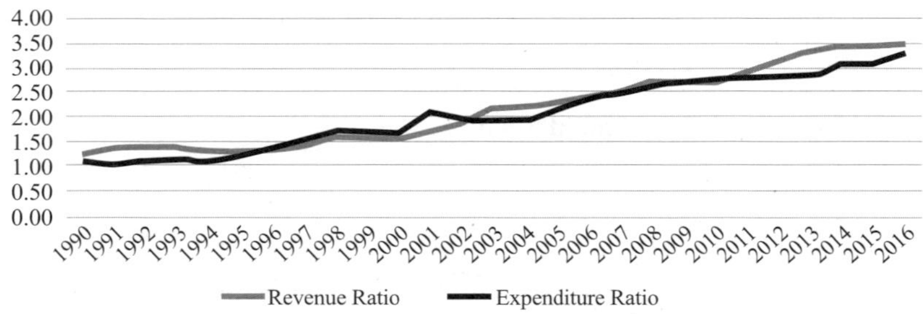

Source: The author created the figure based on the following references: Health Insurance Review Agency & National Health Insurance Corporation (2017; 2010); National Health Insurance Corporation (2001); e-Country Index (n.d.).
Note: The government's budget support is included in revenue.

Figure 2-15 Revenue and Expenditure of National Health Insurance / Nominal GDP (%)

This figure shows the changing ratio of the revenue and expenditure of national health insurance compared to Nominal GDP. The government enacted the Medical Insurance Act in 1963 to enhance public health and promote social security. As seen from the above figure, both revenue and expenditure have been continuously increasing at a similar rate except some period as the insurance develops. During this period, the government has gradually enlarged the coverage of the health insurance with increasing the level of assistance.

1.3. National Pension

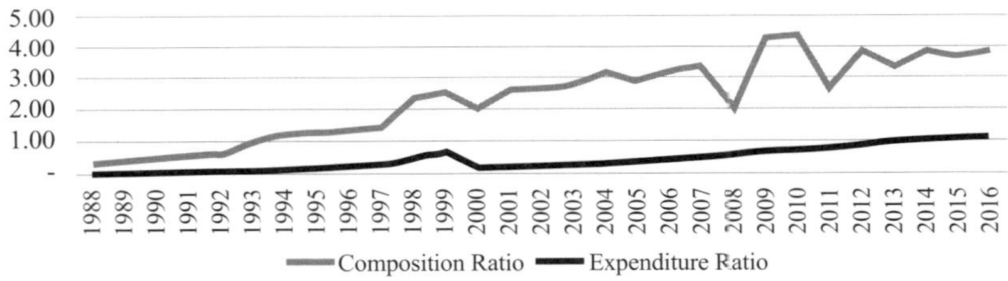

Source: The author created the figure based on the following references: The internal source of the Ministry of Health and Welfare (n.d.); e-Country Index (n.d.).
Note: The government's budget support is included in revenue, and mistaken payment is not included in expenditure.

Figure 2-16 Composition and Expenditure of National Pension / Nominal GDP (%)

This figure shows the changing ratio of the revenue and expenditure of national pension implemented in 1998. Unlike the stable trend of the expenditure ratio, the composition ratio shows a wide fluctuation. One of the reasons why this fluctuation has occurred might come from changing profits from operating national pension fund. However, what we should pay attention to is that the revenue of the national health insurance is largely dependent on the operating profits of the fund. For example, during 1997 to 2012, the operating profits has changed from the minimum -4,191 (2008) to the maximum 249,916 (2012). In other words, this implies the importance of running operating profits by the government.

Table 2-5 Operating Profit of National Pension

(unit: hundred million Korean won)

Year	1997	1998	1999	2007	2008	2009	2010	2011	2012
Operating Profits	21,873	46,356	53,240	137,190	-4,191	262,462	301,058	76,717	249,916

Source: The author created the figure based on the following reference: The internal source of National Pension Service.

1.4. Occupational Health and Safety Insurance

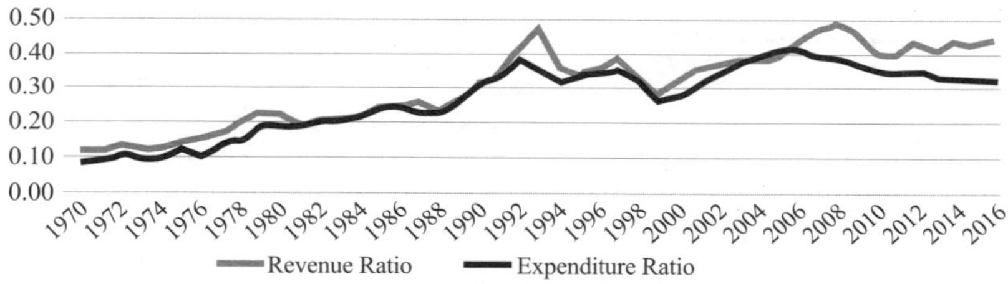

Source: The author created the figure based on the following references: The internal source of the Ministry of Employment and Labor; e-Country Index (n.d.).
Note: The government's budget support is included in revenue, and mistaken payment is not included in expenditure.

Figure 2-17 Revenue and Expenditure of Occupational Health and Safety Insurance Fund / Nominal GDP (%)

This figure shows the changing ratio of the revenue and expenditure of occupational health and safety insurance implemented in 1964 to compensate for a worker's industrial disaster rapidly and fairly. As can be seen in the figure, both lines move in the same direction with little difference. This might be because the government has gradually relieved requirements for joining occupational health and safety insurance, while increasing benefit. Song (2010) mentions that the deficit of occupational health and safety insurance was inevitable because of decreasing insurance fee since 2000.

1.5. Employment Insurance

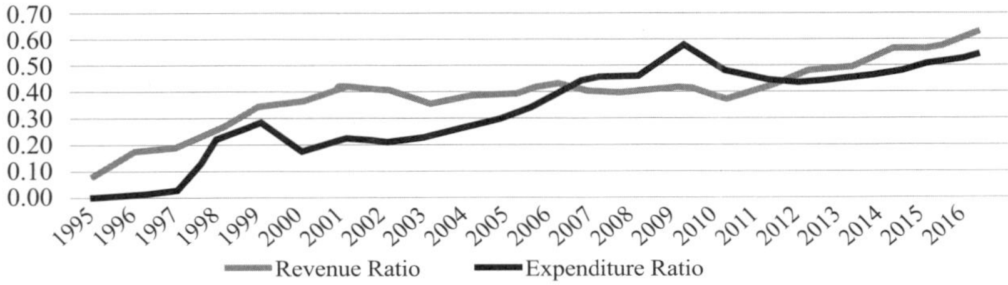

Source: The author created the figure based on the following references: The internal source of the Ministry of Employment and Labor; e-Country Index
Note: The government's budget support is included in revenue.

Figure 2-18 Revenue and Expenditure of Employment Insurance Fund / Nominal GDP (%)

This figure shows the changing ratio of the revenue and expenditure of employment insurance fund compared to Nominal GDP. Overall, both lines have been on the rise, but the expenditure ratio shows more fluctuations. Especially, the expenditure ratio has greatly risen during 1998 to 1999 and 2008 to 2009 because of the Asian financial crisis of 1997 and the 2008 global financial crisis. From this figure, we can verify that many workers were fired at that time, which caused the sudden rise of the expenditure of unemployment allowances.

2. Institutional Aspect

Following the previous section, we are going to discuss the historical progress path of the social welfare system in Korea from the institutional aspect.

2.1. National Basic Livelihood Security Act

Table 2-6 Progress of National Basic Livelihood Security Act

Year	Coverage		Level	Others
	Households	Beneficiaries		
'62	-	-	-	- Implementation of National Basic Livelihood Security Act · Partial implementation of protecting livelihood · Until the mid-1970s, it had not been implemented properly.
'64	-	-	-	- Replacing relief measures for poor people with self-help work programs
'65	-	Nearly 283,000 (actual)	Flour 250g per day	- Targeting the number of the beneficiaries of National Livelihood Protection: Nearly 3,797,000 persons (13.5% of the whole population) - Standards (income per month) for Protection had only been revised upwards for 10 years since 1965.
'68	-	-	-	- Enactment of temporary measures for guidance on self-support · Implementation of job-producing projects for the poor having work capacity · Targeting number of self-support: Nearly 230 million (480,000 households)
'75	-	Nearly 333,000 (actual)	Flour 300g per day	-
'78	-	-	-	- Implementation of Medical Care Act · Separation from National Basic Livelihood Security Act · Applying to the recipients of National Livelihood Protection · It had been implemented as one of the relief work until 1976.
'79	-	-	-	- Provision of tuition fees to middle school students whose parents are the recipients of National Livelihood Protection
'81	-	-	-	- Implementation of job-training programs - Improvement of the National Livelihood Protection programs · Replacement of flour by milled grain & Provision of expenses for side-dishes

‘82	-	-	-	- Implementation of the comprehensive plan for the poor - Complete revision of National Basic Livelihood Security Act · Inclusion of self-support protection & education protection
‘96	-	-	-	- Increasing the level of livelihood protection: 70% → 80%
‘97	-	-	-	- Final revision of National Basic Livelihood Security Act · Increasing the level of livelihood protection: 80% → 90%
‘98	-	-	-	- Increasing level of livelihood protection: 90% → 100%
‘99	-	-	-	- Replacement by National Basic Living Security Act
‘01	698,075	1,419,995	-	-
‘14	814,184	1,328,713	-	-

Sources: The author created the table based on the following references: Ministry of Health and Welfare (2017); e-Country Index (n.d.); National Archives of Korea (n.d.); National Legal Data Center (n.d.).

The National Basic Livelihood Security Act implemented in 1962 had not been implemented properly until the mid-1970s. Even though it is not easy to estimate how the scope and level of this public assistance has been changed exactly, but we can find the government has gradually carried out this program to guarantee protection for those in need while fostering the self-support of poor people. Specifically, the government replaced relief measures for the poor (unconditional benefits) with self-help work programs in 1962 to encourage people’s motivation to work. This kind of approach is very important under the condition that the government does not have enough budget to care for all the poor people, and it is one good way of maintaining fiscal balance. Since then, the Act had strengthened its scope and level of assistance in phases, and it was finally replaced by the National Basic Living Security Act. in 1999, which is more generous.

2.2. National Health Insurance

Table 2-7 Progress of National Health Insurance

Year	Coverage - Members (coverage ratio)	Level (won) - Medical benefits per claim (duration of benefits)	Others
'63	-	-	- Enactment of Medical Insurance Act
'77	-	-	- Applying to workplaces (≥500 workers)
'79	-	-	- Implementation of medical insurance to public servants and educational personnel in private school - Applying to workplaces (≥300 workers)
'80	9,226,365 (nearly 24%)	-	-
'81	-	-	- Applying to workplaces (≥100 full-time workers)
'82	-	-	- Obligatory application to workplaces (≥16 workers) - Facultative application to workplaces (≥ 5 workers)
'85	17,994,913 (nearly 44%)	-	-
'88	-	-	- Expansion of medical insurance to rural areas - Applying to workplaces (≥5 workers)
'89	-	-	- Expansion of medical insurance to urban areas (realization of national-wide medical insurance)
'90	40,180,023 (nearly 91%)	-	- Enactment of National Health Insurance Act
'95	46,005,485 (nearly 95.68%)	Nearly 15,795 (180→210 days)	-
'96	-	Nearly 19,310 (210→240 days)	-
'97	44,925,068 (nearly 96.47%)	Nearly 20,499 (240→270 days) (270→300 days)	-
'98	-	Nearly 22,689	- Launch of National Medical Insurance Management Corporation

‘99	-	Nearly 22,635	- Enactment of National Health Insurance Act
‘00	45,895,749 (nearly 96.69%)	Nearly 21,635	- Launch of National Health Insurance Corporation (full integration of medical insurance)
‘01	46,379,161 (nearly 96.86%)	Nearly 22,680	- Applying to workplaces (≤5 workers)
‘05	47,392,052	-	- Implementation of long-term care insurance for the aged
‘11	-	-	- Integration of collecting social insurance
‘15	50,490,157	-	- Application of insurance benefits to integrated nursing & caregiver services

Source: The author created the table based on the following references: Health Insurance Review Agency (2002); Health Insurance Review Agency & National Health Insurance Corporation (2016); National Health Insurance Service (n.d.).

Note: This table describes the development of the national health insurance system. / The beneficiaries of medical aid are excluded in coverage, and coverage ratio is the percentage of the beneficiaries of total population. / The amount paid by patients is excluded in the level of medical benefits

The government of Korea enacted the Medical Insurance Act in 1963 to improve public health and promote social security. As shown in the table, the government has gradually expanded the coverage of the health insurance while increasing the level of assistance. Like other social insurance programs, major sources of financing are contributions from the insured and government subsidy. When the government expanded medical insurance to people living in rural and urban areas in 1990, 91% of population was to be covered by the health insurance in 1990. To manage the insurance more efficiently and properly, the government launched the National Medical Insurance Management Corporation, and it was replaced by the National Health Insurance Corporation (NHIC) in 2000 when the medical insurance of Korea was fully integrated. The corporation is mainly in charge of imposing money to be collected, providing health insurance benefits, and running various projects for protecting the insured. In addition, the Health Insurance Review and Assessment Service (HIRA) has been evaluating the medical fee and the quality of care institute since 2000 in corporation with the NHIC.

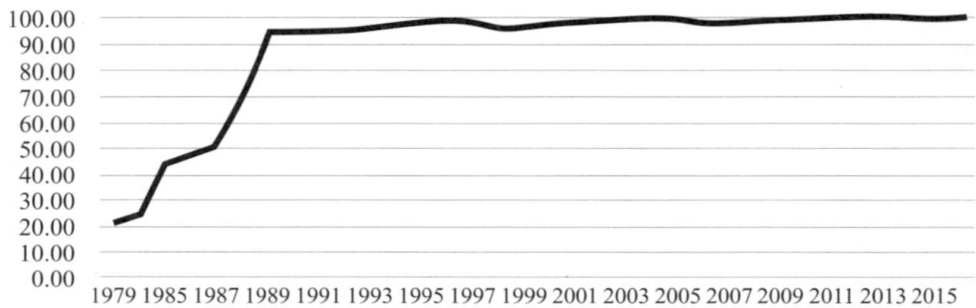

Source: The author created the table based on the following references: National Health Insurance Statistical Yearbook 1998 (National Health Insurance Corporation, 1999);National Health Insurance Statistical Yearbook 2000 (National Health Insurance Corporation, 2001); National Health Insurance Statistical Yearbook 2009 (National Health Insurance Service & Health Insurance Review and Assessment Service, 2010); National Health Insurance Statistical Yearbook 2016 (National Health Insurance Service & Health Insurance Review and Assessment Service, 2017).

Figure 2-19 Revenue and Expenditure of Employment Insurance

This figure shows the coverage ratio of the national health insurance in Korea. As seen from the figure, the coverage ratio had increased abruptly since its first implementation in 1977. Since then, the eligibility for the health insurance has been continuously relaxed. Especially, during 1988-89 when the person is self-employed in rural and urban areas came to be covered, and the employees in a firm with 5 workers or more were covered compulsorily, the coverage ratio reached 94.1%. As of 2016, almost 99% of population in Korea enjoy the national health insurance.

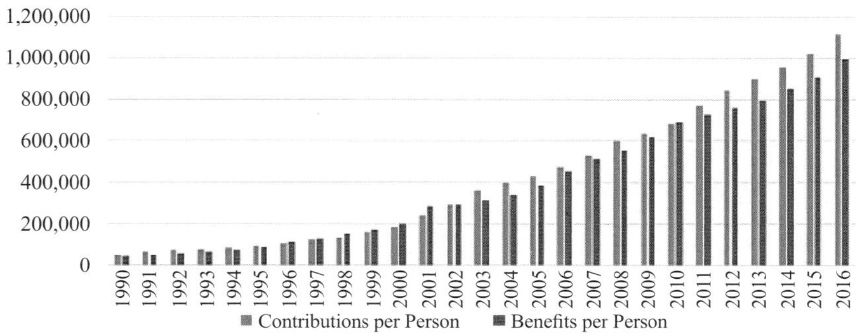

(Unit: Won)

Source: The author created the table based on the following references: National Health Insurance Statistical Yearbook 1998 (National Health Insurance Corporation, 1999); National Health Insurance Statistical Yearbook 2000 (National Health Insurance Corporation, 2001); National Health Insurance Statistical Yearbook 2009 (National Health Insurance Service & Health Insurance Review and Assessment Service, 2010); National Health Insurance Statistical Yearbook 2016 (National Health Insurance Service & Health Insurance Review and Assessment Service, 2017).

Figure 2-20 Yearly Contributions and Benefits per Covered Person

This figure shows the yearly contributions and benefits per covered person of the national health insurance in Korea. As seen from the figure, both contributions and benefits per covered person have been continuously increasing at a similar rate. This implies that, on average, a person receives health insurance benefits as much as s/he contributes to the insurance. However, the gap between contributions and benefits per person began to widen since 2011, which implies that the administration costs are increasing.

This figure shows the yearly national health insurance balance and government subsidies. Since 1995, the balance has been showing an aggravating tendency except 2013 while the subsidies have been showing a rising tendency. The budget deficit mainly comes from rapidly rising expenditure such as an increasing medical fee and expanding the scope of

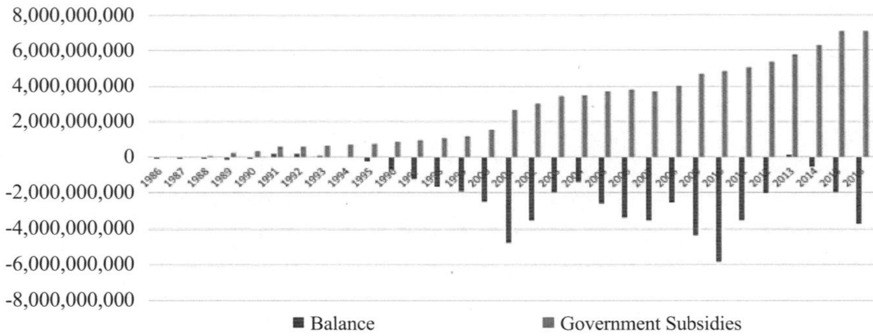

(unit: 1,000 won)

Source: The author created the table based on the following references: National Health Insurance Statistical Yearbook 1998 (National Health Insurance Corporation, 1999); National Health Insurance Statistical Yearbook 2000 (National Health Insurance Corporation, 2001); National Health Insurance Statistical Yearbook 2009 (National Health Insurance Service & Health Insurance Review and Assessment Service, 2010); National Health Insurance Statistical Yearbook 2016 (National Health Insurance Service & Health Insurance Review and Assessment Service, 2017).

Figure 2-21 Yearly Health Insurance Balance and Government Subsidies

the health insurance. In sum, this figure shows the government should also consider various ways to finance for maintaining the health insurance and to expand the level and scope of the benefits at the same time. Especially, under the current Korea government which promotes the increasing coverage of the health insurance, so-called Moon Jae-in Care, the budget deficit is expected to worsen without proper alternatives. The rising aging population might be likely to exacerbate the current situation. For this reason, huge discussions on increasing health insurance rates are currently under way in Korea.

2.3. National Pension

Table 2-8 Progress of National Pension

Year	Coverage		Level (won) - Total Amount of old-age pension per recipient	Others
	Total Members (coverage ratio)	Beneficiaries (old-age pension)		
'86	-	-	-	- Declaration of National Pension Act
'88	4,432,695	3,136	-	- Implementation of the National Pension system · Obligatory application to workplaces (≥10 full-time workers)
'89	-5-	59,438	-	-
'90	--5	257,318	-	-
'91	-5-	383,251	-	-
'92	5,021,159	493,217	-	- Obligatory application to workplaces (≥5 full-time workers)
'93	5,15-5868	584,206 (10,971)	Nearly 587,603	- Increasing contribution rates (3% → 6%) - Beginning of providing Special Old-age Pension
'94	5,4-518	847,199	Nearly 822,201	-
'95	7,257,394	878,102	Nearly 983,109	- Application to the self-employed in the rural areas, farmers, and fishermen
'96	7,42-5,700	945,848	Nearly 1,163,804	-
'97	-5	987,888	Nearly 1,318,420	-
'98	6,580,265	1,268,984	Nearly 1,517,757	- Increasing contribution rates (6% → 9%)
'99	16,261,889	292,9762	Nearly 1,706,378	- Application to the self-employed in urban areas (Implementation of national-wide pension)
'00	16,2-5-81	933,720	Nearly 1,351,267	- Operation of the tele-services system
'02	16,498,932	1,059,365 (717,488)	Nearly 1,748,782	- Construction of the connecting information system for social insurance services

'03	17,181,778	1,177,378 (819,800)	Nearly 1,870,382	- Obligatory application to workplaces (≤5 full-time workers) · Gradual expansion of application (all workplaces shall be covered from 2006)
'04	17,070,217	1,541,630 (1,156,098)	Nearly 1,719,102	- Application to workplaces which are the members of health & unemployment insurance services (≤5 full-time workers)
'06	17,739,939	1,995,984	Nearly 2,044,716	- Application to other workplaces (≤5 full-time workers)
'08	18,335,409	2,375,627	-	- Beginning of paying full old-age pension (terms of subscription ≥20)
'14	-	-	-	- Operation of the basic pension program
'16	21,832,524 (nearly 43%)	1,146,971 (3,412,350)	-	- Ratio of old-age pension: 82.3%

Source: The author created the table based on the following references: National Pension Corporation (2017; 2008; 1999).

Note: This table describes the development of the national pension system. / The coverage ratio is the percentage of the members (subscribers) of total population. / The number of beneficiaries and the number of cases have little difference.

The government implementation the National Pension in 1988 in order to contribute to people's life stabilization and to promote the welfare of the public right after the declaration of the National Pension Act, and it was obligatorily applied to workplaces which hire over 10 full-time workers for the first time in Korea. There are various kinds of benefits from old-age pension and disability pension to survivor's pension, lump sum allowance, and others. Similar to other social insurance systems and public assistance, both coverage and level of the pension has been expanded while contribution rates have been increased to keep budget balance. As of 2016, however, the coverage ratio of the national pension is still 43%, so the government keeps trying to provide financial assistance to enable more people to join the national pension.

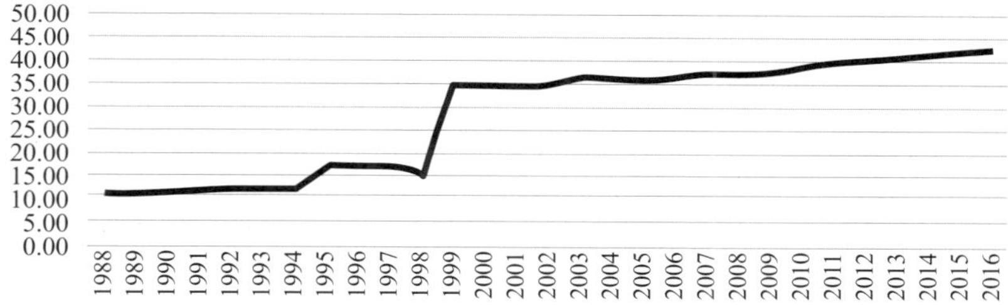

Source: The author created the figure based on the following references: 2002 National Pension Statistical Yearbook (National Pension Service, 2003); 2008 National Pension Statistical Yearbook (National Pension Service, 2009); 2016 National Pension Statistical Yearbook (National Pension Service, 2017).

Figure 2-22 National Pension Coverage Ratio (%)

This figure shows the coverage ratio of national pension. As can be seen from the above, the coverage ratio has been continuously increasing except a few periods since the implementation of the pension in 1988. Especially, in 1999 when the pension was extended to the urban self-employed, employees and employees in workplaces with less than 5 workers, the coverage ratio was increased to 34.9% from 15.4% in 1998. After that period, requirements for joining the pension has been lessened, so, as of 2016, almost 42.6% of population enjoys the pension service.

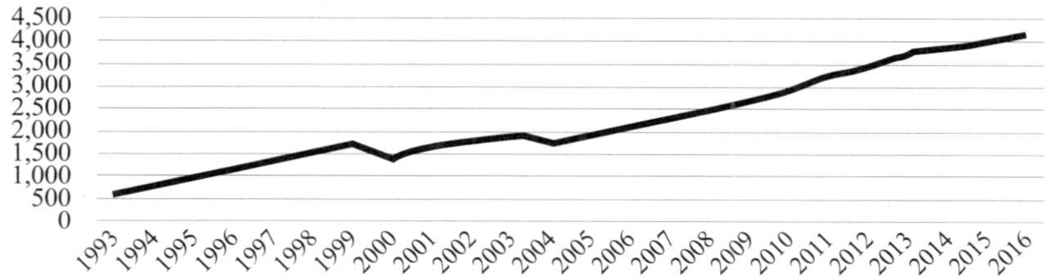

(unit: 1,000 won)

Source: The author created the figure based on the following references: 2002 National Pension Statistical Yearbook (National Pension Service, 2003); 2008 National Pension Statistical Yearbook (National Pension Service, 2009); 2016 National Pension Statistical Yearbook (National Pension Service, 2017).

Figure 2-23 Yearly Old-age Pension Benefits per Beneficiary

This figure shows yearly old age pension benefits per beneficiary (the total amount of old-age pension the number of beneficiaries). Using the old age pension benefits per beneficiary might not be a good proxy to understand the level of the national pension in Korea because the range of receiving the pension is wide depending on the terms of policy. However, from this graph, we can figure out the level of the pension has been on the rise except some specific period even through under the condition that the number of beneficiaries has been growing from 717,488 (2002) to 3,412,350 (2016) (National Pension Service, 2017).

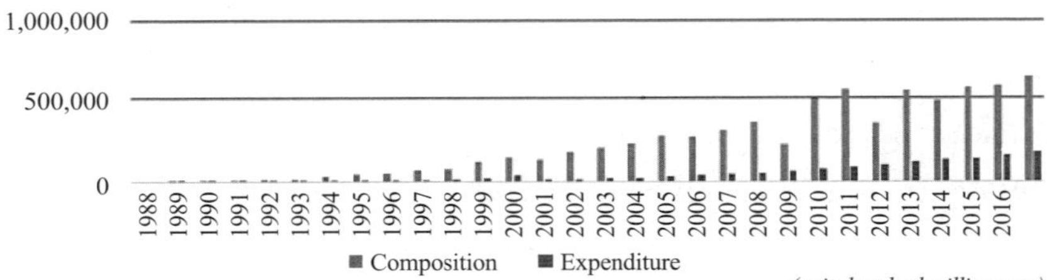

(unit: hundred million won)

Source: The author created the figure based on the following reference: The Internal Source of National Pension Service.

Figure 2-24 Composition and Expenditure of National Pension

This figure describes the composition and expenditure of national pension fund. According to the National Pension Service (2017), the composition of the 2016 national pension fund are mainly composed of contributions (69.91%) and operational profits (29.98%). This implies that the national pension fund can be hugely affected by how the National Pension Service manages its fund. Regarding fund expenditure, as of 2016, 77.12% of the fund is used for investment in the financial section, and 22.74% of the fund is used for the payment of benefits and others (77.12%) (National Pension Service, 2017).

It seems that the national pension fund is run stably because the amount of composition is much higher than that of expenditure. However, many experts argue that the financial burden of the fund will be increased owing to such factors as rapidly aging population. Therefore, it is necessary for the government to take some measures such as strengthening the income security of private pensions.

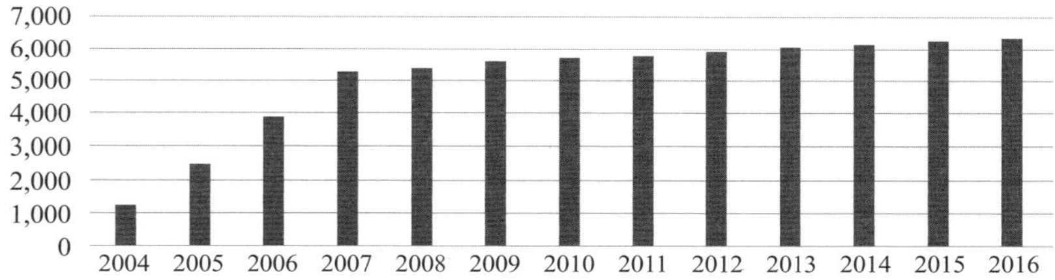

(unit: hundred million won)

Source: The author created the figure based on the following references: 2002 National Pension Statistical Yearbook (National Pension Service, 2003); 2008 National Pension Statistical Yearbook (National Pension Service, 2009); 2016 National Pension Statistical Yearbook (National Pension Service, 2017).

Figure 2-25 Government Subsidies of National Pension

Unlike the national health insurance which has been subsidized by the government for a quite long time because it has been in deficit, the national pension has been in surplus. Despite this reality, the reason why the government subsidies the national pension is that to encourage economically vulnerable people to join the pension more to prevent social problems such as the poverty of the elderly. For example, currently, the government runs the social insurance fee program which provide the employers and employee of small-scale businesses some parts of the insurance fee (national pension and unemployment insurance) to relieve the burden of joining social insurance and to eliminate the blind spot of social insurance.

2.4. Occupational Health and Safety Insurance

Table 2-9 Occupational Health and Safety Insurance

Year	Coverage		Level (won, per capita) - Total benefits (medical care benefits)	Others
	Workplaces	Workers (ratio)		
‘64	64	81,798	-	- Implementation of Occupational Health & Safety Insurance · Applying to workplaces (≥500 full-time workers) · Provision of expenses: If patients are ≥11 days of stay in hospital · Temporary incapacity benefits: 60% of average wage (AV)
‘65	289	161,150 (nearly 0.51%)	-	- Applying to workplaces (≥200 full-time workers)
‘66	594	222,456	-	-
‘67	1,142	336,159	-	-
‘68	2,389	488,628	-	-
‘69	3,696	683,377	-	-
‘70	5,583	779,053 (nearly 2.42%)	48,834 (23,762)	-
‘71	7,799	833,411	-	- Provision of expenses: If ≥8 days of stay in hospital
‘72	9,375	1,077,632	-	- Applying to workplaces (≥30 full-time workers)
‘75	21,369	1,836,209 (nearly 5.20%)	128,837 (64,566)	-
‘79	55,763	3,607,595	414,227 (153,506)	-
‘80	63,110	3,752,975 (nearly 9.84%)	551,308 (213,880)	-
‘81	59,029	3,456,746	-	-
‘82	54,159	3,464,977	-	- Provision of expenses: If patients are ≥4 days of stay in hospital - Applying to workplaces (≥10 full-time workers)

‘85	66,803	4,495,185	1,311,616 (587,921)	-
‘87	88,596	5,356,546	-	- Applying to workplaces (≥ 5 full-time workers)
‘89	118,894	5,743,970	2,753,400 (1,022,400)	- Changing coverage from workplaces under Labor Standards Act to all workplaces - Temporary incapacity benefits: 70% of AV
‘90	129,687	7,542,752 (nearly 17.59%)	4,058,539 (1,328,893)	-
‘95	186,021	7,893,727	8,690,213 (2,103,054)	-
‘00	706,231	9,485,557	12,729,485 (4,386,554)	- Introduction of the maximum coverage - Applying to workplaces (< 5 workers) excluding some businesses (agriculture, forestry, fishing etc.)
‘05	1,175,606	12,069,599 (nearly 25.05%)	15,357,151 (4,812,857)	- Provision of opportunities to the self-employed who do not hire workers - Applying to workplaces (≥1 workers) including businesses (agriculture, forestry, fishing, hunting)
‘10	1,608,361	14,198,748	13,912,562 (4,199,155)	-
‘15	2,367,186	17,968,931	15,113,797 (4,229,199)	-
‘18	-	-	-	- Applying to workplaces (< 1 workers)

Source: The author created the table based on the following references: Korea Labor Welfare Corporation (2016); Ministry of Employment and Labor (2016)

Note: This table describes the occupational health and safety insurance system. / The Coverage ratio is the percentage of the workers (subscribers)) of total population. / Those benefits started to be included in statistics: Temporary incapacity benefits ('90-), injury and disease compensation pension ('99-), disability compensation payments ('99-), bereaved family's compensation pension ('99-), personal care benefits ('00), vocational rehabilitation payments ('08).

Occupational Health and Safety Insurance was implemented in 1964 to compensate for a worker's industrial disaster rapidly and fairly, and it was applied to workplaces which hired over 500 full-time workers. To be specific, the number of workplaces which came to be covered has been continuously increased from 64 in 1964 and 63,110 in 1980 to 129,687 in 1990 and 706,231 in 2000. Especially, the number was abruptly increased to 706,231 in 2000 when the insurance was applied to workplaces which hired at least 1 full-time workers including agriculture, forestry, fishing, and hunting. At this time, the maximum coverage was also introduced for the first time, and, as of 2015, 2,367,186 workers join the insurance and beneficiaries are 17,968,931. Regarding requirements for receiving benefits, it has been gradually relieved while the level of benefit has been continuously increased.

2.5. Employment Insurance

Table 2-10 Progress of Employment Insurance

Year	Coverage		Level (won) (maximum unemployment allowance per day)	Others
	Workplaces	Workers (ratio)		
'95	-	-	-	- Implementation of Employment Insurance Act · Unemployment: Applying to workplaces (≥30 workers) · Other programs: Applying to workplaces (≥70 workers)
'97	47.427	4,280,430 (9.31%)	-	-
'98	400,000	5,267,658	-	- Applying all programs to all workplaces (≥1 workers) - Increasing fixed benefit payment days (age < 25) · 30-210 days → 60-210 days
'99	601,394	6,054,479	-	- Increasing insurance rates: · Unemployment: 6/1,000 → 10/1,000 · Employment stability: 2/1,000 → 3/1,000

'00	693,414	6,747,263 (14.35%)	-	- Increasing fixed benefit payment days: · 60-210 days → 90-210 days - Lessening requ_rements for unemployment benefits - Applying employment insurance to workers in central & local governments
'01	806,962	6,908,888	35,000	- Increasing the maximum amount of unemployment allowance per day (30,000 → 35,000won)
'02	825,531	7,171,277	-	- Applying to daily employed workers
'03	845,910	7,203,347	-	- Decreasing insurance rates: · Unemployment: 10/1,000 → 9/1,000 · Employment stability: 3/1,000 → 1.5/1,000
'05	1,148,474	8,063,797 (16.74%)	40,000	- Increasing the maximum amount of unemployment allowance per day (35,000 → 40,000won)
'06	1,176,462	8,536,967	-	- Integrating employment stability & capability development programs - Applying employment stability & capability development programs to people (age ≥65)
'08	1,424,330	9,385,239	-	- Applying unemployment insurance to extraordinary & contracted-based public workers
'10	1,408,061	10,131,058 (20.44%)	-	- Changing the standards of employment insurant rates: · Wages → Remuneration
'11	1,508,669	10,675,437	-	- Increasing unemployment insurance rates: 0.9% → 1.1%
'12	1,610,713	11,152,354	-	- Applying unemployment insurance to the self-employed
'13	1,747,928	11,571,213	-	- Applying unemployment insurance to people (≥ 65) - Increasing unemployment insurance rates: 1.1% → 1.3%
'15	2,107,071	12,363,063 (24.23%)	43,000	- Increasing the targeting beneficiaries of capacity building programs for workers - Increasing the maximum amount of unemployment allowance per day (40,000 → 43,000won)

Source: The author created the table based on the following references: Korea Labor Welfare Corporation (2016); Ministry of Employment and Labor (2016); Employment Insurance (n.d.).

Note: This table describes the employment insurance system. As shown in the table, the government has gradually expanded both coverage and the level of assistance. Especially, we can see the number of workplaces joining the program was greatly increased in 1998, when the IMF crisis occurred in Korea. / The coverage ratio is the percentage of the insured of total population. / Other programs imply employment stability and capability development programs.

Among social insurance programs in Korea, employment insurance was introduced lastly during the mid-1990s to prevent unemployment and to strengthen the worker's vocational competency development. The program mainly consists of the assistance of the unemployed and the development of worker's vocational competency. Like other social insurance programs, the coverage and requirements of receiving benefit has been gradually improved. Especially, the number of workplaces which came to be covered by the insurance was increased to 400,000 in 1998 when the all employment insurance programs were applied to all workplaces which hired at least 1 worker. In case of the maximum unemployment allowance per day, it was continuously raised from 30,000won at the initial stage to 43,000won in 1995. To keep the balance of budget, the unemployment insurance rate has kept rising from 0.9% to 1.1% in 2011 and 1.3% (an employer goes halves with an employee) in 2013. The rising rate of the insurance was inevitable because expenditure increased hugely during the 2009 global financial crisis while more and more people join insurance as the unemployment system develops.

2.6. Earned Income Tax Credit (EITC)

The earned income tax credit (EITC) which was introduced in 2008 is the income support program providing a refundable tax credit for low-wage working people and the self-employed to encourage them to main their work. The amount of EITC benefit is estimated based on the criteria including family composition, gross income, and property. The ministry of strategy and finance (MOSF) oversees legalizing and planning the EITC, while the National Tax Service (NTS) deal with implementing the ETIC. As of 2018, the maximum EITC benefit is 2.5 million Korean won (won) for a double-income family. The significance of the EITC is that the government not only boosts the employees' motivation to work, but also income redistribution effects are expectable by raising the net income of low-wage working people and the self-employed. Moreover, introducing the EITC extended the double-level social safety net of Korea (National Basic Livelihood Security Act, social insurance) to the triple-level one consisting of National Basic Livelihood Security Act, EITC as the 2nd safety net, social insurance (NTS, n. d).

2.6.1. Quantification for Application

To receive the EITC, as of 2017, a household with earned income or business income should satisfy the following requirements: family composition; gross income; property. Regarding family composition, an applicant should have spouse, dependent children under 18, or one of the parents aged over 70, or the age of an applicant should be more than 30. The annual gross income should be less than 13 million won for a single household, 21 million won for a single-income family, and 25 million won for a double-income family. As for property, as of 2017, the total amount of family property is less than 140 million won. If an applicant falsifies the fact to get the EITC, s/he cannot receive the EITC for the maximum 5 years.

2.6.2. Application Period

The official application period is from the beginning of May to the end of the May. If an applicant fails to apply for the EITC during this time, they can also apply for it by the end of November, but they will receive the EITC with 10% reduction as a penalty. In other words, the EITC is run based on application, so one cannot get the EITC without voluntary application, even if they satisfy the requirements of receiving the EITC.

2.6.3. EITC Benefit

As of 2018, the maximum EITC benefit for a single household with the annual gross income below 13 million won is 0.85 million won, and a single-income family with the annual gross income below 21 million won get the maximum 2 million won. In case of a double-income family with the annual gross income below 2.5 million won can receive the maximum 2.5million won as EITC benefit. The EITC in Korea has been continually improved through revision process and it can be summarized as the following table:

Table 2-11 Progress of ETIC

<table>
<tr><th>Classification</th><th>2008</th><th>2011</th><th>2012</th><th>2013</th><th>2014</th></tr>
<tr><td>Target</td><td>wage earners</td><td colspan="3">+ insurance solicitors, door-to-door salesmen</td><td>+ the self-employed (excluding the professions)</td></tr>
<tr><td colspan="6">Requirements</td></tr>
<tr><td>Gross Income</td><td>couple < 1.7 million won</td><td colspan="2">- no dependent children: < 1.3 million won
- 1 children: < 1.7 million won
- 2 children: < 2.1 million won
- more than 3: < 2.5 million won</td><td colspan="2">- single household: < 1.3 million won
- single-income family: < 2.1 million won
- double-income family: < 2.5 million won</td></tr>
<tr><td>Dependent Child</td><td>≥ 1 dependent child (<18 years)</td><td>If there is spouse, possible despite having no dependent child</td><td colspan="3">If applicant's age ≥ 60, available for a single-household</td></tr>
<tr><td>Housing</td><td>no house or 1 house ≤ 50 million won</td><td colspan="3">no house or 1 house ≤ 60 million won</td><td>no house or 1 house</td></tr>
</table>

Property	gross property ≤ 100 million won		gross property ≤ 140 million won
Maximum Benefit	1.2 million won	- no dependent children: 0.7 million won - 1 children: < 1.4 million won - 2 children: < 1.7 million won - more than 3: < 2 million won	- single household: 0.7 million won - single-income family: 1.7 million won - double-income family: 2.1 million won

Source: The author reorganized the table based on the following reference: Song, H, J, and Shin, U, R (2018)

As can be seen from the above, supporting targets and requirements for receiving the EITC have been continuously lessened since the introduction of the EITC in 2008, and the maximum benefit has been also increasing and specified based on family composition. As mentioned above, as of 2018, the maximum benefit for each household is 0.85 million, 2 million, and 2.5 million won respectively. Moreover, an applicant aged over 30 is also available for the applying for the EITC.

3. Lessons

There are things that Korean government did well. First, Korea started focusing on the social welfare after 1980s, and it was a right timing. After a growth-oriented drive during 1960-70s, demand for social welfare was rising around 1980s. Second, it expands the social welfare gradually so that it can maintain fiscal balance. As we have seen in the previous section, the expansion of the social welfare was very gradual although there were some turning points with an introduction of new systems. Third, in terms of financing, the social insurance which mandates contribution of both employees and employers has been the dominant form of social welfare before 2000. If social welfare depends too much on the general account of the government budget, the size of the social welfare may expand too fast because the tax payers and beneficiaries are often different. Fourth, universal and mandatory health insurance system was a good choice to avoid adverse selection. If the health insurance is not mandatory for all people, only high-risk people will be a member of the insurance causing a high insurance premium, which in turn will deter low risk people even more. This was what happened in the U.S.A. before Obama Care.

However, there were mistakes that Korea has committed. First, when it first introduced the national pension system, it did not carefully predict the future trend of aging society. To attract people's support, the government created too generous pension scheme. Since the pension system in Korea is still at a fledgling stage, the pension fund is around 600 billion USD now and it will reach its peak of 2 trillion USD around 2040, but will be rapidly depleted around 2060. Second, due to many tax exemptions, 48% of workers are not paying income tax compared to OECD average of 16%. When tax is financed by only 52% of the population, 48% will consider the social welfare a free lunch. When unemployment becomes a serious issue, social welfare relying on tax and general account will play a more important role. Without a cost awareness, it may result in too fast expansion of social welfare. Third, there are too many subsidized in-kind service which is not considered a social welfare by the beneficiaries. Such examples include low electricity for the low-income families, low rented apartment for the poor, free childcare service etc. This is one of the reasons that people do not recognize the benefit they enjoy despite costs borne by the government for the in-kind service. It is better to provide cash to the needy rather than free in-kind service. This is not welcomed by the ministries who want to maintain the service they provide as form of social welfare.

IV. Current plan for the Social Welfare System in Vietnam (Dr. Phan Thi Song Thuong)

1. Poverty alleviation

The current plan for poverty alleviation is mainly documented in the National Target Program on Sustainable Poverty Reduction for the 2016-2020 period (Decision No.1722/QĐ-TTg dated on September 2nd, 2016). According to the program, the targets on sustainable poverty reduction toward 2020 include:

- Reducing the national poverty rate by 1-1.5% per year based on multi-dimensional poverty measurement. Moreover, the proportion of poor households in disadvantaged districts must reduce by 4% annually, and the proportion of poor households in districts inhabited by national minorities must drop by 3-4% per year for the period of 2016-2020.
- Improving income and living conditions for the poor, for instance increasing per capita income of poor households by 1.5 times and of those living in disadvantaged districts by two times from 2015 to 2020.
- Building essential infrastructure including irrigation systems, transport systems, and many other indispensable facilities to increase the livelihoods of low-income people.
- Gradually improving the living conditions for the poor, particularly the ethnic minorities and disadvantaged residents in poor districts, borderline communes, especially disadvantaged localities, coastal areas, and islands.
- Creating a strong, comprehensive and sustainable advance in poverty

reduction; contributing to narrowing the gap in living standards between urban and rural areas, as well as among regions and ethnic communities.

The total budget for the program implementation is VND 48,397 billion (about US$2.1 billion), VND 41,449 billion (US$1.9 billion) and VND 4,484 billion of which is sourced from the central government budget and the local government budget, respectively. In addition, total minimum investment for the national target program on new-style rural area building is VND 193.1 trillion (US$8.7 billion), VND 63.1 trillion (US$2.8 billion) of which will be sourced from the central government budget and the rest is to come from the local government budget.

As mentioned in part I, Decision 1557/QĐ-TTg documents a number of targeted indicators for ethnic minority communities as a basis for sustainable development. For instance, rate of poor ethnic minority households (%) is aimed to reduce about 3% - 4% per year for the period 2020-2025. Malnutrition percentage of children under 5-year-old is targeted to 14% in 2020 and 8% in 2025. Furthermore, the Vietnamese government has implemented two main programs on "The National Target Program for Development of the Social Assistance System for the 2016-2020 period" and "Renovation, development of social assistance for the 2017-2025 period, with a vision toward 2030" (table 2-12). These official documents show the national plans and targets on poverty alleviation and development of social assistance system with a vision 2030. Almost all budgets for implementing these plans (above 90%) come from the state budget.

Table 2-12 Current Plan for Poverty Alleviation and Social Assistance in Vietnam

Official Documents	National plan/targets	Sources of budget Total budget (billion VND)
Decision No.1722/QĐ-TTg (Sept 02, 2016): "The National Target Program on Sustainable Poverty Reduction for the 2016-2020 period"	<2016-20> - Reducing the national poverty rate by 1-1.5% per year - Annually reducing the proportion of poor households in disadvantaged districts by 4% - Increasing per capita income of poor households by 1,5 times and of those living in disadvantaged districts by two times from 2015 to 2020	Total: 48,397 Central: 41,449 Local: 4,484 Others: 2,100
Resolution 73/NQ-CP (8/26/2016): "The National Target Program for Development of the Social Assistance System for the 2016-2020 period"	<2016-20> - 55% of total social assistance offices are non-public. - 30% of total poor and disadvantaged people are supported by social assistance offices. - 90% of total children in special living condition are supported and taken care by social assistance offices.	Total: 11,655 Central: 4,345 Local: 4,980 Others 2,330
Decision 488/QĐ-TTg (4/14/2017): Project on "Renovation, development of social assistance for the 2017-2025 period, with a vision toward 2030"	<2016-20> - 100% of people who face sudden difficulties are timely supported - 50% of people who have special difficulties of living condition are provided social assistance services based on their demand, 10% of which are provided full package of social assistance services. <2021-25> - 100% of that - 70% and 30%, respectively <2030> 100% of that - 90% and 50%, respectively	-
Decision 266/QĐeTTg (5Oct, 2017): The 2030 Agenda for Sustainable Development	<2021-25> - Eliminate extreme poverty and hunger - Adopting poverty line is a per capital income of USD1.25 a day or less. <2030> - Poor and vulnerable people are significantly benefit from social welfare policies	-

Source: Author's synthesis

2. Old-age: Pension and other Old-age Assistance

The government has implemented several policies on pension and other old age assistance with the aim of maintaining the balance of revenues and expenses of the social insurance fund. *Firstly, the government has applied a roadmap to change method of national pension calculations* since January 1st, 2018. According to Clause 2 of Article 56 of the 2014 Law on Social Insurance (SI), there are two main adjustments:

- Men and women who have contributed social insurance premiums for a minimum of 20 and 15 years, respectively, are eligible for 45% of their average monthly wages. For every additional year, men and women receive 2% and 3% increment, respectively, until it reaches the maximum of 75%. The new Law changes the increment to 2% every additional year for both men and women.
- The duration of social insurance benefits for up to 75% of the average monthly salary as pension will be extended for 5 years. A woman must be at least 55-year-old and retire after January 1, 2018, and she has to pay social insurance premiums for at least 30 years to receive 75% of pension. The corresponding time for males is 35 years.

Table 2-13 Years of Social Insurance Premium Contribution to Receive

Gender	Before 2018	After 2018
Female	25 years	30 years
Male	30 years	35 years

Source: The 2014 Law on Social Insurance

Based on this new national pension calculation, the Vietnam Social Security states that there are about 21,000 female labors in 2018, equivalent to 43% of total retired female labors, who have paid social insurance premiums less than 30 years. These female labors must have contributed social insurance premiums for at least 26 years in 2018, 27 years in 2019, 28 in 2020, 29 in 2021 and 30 in 2022 to get 75% of their average monthly salary. This new retirement policy may negatively affect the female labors.

According to Resolution No. 28-NQ/TW dated 23/5/2018 on Reform of the Social Insurance Policy, the government plans to reduce time of paying social insurance to enjoy a pension from 20 years to 15 years and towards 10 years, to modify equality of pensions between women and men, to increase the retirement age, and to mandate foreigners working in Vietnam to participate in social insurance. The retirement age is unofficially planned to extend from 60 to 62 for male and 55 to 60 for female according to the roadmap of extending retirement age from 2021.

Secondly, the government has set out a wide-ranging social protection and basic social services agenda which is documented on the Resolution No. 15-NQ/TW dated on June 1st, 2012 on number of issues relating to social policies for the period 2012-2020. The Resolution provides general guidance, but acts more to identify aspirations than as a concrete set of challenges, trade-offs, financing constraints, and sustainable solutions in social protection. More specifically, the government has set a target of 50% coverage of pensions and about 2,5 million people, 30% of which are elders, will receive annual social assistance by 2020. However, a big challenge is extending coverage to the informal sector in Vietnam. In fact, there are only two-thirds of formal private sector employees participating in social insurance (as against around 90% of FDI and 93% of state-owned sectors) (Vietnam Social Security, 2013). The coverage expansion achieves fuller coverage of formal sector workers, but not for informal sector workers. The targets are unlikely to be reached under the current policy and financing approach. The feasibility of targets cannot happen without major improvements in social security administration, and the current rate of pension contributions creates incentives to evade. Essentially, Vietnam is "losing the race" between pension coverage expansion and rapid aging in the coming years.

Thirdly, the government has established Voluntary Pension Fund since 2016 by issuing Decree 88/2016/NĐ-CP on Program of Voluntary Supplementary Pension. This program points out that, by 2020, there are about 150,000 people from 400 to 500 firms buying retirement insurance products or contributing to voluntary pension fund in the form of investment trust. The voluntary pension fund will be reinvested on the stock market and the capital market. As a result, the reinvested revenue of the fund is accumulated about 10,000-12,000 billion by 2020. In Vietnam, pension funds contributed by workers, individuals and employers will be invested in financial products. The government believes that the capital market, especially the government bond market will be developed in a sustainable way by using pension funds to invest on the markets.

3. Health: National Insurance and Health Care

The government has set out a new goal to raise health insurance coverage rate to 90% by 2020 (this rate was 76.5% at the end of 2015). Accordingly, the major current plans for the national health insurance are as following:

(1) *Adopting the Universal Health Coverage Strategy which is stipulated by Constitution and Laws*. For instance, The Law on Health Insurance

in 2008 (Revised Health Insurance Law in 2014) makes universal health coverage as a national goal. Implementation of universal health coverage ensures that all people have access to basic and quality health care services; to prevent occurrence of major epidemics; to gradually control health hazards related to the environment, food safety, lifestyle and behaviors of people. According to the Revised Health Insurance Law in 2014 (effected since 01/01/2015), (i) all Vietnamese citizens compulsorily participate in the national health insurance scheme; (ii) Family based members compulsorily participate in health insurance: from second member, health insurance contribution reduce to 70%, 60%, 50% 40% of the first member's contribution; (iii) The employees of the army and police forces compulsorily participate in health insurance; (iv) Increase health insurance benefits of some beneficiaries.

(2) *Managing expansion with horizontal equity, in which pro poor policies as core for equity and for expansion of coverage.* The government is strongly committed to developing and to implementing pro poor health programs toward equitable coverage. The targets of national health insurance include (i) enhancing communication on the obligations and benefits of participation in health insurance; (ii) promoting the use of state budget and local budget to pay full/partial health insurance premium for vulnerable groups; (iii) expanding health insurance participants towards household-based health insurance, particularly among households working in agriculture, forestry, fishery and salt production; (iv) developing health care in poor, mountainous, remote areas; (v) and having preferential treatment in health care for poor people and beneficiaries of social policies.

(3) *Maintaining momentum for continuous health insurance reform.*

Regarding health financing reform, in 2016, the government documented the Health Financing Strategy of Vietnam for the 2016-2025 period. The strategy clearly defines objectives and targets to be achieved by the health financing system as well as comprehensive and effective solutions. According to "Plan for people's health protection, care, and promotion for the 2016-2020 period" (Ministry of Health, 3/2016), the plan sets goals to rapidly increase proportion of public expenditures on health and on achievement of universal health insurance coverage; to improve the efficiency of budget allocation and utilization; to develop health infrastructure; to mobilize resources in the society for investment in health, to create new revenue sources for health budget such as sin taxes on tobacco, alcoholic drinks, etc.; to develop and scale up models of investment loans, cooperative investment and public-private partnership (PPP) in health care. By 2020, the proportion of public expenditures on health (including state budget, social health insurance, and grants) reaches at least 60% of the total social spending on health. In addition, the shift of recurrent budget allocated to health facilities to support people's participation in health insurance along with the process of calculating service prices correctly and fully are completed by 2020. Estimated budget for people's health protection, care and promotion for the 2016-2020 period is 742,320 billion dongs (equivalent to 8.4% of the total state budget expenditures), of which:

- Spending on investment and development: 176,148 billion dongs to complete the health system as planned by 2025 and vision to 2035
- Non-business health expenditures: 550,314 billion dongs (530,922 billion dongs as recurrent expenditure and 19.392 billion dongs for national targeted programs on health and population)

- Health expenditures in national security, defense and reform of salaries: 19,750 billion dongs
- Expenditures from the retained revenue: 625,641 billion dongs, of which direct service fee is 164,402 billion dongs, HI reimbursement is 455,462 billion dongs and other non-business revenue is 5 776.5 billion dongs.

(4) *Implementing the roadmap of adjustment of health service prices.* The health service prices are to include wages and direct costs in the service prices by 2016, to include wages, direct costs and management costs in the service prices by 2018, and to include wages, direct costs, management costs and depreciation of fixed assets in the service prices by 2020. Furthermore, health insurance has been adjusted since 2018 by annual increase of 0.3% of the minimum wage.

(5) *Enhancing investment in development of local health care system.* In 2017, the Prime Minister approved the target program for investment in the development of the local health system for the 2016-2020 period (Decision No.1267/QĐ-TTg dated on August 25th, 2017). This program aims to increase investment in local public health facilities, to upgrade infrastructure and medical equipment, and to improve the quality of medical examination and treatment services. The program sets the target of 26.5 beds per 10,000 people by 2020. The total budget of the program is VND 22,500 billion, 67% and 22% of which comes from the state budget and ODA, respectively. The program continues to complete 64 projects which are invested in the 2011-2015 period and to conduct 52 new investment projects.

4. Work: Unemployment Insurance and Worker's Compensation

According to the development strategy of the Vietnam social insurance sector in the period of 2013-2020 (Decision No.1215/QetTTg dated on 23/7/2013) and the strategy for international integration of the social insurance sector to 2020, with a vision to 2030 (Decision No.146/Q -TTg dated on 20/01/2016), Vietnam sets a goal that by 2020, 35% of the labor force participate in unemployment insurance, around 50% of the labor force participate in social insurance, and more than 80% of the population participate in health insurance. The overall objectives of the strategy are to build a sustainable, effective and modern model of social security management in line with global labor mobility and trends by 2030. Accordingly, all Vietnamese citizens, including Vietnamese citizens living abroad, will be provided with adequate social insurance and health insurance schemes. The international corporation on social insurance and health insurance has been expanding in the region and the world. Vietnam's social insurance has been enhanced to cooperation with Europe, South America, Middle East and Africa.

To achieve the goal of 35% of the labor force participate in unemployment insurance, the Vietnam General Confederation of Labor has directed trade unions at all levels to encourage more workers to join the social insurance as well as employment insurance. In addition, Law on Employment (No.38/2013/QH13) issued on November 16th, 2013 states that all enterprises, business households and individuals that hire or employ labors (no limited 10 employees or more as before) under labor contracts are compulsory for unemployment insurance. Recently, the government has proposed to reduce contribution by employers to workers' unemployment insurance premiums from 1% of employees' monthly salary to 0.5%. The adjustment proposal will take effect right when the National Assembly's resolution on adjusting unemployment insurance premiums comes into force, and will remain until the end of 2019.

Regarding the unemployment fund, according to existing law, the fund will be jointly raised by the state, employers and employees. However, due to a large surplus of the fund witnessed year by year, the fund no longer enjoyed contribution from the state budget starting from 2015 and likely in the coming years. In other words, the fund comprises entirely of the premiums paid by employees and employers. Furthermore, Vietnam is striving towards the target of 50% of the workforce benefiting from social insurance and 35% being covered by unemployment insurance by 2020, according to Resolution No.15-NQ/TW and Resolution No. 21-NQ/TW.

V. Vietnam's Vision and Reform (Prof. Jin Park and Dr. Phan Thi Song Thuong)

1. Aggregate Reform

According to the Resolution No. 28-NQ/TW dated 19/5/2018 on the reform of social insurance policy, the Vietnamese government sets objectives of social welfare system from now to 2030. For instance, about 60% of labor force participate in social insurance; 5% of which are farmer and labor working in informal sector participate in voluntary social insurance; about 45% of labor force participate in unemployment insurance; about 60% of retired person receive pension, monthly social insurance and social pension subsidy; 90% of the participants are satisfied with the quality of social insurance services. The government has to conduct an aggregate reform on social welfare system in order to achieve these objectives. As mentioned earlier, the state budget deficit has been recently increasing since the budget expenditure has often outpaced budget revenue. Despite chronic budget deficit, the government has not reduced its budget expenditure for social welfare programs. This is one of the reason why the financial sustainability is at risk.

Other reasons are that the number of pension is increasing; many people are still outside social welfare scheme, especially those in informal sectors; the number of workers who join voluntary social insurance program is insignificant; employers are reluctant to pay social insurance because of poor regulation implementation on social insurance; and the risk of aging population in Vietnam in the near future. From fiscal balance point of view, therefore, we can draw an aggregate reform on social welfare expenditure with the aim of reducing government budget constraint and achieving financial sustainability as below.

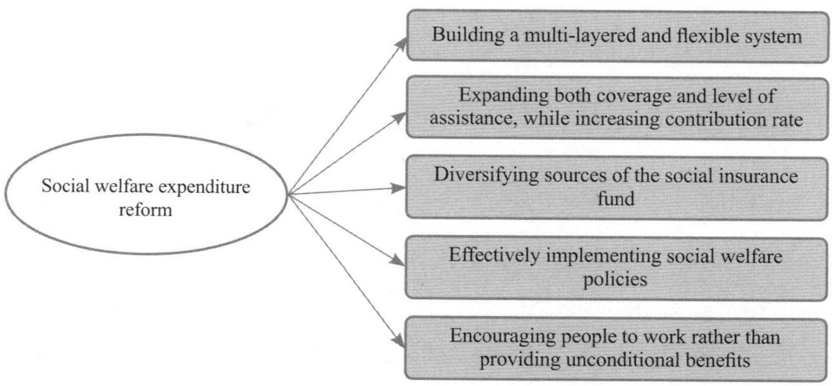

Figure 2-26 Social welfare expenditure reform

First, building a multi-layered and flexible social welfare system. Reforming social insurance system is the main pillar of social welfare reform by building a multi-layered and flexible social insurance system. The system should be developed based on the principle of equality, equity, and sustainability. As for social pension, the state budget provides pension allowances for elders who do not receive monthly pension or monthly social insurance benefits. In case of Korea, the government has implemented the basic old-age pension in 2008 for those who do not join the national pension or who do not receive the enough amount of the pension because of the short duration of entitlement to the national pension. As for social insurance, the coverage of compulsory social insurance based on contributions of employees and employers and that of voluntary social insurance based on contributions of people who do not have labor contract. Furthermore, the government provides appropriate supports for farmers, the poor, low income people, and workers in informal sectors in line with the budget's capability. The social welfare expenditure should be adjusted in the direction of harmonizing the interests between employers and labors, and among people in all types of social classes. Although the social welfare system should be flexible, its implementation should be very strict. There are many companies that do not comply with their obligation of social insurance contribution, and the government should penalize those companies. The Korean government has punishment regulations for the uninsured companies and workers. For example, if an employer does not join the national pension, the government can impose penalty up to 0.5 million Korean won while 5 million Korean won will be charged to the uninsured workplaces.

Second, gradually expanding both coverage and level of assistance while increasing contribution rates. The coverage of social insurance, including compulsory social insurance and voluntary social insurance, are expanded in line with the budget's capability and the roadmap for adjustment of retirement age. Supplementary pension insurance of a voluntary retirement scheme is based on market principles, for example the more additional contributions to pension insurance, the higher pension allowances to enjoy. The government conducts financial policies and job security to support production development in order to increase the social insurance contribution rate. Social insurance should maintain self-sufficient financing without fiscal support from government's general account. As we have seen in Korea's experience, gradual expansion of social insurance is very important to maintain fiscal soundness. In the process of expanding income gap after 2000, Korea hastily expanded social insurance benefits which has caused a serious dependence of social insurance such health insurance system, civil servants' pension upon the general account, which will become even more serious issue in the future.

Third, diversifying sources of the social insurance fund. The fund comes from a variety of resources, in which the main resources are from the state budget, external resources (such as ODA, non-refundable aid programs from foreign countries), and the society such as enterprises, organizations, people. In addition, expending investment of the fund on the principle of safety, sustainability and efficiency should be considered to generate great resources for ensuring social welfare expenditure. The portfolio investment of the fund should be at the hands of the experts rather than government officials. The managing organization of the fund should be separated to an independent agency whose CEO should be recruited from among private sector experts.

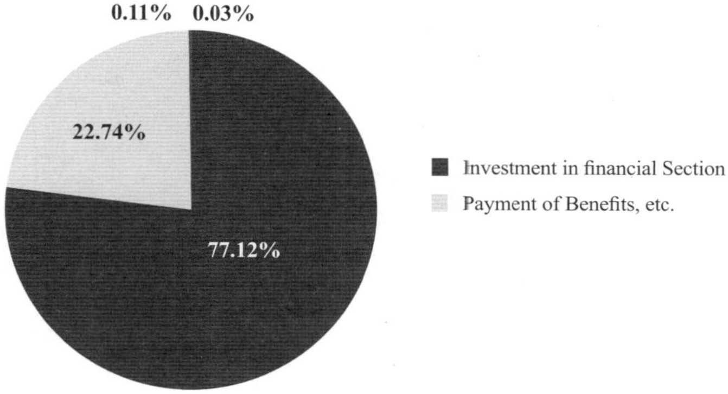

Source: The author reorganized the figure based on the following reference: National Pension Service (2017)

Figure 2-26 Operation of National Pension Fund in Korea (2016)

As can be seen from the above, almost 77% of the national pension fund is operated for investment in the financial section (domestic bond, domestic and foreign stocks, and others) to secure finances necessary for running the national pension. Also, the government has the operation center of managing the national fund with the National Pension Corporation to operate the national fund more efficiently while recruiting many professional personnel from the private sector.

Fourth, effectively implementing social welfare policies to encourage participation of the whole society. Currently, many social welfare programs and policies are overlap, especially more than 150 policies of poverty reduction. Formulation and implementation of social welfare policies should be reformed to strengthen confidence and to increase satisfaction level of participants in the social welfare system. Especially, distribution of social welfare expenditure is to ensure fairness and non-discrimination among the target groups. The reform aims to improve the quality of social insurance services, accelerate the administrative reform, and create favorable conditions/environment for people and enterprises to participate in the social welfare system. Although the supplementary pension can be open to people's voluntary choice, the basic national pension should be compulsory to all people in the long run with an exception of those who cannot afford it. If the basic pension is optional, those who are expected to live longer will have a stronger incentive to take the basic pension, which will cause a serious fiscal problem. Since 2011, the National Health Insurance Corporation in Korea has been in charge of collecting the premium of 4 social insurance programs and other related work to reduce overlapped administrative actions of each corporation and to improve the accessibility of people to all social insurance service. This kind of integrating social insurance service can be one way of effectively implementing social welfare programs.

Fifth, encouraging people to work rather than providing unconditional benefits. The reform should aim to improve the quality of social welfare programs and balance of social welfare expenditure. For instance, modernizing labor markets; developing small and medium enterprises to create jobs and ensuring labor standard; enhancing employees' training and skills; strengthening sanctions for non-compliance; supporting the poor and labor in informal sectors to participate in social insurance and unemployment insurance; and at the same time, create opportunities for pensioners to diversify their pension benefits. In this respect, EITC (Earned Income Tax Credit) is a very useful tool to support people's work incentive. It is a refundable tax credit for low income working population which depends on individuals' income and size of the family. If an individual works and makes less money than the threshold level, the government compensates the gap through tax refund. As seen in the case of Korea which introduced the EITC in 2008, the Vietnam government can not only boost the employees' motivation to work, but also income redistribution effects are expectable by raising the net income of low-wage working people if the government runs the EITC properly.

2. Institutional reform

2.1. Old Age: Pension and Old-age Assistance

In recent years, Vietnam has improved social welfare for old people thanks to implementing many policies and programs for them in different target groups. However, ensuring social security for old age person has been facing many challenges, especially when Vietnam is in the period of population aging. The government should formulate pension and old age assistance reform based on the achieved results as well as challenges of population ageing. The following institutional reform on pension and old age assistance should take into account.

First, creating opportunities for old people to participate in economic activities in order to diversify their pensions and improve their living standards, especially for those who have working skills and experiences. At the same time, old people could transfer their skills and experiences to young people who need to be trained. In fact, the retirement age is planned to increase according to the roadmap of extending retirement age from 2021. Although it does not attract people's support, the plan should be implemented for fiscal soundness. The gender difference in retirement age and pension scheme should be abolished in the long run. To deal with this issue, some companies in Korea have introduced the salary peak system to guarantee retirement age with income reduction since

2003. Until now, this system is not widely used by most of the companies, and discussions on effectiveness are underway, the government keeps pushing the introduction of the salary peak system targeting public institutions. Other than the salary peak system, the government has also tried to provide various job opportunities for the elderly through the Korea Labor Force Development of for the aged affiliated with the Ministry of Health and Welfare since 2005.

Second, the pension insurance regime should be built more multi-layered and flexible. The pension insurance regime includes old-age assistants are financed by the state budget, retirement pension is financed by the social insurance fund, and voluntary pension benefits based on voluntary supplement contribution to the fund. Regulations of pension insurance regime are modified to encourage employees to participate in social insurance in the long time and to reduce the rate of retirement pension for people who want to receive one-time social insurance pension.

Third, adjusting formula of retirement pension rate in line with international standard. It is necessary to draw a roadmap for adjusting retirement pension rate and the length of time for participation in social insurance. The way of calculating pension rate is based on ensuring the balance of pension funds in long-term and considering the tradeoff between level of benefit and eligibility. The adjustments of retirement pension rate are on the basic of the principle of equality and fairness. The adjustments of social pension allowances are relatively independent and incorporated with monthly wage of employed person.

Fourth, expanding coverage of the pension scheme. There are some measures that should be considered, for instance extending compulsory social insurance to all employed labors; encouraging voluntary participation; increasing employees' awareness about their pension benefits if they participate in social insurance in their early working life. Furthermore, it would be more prudent to allow workers to buy missing years of contributions as well as to provide opportunities for workers having pension income. We may have to consider non-contributory pensions for elderly as Korea does. This should be, however, paid to those who are in the lower income bracket. In Korea, lower 70% of old aged people are recipients of the non-contributory pension paid by the general account of the government, but this over-generosity is becoming a serious fiscal burden.

Fifth, promoting socialization for old-age people in terms of provision of health care services and old-age assistants which are to ensure minimum standard of living them. The government should pay attention to enhance the role of political and social entities to conduct and participate in policies/ programs for old-age people. It is necessary to encourage these entities to provide old-age care services and the elderly's family and social communities to care for them. In addition, it is appropriate to regularly conduct social activities for the elder with the aim of improving their quality of life and increase their awareness about government policies as well as accommodate their comments.

2.2. Health: Insurance and Health Care

Development of health care system is the most important part of social welfare reform. In recent years, the health system in Vietnam has generally improved, especially health care services for the elderly. However, as mentioned above, there are many shortcomings and challenges in the health care system. This paper suggests some reform directions for improvement of health insurance scheme and health care services.

First, the reform progress towards developing the benchmarks of fairness. Patients' co-payment structure for private hospitals is not yet standardized. A more standardized fee-for-service payment scheme should be introduced. In the long run, the payment method of health care services may consider pay-for-performance as a prospective payment method.

Second, the reform focuses on gradually expanding both coverage and the level of assistance while lessening requirements for receiving benefits. The most important role of the health care system is to prevent financial collapse of a family due to serious diseases. The health insurance should fully cover serious diseases whereas impose relatively high copayment rate for less serious diseases such as cold, stomachache. For example, in case of Korea, the duration of medical care benefits has been gradually changed from 180 days to 300 days per year while extending the scope of dependents. Also, the government announced strengthening measures for the coverage of the national health insurance to extend its coverage and to reduce the burden rate through accumulated contributions in August 9th, 2017 (NHIC, n.d.).

Third, strengthening awareness of health insurance and health care to the people. Promoting communication activities on health insurance and health care information to increase the people awareness with the aim of encouraging people and communities to actively participate in the health system. Health insurance should be mandatory, and it should be implemented without exception. If it is open to people's choice, it will create adverse selection as we have seen in the case of U.S.A. The National Health Insurance Corporation in Korea has the department of public relations which is in charge of developing various public relations strategies and implementing different types of public relations work to encourage more people to easily have access to the health insurance. For example, the department uses Social Network Service (SNS) as

Facebook and a blog to easily approach more people.

Fourth, improving the quality and effectiveness of the health system. The reform is suggested to improve attitudes and serving styles of health workers toward increasing the satisfaction of patients and to strengthening communication and counseling skills in health services for medical staffs. In order to achieve this goal, competition among public hospitals should be introduced. At the same time, medical hospitals should be expanded to overcome the current lack of labor supply in the health market.

VI. Conclusion

The social welfare system is a very important part of the economic system. Depending on the total tax revenue ratio [(tax + social insurance compensation)/GDP], the social welfare system in the world can be divided into the following: the Nordic model with very high total tax revenue ratio around 50%, the continental model around 40%, the Anglo-saxon model around 30%, and the E. Asian model around 25%. How much people are willing to pay for their tax and social insurance contribution depends on three factors. First is the level of GDP per capita. In a poor country, people cannot afford to assume high total tax. Since Vietnam will maintain steady growth rate in the coming years, this income factor will not be a serious constraint to the rising tax burden. Second is the level of people's trust for the government. When people cannot trust the government, their willingness to pay tax will be very low. By the Transparency International, the corruption perception index of Vietnam in 2017 is 35 out of 100 with the world ranking of 107th. Since the ranking is on its rising trend from 123th at the year of 2012, the trust level for the government will be improved in the future. But it will not be an easy job to increase its tax burden in a short period of time. Third factor that affects willingness to pay tax is the size of the population and the level of fiscal decentralization. When your tax money is pooled in a big pot and is shared with many people, you do not think that you are going to be the beneficiaries of your contribution. All the Scandinavian countries are small in their population size, and most of the European countries are very much decentralized in their social welfare system. Considering Vietnam's big population and the strong role of the national government in the social welfare system, high tax burden does not seem to be appropriate in Vietnam.

Vietnam should gradually expand its coverage and benefits so that it can maintain the fiscal balance. Korea has respected this principle until 1990s, but speeded up too much after 2000 causing a fiscal imbalance now. Social welfare should be expanded, but at a pace that the public finance can handle. In this respect, the South European model should not be the choice of Vietnam. And the optimal level of the social welfare in Vietnam depends on the decision of the Vietnamese people.

CHAPTER THREE:

INDENTIFYING AND PROMOTING SOUND ECONOMIC POLICIES FOR GROWTH AND FINANCIAL MARKET DEVELOPMENT

Ki Young Park
Professor, School of Economics, Yonsei University

CHAPTER THREE:

IDENTIFYING AND PROMOTING SOUND ECONOMIC POLICIES FOR GROWTH AND FINANCIAL MARKET DEVELOPMENT

I. Introduction

In this chapter, we focus on the issues related to financial markets. There are so many important topics that touch both financial markets and economic growth. Rather than skimming all related issues, we examine a few issues in more detail. Our criteria of choosing the topics are as follows: (1) it is relevant to the main challenges the Vietnamese economy faces, (2) it is not much discussed by other programs such as Vietnam 2035 and KSP (Knowledge Sharing Program), (3) South Korea has precedents or has experienced the similar situations. More specifically, we attempt to provide "bad" examples where South Korea should not have done or would have avoided. By examining those "bad" examples, we identify what policy options South Korea should have used in the past and make policy recommendations by combining South Korea's precedents with the current situation of Vietnamese economy.

Based on these criteria, we choose two main topics. The first topic we discuss is on capital market liberalization (CML). The second is on financial resource allocation during the transition toward more market-oriented economy. As to the first topic, we first examine the main arguments for CML and their weaknesses, along with explaining some myths on CML and prerequisites for

CML. Then, we provide a brief history of South Korea related to CML and key policy changes and deregulations. We examine the mechanism in which the policies of different motivations lead to maturity mismatch of foreign funding and the liquidity crisis during the period of Global Financial Crisis (GFC). We will see the unintended consequence of a set of policy changes that are seemingly innocuous by themselves. For the second, we focus on financial resource allocation issues during the transition period in which bank privatization takes place. During the processes of bank privatization in South Korea, two key issues have emerged: allocation of financial resource toward households (at the same time, away from small and medium enterprises (SMEs)) and extremely high share of foreign ownership in domestic banks. Based on the experience of South Korea, we examine what the Vietnamese policy makers should consider when the roles of private banks become more critical compared to government-owned banks, based on South Korea's experiences.

The rest of the section is structured as follows. Section 2 reviews the current state of the Vietnamese economy related to financial market issues. It discusses the topic of CML, domestic financial markets, and monetary/macroprudential policy one by one. Section 3 examines the case of South Korea related to CML and Section 4 examines issues that have emerged in bank privatization. Section 5 discusses the lessons and policy options that the Vietnamese economy needs to consider. Section 6 concludes with a summary.

II. Evaluating the Current State of the Vietnamese Economy and Financial Markets

1. Issues in Capital Market Liberalization

1.1 Current Issues

The development of capital markets depends significantly on the level of capital market liberalization, which can be understood as the degree to which the government loosens the conditions and control access to capital market, the discrimination between domestic and foreign stakeholders. In the process of economic development and integration with the trend of globalization, the financial market in general and the capital market in particular in Vietnam has gradually been removed from the administrative and limitative in the legal regulations.

In relation to the world, so far Vietnam's current account has been fully liberalized according to the International Monetary Fund (IMF) standards. The capital account has been significantly liberalized in terms of capital inflows into Vietnam, especially foreign direct investment (FDI). Foreign firms are almost uninhibited in terms of industry, capital withdrawal and profit transfer. For Foreign Indirect Investment (FII), foreign investors are free to invest and withdraw capital in the Vietnamese stock market, but their investment size is restricted to listed companies as well as in some special areas such as banking and insurance sector. However, for investment abroad, the current regulations are still tightly controlled. Enterprises have to do a lot of procedures for direct and indirect investment abroad. Indirect investment abroad, not prohibited by law, but there is no document to guide domestic investors open accounts as well as transfer money overseas investment.

Credit markets were strongly reformed in the 1990s, allowing for the involvement of private commercial banks domestically and internationally. The State Bank of Vietnam (SBV) gradually reduced its intervention in credit decisions and interest rate agreements at commercial banks. As a result, competition among banks has been increasing, helping banks to operate more effectively, the gap between deposit and lending rates has been narrowed. As a result, the private sector is increasingly accessing credit from the commercial banking system for investment and business purposes. In addition, domestic enterprises are free to borrow medium- and long-term loans from foreign countries, provided that they are included in the total loan limit set up by the SBV. People are also entitled to foreign loans for business and consumption. To some extent, the SBV uses state own commercial banks as a tool to guide the credit policy and preferential interest rates for the SOE sector. As a consequence, the private sector, especially small and medium enterprises, still has difficulty accessing credit and has to borrow at higher interest rates than SOEs.

The stock market has officially become a new capital mobilization channel for businesses and the government since 2000. However, it was not until 2006 that the market actually developed in terms of both market size and transaction value. HOSE and HNX listed nearly 700 shares of the company and more than 100 government bonds as well as corporate bonds. This is the place to attract 1.5 million investors, individuals and organizations, both domestic and foreign participants. During the uncertain macroeconomic period and the domestic economy went down in the period 2008 - 2011, the stock market has experienced sustainable development since 2012. However, the recovery the stock market is quite slow, businesses still cannot issue bonds to raise capital. This is partly due to the slow recovery of the economy, but one important reason is that Vietnam maintains prudent restrictions and has not had strong reforms to boost the stock market.

Up to now, Vietnam's capital market has developed significantly and has all kinds of markets including credit markets and stock markets. Following sections, each market will be analyzed in detail.

1.2 Credit Markets

1.2.1 Overview

In 1990, Vietnam's banking system was transformed into a two-tier banking system instead of a one-tier banking system[18]. Since then the banking system has been operated according to market rules. The reform of the banking system has led to a dramatic change in credit activities of credit institutions, allowing for the involvement of private and foreign banks. The State Bank of Vietnam (SBV) has gradually reduced its intervention in credit decisions and interest rate agreements at commercial banks. So far, Vietnam's credit market has contributed significantly to the development of the multi-sector commodity economy and Vietnam's economic growth.

The rapid increase in the number of credit institutions has contributed greatly to the development of the credit market. Since the beginning of the reform, the number of credit institutions has increased sharply and diversified in terms of ownership. In the first years of reform (1990-1991),

18 The State Bank of Vietnam implemented both monetary policy and commercial banking operations.

credit institutions in Vietnam consisted of only four state-owned commercial banks and 10 joint stock banks and a few credit cooperatives (there was no foreign credit institutions). In 2000, the number of joint stock banks was 48. However, in recent years, as a result of the government's implementation of the restructuring program of credit institutions, the number of joint stock banks has reduced significantly. By the end of 2017, the number of financial institutions was up to 95 banks (including 7 state-owned commercial banks, 1 social policy bank, 1 development bank, 55 branches of foreign banks and banks with 100% foreign capital, 3 joint venture banks, and 28 joint stock commercial banks.

In the period from 2000 to 2010, credit grew rapidly at average rate 30% year-on-year, peaking at nearly 54% in 2007. High growth rate of credit in this period was one of the main reasons for the high inflation in 2008. To curb inflation, the SBV had to tighten credit control. As a result, total credit outstanding in 2011 went down to 16%, thus significantly shrinking from the level of 31.19% of 2010 (Figure 3-1).

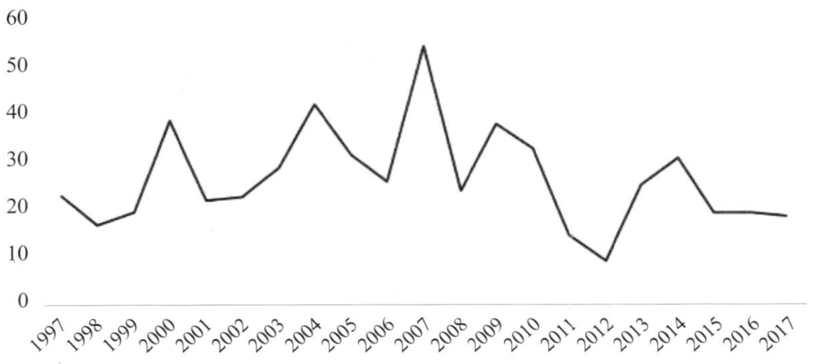

Source: State Bank of Vietnam

Figure 3-1 Credit Growth Rate

The state-owned sector account for over 50% of the total credit, however, the private sector, especially small and medium enterprises (SMEs), still has difficulty accessing credit and has to borrow at higher interest rates than SOEs. SMEs, mostly micro enterprises and accounting for up to 98% of the total number of enterprises, are usually not the subject of interest for commercial banks while their loans might be too large to borrow from microfinance institutions (Nguyen, Gan, & Hu, 2015).

As we can see in Table 3-1, Vietnam has all kinds of credit institutions, however, sate-owned commercial banks account for a large share not only of credit market but also of capital mobilization market. Although in recent years, the market share of state-owned commercial banks has been declined, these banks still play a dominant role in both capital mobilization and lending. In 2005, state-owned commercial banks had a credit market share of 75.2% and capital mobilization market share of 80%. By the end of 2016 these banks account for about 52.9% of credit market share and 49.1% of mobilization market. Joint stock commercial banks, foreign commercial banks mainly provide loans to private enterprises and foreign invested economic sectors, meanwhile the state commercial banks often focus on lending to SOEs.

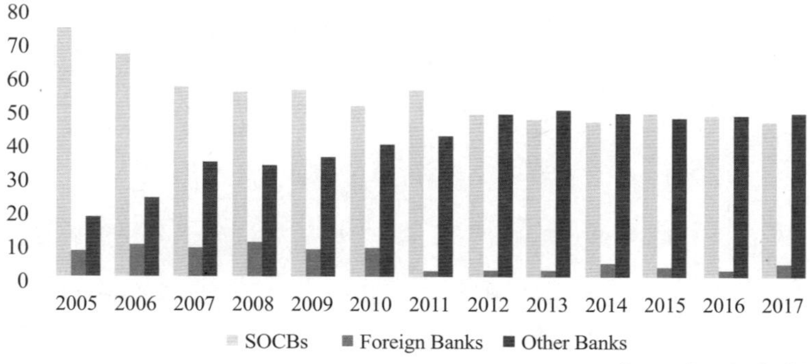

Source: State Bank of Vietnam

Figure 3-2 Credit Market Share

In short, the credit market of Vietnam has contributed significantly to the development of multi-sector commodity economy and economic growth in Vietnam. However, credit markets are relatively mature and are moving towards Basel II risk management standards. More importantly, in credit market, the state-owned commercial banks account for a large share of total credit outstanding. Private sector and SMEs still face many difficulties in accessing formal credit.

1.2.2 Credit Liberalization Process

The formation of a two-tier banking system has allowed the private sector to engage in the banking sector. In the early years, the SBV used credit ceilings as a monetary policy tool to control credit. Credit ceilings, which have been utilized by the SBV since 1994, had effectively limited the growth rate of total liquidity during 1995-1997 period. Initially, credit ceiling was only applied for four stated owned commercial bank (including Bank for Foreign Trade, Bank for Industry and Commerce, Bank for Agriculture and Rural Development, and Bank for Investment and Development), it then expanded to about two thirds of banking system in 1996. However, in 1997 and early 1998, credit ceilings gradually became less effective in constraining the increase of total liquidity. Furthermore, credit expansion during this period was necessary for the promotion of economic growth (which was then showing signs of slowdown). If credit ceilings had been continued to be applied, there would have been more difficulties for commercial banks to expand credit. Therefore, since the second quarter of 1998, the SBV has ceased to use credit ceilings as a regular instrument in conducting monetary policy.

To support the economy after the Asian financial crisis of 1998, the SBV began implementing an expansionary monetary policy from 1999. Accordingly, the SBV almost did not do anything to control total credit outstanding for the economy. As a result, in the period 1999-2010, credit growth rate was always above 30%. It peaked at over 50% in 2007 because SBV failed to sterilize large inflows of portfolio investments, which then surged due to the exuberance of foreign investors in the first year of Vietnam's accession to the WTO. Due to the resultant high inflation, the SBV shifted from expansionary monetary policy to tightening monetary policy from 2011. Since then credit growth rate has been closely monitored to enable SBV take prompt actions in case of too expansionary credit growth.

According to current practice, at the beginning of the year, on the basis of credit growth target approved for the year, the SBV assigns the maximum credit growth targets for credit organizations, which can be adjusted on the basis of assessment of credit quality and credit capacity of credit institutions. Credit institutions are required to control the credit growth rate, giving priority to the real sector. The SBV also stipulates that the proportion of outstanding loans in non-priority sectors to total loans should not exceed 16%, but allows for exceptions according to the market conditions (the SBV's annual reports).

For foreign currency denominated credit, the SBV implements measures to strictly control the growth of credit, in foreign currency. It narrows the scope of foreign currency lending by credit institutions by issuing regulations[19] on lending in foreign currency as well as borrowers in foreign currency. It inspected and examined a number of credit institutions with highgrowth of foreign currencies denominated credit. However, the SBV also flexibly handles

19 Circular No. 03/2012 / TT-NHNN dated 08/3/2012 and Circular No. 29/2013 / TT-NHNN dated 06/12/2013 regulating lending in foreign currency of credit institutions, foreign bank branches with resident borrowers

cases where it is necessary to lend in foreign currencies to reduce the cost of borrowing, thus lessening difficulties for enterprises.

1.3. Stock Market

The Vietnam stock market includes two stock exchanges: Ho Chi Minh City Stock Exchange (HOSE) and Hanoi Stock Exchange (HNX). In 2000, the Ho Chi Minh City Securities Trading Center (HoSTC) was established, later, it was renamed and upgraded to become HOSE. Five years later, in 2005, Hanoi Securities Trading Center[20] was launched. The first trading section was conducted in 2000 with only two stocks REE and SAM. To date, after 20 years of development, the Vietnam's stock market has developed strongly. Hereafter,

Vietnam's stock market will be analyzed in more detail in terms of legal and institutional frameworks, the size of the market, and the management and supervision of the market.

1.3.1. Legal and Institution Framework

Since the Law on Securities came into effect on 2007, it has created a highly consistent and uniform legal framework. The Law is in line with international practice, providing the basis for Vietnam's stock market to integrate into international and regional capital markets, enhancing the transparency of the market and improving the market surveillance and management capabilities of state management agencies. However, besides the results obtained, the Law on Securities remains under-developed in terms of scope, which only covers

20 It is renamed as Hanoi Stock Exchange (HNX) in 2009.

the basic contents. The issuance of legal regulations generally has a time lag compared to the goal set, and many provisions in the Securities Law have not been supported by detailed guidelines. According to Farber, Nguyen, and Vuong (2006), policies on trading and disclosure practices have had profound impacts on Vietnam's stock market. The excessive use of policy tools can harm the market and confidence of investors.

Box 1 Major milestones mark the development of the stock market in Vietnam

Date	Events
1990	The Enterprise Law was passed and came into effect.
1993	Decision No. 207 / QD-TCCB of the Governor of the State Bank on the task of studying, developing projects and preparing conditions for establishment of the securities market
1995	Decision No. 361 / QD-TTg on the establishment of the Preparatory Committee of the stock market organization to assist the Prime Minister in directing the preparation of necessary conditions for the development of the securities market in Vietnam.
1996	Decree No. 75 / CP of the Government on the establishment of the State Securities Commission
2000	Opening Ho Chi Minh City Securities Trading Center
2000	The first trading session of the Securities Trading Center Ho Chi Minh City with 2 shares coded REE and SAM
2005	Secondary trading at Hanoi Securities Trading Center was established
2006	The XIth National Assembly's passed of the Law on Securities. This is the document defining the highest legal framework in the securities sector
2007	Ho Chi Minh Stock Exchange (HCMC) officially came into operation
2008	Special bond market was formed under Decision No. 352 / QD-UBCK dated 16/5/2008.
2009	Hanoi Stock Exchange was established
2009	Open Market for Unlisted Public Companies (UPCoM) with 10 public companies registered for trading.

1.3.2 Market Size

Market size experienced consistently strong and solid growth, acting as an important medium and long-term capital channel, thus contributing positively to the industrialization and modernization of the country. During the period 2000-

2005, market capitalization was less than 1% of GDP, it jumped dramatically to 22.7% of GDP in 2006 and continued to rise to over 43% in 2007. Due to the negative impact of the Global Financial Crisis (GFC), the stock price index dropped continuously in 2008 and as a result the market capitalization dropped by more than 50% to just about 18% of GDP. As the economy recovered since the second quarter of 2009, stock price index has gradually increased, the number of companies listed on the market also increased rapidly. As a result, according to the State Securities Commission (SSC), by 30 November 2017 the market capitalization reached as high as 96.3% of GDP.

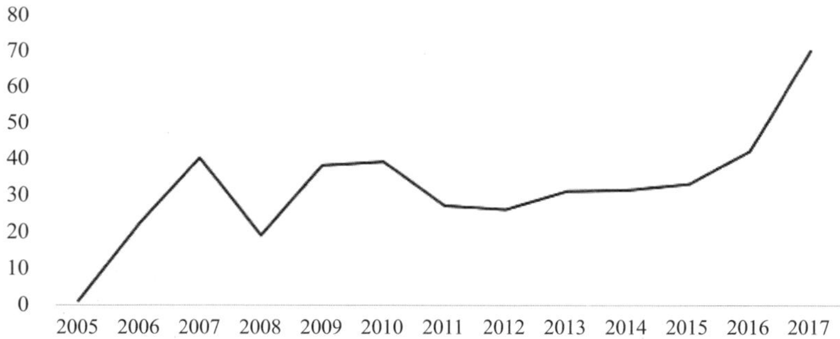

Source: State Securities Commission

Figure 3-3 Stock market size (% of GDP)

The market size increases not only in terms of market capitalization and the number of listed companies but also in the number of investors involved in the transaction. Vietnam's stock market is an attractive destination for foreign investors. Foreign capital inflows increase quickly every year. The number of foreign investors has increased consistently, from about 3,000 accounts in the year 2000, to 21 - 685 as of 31 October 2017.Foreign investors tend to invest in large firms, firms with high book-to-market ratio and firms with low leverage (Vo, 2011).

In 2000, there were only two companies listed on the HOSE and until 2005, after the Hanoi Securities Trading Center (HASTC) came into operation, the total number of companies listed on both markets were 44 companies. In general, in the period from 2000 to 2005, the stock market developed very slowly because of the lack of fully developed financial and legal institutions that are required to support a stock market (Ando & Scheela, 2005). However, since 2006, Vietnam's stock market has started to flourish and has seen strong growth in both the number of listed companies and transaction turnover. By November 2017, there were 2.016 listed companies on both stock exchanges

1.3.3 Management and Supervision of the Market

A supervision mechanism has been established in a professional manner according to international practices. Inspection and supervision by the SSC focuses on monitoring compliance with market intermediaries; supervising the compliance with issuing organizations and listing organizations. In addition, supervision of transactions in the stock market aims to detect acts of market abuse; the inspectors perform enforcement functions.

Although the stock market in Vietnam has achieved encouraging results in the last 20 years, Vietnam's stock market is still at an early stage of development. When compared to the Chinese stock market, Chu (2017) find that Vietnam's stock market is heavily underdeveloped although the two markets were formed under similar backgrounds. Capital mobilized through the stock market is small compared to credit channels. The size of the stock market is also small compared to the economy, and more importantly, the Vietnam's stock market has no contribution to the country's economic growth (Vo, Nguyen, & Pham, 2016).

1.3.4 Vietnam Stock Market Liberalization

A stock market liberalization is a decision by a country's government to allow foreigners to purchases shares in that country's stock market (Henry, 2000). Stock market liberalization brings many benefits to the domestic economy. Kinuthia and Etyang (2014) argue that stock market liberalization indirectly impacts on economic growth through investment. The liberalization of stock market is also found to have effect to stock returns (Auzairy & Ahmad, 2009), it also renders equity markets more liquid and efficient (Jain-Chandra, 2002).

Although certain achievements have been achieved in managing, operating and monitoring the market, the management and operation of the stock market over the last time still have some shortcomings and limitations such as: The promulgation of legal documents, market management policies have not been flexible, still passive and slow compared with the requirements of real development of the stock market. The capitalization of the market is concentrated in a few enterprises where the State holds dominant shares. The ability to raise capital from the issuance of bonds is very low. The State still holds a large number of shares in many listed companies (even over 90% in some stocks); unlisted or listed large-scale SOEs; lack of strategy as well as policies to encourage domestic and foreign investors to participate; no funds from pension funds, social insurance ... to participate in the market; There are no independent credit rating agencies to assist bond issuers. The strong fluctuation of the market in the period 2006-2012 indicate that the risk control capacity of the authorities is still weak.

Vietnam joined the World Trade Organization (WTO) in January 2007 and became an official negotiating partner in the Trans-Pacific Partnership (TPP) trade agreement in 2010. As a member of the WTO, Vietnam commits to allow foreign investors to provide several securities services in Vietnam. Under current regulations, foreign investors are allowed to own up to 49% of shares in a company, 30% in a bank. Recently, in 2015, the Government issued Decree No. 60/2015/ND-CP, which amends and supplements a number of articles of Decree 58/2012/ND-CP detailing and guiding the implementation of a number of articles of the Law on Securities. This decree removed caps on foreign share of public companies that do not fall into a few specified categories.

Although the government has many solutions to encourage domestic and foreign individuals to participate in the stock market, the stock market is still under strict control of the government. The Vietnamese government should further relax control on the market and open the market more widely to the world (Chu, 2017).

Box 2. Commitments to open the securities services market

Regarding securities services, Vietnam commits to allow foreign investors to provide the following securities services in Vietnam:

1. Transactions for their accounts or customer accounts at the stock exchange, the OTC market or other markets on the following products:
   - Derivatives, including futures and option contracts;
   - Transferable securities;
   - Other negotiable instruments and financial assets, other than gold bullion.
   (These include brokerage services.)
2. Participating in the issuance of all types of securities, including issuance underwriting, and acting as a selling agent (offering to the public or private offering), providing services related to the issuance there);
3. Asset management (including portfolio management, all forms of collective investment management, retirement fund management, depository and trust services);
4. Payment and clearing services for securities, derivatives and other products related to securities;
5. Providing and transferring financial information and related software of securities service providers.

Foreign securities companies, foreign investors can provide securities services in Vietnam in what form?

Vietnam commits to allow foreign securities companies and foreign investors to operate securities in Vietnam in the following forms and conditions:

- Representative office (provided that the representative office is not allowed to carry out direct business activities);
- Joint venture with Vietnamese partners (provided that the foreign capital contribution ratio does not exceed 49%);
- Securities companies with 100% foreign capital (as from January 11, 2012);
- Branches of foreign securities companies (as of January 11, 2012) and their operating conditions are limited to the provision of asset management, payment and clearing services. Supply, transfer and delivery of financial information, related software.

1.3.5 Concerning Issues

Although certain results have been achieved in managing, operating and monitoring the market, the management and operation of the stock market over the last time still have some shortcomings and limitations. They include:

- The promulgation of legal documents, market management policies have not been flexible, still passive and slow compared with the requirements of real development of the stock market.
- The capitalization of the market is concentrated in a few enterprises where the State holds dominant shares. The ability to raise capital from the issuance of bonds is very low.

In addition to the achievements, the development of the capital market has shown some limitations and shortcomings, reducing the role of the capital channel of the economy. First, the capital market still depends heavily on bank credit. The banking credit market is still the main source of capital for the economy. Bank loans are the main source of capital in enterprises. Even with the developing stock market, commercial banks are also the key and direct investors on the stock market, playing a domination role in the bond market. Although bank credit is the main source of capital, capital mobilization of the banking system is mainly short-term and demand capital, so the stability is not high. On the other hand, banks' derivative products and other banking services have not really developed, the revenue of the banking system still relies heavily on credit operations; many local commercial banks do not comply with Basel II risk management standards. In the context of slow recovery in domestic and world economy, production and business activities are affected, making credit activities of the bank difficult to maintain. Meanwhile, the informal credit market still exists in parallel with the banking credit market. Small and medium enterprises (SMEs) have difficulty accessing formal credit resulting in credit misallocation problem (IMF, 2017).

Second, during the period of macroeconomic environment fluctuations, the SBV has implemented many discretionary policies such as imposing ceiling deposit and lending interest rates, restricting credit to non-manufacturing sectors, and limiting the formation and the existence of small commercial banks. These policies only have short-term effects. However, extending it after a period of turmoil caused the financial and credit markets to be stagnant or develop distorted.

In addition, the size of the stock market has rapidly increased. However, the quality of the market has not been as expected. The number of listed shares and the number of investor accounts has increased significantly however, many large listed stocks increased erratically, large stocks increased but low liquidity seriously affected the index and did not reflect the real value of stocks. More importantly, investors on the stock market are not professional and have developed quite diversified capital from individual investors is quite large but lack sustainability when easily affected by psychology, rumors or activities of foreign investors. Meanwhile, potential investors such as investment funds and insurance companies are not fully exploited. In the bond market, the main investor is the commercial banks who are dependent on business activities (lending), which makes the capital unstable and cannot bring sustainable development to the market. Moreover, different from developed countries, such as Korea, corporate bonds is equal to 74.3% of GDP and government bond is about 53.2% of GDP, in Vietnam, the government bonds account for the majority market share.

A recent financial development index released by the International Monetary Fund indicates that Vietnam's financial sector development has improved during the last two decades but remains below most of ASEAN countries (Figure 3-4).

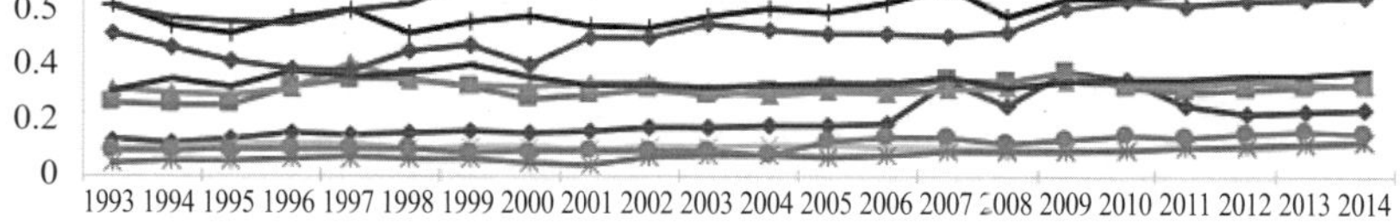

Source: International Monetary Fund

Figure 3-4 Financial Development Index in ASEAN Countries

However, if we examine other indicators related to financial markets such as, Financial Institutions Efficiency Index and Financial Markets Efficiency Index, we can see that these indicators are quite high.

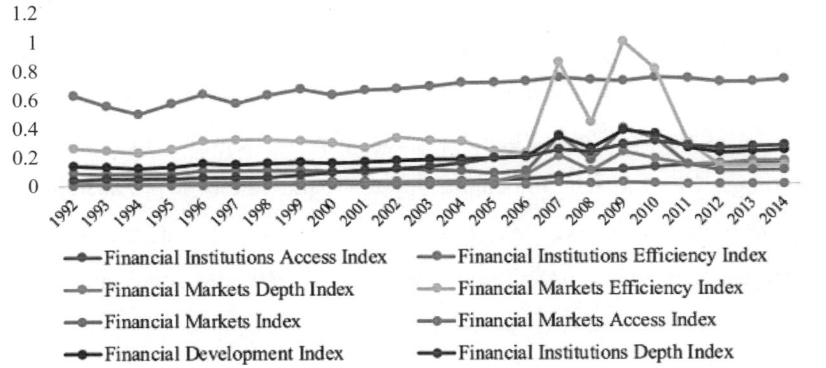

Source: International Monetary Fund

Figure 3-5 Selected Financial Indices

2. Issues in Domestic Financial Markets

In 1986, Vietnam launched its economic renovation, starting the process of deep integration into the world economy. Along with the broader economic reform, Vietnam's financial market has started a comprehensive reform in which administrative interventions have been decreasing, accompanied by more expansion of the market size and quality of services. The introduction of two ordinances on banking in May 1990 marked the important milestone of the financial markets reform. Vietnam's financial market has been gradually developed since then.

By the end of 2011, as noted by the World Bank (2014), the structure of the financial markets of Vietnam has the features as follows:

- The banking sector dominated financial system, with total assets equivalent to 183 % GDP and 92% assets of financial institutions.[21]

- Non-bank financial institutions account for only 17% of GDP and 8% of total assets of financial institutions.
- Financial companies are the most significant group in the non-bank institutions with a size equivalent to 6% of GDP; insurance companies accounted for 4% of GDP, the rest belong to the social insurance funds, and mutual funds which account for less than 1% and private pension funds is negligible.

2.1 Banking Sector

Vietnam banking' industry has grown from a mono-banking system to a massive network of banks and financial institutions (Hung, 2016). Banking sector witnessed significant efforts by the Vietnamese government in initiating many banking reforms during the last few decades.

Before 1990, the State Bank of Vietnam (SBV) functioned as both a central bank and a commercial bank implementing the tasks of unifying the currency after the war against United States in 1975. From 1986 to 1990, reforms began as a premise for a basic and then comprehensive banking system in Vietnam (Du, Kieu, and Tuan 2013). The SBV separated the central bank's functions and delegated its banking activities to four newly created state-owned commercial banks (SOCBs), each targeting a different segment of the economy.[22] In 1991, Banking ordinances took effect allowing foreign banks to establish their

21 Include two policy banks

22 The central bank's industrial and commercial lending department was converted to the Vietnam Industrial and Commercial Bank (formerly Incombank, now Vietinbank), its agricultural department to the Vietnam Bank for Agriculture and Rural Development (Agribank), its international trade department to the Bank for Foreign Trade of Vietnam (Vietcombank), and its infrastructure department to the Bank for Investment and Development of Vietnam (BIDV)

branches and representative offices in Vietnam and joint stock commercial banks (JSCBs) started to emerge (Du, Kieu, and Tuan, 2013).

From 1991 to present, the state remains as the controlling stakeholder to these SOCBs, holing at least 65% ownership in them, while the role of the SBV is narrowed to that of a central bank, which includes the formulation of monetary policies, management of foreign exchange reserves, licensing and supervision of credit institutions. Even though there is a significant shift of credit mobilization and allocation from SOBs to JSCBs, SOBs remain a significant market share. Furthermore, the integration process of Vietnam such as US-Bilateral Trade Agreement in 2001, accession to World Trade Organization (WTO) in 2007 has led to an increasing presence of foreign banks in Vietnam. There has been growing partial privatization of the SOCBs and more considerable efforts to achieve compliance with the international capital standards under the Basel capital accords.

Nevertheless, reforms of the banking sector have been slow, and banks are still undergoing a restructuring program to address the high level of non-performing loan ratios (NPLs) and other structural problems (Tran, Ong, and Weldon, 2015).

The abolition of the state monopoly in 1990 has contributed significantly to the diversification of banking activities and increased the number of JSCBs from 4 to 41 in the period 1991-1993, subsequently reaching a peak at 51 in 1995. However, after the financial crisis in 1997, this figure declined because of business failures, bankruptcy or license withdrawal of some JSCBs. High fragmentation posed a challenge to the stability of Vietnam's banking industry. In comparison to the country's population and size of the economy, the banking sector has become overly dense by their NPL ratios, which were particularly vulnerable as they could not adequately assess the risk of loans to very small businesses and individuals. Due to their relatively small asset size, these small banks were not able to properly price loans, lowering the overall profitability of the industry. A large number of banks in the industry also increased the difficulty for regulators to monitor and supervise.

From 2000 to 2007, Vietnamese banking system underwent a restructuring process. The dissolution, M&A of weak JSCBs happened which continuously decreased the number of JSCBs to 34 in 2007. From 2007 to 2015, at the former stage, the number of JSCBs increased as the equitization of some SOCBs such as Vietinbank, Vietcombank, and BIDV. At the later stage, this figure again witnessed a decreased tendency due to restructuring process in some recently detected weak banks like ACB, Ocean Banks, MHB, Habubank, and so on. On the contrary, the number of branches of foreign bank has escalated since the reforms of the banking sector. This phenomenon is attributed to integration process and economic development in Vietnam.

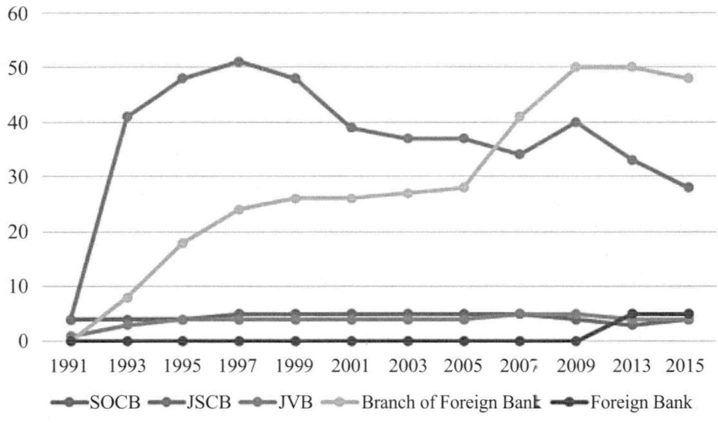

Source: Compiled from Truc & Danh (2012), VP Bank Securities (2014) and SBV

Figure 3-6 Number of SOBs, JSCBs, JVBs, FBs, and Branch of FB, 1991-2015

Along with the increase in quantity, the banking sector also experienced significant growth in asset size. From 2007 to 2010, the total assets of the banking sector doubled from 1,097 trillion VND ($52,4 billion) to 2,29 trillion VND ($128,7 billion). By the end of 2016, this figure was 8,113 trillion VND ($456 billion).

The market share of JSCBs has changed considerably since 2004. Previously to 2004, SOCBs were normally dominant with the average market share of capital mobilization and allocation of above 78%. There was a sharp rise of JSCBs from 12% of the lending market, and 13% of credit mobilization market in 2004 to 47% and 35% respectively. On the other hand, the market share of SOCBs has narrowed significantly. Figure 3-7 & 3-8 have shown the increasingly important role of JSCBs in Vietnamese financial market in particular and economic development in general.

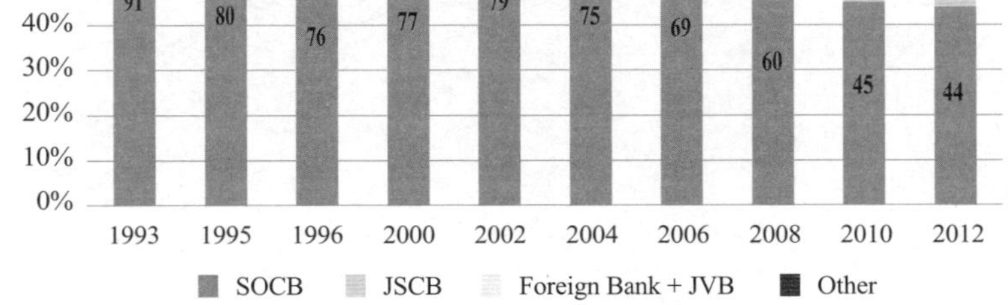

Source: VP Securities (2014)

Figure 3-7 Market Shares of SOCB, JSCB, Foreign Banks + JVB in Credit Mobilization Market

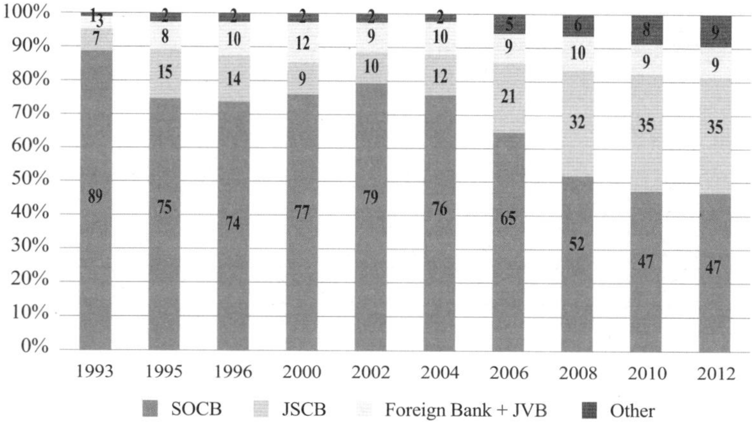

Source: VP Securities (2014)

Figure 3-8 Market shares of SOCB, JSCB, Foreign Banks + JVB in Credit Market

Domestic banks have expanded their network through opening new branches, transaction offices, ATMs. In this term, SOCBs are more advantageous than JSCBs and foreign banks because they have a longer history, more significant capital resources, and broader customer network. In 2013, SOCBs had 1,320 branches and 3,154 transaction offices nationwide. Meanwhile those of JSCBs were 1,083 and 3,154 respectively. This numbers of JVBs and foreign banks were even much smaller. In general, it can be seen that the majority of JCSBs only focuses on their networks on urban areas where the economic and infrastructure conditions are better. Consequently, this leads to increasing competition in urban areas among banks and causes an imbalance in banking services between urban areas and rural areas.

Table 3-1 Network of the Banking System in Vietnam

Network	SOCB	JSCB	Foreign Bank + JVB
Ha Noi	692	892	25
HCMC	495	1.248	30
Da Nang	84	179	3
Can Tho	54	137	7
Other	3,149	1,808	27
Total	4,474	4,241	92

Source: VP Securities (2014)

Table 3-2 Density of Banking Facilities in Vietnam

Density	Ha Noi	HCMC	Vietnam
Average km² per bank point	1.6	1.0	47.3
Average bank point per people	3.2	3.6	12.4
Average ATM per people	2.7	2.0	6.4
Average POS per people	450	420	1,048

Source: VP Securities (2014)

One potentially critical threat lies in non-performing loans in banking sector.[23] Although non-performing loans have been in existence for long time in Vietnam, they surged sharply in the post-WTO accession period. Statistics show that the period of high and prolonged macroeconomic instability began in 2007, as evident by slowing growth and rising inflation. Upon becoming a member of the WTO, Vietnam became a favorite destination for capital inflows due to the exuberance of international investors, including managers of speculative funds about the bright prospects of the economy. This resulted

23 In Vietnam, the State Bank of Vietnam (SBV) defines non-performing loans as those falling into groups 3, 4 and 5, which correspond to substandard, doubtful, and potentially lost loans in accordance with Article 10 and 11 of Circular 02/2013 /TT-NHNN on the classification of assets, the method, level and use of loan loss provisioning to deal with risks in operations of credit organizations and foreign bank branches. Although such definition may fall short of international standards, Vietnam is in a transition towards meeting them.

in a surge of foreign investment, both direct and indirect. The large amount of money that had been poured into the economy then was not neutralized by appropriate measures, thus resulting in excessive money supply. In 2007, M2 increased by over 30% while credit growth exceeded 50%. A bubble economy followed, and as a consequence, the value of not only goods and services, but also many assets (stocks, real estate, gold, foreign currency etc.) was inflated, which misguided the behavior of many players in the market and members of the society. There are several reasons. First, numerous households changed from savings to excessive consumption. If the gap between domestic savings and investment in the period 2001-2005 was only 1.83% of GDP, this difference rose to 7.51% of GDP in the 2008-2010 period, thus resulting in substantial risks to macroeconomic stability. The number of private luxury cars and luxury goods soared in the post-2007 period, which was evidence of changes in the consumption behavior among the elite and the emerging middle class. This in turn was explained by the well-known wealth effect overwhelming the income effect. The latter are considerably more sustainable than the former.

Second, many participants of the market changed their behavior from investment to speculation. Their engagement in risky activities escalated during the 2007-2010 period because of the heard mentality. As a consequence, resources did not flow into the real economy to upgrade production capacity, technological capabilities and worker skills towards improving Vietnam's international competitiveness. This in turn resulted in a sharp decline in efficiency as evident by significant deterioration of ICOR and TFP. Many enterprises engaged in rent seeking activities to exploit gaps in legal and policy frameworks at the expense of healthy competition in the economy. Numerous enterprises, state-owned and private firms alike, were excessively leveraged. Many firms made excessive investment in non-core business activities. Industrial policy in support of some large state corporations was also to blame. Notably, the collapse of Vinashin – a state-owned shipbuilding giant, which received strong support from the government without proper oversight, contributed to the build-up of non-performing loans.

Third, cross-ownership prevalent in both the financial and banking systems also raised systemic risks in the economy. Furthermore, moral hazard in the banking and financial system rose substantially. When there is too much money in the economy, it is understandable that commercial banks went easy with their lending, focusing on disbursement rather than efficiency and risk management. In fact, moral hazard increased significantly in the financial-banking system, especially in commercial banks that set up and used connected companies to perform many of the functions of the investment banking. As a consequence, excessive investment was made in risky assets such as stocks and real estate. Many financial and banking institutions fail to adhere to the principles of professional ethics and strict compliance with the laws. We discuss some policy measures to address these issues below.

2.2 Stock Exchange Market

Vietnamese stock exchange market has become an indispensable capital mobilization channel for domestic enterprises and an investment channel for domestic and foreign investors. Established in 1998 by Decision No. 127/1998/QD-TTg (but officially in operation in 2000 as the Ho Chi Minh Securities Trading Center (HOSE)), the Vietnamese stock exchange market only had two securities of two companies: Refrigeration Electrical Engineering Joint Stock Corporation (REE) and Saigon Cable and Telecommunication Material Joint Stock Company (SACOM)), and two trading days per week. Since then, it has experienced a continuous and robust expansion with the establishment of Ha Noi Stock Exchange (HNX) in 2005 and the Unlisted Public Company market (UPCoM) (Stock online 2017; Stock investment 2016).

After more than 20 years of establishment, the volume and size of Vietnamese stock market have been growing strongly which acts as a vital capital mobilization channel for the development of Vietnam economy (Bang, 2017). The total value of mobilized capital from the stock market has reached form 986 billion VND accounting for 0.28% of GDP in 2000 to over 1.9 trillion VND accounting for over 69% of GDP in 2017 (of which in the 2011 period, the capital mobilization through the stock market was 1.5 trillion VND which was 5 times higher than the that of 2005-2010 period).

The number of companies listed on the stock market has escalated from 2 companies in 2000 to over 1,000 companies in 2016 (of which, 659 companies were listed on Ha Noi, and HCMC stock exchange and over 400 companies were listed on UPCoM). Meanwhile, the number of accounts has increased from 3,000 to 6,9 million, of which the number of foreign accounts has increased by 2.3 times compared with that of 2007. This means that Vietnamese stock market is attracting more and more foreign as well as domestic investment. While the foreign investment flows tend to withdraw from emerging markets, the Vietnamese stock market remains and destination for foreign investors. Also, the average trading value of the Vietnamese stock market in 2016 was 6.89 billion VND increasing by 4.9 times compared with that of 2000. In general, Vietnamese stock market has contributed to the economy an average of 23% of the total investment capital and equivalent to 60% of the capital supply of the banking system.

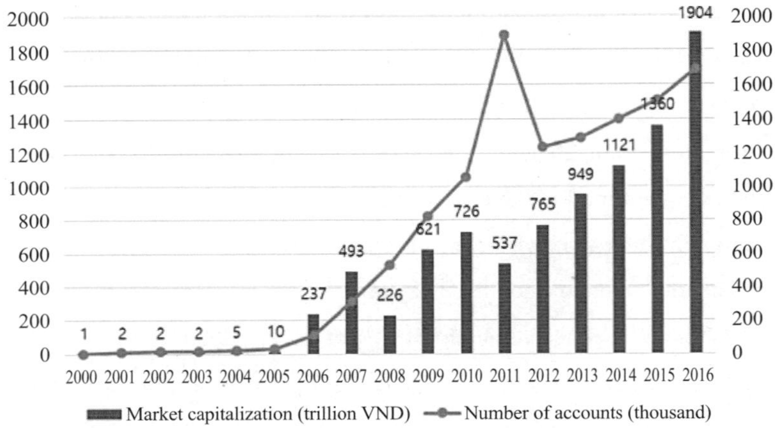

Source: Bang (2017)

Figure 3-9 Size of Vietnamese Stock Market and Number of Foreign Accounts

The number of securities companies are flourished in line with the development of Vietnamese stock market. However, this figure is under restructuring process to improve service quality, management, risk management, technology, widen capital scale, and apply Basel II financial standards as well as CAMEL early warning criteria. As a result, it had reduced from 105 companies to 79 companies.

2.3 Insurance Market

The insurance market in Vietnam is also increasing. Initially, insurance market in Vietnam has only one insurer (insurance companies) owned by the State's Insurance Company of Vietnam established in 1965. In 2015, the insurance market in Vietnam has insurance companies as follows:

Table 3-3 Number of Insurance Enterprises

Types	Year			
	2011	2012	2013	2015
Non-life insurance	29	29	29	29
Life insurance	14	14	16	17
Insurance brokerage	12	12	12	12
Reinsurance	2	2	2	2
Foreign non-life insurance branch				1
Total	57	57	59	61

Source: Insurance Association of Vietnam

According to the annual report of the Insurance Association of Vietnam in 2016:[24] (i) total revenue reached VND 84,374 billion in which the premium revenue reached VND 70,190 billion (increase by 25.75%), revenue from investment activities reached VND 14,185 billion. Life insurance revenue was VND 38,180 billion, increased by 34.4%. Non-life insurance reached VND 32,010 billion, increased by 15%; (ii) total assets reached VND 200,023 billion, increasing 17,48%; in which non-life insurance assets were VND 56,785 billion; life insurance assets were VND 143,238 billion; (iii) contingency funds were VND 130,391 billion, increased by 21.09%, of which life insurance was VND 103,901 billion, non-life insurance reached VND 26,490 billion; (iv) insurance benefits reached 26,797 billion, increased 4%, of which non-life insurance reached 13,231 billion , life expectancy reached 13,566 billion; (v) the sector's investment reached VND 157,266 trillion, increased by 24.9%, of which non-life insurance reached VND 30,433 trillion and life insurance was VND 126,266 trillion; (vi) total equity reached VND 47,917 billion, increased by 7.82%, of which VND 21,251 billion was non-life insurance and

24 http://iav.vn/News/Item/2437/195/vi-VN/Default.aspx

VND 23,666 billion was non-life insurance; (vii) total insurance premium paid through brokerage reached VND 7,733 billion, increased by 18.5%.

In general, the insurance market of Vietnam is still small and mainly non-life insurance, with 62 insurance companies but total assets are only about 4% of GDP, and total insurance premium was about 1.8% of GDP in 2011. In addition, the rate of market penetration tends to increase in recent years. It was 0.57% in 2005 and reached 1.48% in 2011 (Nhung and Luu, 2015). This is a very modest figure compared with other countries in the region such as Malaysia (3.47%), Thailand (2.19%), Singapore (5.52%).

2.4 Real Estate Market

The real estate market is an important market of Vietnamese economy because it has a close relationship with financial markets, which is the primary source of investment capital for real estate market. Therefore, the up and down of financial market have significant impact on the real estate market.

The history of Vietnamese real estate industry is divided into eight stages (VP Bank Securities 2014):

Before 1990: Vietnamese economy had not yet developed, the land fund was still abundant, the urbanization process was low. Thus, the demands for land use of organizations and individuals were not high. In this period, the property market did not almost exist. The majority of real estate transactions was informal and non-market.

The first land fever (1993-1994): There was a fever in residential land segment and the land use right. This was due to the increasing demand of properties for residential, manufacturing and commercial purposes. The heat of land demand was even hotter in urban areas, especially big cities.

The Land Law was formed and came into effects in 1993.

The first land freeze (1995-1999): To cool down the first land fever and prevent speculation phenomenon, the government had to invented by Decrees No. 18 and 87 on land for lease. Accordingly, the owners had to pay twice for their properties (fees for land use right transfer and land lease). The impact of these Decrees forced speculators who use financial leverage had to sell off their properties to pay for lending interest and bank loans. Such massive discharge makes the real estate plummeted as the supply exceed the demand. Besides, the economic crisis in Asia deriving from Thailand had frustrated some foreign real estate projects in Vietnam which contributed to the collapse of the real estate market.

The second land fever (2001-2002): After a dormant period, the land price began to fluctuate in 2000 and then escalated to a peak in the second quarter of 2001. The second land fever happened because speculators predicted that the favored policy for overseas Vietnamese to by properties and the promulgation of new land price would be motivators for real estate market. Consequently, the speculation occurred across suburban areas.

The second land freeze (2000-2006): From late 2000 to 2006, the real estate market was quiet and even frozen. The market next year was even colder than that of last year. According to statistics, the successful transactions in 2003 fell by 28%, and 56% and 78% in 2004 and 2005 respectively. In the second land fever (2001-2002), the State had to regulate the real estate market by promulgating the Land Law (2003) and Decree No.181 to guide implementation of this Law. These changes eliminated benefits deriving from speculation and cooled again the real estate market. However, because most of the capital investment in this period was equity capital, the pressure to sell properties to repay bank loans did not happen as the first fever. Hence, the land price did not go back to that of the first land freeze. This subsequently lead to the movement of investment from real estate market to stock market.

The third land fever (2007-2008): Unlike the previous fever, this fever concentrated significantly on apartment and villas segment. It is because FDI poured into Vietnam considerably, generating impressive economic growth during the 2003-2007 period. In addition, the period of 2006-2007 were fruitful years of Vietnamese securities market where all participants could easily make money. The significant amount of surplus capital of investors from securities market was then transferred to the real estate market which elevated the land price in the high-end segment.

The third land freeze (2008-2013): in the context of real estate bubble and ever-rising inflation, the government had to regulate the market with a tight credit policy, especially for non-manufacturing credit. In addition, some measures had been taken to stabilize the market and curb inflation rate. Immediately after such policy and measures, the real estate market in the South of Vietnam had been heavily affected, and the reduction in price and transaction were inevitable. Regarding the North which had stronger capital flows, real estate market was affected temporarily. Although the transactions were leveled off, the land price only decreased by about 10% in 2008.

Decrees 69 and 71 were issued in 2010 guiding the implementation of the amended land law in 2009, and the land use tax collection made the real estate market more depressed. In 2011, the risk of high inflation and the escalation of the gold and USD prices had forced the government to issue Resolution No. 11, which took action to curb inflation as well as stabilize the macroeconomic situation. Accordingly, credit growth in

2011 was limited to 20%, while outstanding loan balance was limited to 16%, worsening the real estate market and dispel the market recovery expectations of investors.

In 2012, the real estate market became more unstable as some real estates firms had to go bankrupt or sell their projects. In 2013, the real estate market hit bottom as quiet transaction, high inventories and bad debt have not been solved. Some experts claimed that the land price had reduced by 15-30%, and even 50%, while the other pointed out that the price was unchanged, especially in Ha Noi. In this situation, the government has promulgated a number of measures to improve the market. Particularly, Vietnam Asset Management Company (VAMC) was established to deal with bad debts of credit institutions; 30 trillion VND package was created under the Resolution No.2 to promote workhouse and subsidized housing markets. Real Estate Investment Trust (REIT) was also established.

Recovery (2014-present): The real estate market has begun to show signs of recovery in the late of 2013. In 2014, the recovery momentum was continued. Specifically, there were 11,450 successful transactions in Ha Noi (doubled that of 2013), while that of HCMC was 10,350 (increased by 30% compared with 2013). The land price remained stable instead of plummeting like what were happened in 2013. In some projects locating in good positions, the price was even higher by 1-2%. The total value of real estate inventories in 2014 was 73,889 trillion VND, decreasing by 20,569 trillion VND (21.8%) compared with 2013. The structure of real estate market was adjusted towards workhouse and subsidized housing markets by reducing the area of the apartments.

Continuously, in 2015, there was a massive recovery in all market segments such as properties for low, middle, and high income, rental housing, apartments, and resorts. The low lending rates of 8-10% helped real estate companies to access to capital in order to keep going with their projects but maintain reasonable profits.

In 2016, the market continued to develop. The successful number of transactions in Ha Noi and HCMC was 27,565. The total value of real estate inventories halved to 33.6 trillion VND. In sum, the Vietnamese real estate market are warmer, healthier and growing in compatible with the real demands of homeowners, not the speculators.

2.5 State-Owned Enterprises (SOEs) Equitization

In the 1980s, the Vietnamese economy was dominated by SOEs that enjoyed numerous privileges but that was largely inefficient (Hiep 2017). The demand for restructuring SOEs stems from the fact that this type of firms requires more resources while generating less desirable outcomes compared with other firm types. After the official introduction of the non-state legal and policy reforms to create an equal playing field for all economic players. It also began to restructure SOEs to make them more efficient and competitive. Nevertheless, it remains mostly a work in progress.

The SOE equitization process can be divided into three phases (see). The first phase from 1992 to mid-1998 witnessed only 123 SOE equitized, reflecting the government's cautious approach towards this issue. Moreover, the lack of stock exchange market which was not set up until 2000, also discouraged SOEs from being equitized.

The second phase from mid-1998 to 2011 experienced a great number of wholly SOEs and sections of SOEs were converted into multi-ownership or non SOEs. This period experienced a greatest number of equitized SOEs which was 3.585 enterprises. Methods of equitization include selling part of state ownership, selling state ownership, keeping state's equity capital and selling more stocks to outsiders. The main method of equitization for firms with capital larger than 10% billion VND was auction which helped shoot stock price of previously SOEs and brought cash flows to the government. The surge in this period also coincided with Vietnam's preparation for WTO accession in early 2007 and was assisted by its growing stock exchanges.

The third phase from 2011 to 2016, the equitization pace has slowed down with only 535 equitized SOEs. A few reasons accounted for this tendency. First, after the 2007-2008 global financial crisis, the poor performance of Vietnamese stock exchanges discouraged SOEs from doing Initial Public Offerings (IPOs). Second, most of remaining SOE planned for equitization during this period were corporation of large scales so vigilant examination of firm value is prerequisite. Moreover, it was also more difficult for them to find strategic partners given their large size as well as the adverse economic conditions during this period. Third, certain ministries and SOEs themselves were slow and not active enough in meeting equitization targets set by the government (Sjöholm, 2006). Finally, the government's retention of majority stakes in most equitized SOEs and many equitized SOEs' failure to promptly get their shares listed on stock exchanges, caused investors, especially foreign one to lose confidence in the government's equitization programme. The majority of strategic investors claim that the holding of less 51% of stocks at the SOEs make them uncomfortable, and such limitations risk equitization being able to attract only domestic investors (Hung, Thien and Liem 2017).

Table 3-4 Number of Equitized SOEs during 1992-2016 Period

Phase	Legal bases	Number of equitized SOEs and sections of equitized SOEs
Pilot phase (1992 to mid-1998)	Decisions 202-CT (1992), 28 (1996), 25 (1997) Decrees 28 (1996), 25 (1997)	123
Accelerated phase (mid-1998 to 2011)	Decrees 44 (1998), 64 (2002), 187 (2004), 109 (2007)	3,858
1999-2002		834
2003-2006		2,649
2007-2010		356
2011		19
Economic restructuring phase (2011-2016)	Decision 929 (2012), Decrees 59 (2011), 189 (2013)	535
2012		20
2013		77
2014		144
2015		239
2016		55
Total		4,516

Source: Linh (2017)

From 2011 to 2015, the State Capital Investment Corporation (SCIC), which manages the State capital in SOEs, conducted divestment worth 8,726 billion VND ($402 billion) while the number of SOEs had reduced remarkably from 6,000 enterprises to over 500 enterprises.

In May 2017, the government approved a blueprint for SOE restructuring in the 2016-2020 period, under which the government aimed to equitize 137 more SOEs by 2020, most of which are large ones. It also stressed the plan to undertake divestments worth at least 250 trillion VND ($ billion) from equitized SOEs during this period. In the same month, the Fifth Plenum of the CPV

Central Committee passed a resolution on SOE restructuring, stressing again the task of accelerating the equitization and divestment of SOEs. As a result of these measures, from 2016 to 2017, the government approved the equitization proposals of 56 and 69 SOEs with the value of divestments reach 4.116 billion VND ($190 million) and 8.915 billion VND ($412 million) respectively (Ministry of Finance 2016, 2017). More than 10 Major SOEs, including Vietnam Engine and Agricultural Machinery Corporation, Vissan, Reconha, Vinapharm, Vinafor and FI (CO did their IPO in 2016. More Major SOEs are earmarked for IPO 2017 and subsequent years. These include big names in various industries such as Agribank, Vinacomin, Vietnam Rubber Group (VRG), Vinafood 2, PV Power, PV Oil, Binh Son Refining and Petrochemical Company (BSR), Mobifone, Vietnam Posts and Telecommunications Group (VNPT), Vinataba, Vinachem, Vinacafe, VTV Cab, Vietnam Multimedia Corporation (VTC), Saigon Jewelry Company (SJC), Saigon Trading Group (Satra), and Saigon Tourist.

Four major factors account for the Vietnamese government's decision to accelerate the equitization and divestment of its SOEs at present (Hiep 2017) are as follows. First, Vietnam's expanding budget deficit and public debt have made it increasingly difficult for government to find funding for its development projects. Therefore, financial resources in the form of SOE stakes have become a valuable source of funding that the government wants to tap to support its growth target.

Second, the majority of SOEs are technological outdated and hence, their products cannot be able to compete in the market (if not receiving assistance from the state such as easily accessing to bank loans, exclusive suppliers, etc.). Following the collapse of major SOEs such as Vinashin and Vinalines in 2011, the inefficiency of SOEs has recently been cast into the spotlight again after 12 major capital projects developed by SOEs were found to cause substantial loss to the State capital. In addition, the leaders of SOEs are not willing to equitize as they fear that they will lose their powers, the companies' privileges which have long been a hotbed for corruption. Equitizing and subjecting them to public scrutiny is essential for the government to fight corruption.

Third, a number of high-quality free trade agreements (FTAs) such as the Comprehensive Progressive Agreement for Trans-Pacific Partnership (CPTPP), and Vietnam-EU FTA (that Vietnam is pursuing) provide for a level playing filed among economic actors. Under the CPTPP, for example, Vietnamese SOEs will have to operate on market principles and in a transparent manner. They won't be able to discriminate against the enterprises, investments, goods, services of other member states. As such, equitizing SOEs and reducing th e government' stake in these enterprises become a measure to keep Vietnam compliant with its international obligations under these free trade agreements.

Finally, Vietnam stock exchanges have recovered significantly in recent years. The VN Index is one of the five leading growth market in the world and the highest in Asia regions. The equity market is growing due to government's determination in divestment the state capital from and listing large SOEs on the stock market. gives details about the size and the proportions of the SOEs that have been equitized in Vietnam. In 2014, firms with major shareholder being the State accounts for 22% of the number of listed firms, but their size is 48% of the total market capitalization. The equitized SOEs in general are larger than the other firms.

Table 3-5 Proportions of State-owned Enterprises in Vietnamese Stock Market

Year	Equitized SOEs	Listed firms	Percentage of total firms (%)	Percentage of total market cap (%)
2006	85	318	27%	37%
2007	103	414	25%	35%
2008	134	540	25%	45%
2009	142	599	24%	39%
2010	144	615	23%	32%
2011	151	666	23%	39%
2012	156	695	22%	46%
2013	155	718	22%	52%
2014	156	721	22%	48%

Source: Hung, Thien and Liem, 2017

2.6 Financial Issues of Urban and Rural Areas Development

According to World Bank (2018), the getting credit index of Vietnam ranked 29/190 surveyed countries which scored 75/100 points. The getting index was assessed based on the strength of legal rights, the depth of credit information, and the coverage of information public credit (51%). Compared with 2017, this index increased by 5 points and improved 3 levels, which was lower than that of Malaysia (20), and higher than those of Thailand (42th)) Indonesia (55th), Lao PRD (77th), and Philippines (142th). In general, this result suggests that the access to credit in Vietnam has improved in both rural and urban areas.

While the urban areas are heavily relied on formal credit institutions of which commercial banks play central role, rural areas are not only relied on formal credit but also informal credit. As mentioned above, the nationwide network of SOBs renders their credit accessibility in rural area better than JSCBs. On the other hand, the JSCBs are likely to focus their target market on urban areas and leave this market pie to SOBs.

In urban areas, the credit accessibility is quite high as it becomes economic hubs where most of banks are located. The citizens can easily access to the capital provided by banks whose transactions points are adjacent to their living areas. Besides, they also benefit from dedicated customer services and guidance from bankers as the market becomes more and more competitive. In general, there is no different between lending procedures in urban and rural areas. However, since the citizens are higher educated, have higher and more stable incomes as well as valuable secured assets, they have more advantages in borrowing money from the banks. On the other hand, the informal credit is less developed in cities because of high lending rates and lack of availability.

In rural areas, formal credit is provided by SOBs such as Agribank, Vietnam Bank for the Poor (VBP), and the People's Credit Fund. Argibank only has a network spreading to district and commune levels, hence, the coverage of credit accessibility to remote areas is limited. In addition, the complicated administrative procedures have contributed to the underdevelopment of Agribank.

The VBP began operations in 1996, providing low-interest credit through micro-credit programs to the rural poor who were ineligible for individual loans because of limitation in mortgage. In 2003, this VBP was renamed as the Vietnam Bank for Social Policy (VBSP). The major mission of VBSP is lending to the poor households by cooperating with local organizations in lending procedures. Particularly, the Commune People's Committee helps VBSP verify poor households. The Women's Union and the Farmer's Association help VBSP establish and monitor loans. There is no need for collateral but such organizations play as guarantee funds for borrowers. In order to ensure the return of lending capital, such social organizations group borrowers into a credit team and the whole teams will be responsible for their repayment. Later, this method of lending was replaced by a more flexible one, in which the individual are solely responsible for his/her loan instead of the group's loan (Bhole and Ogden, 2010). By the end of 2015, 11,068 mobile transaction points were established out of total 11,162 communes nationwide, which currently cover 90% of VBSP transactions. The rest communes with no transaction points are communes where VBSP's offices are located (VBSP 2015).

While the two main sources of loans in rural Vietnam are formal sources, Agribank and VBSP. Combined these two count for over 62% of all the loans. Informal resources includes, relatives, friends, neighbors, "hui" rotating savings and credit associations (ROSCAs) account for a smaller share of household loads at 20% (see). The existence of informal credit means that there is a proportion of rural rural households who cannot borrow money from formal channel (Duong & Izumida, 2002). This is because formal credit institutions only evaluate credit risk based on the borrowers' lending history, lending rates, regular incomes, and value of collateral (Huong 2016). Furthermore, rural borrowers find themselves difficult to get used to lending procedures. These limitations have led them to informal credit including loans from relatives, friends, neighbors, "hui" rotating savings and credit associations (ROSCAs), and money lenders.

Table 3-6 Loan Amount over Time, by Source and Usage

Source of loan	Main loan (%)	Second loan (%)	Third loan (%)
Formal sector	62,7%	28,2%	20,6%
VBSP	36,3%	13,7%	2,9%
Agribank	26,4%	14,5%	17,7%
Informal sector	20%	53,1%	70.6%
Friends/relatives	14,1%	26,2%	35,3%
ROSCA	0,4%	2,1%	2,9%
Money lender	2,6%	11,7%	5,9%
Other sources	17,5%	18,6%	8,8%

Source: Tarp, 2017

Relatives, friends and neighbors are the first sources when seeking for credit. They lend to others at negotiated rates depending on social relationships and reputation. Taking advantage of personal information, relatives and friends in general provide loans without collateral or any other written loan contract. The purpose of the loans is generally for emergency consumption such as illness, funeral and wedding, and for the building or repairing of houses.

ROSCAs have a very long tradition in Vietnam. Although they exist for many generations already, they have never been recognized officially. Usually these groups are referred to as "Ho" in the Noth and "Hui" in the South. The savings and credit can be made either in cash or in kind. In general, the average membership is around 10-15 persons. Decision on interest rates, membership and loan amounts are made either jointly by all members, by a bidding process or made solely by the organizer. The life cycle of a savings and credit association ends when every participant has obtained once the total fund collected at each turn.

Private money lenders are widespread and seem to be important sources of loans for households. They are usually rich households with surplus of money and goods in rural areas, who lend money for long-term periods against sometimes very high interest rates.

3. Issues in Monetary Policy and Macroprudential Policy

This section aims to overview the monetary policies controlled by the State Bank of Vietnam (SBV) since the early 1990s. It is divided into two sub-sections with the first one reviewing monetary policies of Vietnam through different periods and its influence on economic growth, and the second one analyzing monetary policy tools.

3.1. Monetary Policies of Vietnam: An Overview

In general, the objectives of monetary policies have changed over time, to be in line with the socio-economic development objectives. Historically, Vietnam's monetary policies can be divided into three periods:from 1990 to 1998, from 1999 to 2010 and from 2011 to date.

3.1.1 1990-1998 Period

Prior to 1990, Vietnam had a so called single-tier banking system, which was owned and controlled by the state. The SBV provided nearly all domestic banking service to economic units through its vast branch network.

In 1990, the State Council promulgated two important ordinances. The first one was the ordinance No. 37-LCT/HĐNN8 on the State Bank, and the second one was Ordinance No. 38-LCT/HĐNN8 on credit institutions. These two ordinances launched a new era of banking system reform in Vietnam. Since then the banking system of Vietnam has been transformed from single-tier to two-tier banking system, similar to the banking system of other countries with market economy, including:

- The State Bank plays the role of central bank
- Credit institutions, including commercial banks, investment banks, finance companies and credit cooperatives.

In the period from 1990 to 1998, the SBV implemented its monetary policy in accordance with the Ordinance of the State Bank of Vietnam. Article 1 of the Ordinance clearly states that "The State Bank of Vietnam has the function of exercising state management over monetary, credit and banking activities throughout the country in order to stabilize the value of money" (State Council, 1990). However, in specific time, the SBV determines the objectives of the monetary policy based on the socio-economic development objectives set by the Communist Party of Vietnam and National Assembly and the performance of the banking system.

In the period of 1990-1995, for example, based on the economic objectives defined in the Resolution of the Seventh Party Congress as "control the inflation at reasonable rate in order to stabilize macro-economy, develop and improve the efficiency of production; stabilize and gradually improve the citizen's living standard", the objective of monetary policy to focus on stabilizing the value of currency, and ensuring favorable institutional environment for the banking system and capital for economic development. The main objective of SBV is highlighted as stabilizing monetary value, controlling inflation.

To achieve this goal, the SBV implemented a prudent credit policy, which adjusted the credit structure toward enhancing lending to profitable non-state enterprises and reduce loans to state-owned enterprises. This helped to avoid excessive credit growth and keep down inflationary pressures. The State Bank of Vietnam reduced lending to the economy by promoting commercial banks to mobilize capital from citizens to meet the credit needs of the economy. The SBV implemented a strict foreign exchange policy in order to mobilise foreign currencies for the government, established two foreign exchange centers, in which the official exchange rate was determined closer to the market conditions.

In the next period of 1996-1998, the monetary policy objective was to control inflation at a single digit level and to support economic growth. The objective was also set in line with the actual situation of growth slowdown. In 1998, due to the impact of the Asian financial crisis, GDP growth rate was only 5.8%, a sharp decrease from 8.8% in 1997. In order to mitigate the negative impact of this crisis, the SBV implemented a prudent monetary policy aimed at stabilizing the value of Vietnam currency (VND), the exchange rate and the foreign exchange market. Throughout the period 1996-1998, the executive objectives were set out in a more concrete way than in the 1990s. Specifically, the SBV set the annual target on money supply growth (M2), credit growth and deposit growth as prerequisites to achieve the inflation target.

Figure 3-10 presents some economic performance indicators of Vietnam in the period 1990-1998. It shows that controlling inflation policy in this period kept the inflation rate from 67 percent in 1990 down to 9.2 percent in 1998. The decreasing inflation rate was considered one of the causes leading to the decrease in GDP growth from the peak of 9.5 percent in 1995 to 5.8 percent in 1998.

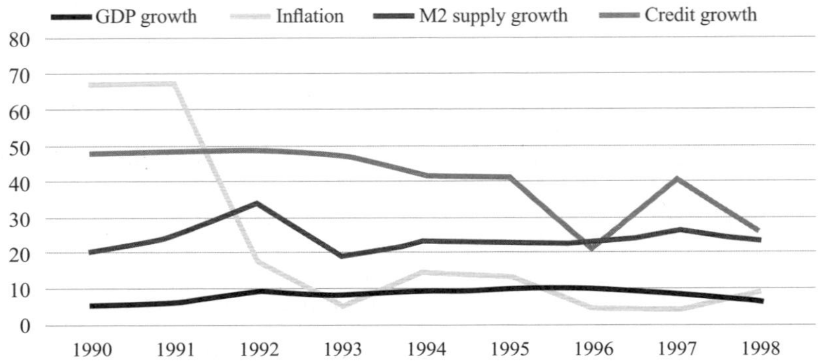

Source: SBV and GSO, unit: annual percentage rate

Figure 3-10 GDP Growth, Inflation, M2 Supply Growth, and Credit Growth in 1990-1998

3.1.2 1999-2011 period

In this period, monetary policy was implemented in accordance with the Law on State Bank of Vietnam, promulgated in 1998. Specifically, Article No.2 of the Law stipulates that "the national monetary policy is a part of the State's economic and financial policies in order to stabilize the currency value, and control inflation, contribute to socio-economic development, to ensure national defense and security, and improve people's living standards". In addition, in a certain year, the SBV pursued the goal of consolidating banking system. In general, there were so many goals of monetary policy in this period that caused difficulties in executing monetary policy.

During the period of 1999-2000, in the context of currency scarcity due to the impact of the financial and monetary crisis in Asia, the SBV applied the stimulus policy to increase economic growth and control GDP deflation.

The SBV shifted from prudent, curbing inflation monetary policy into a loose monetary policy aimed at economic growth and low inflation. However, due to the lagging effect of stimulus policies, in 1999 the inflation rate was as low as 0.1%, and in 2000 deflation rate was at 0.6%.

In the 2001-2010 period, the objectives of monetary policy were guided by 9th Party Congress document as to stabilize macro-economy, control inflation, promote production and consumption, stimulate investment. In the first three years of the period, SBV implemented a prudent loosing monetary policy. This contributed to achieving the objective of economic growth but also took inflation on increasing trend. In 2004, in the face of relative high inflation, the SBV made adjustments in the implementation of the monetary policy toward a carefully and flexibly controlled inflation policy.

Figure 3-11 shows four economic indicators in the 1999-2010 period. It fails to demonstrate closed relationship between GDP growth and inflation. The figure presents a recovering trend of Vietnam economy in the 2001-2005 period. GDP growth rate gradually increased from 6.9% in 2000 to 8.4% in 2005, with the average pace was 7.5%. The inflation rate was low but unstable over the years. It increased from low rates of below 5% in 2001-2003 period to a high of 9.5% in 2004, and 8.4% in 2005. The high inflation rate in these two years can be attributed to the rising tendency of commodities, raw materials, and energy prices in the world, and domestic natural disasters, which made production costs increase.

The main objective of Vietnam economy set by National Assembly in the 2006-2010 period was high economic growth. Therefore, the monetary policy implemented during this period was a losing monetary supply. In 2006 and 2007, total liquidity increased by 33.59% and 46.12% respectively; capital mobilized by credit institutions increased 36.53% and 47.64%, respectively;

credit loans increased by 25.44% and 53.89%, respectively. The implementation of loose monetary supply in consecutive years coupled with capital flows (both direct and indirect investments) increased sharply, but the low efficiency use caused the risk of high inflation. High inflationary pressures was also attributed to poor performance by SBV in dealing with foreign capital inflows. As this capital flows rushed into Vietnam in the late 2006 to the early 2008, with the desire to stabilize the exchange rate, the SBV buy foreign currency. This lead to an increase in foreign exchange reserves, but also increased the amount of money in circulation. Therefore, the money supply increased sharply in the period 2007-2008. Along with the high credit growth, inflation has started escalating and peaked in 2008 by 19.9%.

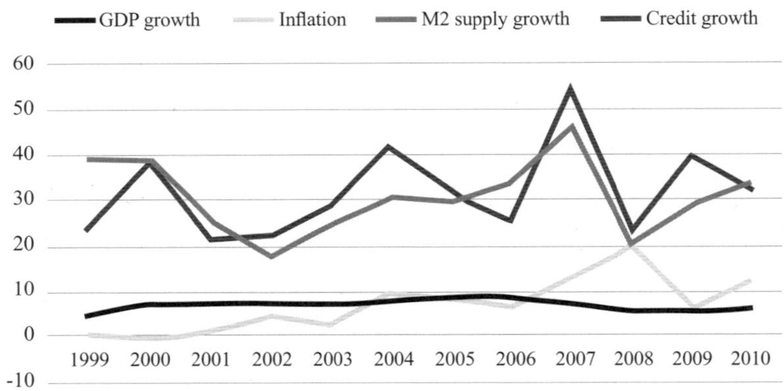

Source: SBV and GSO

Figure 3-11 GDP Growth, Inflation, M2 Supply Growth, and Credit Growth in 1999-2010

After fluctuation of inflation in the 2006-2008 period, in 2009 the SBV decided to implement a series of tightening measures: (i) increasing the reserve requirement ratio; (ii) issuing VND 20,300 billion of bonds to withdraw money from circulation; (iii) control the credit growth rate at 30%. Tightening monetary policy has brought inflation from 19.89% in 2008 to 6.52% in 2009. This tightening monetary policy led to a decline in aggregate demand, leading to a low GDP growth, reached 5.66% in 2008.

After 2009, when fundamental inflation was restrained and the exchange rate was stable, monetary policy was relaxed by reducing the refinancing interest rates in period 2009 - 2010 to promote economic growth. Rediscount interest rates fell sharply from 13% in June 2008 to 6% in December 2009 and remain unchanged until November 2010. The compulsory reserve ratio of VND for credit deposits decreased from 11% to 10% (in November 5th, 2008), to 8% (in November 20th, 2008), to 6% (in December 5th 2008), 5% (in January 2009) and 3% (in March 2009).

Simultaneously, the government also took many measures to stimulate economic growth. Specifically, on January 23rd, 2009, the Prime Minister issued a decision to subsidize interest for 8 month or less loans under credit contracts signed and disbursed from 01/02/2009 to 31/12/2009. The interest rate support for borrowers is 4% per annum. Furthermore, on April 4th, 2009, the Prime minister issued Decision No. 443/QĐ/TTg providing interest subsidy for medium and long term loans of organizations and individuals making new investment to develop production, infrastructure development. In the end of 2009, the prime minister issued Decision No. 2072/QĐ-TTg stipulating interest rate support of 2% for medium and long-term loans.

However, the implementation of losing monetary policy led to high inflation again, which peaked 18.58% in 2011. And under pressure of inflation, the SBV once again had to change its monetary policy from loosening to tightening in the end of 2010 with a series of measures taken such as raising refinancing interest rates, increase net withdrawal in the open market, control credit growth through credit limit tool.

3.1.3 2011-Present

Figure 3-12 presents economic indicators in the 2011-2015 period. It shows that inflation decreased sharply from nearly 20% in 2011 to below 5% in 2015. Simultaneously, GDP growth rate slightly increased and go around 5 to 6%. In this period, monetary policy was implemented in accordance with the amended Law on State Bank of Vietnam promulgated by National Assembly in 2011. Article 3, Chapter 1 states that "the national monetary policy is the monetary decision made by competent authorities, including decisions on stabilizing the value of the currency, decision on the use of tools and measures to achieve the objectives." Thereby, it was clear that the difference between amended Law on the SBV in 2010 and the Law on the SBV issued in 1998 is that the sole objective of monetary policy is to stabilize the currency value reflected through inflation index. It meant that monetary policy in this period only focused on stabilizing monetary value instead of pursuing multi-targeting such as stabilizing the currency as well as boosting the economy.

In 2011 and early 2012, the goal of monetary policy is to control inflation and stabilize monetary values in response to high inflation due to excessive loosing monetary policy loosening in the 2006-2010 period. In 2012, the core inflation seemed to be controlled, the inflation rate in 2012 dropped to 6.81%. However, economic growth started slowing down, the SBV started loosening monetary policy. Specifically, the refinancing interest rate was adjusted down 9 times (from March 2012 to March 2014). Simultaneously, the ceiling interest rate for short-term deposit was reduced from 14% per year to 7% per year, contributing to reduce the lending interest rate and help businesses to reduce the borrowing cost.

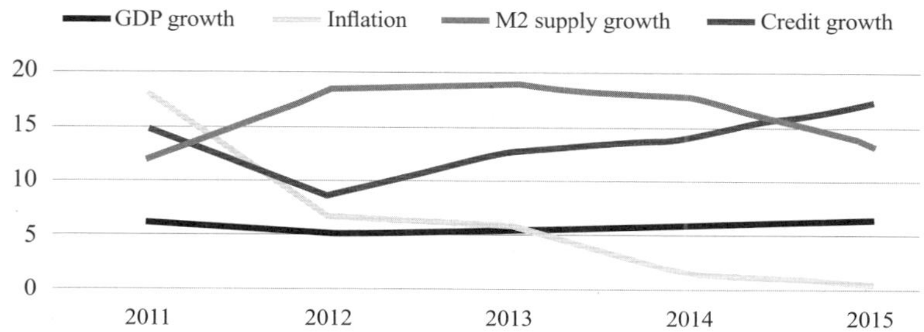

Source: SBV and GSO

Figure 3-12 GDP Growth, Inflation, M2 Supply Growth, and Credit Growth in 2011-2015

In the nutshell, monetary policy in this period was carried out carefully, flexibly and proactively in order to ensure the main objective of stabilizing inflation. Thus, since 2011, inflation has been below 7%. The economic growth has been stable, and in a good shape. In 2017, for example, the economic growth peaked at 6.81%.

It can be said that, since 2011, monetary policy has been flexible and active. The good performance of monetary policy has helped secure banking system, increase the foreign exchange reserves, and curb inflation pressure, while maintaining the stable economic growth.

3.2 Tools of Monetary Policy

3.2.1 Interest tool

In June 1992, the SBV shifted from the negative interest rate mechanism into the positive interest rate mechanism, and the financial institutions started to be managed under the interest rate framework.[25] Under the positive real interest rate mechanism, the SBV regulated the interest rate framework including the minimum interest rate for capital mobilization and the maximum interest rate for borrowing in VND. The SBV also regulated that the average lending interest rate must be higher than the average mobilizing interest rate, and the capital subsidy via bank credit channel would be terminated. It can be said that the implementation of interest rate management during this period has contributed positively to the achievement of monetary policy in this period.

In the period of 1996 - 2000, the interest rate tool continued to be renewed for lending interest, and mobilizing interest. The SBV stipulated that short-term loan interest ceiling must be lower than the mid-term one. Regarding mobilizing interest, the SBV did not set a minimum rate, but specified the average gap between deposit rates and lending rates must be lower than 0.35% per month.[26]

Since May 2000, the SBV has issued and applied the base interest rate to replace the regulations on the lending interest ceiling. Accordingly, lending interest rates of commercial banks had not to exceed the permissible fluctuation range (0.3% per month for short-term loans and 0.5% per month for medium-

25 Le Quoc Ly (2013), *Financial and Monetary Policy – Theory and Practice,* Ha Noi, National Political Publishing House.

26 Le Quoc Ly (2013), Financial and Monetary Policy – Theory and Practice, Ha Noi, National Political Publishing House.

term and long-term loans).

In essence, the management of banking activities through the base interest rate plus the amplitude of the fluctuation is quite similar to the regulation of the lending interest rate ceiling applied in the previous period. Controlling interest rates has made interest rates do not properly reflect the relationship of supply and demand on the market. For instance, both base interest rates and lending rates by commercial banks declined in 2000 and 2001. However, competition among banks led to an increase in deposit rates (lending interest did not increase because the base interest rate was reduced in order to stimulate economic growth and overcome deflation). This clearly reduced the gap between deposit rates and lending rates of commercial banks, creating a great pressure on commercial bank system.

From June 2002 to 2007, the SBV implemented the negotiable interest mechanism in credit activities of commercial banks.[27] In particular, commercial banks are allowed to determine lending interest rates on the basis of supply and demand on the market (between the borrower and the lender). Nevertheless, the State Bank still announced the base interest rate for market orientation. As a result of monetary policy, the period 2000-2005 was considered a period of positive changes in Vietnam's economy, with high growth in GDP and low inflation.

In the 2007-2008 period, when the global economy suffered from crisis, the SBV did change its monetary policy continuously, causing enterprises difficulties. Specifically, the SBV tightened monetary supply in the early 2008 and loosened gradually in the end of the year[28]. As a result, the interbank interest rates were cooled down in line with the downward trend of the SBV's base interest rate. During this period of time, the base interest rate became

27 SBV's 2002 report.

28 SBV's 2008 report.

a tool to transfer information of interest policy for the economy and as a basis for commercial banks to determine lending interest rates. This made easier for businesses to access loans and boost production and business in order to curb economic recession. The adjustment of interest in the end of 2008 was also seen as a measure to support the stock market against the decline. In general, banking activities had positive changes after strong interventions by the SBV. From mid-July 2008 to the end of the third quarter of 2008, the available capital of commercial banks was somewhat less concerned, with deposit interest rates tending to decrease and maintaining relatively stable.[29] Under the tighter control of the SBV, no commercial banks had lending interest rates above the ceiling, and commercial banks also stopped collecting all fees associated with the loan.

From 2009, interest policy has been flexible, increasing or decreasing in line with market movements. Specifically, in order to ease interest posed on lending of commercial banks, the SBV ran the interest policy aimed at reducing the interest rate for business loans, but tending to float interest rates for consumption lending contracts (according to Circular 01/2009 / TT-NHNN issued on 23/11/2009). The SBV step by step eased the interest rate regulations for commercial banks by allowing commercial them to apply negotiable lending interest rates for medium and long term lendings (Circular 07/2010 / TT-NHNN issued by the SBV on 26 February 2010) and for all types of loans (Circular 12/2010 / TT-NHNN, dated 14 April 2010), aimed at facilitating capital markets for businesses. The negotiated interest mechanism between the borrower and the lender has significantly reduced the role of the base interest rate because it has terminated the ceiling interest rate policy (up to 150% of the base interest rate).

29 SBV's 2008 report.

In general, in the current period, the SBV controls the base interest rate, the refinancing rate and the discount rate relatively flexible, in line with the objectives of monetary policy and supply and demand of capital market, ensuring the harmony between interest rates in VND, exchange rates, and foreign currency interest rates.

3.2.2 Compulsory Reserve Ratio

The SBV started to use compulsory reserve instruments in 1992, with an initial compulsory reserve ratio of 10% of total mobilized deposits, with no distinction between different types of deposits. However, the compulsory reserve instrument at this stage did not really play a role in regulating currency, as credit institutions often maintained excess reserves to obtain interest (because excess reserves also enjoy interest rates); thus, limiting activities in the monetary market and limiting the role of regulating and controlling the SBV.[30]

Since 1999, the compulsory reserve ratio was adjusted more and more flexibly in accordance with the monetary policy objectives in each period, which was due to the establishment of the SBV Law in 1998 which specified that The State Bank of Vietnam (SBV) was entitled to regulate the compulsory reserve ratio in the band of 0% - 20%. SBV revised the regulation on compulsory reserves from daily maintenance to average maintenance during the period. For example, from 1999 to 2003, the SBV adjusted its reserve requirement ratio to stimulate economic growth. In 2004, when the economy showed signs of inflation, the State Bank of Vietnam reduced the compulsory reserve ratio (applied from July 2004). Also in 2004, the SBV changed the

30 Le Quoc Ly (2013), Financial and Monetary Policy – Theory and Practice, Ha Noi, National Political Publishing House.

method of paying interest on compulsory reserve deposits. The State Bank of Vietnam (SBV) only paid interest on compulsory deposits in VND instead of paying interest on deposits in excess of the compulsory reserve. This had the effect of encouraging credit institutions to use capital more effectively, being limited to capital surplus at SBV.

In general, the compulsory reserve ratio has been used flexibly by the SBV at different stages of the economy, corresponding to the objective of monetary policy for those periods, contributing to stabilizing the value of money and stimulating the economic growth.

3.2.3 Open Market Operations (OMO)

The open market operation (OMO) was officially started in July 2000. Since then, open market operations have been constantly improved and become the main tool of the SBV. Open Market Operations helped to solve the liquidity problem of credit institutions quickly, thus increasing business ability of credit organizations. After more than 15 years of operation, OMO has confirmed its role as a key tool in managing the monetary policy of the SBV.

OMO is increasingly being finalized by the SBV in accordance with international practice to become an important instrument of monetary policy, which has a regular and widespread impact on the market, thus enhancing SBV's regulatory capacity to maintain stability and to stimulate development of the currency market. From 2000 up to now, the trading frequency of open market operations has been increasing. From 10 days / sessions in 2000 to 1-3 sessions / week in the period 2001-2006, and from 2006 to now are carried out regularly on a daily basis. However, there was a special period in 2008, due to the context of the global economic and financial crisis as well as the fluctuations of the financial and monetary market of Vietnam, the SBV carried out 1-2 sessions per day to meet the actual demand for restructuring of credit institutions.[31]

Commodities traded on the OMO have become more diversified, which are valuable papers with high liquidity and in accordance with the common practice of the world, mainly including treasury bonds, treasury bills, SBV bills, government guaranteed bonds (issued by the Vietnam Development Bank and the Social Policy Bank), local government bonds of some provinces and cities and some other valuable securities allowed to be traded in accordance with regulations of the SBV. Open market development has attracted many credit institutions to increase the possibility of spillover effects of monetary policy to monetary market and credit system. From only 4 state-owned commercial banks in 2000, 31 credit organizations were admitted as members in open market operations by December 31, 2005. By 2008, 53 members were active in the open market operations, and until now most credit institutions have been recognized as members of the banking system (about 70).[32]

The OMOs were conducted flexibly daily, combined with the adjustment of trading volume, interest rates and trading terms, which helped the SBV to manage the currency quickly and timely in order to achieve the objective of monetary policy in each period. In the period 2007 - 2008, in the context of high inflation, the SBV actively and flexibly used the open market tools to ensure the inflation target without affecting liquidity ability of credit institutions, which are: (i) the SBV offered SBV bills with terms of 14 and 364 days to assist with the objective of taking money back; (ii) In addition, the SBV held regular buy-sell sessions for short terms valuable papers(7, 14, 21, 28

31 Summary from the SBV's reports.

32 Summary from the SBV's reports.

days) in order to support capital for credit institutions having capital shortages to ensure liquidity, especially at times of changing the compulsory reserve ratio and times of changing interest rates announced by the SBV. In the period from 2009 to 2011, with the expansionary monetary policy for overcoming economic recession, the SBV made bids for short term valuable papers (7, 14, 21, 28 days),[33] the volume and interest rate of bids were adjusted to the situation of market in order to support the liquidity ability of credit institutions, facilitating the reduction of mobilizing and lending interest rates, stabilizing the monetary market and controlling the inflation and monetary targets.

OMOs are increasingly becoming the main liquidity support channel for credit institutions as demand for payment increases due to market fluctuations, ensuring that the banking system operates safely and smoothly, meeting all payment needs in the economy. With the fast-paced transaction procedures through the online bidding software system, money transfer transactions took place during the day; therefore, credit institutions could access liquidity support funds in time from the SBV. Apart from offsetting the deficit liquidity, OMOs have been operated timely and have met the needs of credit institutions, especially in times of high liquidity demand or unpredictable market fluctuations such as on the occasion of the Lunar New Year, or the annual long holidays. Accordingly, on the basis of adhering to market movements, the SBV actively raised the volume of tender offer for valuable papers, and even increased the number of tender sessions to two sessions per day in order to support temporary liquidity shortage for the credit institutions, ensuring stability in the currency market.

33 SBV's 2008 report

3.2.4 Exchange Rate Policy

Before 1989 the exchange rate regime was a fixed one, with 1 USD being fixed at 19 VND. In the process of banking innovation, from the one-level banking system to the two-level one, the exchange rate management mechanism has been gradually reformed.

The period of 1989-1999 experienced the new exchange rate mechanism, which was the official exchange rate plus band. Particularly, the SBV announces the official exchange rate between the foreign currency and the VND, whereby the buying and selling rates on the market are allowed to fluctuate within the permitted band against the official rate. The exchange rate was adjusted flexibly by the SBV in accordance with the fluctuation of the economy. In order to avoid adverse effects from the financial crisis in Southeast Asia, from the beginning of 1997 to 1998, the SBV twice adjusted the exchange band, widening from +/- 0.5% to +/- 5% and up to +/- 10%, then raised the official exchange rate from 11,175VND / USD to 11,800VND / USD (5.6% devaluation); after that the SBV continued to devalue 9.2%, with the official exchange rate being raised from 11,815 VND / USD to 12,998 VND / USD and the permitted band being adjusted to +/- 7%. By August 1998, the official exchange rate was close to the free market exchange rate.[34]

From February 1999 to 2015, the SBV applied the average exchange rate policy in the inter-bank foreign currency market plus the permitted trading band. Instead of announcing the official exchange rate, the State Bank announced the average exchange rate on the interbank market of the last working day, and commercial banks were allowed to trade at rates not exceeding the SBV's

34 Summary from the SBV's reports.

published rate of 0.1%. With the new exchange rate regime, the exchange rate of the VND was formed on the basis of foreign currency supply and demand in the market and exchange rate in the inter-market was close to the free market exchange rate. The exchange rate administration under this new mechanism has contributed significantly to improving the balance of payments, contributing to the increase of foreign currency reserves.

From January 2016, the SBV officially applied the new mechanism, a flexible central exchange rate mechanism, replacing the previous interbank average exchange rate mechanism.[35] Accordingly, the exchange rate of the Vietnam dong against the US dollar was determined on the basis of the reference exchange rate movements in the interbank foreign exchange market, exchange rate movements on the international market of a number of foreign currencies which Vietnam had commercial relationships, as well as the monetary policy objectives. Over the two years of 2016 and 2017, the new exchange rate regime has made the exchange rate relatively stable, limiting the impact of large external shocks.

4. Other Issues of Monetary and Macroprudential Policy

4.1 Monetary Policy

Generally, monetary policy management has been improved constantly, with the reforms in management and operation of money supply mechanism through the use of synchronized monetary policy tools. State Bank of Vietnam

35 SBV's 2016 report.

has gradually moving from using direct tools such as administered interest rates to indirect tools such as open market operations (OMO) to improve the effects of monetary policy. In general, monetary policy instruments have been being established and gradually perfected in accordance with the international practice. Capital mobilization of the banking system has been also promoted constantly, meeting the capital for development investment objectives of Vietnam. Business activities of credit institutions continue to be strengthened, contributing actively to the goal of curbing inflation, stabilizing macroeconomics, ensuring social security and sustainable growth.

Depending on the stages of development, the objectives of monetary policy of Vietnam have had different priorities. Before 2011, for example, the priority of monetary policy mainly focused on promoting economic growth, which contributed to the rapid growth in the period between 1992 and 1997 and in the period between 2005 and 2007. However, this could also lead to the instability for the economy, with the high inflation rates in 2008 and 2011. From 2010, the prioritized objective of monetary policy had been clarified, with the primary goal of curbing inflation and stabilizing currency. This clarification of monetary policy objective has contributed greatly to the success of monetary policy of Vietnam in recent years.

Based on the objective of stabilizing inflation, the management of monetary policy in Vietnam could be divided into two phases: the pre-2012 period and the post-2012 period. While the former period had high inflation and complex developments, the latter one has had certain success in curbing inflation at a one-digit level, contributing to the stabilization of the economy. This success comes from the following reasons: (i) The primary objective of monetary policy has been clarified: Remaining inflation rate at a low and stable level; (ii) Interest rates and exchange rates have been more focused as an intermediate objective of monetary policy; (iii) SBV have been become more active in managing monetary policy, formulating the short-term monetary policy within a framework of long-term monetary policy.

However, there are still a number of challenges that need to be addressed to further improve the quality of monetary policy: (1) SBV is not totally independent in making decision, leading to the ineffectiveness in the implementation of monetary policy; (2) There is a lack of effective coordination between SBV and Ministry of Finance (MOF); (3) The commercial banking system is still limited in terms of risk management ability and financial capacity; (4) The information system is not complete; hence there is a lack databases to make accurate monetary policy decisions; (5) Money market and bond market are still developing at low level; (6) The economy is still at risk of dollarization.

In order to solve these above challenges, there are some issues: (1) continuing to improve the monetary and banking institutions, ensuring that SBV effectively implement its objectives; (2) improving the quality of informatics system and producing models with more accurate forecasting capabilities; (3) continuing to innovate and improve monetary policy; using direct and indirect tools more flexibly; (4) managing flexibly the exchange rate, stabilizing the foreign exchange market and gold market and reducing the dollarization; (5) maintaining reasonable credit growth to contribute to achieving inflation control objectives, supporting growth, improving credit quality.

4.2 Macroprudential Policy

Along with the economic development, Vietnam has also experienced the significant growth in the financial market with the expansion of the commercial banking system as well as the improvement in the stock market. This development also set requirements for macro-financial security management or requirements for implementing macroprudential policy. However, the implementation of the macro prudential policy has been still at an early stage, and there are many issues need to be improved.

First of all, macroeconomic surveillance of the financial system in Vietnam involves multiple agencies. In particular, the SBV supervises the system of credit institutions, while the Ministry of Finance (MOF) supervises the securities sector and insurance. Thus, each agency only focuses on its own specialized supervision and does not perform consolidated supervision of financial corporations. Moreover, there are other two agencies participating in supervising financial system in Vietnam, namely National Financial and Monetary Policy Advisory Council (NFMPAC) and National Financial Supervisory Commission (NFSC).

The National Financial and Monetary Policy Advisory Council was established in 2011 with the task of drafting, discussing, consulting and proposing to the Government and the Prime Minister in planning and making decision relating to important issues of financial and monetary policies and policies under the tasks and powers of the Government and the Prime Minister. This council does not play any role in coordinating between the macroeconomic policy with the macro prudential policy, and its main tasks are to give policy recommendations and policy advices.

National Financial Supervisory Commission (NFSC) was established in 2008. Beyond the policy advisory function, NFSC is also empowered to implement the general supervision with the financial market. However, NFSC does not have tools for supervising, and is not empowered to inspect the financial organizations; hence, its ability is rather limited in overseeing the financial system. In addition, NFSC is also assigned the task of coordination between sectoral supervision, general supervision of the financial market and the observance of international practices and standards on supervisory activities of inspection agencies. However, there should be more specific regulations in the coordination mechanism among agencies so that the NFSC can effectively implement this task.

From the analysis of the functions and duties of the agencies involved in the process of enduring financial security, the macroprudential policy is implemented by the supervision and inspection of specialized management agencies (SBV and MOF) accompanied with the general supervision of NFMPAC and NFSC mainly through the policy recommendations and policy advices.

In the implementation of the macro prudential policy, there are a number of emerging issues that need to be addressed to improve the effectiveness of this policy:

- There should be a change in the monitoring method, from compliance monitoring (for example, compliance with CAMEL, BASEL standards) to risk monitoring.
- Regarding the content of the monitoring, it is necessary to develop monitoring standards, especially monitoring standards for financial groups.
- Establishing the informatics system for monitoring; the tools for monitoring need to be supplemented, standardized and consistent with international practices.
- Strengthening the coordination among the agencies being responsible for monitoring.

• Continuing to restructure the banking system and credit institutions.

5. Summary

Since 1990, the monetary policy of the State Bank has been continuously improved, contributing to stabilize the macroeconomic environment, curbing inflation, promoting economic growth.

Regarding the objective of monetary policy, the ultimate goal of monetary policy has been clearly defined as inflation controlling and monetary stability, instead of two parallel objectives (controlling inflation and supporting economic growth). The ultimate goal of monetary policy has facilitated the implementation of monetary policy more easily and conveniently, limiting the conflict between the objective of curbing inflation and the objective of supporting economic growth.

Furthermore, monetary policy tools have been used flexibly and effectively in the direction of increasingly using indirect tools instead of direct tools. Instruments of monetary policy have been established, gradually improved in accordance with international practice. The OMOs is a clear demonstration of this. From a tool that was put into use later (since 2000), OMOs has been one of the most effective instruments of the SBV in regulating the money market, contributing to macroeconomic stability.

Regarding the administration of monetary policy, the SBV has been more active in managing monetary policy. Specifically, since 2012 the governor of the SBV has been actively deciding the plan to provide additional money for circulation and actively operating monetary policy instruments to control credit and M2.[36] In addition, monetary policy has worked more closely with fiscal policy, contributing to improve the effectiveness of monetary policy.

In addition, the business activities of credit institutions have been continuing to grow, and the capacity of credit institutions has been increasingly enhanced, contributing positively to the achievement of the goal of curbing inflation and stabilizing macroeconomic.

However, there are still some issues that need to be addressed in the near future. Firstly, the implementation of monetary policy requires closer coordination with other macroeconomic policies such as fiscal policy. Short-term monetary policy needs to be formulated within the framework of medium-term and long-term monetary policy, avoiding the case of changing monetary policy as in the period between 2008 – 2010 continuously, which makes difficult for the economy as well as for business operations of enterprises. Secondly, the SBV needs to improve the quality of information systems and databases for forecasting. Making the right forecasts will help make monetary policy more active and effective. Thirdly, the SBV also needs to continue to perfect the tools of monetary policy in the direction of modernization, meeting the standards and international practices.

36 SBV's 2012 report.

III. Capital Market Liberalization

1. Arguments for CML, Their Weaknesses, and Some Myths

Capital market liberalization (CML), which integrates a country's local financial system with international financial markets and institutions, has been a key issue in the debate on globalization. (Schmukler 2008) defines financial globalization as the integration of a country's local financial system with international financial markets and institutions. In this regard, the result of CML is equivalent to financial globalization. It enhances the functioning of the financial system through two main channels: one is to increase the availability of funds. The other is to improve financial infrastructure. There are many ways for the second channel to work: (1) efficiency gains through greater competition, (2) increased transparency through the adoption of international accounting standards, (3) improved corporate governance and monitoring, and so on.

While advocates of CML believe that it would increase economic growth by allocating funds efficiently and reduce risk by stabilizing consumption and investment, those benefits of CML is predicated on perfect capital market and perfect intertemporal smoothing, as (Ocampo, Spiegel, and Stiglitz 2008) argue.[37] As long as the theoretical assumption of perfect capital market is not met, free capital mobility may lead to excessive capital inflows, overvalued currency, and a shifting of resources from tradable to non-tradable

37 See also (Kose, Prasad, and Terrones 2006).

sectors.[38] In developing countries with small and thin markets, and weaker prudentialregulation, bubbles are easier to create ((Ocampo et al. 2008)). And, as we will examine the case of South Korea below, a poorly designed or hastily implemented CML often leads to financial crisis. The crisis can bring about not only an extended period of output loss but also shift the trajectory of economic growth, leaving a permanent scar on the economy.

There have been several myths on CML. The first myth is that the immediate CML is the best for all countries and in all circumstances. Even the IMF that heralded financial globalization retracts their previous assertion that the immediate CML is the best policy for all countries. ((IMF 2000), (Eichengreen 2002), (Fischer 2002)) The top scholars in mainstream economics such as (Krugman 1998), (Tobin 2000), and (Stiglitz 2000) also advocate the government intervention to restrict cross-capital movements because they can be socially beneficial. The second is that, even if there is intervention, priced-based controls are better. After the financial crises of 1990s, even strong advocates of CML have admitted that some countries that used capital controls could have avoided the worst scenarios. (Epstein, Grabel, and Jomo 2008) well illustrate that China, India, and Malaysia were able to use quantity-based regulations to achieve important macroeconomic objectives (for example, reducing the severity of maturity mismatch, attracting foreign investment in favorable terms, insulating from speculative attacks). The third is that increased tolerance for capital controls applies only to inflows, not outflows. Malaysia is another example that shows the controls on outflow could work. They did not 'deter future inflows of all kinds' ((Economist 2003))

38 Using various econometric techniques, (Shin and Wang 2000) find that there is at best a modest degree of international risk sharing, and far from the levels predicted by theory. According to their results, even emerging market economies, which have experienced large increases in cross-border capital flows, have not much benefitted from CML in terms of risk sharing.

2. Prerequisites for CML

The above discussion implies that, in many cases, the relative size of benefits and risks associated with CML depends on the specific history and economic environment of a country. (Schmukler 2008) emphasizes that CML can be beneficial with some conditions: a country with sound fundamentals and strong institutions. An empirical study by (Eichengreen, Gullapalli, and Panizza 2011) finds evidence that financial openness has positive effects on the growth of financially dependent industries, although these growth-enhancing effects evaporate during financial crises. Further, the positive effects of capital account liberalization are limited to countries with relatively well-developed financial systems, good accounting standards, strong creditor rights and rule of law. It suggests that countries must reach a certain threshold in terms of institutional and economic development before they can expect to benefit from capital account liberalization.

Since CML requires strong and stable financial institutions, a strong regulatory framework needs to be in place before CML takes place. For this purpose, many researchers suggest the use of capital management technique (CMT), which is a combination of capital account regulation and prudential regulations. More specifically, (Epstein et al. 2008) define capital management techniques as the combination of two complementary and often overlapping types of financial policies: capital controls that govern international private capital flows and prudential regulation of domestic financial institutions. For example, prudential regulation may reduce the need for more direct capital controls. They emphasize the synergy between prudential financial regulations and traditional capital controls.[39] CMT has many aspects: residents vs. non-residents, financial vs. non-financial corporations, FDI vs. portfolio investment, short-term vs. long-term, and on-shore vs. off-shore markets. Among these, we will examine issues related to FDI vs. portfolio investment, and short-term vs. long-term investment in the following sections.

While CMT is more closely related to short-term strategic and portfolio investment, it is also important to entice FDI, which is crucial for long-term and stable growth. (Uthoff and Titelman 1996) point out that, in order for CML to promote economic growth, capital inflows need to be used as investment. However, in 1970s and even more in 1990-1997, increased capital inflows were used as consumption. Even if they were used as investment, they were for non-durable that did not earn foreign exchange. In this regard, it is important to distinguish between 'greenfield' investments and M&As since much of what is classified as FDI is sometimes really 'finance'. ((Ocampo et al. 2008)). In the following sections, we discuss the measures to stabilize capital flows and entice FDI.

3. Experiences of South Korea

3.1 A Brief History on Capital Market Liberalization

A typical procedure of CML takes the following steps:

1. liberalizing the trade account
2. relaxing FX restrictions
3. relaxing the long-term capital account

39 However, even authors admit that it is often difficult to draw a firm line between the two.

4. relaxing the short-term account

For example, major players in global trade such as Germany, Japan, Taiwan, and China have accumulated foreign reserves through trade account surpluses of several straight years and then decided to open short-term capital markets in the last step.

South Korea followed a different path.[40] Before 1997 Asian crisis, the government loosened up the regulation on short-term borrowing despite frequent current account deficits.[41] While there might have been the benefits of this unique process of CML, its cost turned out to be huge. Figure 3-13 shows the real GDP growth rate and Korean won/US dollar exchange rate during the period of 1990Q2-2017Q4. There are two major economic crises on the solid growth path of Korean economy. One is 1997 Asian financial crisis and the other is a liquidity crisis resulting from the global financial crisis (GFC). As Figure 3-13 clearly shows, there were two huge drops in real GDP growth rate around 1997 and 2008. At the same time, there are two spikes in won/dollar exchange rate around those periods, suggesting sudden outflows of foreign capital. Evidently, the real economy was hit hard by those crises. For example, the average of annual real GDP growth rate during the period of 1990-1997 is 7.5%, but the annual real GDP rate of 1998 amounts to -6.9%.

There exists a common cause at the heart of the two crises. It is maturity mismatch (along with currency mismatch), which took place in the process of CML. Despite an increase in net capital inflow in the early- and mid-90's, South Korea were not able to restrict capital inflows because of OECD membership

40 See (Johnston, Darbar, and Echeverria 1997) and (Blustein 2003) for the proper path of CML based on the experiences of South Korea and other countries.

41 Since our discussion is not related to the overall economy growth strategy of South Korea, it is too long to discuss here. For a recent and short summary on this, see (Lee, 2017), for example.

in 1996. That is, the OECD membership tied one hand of policymakers. South Korea instead decided to encourage capital outflow, which prompted domestic banks and financial institutions to borrow short-term loans mainly from Japan and invest abroad, leading to maturity mismatch and high leverage. Meanwhile, there were few regulations to address this change of borrowing behavior. Regulations on banks' foreign currency (FX) liquidity started too late in 1997 June. Even worse, there was no regulation on non-bank financial institutions. Japanese banks suddenly asked for repayment of trade finance and inter-bank loans or refused to roll-over existing loans, which started the liquidity crisis in 1997.[42]

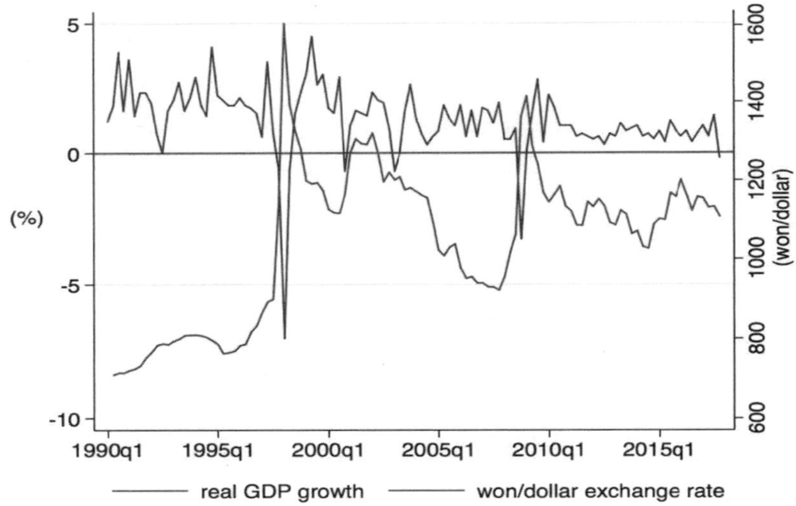

Source: Economic Statistics System (https://ecos.bok.or.kr), Bank of Korea

Figure 3-13 Real GDP Growth Rate and Won/Dollar Exchange Rate, 1990-2017

42 Regarding the origins of 1997 Asian financial crisis and the role of IMF, refer to (Kim 2014). While we emphasize the role of maturity mismatch, there are other reasons to prompt and/or aggravate the crisis such as low level of foreign reserves (only $20 billion just before the crisis), weak regulation, and external shocks.

Even after South Korea has learnt hard lessons from 1997 Asian crisis because of poorly managed maturity structure, South Korea has taken steps toward CML without fully considering the consequence of those measures. shows key changes related to CML after 1997 crisis.[43] Note that policy changes in 2006 are related to capital outflows. In the following section, we examine how these policy changes combined with seemingly unrelated factors brought about another liquidity crisis in 2008 and 2009.

Table 3-7 A Summary of Key Changes related to CML after 1997 Crisis

December 1997	Adoption of free-floating exchange rate
	Full liberalization of bond markets
May 1998	Opening of all money market instruments (CP, CD, etc.)
	No limit on foreigners' stock investment
July 1998	Deregulation on FX position
April 1999	Adoption of negative list on capital account transactions
October 2001	No limit on foreign currency loans
January 2006	Abolition of capital transaction licensing system
March 2006	No limit on outbound FDI
	No limit on types and items of overseas securities investment
May 2006	Raising the limit of overseas real estate acquisition for investment purpose From $1 million to $3 million dollars.

3.2 Unintended Consequences of Various Policies/Phenomena

South Korea has experienced another crisis in 2008. While it was triggered by the GFC, resulting from bad mortgage loans in US and Europe, in essence,

43 Appendix Table 1-Appendix Table 3 provides a summary of South Korea's financial deregulation since the early 1980s, along with those of Vietnam's.

it was a liquidity crisis in South Korea. Again, the main culprit is maturity mismatch. How did South Korea suffer from another crisis because of the same reason? In this section, we examine the several underlying factors that lead to the crisis again in 2008: outstanding performance of shipping industry in the 2000s, allowance of capital outflows through overseas investment (see), regulation on FX risk, and bank size competition. Interestingly, all these do not look harmful themselves, but the combination of these made the unintended consequence of maturity mismatch, leading to another crisis. We will see one by one and how they are connected.

3.2.1 Performance of Shipping Industry

The period of 2003-2008 was a good time for shipping industry as a whole. The total value of orders has increased from $10 billion in 2003 to $98 billion in 2007. The relative share of shipping industry to total GDP has increased from 4.8% in 2000 to 11.7% in 2009. Despite the increased overseas orders, domestic shipping companies have exposed themselves to FX risk inherent in the characteristics of shipping industry: time lag (typically, 3 years) between contract and delivery. Companies suffer from losses if won appreciates at the time of payment. Furthermore, as the current account surpluses and foreign capital inflows continued, the value of Korean won started rising and market participants expected that this pattern would continue. It is natural for domestic shipping companies to sell the significant amount of FX forward to hedge FX risk. FX currency forward contract is an agreement that obligates its parties to exchange given quantities of currencies at a prespecified exchange rate on a certain future date. For example, assume that a Korean company A who is expecting to receive a payment of US $1 million after 6 months. Since A will need to covert these dollars into Korean won, there exists exchange rate risk. To hedge this risk, the company A sells a FX forward to a bank B. The company A makes a FX forward contract of $10 million into Korean won after 6 months at a fixed exchange rate of $1 = 1,200 won. After six months, A pays $1 million to B and B pays 1.2 billion won (1 million*1,200 won) to A.

Figure 3-14 summarizes this transaction. In the viewpoint of shipping industry that expose itself to FX risk, it is desirable to sell forward contracts. During that time, the main buyers of these forward contracts are domestic banks. In the context of South Korea's experience, it is important to understand the banks' main motivation of buying forward contracts. We will examine this in the following discussion.

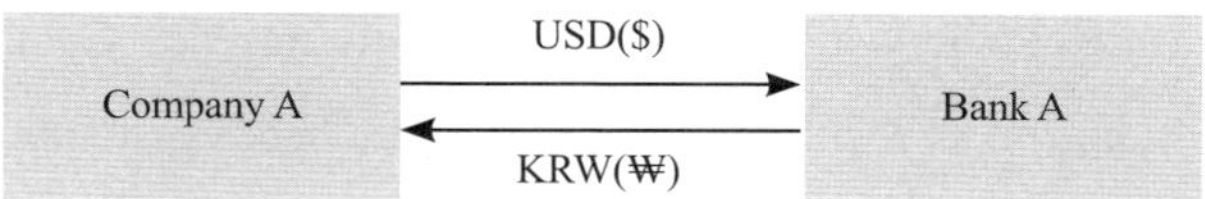

Figure 3-14 Basic Structure of Forward Contract

3.2.2 Bank Size Competition

From the early 2000s, the government has looked for the new engine growth that would guarantee stable economic growth and found an answer in the role of financial markets. It designated finance as new growth engine and emphasized that South Korea should be "Northeast financial hub." And it promoted size competition among financial institutions in order to equip them with global competitiveness.[44]

The easiest way to increase bank size is to expand one's balance sheet by borrowing more and lending more, as long as capital adequacy is maintained. Deregulation took place in favor of bank size competition, too. The government lifted regulation on loan-to-deposit ratio on November 1998. In addition, size competition among domestic banks has expanded to the area of foreign currency from 2006 as many regulations on foreign investment have been lifted (see). One bottleneck to borrow as much as a bank would like was FX regulation that aims to prevent currency mismatch. Before 1998, if a bank buys FX forward, it should sell the same amount of FX forward, resulting in zero FX position. However, after 1998, deregulation gives another option: a bank can borrow up to the amount of FX forward.[45] That is, once a bank buys FX forward, it can sell FX forward or borrow in the same currency. Combined with size competition, this deregulation made domestic banks buy more forward contracts and borrow more from abroad. Even worse, since domestic banks were not capable of borrowing long-term funds in favorable terms, they relied on short-term loans and lent them in long-term, leading to maturity mismatch.

FX forward is an effective tool for hedging FX risk to companies in shipping industry. At the same time, to domestic banks, FX forward is an attractive tool not only to raise fee income but also to increase bank size. Banks' attempt to increase their size resulted in higher leverage and maturity mismatch.

44 See (Kim 2014) for more detail. This also happened in Vietnam in the late 2000s when commercial banks are required to raise their equity according to a roadmap.

45 Even if a bank borrows from abroad in FX, it can pay back using the money it will receive from FX forward. For example, if a bank buys 3-year US dollar forward and expect the payment of US dollar in 3 years, it can borrow US dollars whose maturity is 3 years and pay back using the payment from the forward.

3.2.3 Allowing Capital Outflows and the Case of Unnecessary FX Regulation

During 2000-2007, South Korea has experienced continuing large surpluses in current account and had net surplus in financial account ("twin surpluses").[46] Since the twin surpluses have exerted pressure toward the appreciation of Korean won and global competitiveness, the government has devised various policies/deregulations to promote capital outflows since 2006.[47] shows the deregulation related to FDI and overseas securities investment that took place in 2006

Following this, domestic asset management companies started large-scale overseas investment. Figure 3-15 clearly shows the sharp increase in overseas equity investment around 2006 and 2007. In principle, domestic asset management companies fund themselves with the money from domestic investors and make overseas investment.

However, there was an unnecessary FX risk regulation. Strangely, the government encouraged FX risk hedging on overseas investment by using FX forward. It is unnecessary because investors also consider FX risk and invest accordingly. For some investors, FX risk can be a source of extra returns. (Lim 2011) empirically compares the performance of various currency hedging strategies using the data of multiple countries from 2000 to 2009. He finds that the unhedged strategies yield higher risk-adjusted returns for Korean residents to invest foreign equities. It is more unnecessary in the long run because exchange rates move around the equilibrium rates. But, as the government

46 In contrast, the share of FDI is small relative to portfolio investment, making the economy very susceptible to external shocks.

47 (Chung and Kim 2014) discuss the policy responses to capital inflows and perform econometric analysis.

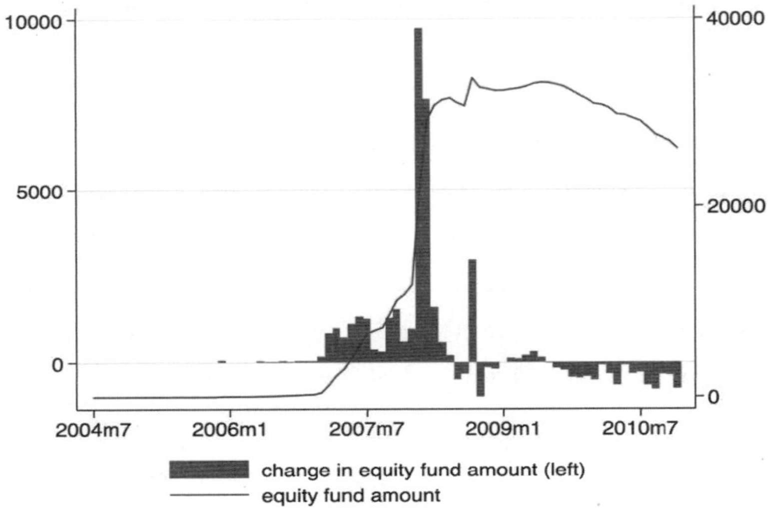

Source: Economic Statistics System (https://ecos.bok.or.kr), Bank of Korea

Figure 3-15 Trend of Overseas Equity Fund

strongly urged domestic asset management companies to hedge FX risk, they sold a large amount of FX forwards to domestic banks, enabling banks to borrow more from abroad. That is, FX forwards, (unintentionally) combined with bank size competition, have contributed to an increase in short-term foreign debt. Domestic banks purchased a large amount of FX forward from shipping industry and domestic asset management companies and increased their foreign currency loans. The supervisory authorities failed to understand the unintended consequences of these factors. An important consequence is maturity and currency mismatches.

3.3 Lessons to Be Learned

We have examined various phenomena with different motives that led to maturity/currency mismatches and, ultimately, another liquidity crisis in 2008. To sum up, there are several causes that are seemingly innocuous by themselves:

(1) Outstanding performance of South Korea's shipping industry in 2000s and high demand for hedging FX risk through FX forward
(2) Twin surpluses of trade and capital accounts and allowance of capital outflows through FDI and portfolio investment in order to alleviate pressure on the appreciation of Korean won
(3) Regulation that urge to use FX forward for overseas portfolio investment and a change in regulation related to FX forward
(4) Domestic banks' drive to increase their sizes and reliance on foreign borrowing

Figure 3-16 shows the part of this mechanism. (1), (2), and (3) make shipping industry and domestic asset management companies sell FX forward contracts. Given the huge demand of FX forward, banks readily became the buyer of those FX forward because of (4). Following a change in FX forward regulation, which is a part of (3), banks can borrow from abroad to the amount that they hold FX forward. Ironically, though South Korea aimed to be "Northeast financial hub," the global competitiveness of domestic banks was relatively low and, as a result, they could not finance long-term funds in favorable terms and had to rely on short-term funding. Thus, the unintended consequence of (1)-(4) is maturity and currency mismatches. Large maturity and currency mismatches before the GFC were the key source of systemic risks in the financial sector.

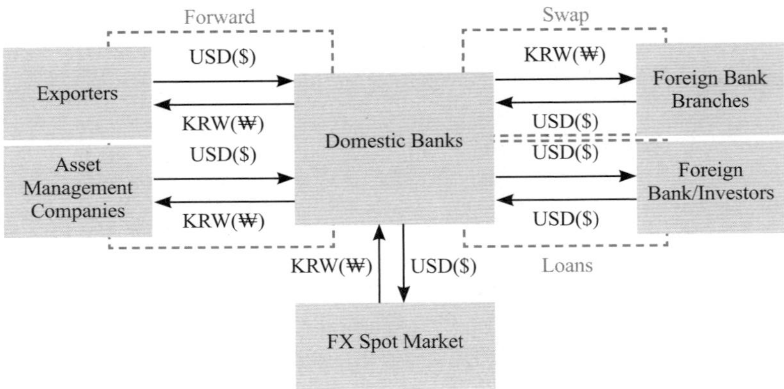

Figure 3-16 Fund Flows related to FX forward and Overseas Investment

Note that the branches of foreign banks also contributed to an increase in short-term funding and maturity mismatch. It is because they financed short-term debts from foreign banks and invested them in long-term bonds in South Korea. displays the trends of foreign debts by domestic banks and foreign bank branches in long-term and short-term. One can easily see the sharp increase of foreign debt and short-term debt.

Table 3-8 Trends of Foreign Debt in Banking Sector

	2004	2005	2006	2007	2008.9
domestic banks	505.7	583.9	821.1	1089.6	1200.5
(share)	67.9	70.0	60.1	56.5	55.6
long-term	271.2	304.2	378.5	543.2	566.1
short-term	234.5	279.7	442.6	546.4	654.4
foreign bank branches	239.2	250.4	544.2	839.2	974.0
(share)	32.1	30.0	39.9	43.5	44.4
long-term	29.2	17.3	25.9	45.8	34.7
short-term	210.0	233.1	518.3	793.4	939.3
total	744.9	834.3	1365.4	1928.8	2194.5

(Unit: $100 million)

Source: Economic Statistics System (https://ecos.bok.or.kr), Bank of Korea

To better see these patterns, Figure 3-17 shows the degree of maturity and currency mismatches. 'Currency mismatch' is defined as (foreign liabilities – foreign assets) and 'maturity mismatch' is defined as (short-term foreign liabilities – short-term foreign assets). Figure 3-17 clearly shows that the degrees of maturity/currency mismatches have increased from 2004 and they dropped sharply after the GFC.

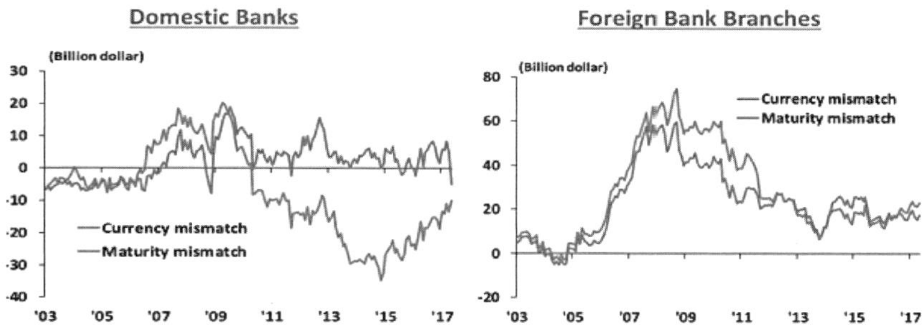

Source: Economic Statistics System (https://ecos.bok.or.kr), Bank of Korea

Figure 3-17 Maturity and Currency Mismatches

Figure 3-18 highlights the degree of maturity mismatch in banking sector. It shows the relative ratio of short-term to long-term debts for total amount of loans and loans in banking sector. Note that the shares of short-term debt both in the overall financial sector and banking sector increased before the two crises in 1997 and 2008. In addition, one can easily see the sharp increase of short-term loans in banking sector that started around 2006.

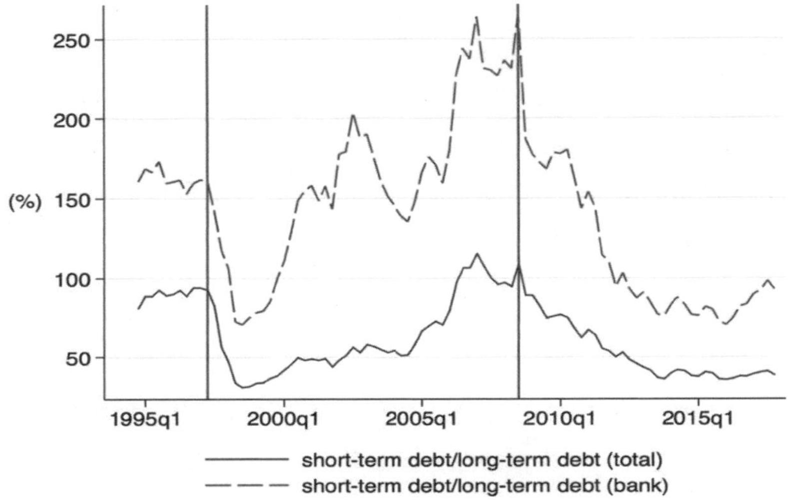

Source: Economic Statistics System (https://ecos.bok.or.kr), Bank of Korea

Figure 3-18 Ratio of Short-term to Long-term Debt

Then, what can we learn from the experience of South Korea prior to the GFC? There are several things to learn:

(1) Managing currency/maturity mismatches matters.

(2) Consolidated prudential supervision is necessary and important.

(3) Managing capital outflows is important not only in bad times but also in good times.

It is needless to say that managing mismatches is important. However, it is also important to recognize that FX forward is not a cure-all for currency mismatch. Based on South Korea's experience, hedging FX risk through FX forward in one sector (shipping industry) can result in maturity/currency mismatches in another sector (banking sector). In this regard, it is important to have consolidated prudential supervision. Since the "micro-stability" of individual institutions cannot guarantee the "macro-stability" of the whole system, it is imperative to have a supervisory authority or a collective board that are entitled to oversee the whole financial system.[48][49] Remember that, facing capital inflows in 2000s, the government allowed capital outflows without fully catching its implication on maturity/currency mismatches in banking sector. The supervisory authority should have monitored the whole system and should have allowed capital outflows more carefully even in good times. We suggest the feasible policy options in Section 5.

IV. Financial Resource Allocation

In this section, we examine the factors to consider for more efficient financial resource allocation during the process of bank privatization. There can be many issue during the transition, but we will focus on the experience of South Korea. We start by briefly discussing the pros and cons related to the government ownership of banks and examine the various hypothesis related to bank privatization by summarizing the related literature. Then, we analyze the case of South Korea and draw some lessons.

48 (Ocampo et al. 2008) also emphasize that the accelerated growth of derivative markets has helped to reduce 'micro-instability' but might have increased 'macro-instability.'

49 Refer to (Calvo et al. 2018) on the changes in financial supervisory architecture after the GFC.

1. Arguments on the Government Ownership of Banks and Empirical Evidence

The government ownership of banks has both pros and cons. Arguments for government ownership include that it can jump-start both financial and economic development by strategically allocating financial resources to the most needed areas. At the same time, the government can play a role of "commanding height" of overall economic growth strategy. Meanwhile, the biggest concern on government ownership is that there exists a large room for politicians' intervention, which would lead to the inefficient operation in most cases. In related studies, (La Porta, Lopez-De-Silanes, and Shleifer 2002) and (Clarke, Cull, and Shirley 2005) show that government ownership is large and pervasive, and higher in countries with low levels of per capita income, backward financial systems, interventionist and inefficient governments, and poor protection of property rights. (Boehmer, Nash, and Netter 2005) also show that higher government ownership of banks in 1970 is associated with slower subsequent financial development and lower growth of per capita income and productivity, supporting "political" theories of the effects of government ownership of firms. While there are many empirical studies to estimate the benefits and costs related to the ownership, it is hard to estimate the overall effect of bank privatization on growth because it has spill-over effects on the whole economy. In addition, it is hard to generalize the empirical results because of different performance measures, privatization methods, stages of development, and so on. In this regard, we succinctly review the related empirical literature on bank privatization.[50][51]

(Barth, Caprio, and Levine 2001) and (Boehmer et al. 2005) examine what kinds of banks are to be privatized. (Barth et al. 2001) examine the sales of 13 banks in Argentina and find that small banks and poorly capitalized banks were more likely to be privatized. And overstaffing tended to reduce the probability of privatization and higher levels of provincial unemployment and higher shares of public employees reduced the probability of privatization. (Boubakri et al. 2005) examine how political, institutional, and economic factors are related to a country's decision to privatize state-owned banks. They specifically test the hypothesis of whether those determinants are the same in OECD and non-OECD economies. Using a panel of 101 countries from 1982 to 2000, they find that political factors significantly affect the likelihood of bank privatization only in developing countries. In non-OECD countries, bank privatization is more likely with the more right-wing government. In contrast, none of their political variables affects the bank privatization decision in developed countries. However, economic factors such as the quality of the nation's banking sector are significant determinants of bank privatization in both OECD and non-OECD nations.

Regarding the methods of privatization, there are three options for governments to privatize: asset sales, share-issue privatization (SIP), and voucher privatization. Asset sales refer to the case in which the government

---

50 See (Clarke and Cull 2002) for a nice survey on bank privatization in developing countries. A whole issue of *Journal of Banking and Finance* 29 (2005) devotes to the issues of bank privatization.

51 (Bonaccorsi di Patti and Hardy 2005) use data from 81 privatizations in 22 low- and middle-income countries and find that several, but not all, performance measures improved after privatization. But the results are not uniform. It depends on how you measure 'performance' (e.g., profitability, cost efficiency, non-performing loans (NPL), ROA, ROE, total factor productivity, etc.) and how long you measure (some changes such as loan portfolio quality can take more time). In addition, one cannot evaluate the effect of privatization by looking at only the banking sector. It may have spill-over effect on the economy as a whole. For example, privatization results in increased prudence. In Argentina, privatized banks reduce total lending and loans in local currency. They also cut mortgage lending and agricultural lending.

sells ownership of the state-owned banks to a small group of investors or an existing private bank. It may sell all or a fraction of ownership. Typically, it is implemented through an auction. In SIPs, the government sells equity shares in the public capital market. The form of SIPs is frequently used in advanced economies and large-scale privatization in developing countries. Voucher privatization has been used in former communist nations in East Europe such as Russia, the Czech Republic, and Poland. While it is similar to SIPs in that shares of ownership are widely distributed, it is different because vouchers are available to many citizens at a very low price.

As mentioned above, it is not easy to answer to a question like "will bank privatization do good to the economy?" because the answer can differ depending on the specific environments of countries. It is better to ask in what conditions has bank privatization turned out be beneficial? Researchers have identified several factors. They find that the effect of bank privatization depends on (1) the amount of the government shares in the privatized banks, (2) whether to be bought by strategic buyers, (3) foreign ownership, and (4) competitiveness of banking sector. According to (Otchere and Chan 2003), the common rationale behind these factors is that privatization can enhance bank performance by limiting harmful government intervention in state-owned enterprises.

Firstly, as to the amount of the government ownership, it suggests that less government ownership is desirable because it allows smaller room for political intervention. (Boubakri et al. 2005) show that, when Pakistan government started privatization and lifted entry restrictions at the same time, new private banks that enter the market outperformed privatized banks in the period of following privatization, suggesting that the continued government ownership is associated with poor performance.

Second, the role of strategic investors is important. Drawing upon the corporate governance literature, concentrated strategic owners are in a better position to deal with agency problem, which results from information asymmetries. Thus, case studies show that the performance of most banks privatized through sales to strategic investors improved while the performance of those through share-issue privatization did not. It is mainly because governments use share-issue privatization to ensure that private owners do not gain full control over the privatized bank. However, what is essential is the existence of informed investors that can resolve agency problem and it needs not be strategic investors in all cases. Based on the case of the Commonwealth Bank of Australia, (Djankov, Jindra, and Klapper 2005) emphasize that market monitoring by informed investors is important.

Third, foreign ownership can increase the gain from privatization.[52] The logic is that foreign owners have more experience and know-how than domestic investors. Alternatively, foreigners invest only when there is little risk related to government intervention. (Megginson 2005) find that banks that were privatized to foreigners are better in terms of capital ratio and economic efficiency. (Otchere and Chan 2003) show that the firm value of distressed banks in East Asia that were sold to foreigners has increased in the long run. However, note that higher firm values of privatized banks that are under foreign ownership do not necessarily imply enhanced welfare of a country. We discuss the related issue in Section 4.

Fourth, the competitiveness of banking sector affects the gain from privatization and privatization will subsequently affect the competitiveness of banking sector. While competition in the bank sector may encourage excessive risk taking, restrictions on competition may do harm to banking sector stability and performance. (Clarke and Cull 1999) show that some of the banks and

52 (Chen, Li, and Moshirian 2005) points out that it is perhaps the most controversial issue related to bank privatization.

non-bank financial institutions reacted negatively to the partial privatization announcements of the Bank of China Hong Kong (BOCHK). (Park 1996) show that stock returns of major rival banks reacted negatively to the privatization announcements of the Commonwealth Bank of Australia (CBA). However, there are not many case studies because it is hard to assess 'competition' between state-owned banks and private banks.

(Megginson 2005) also add additional conditions. Governments should avoid setting up 100% deposit insurance to avoid well-documented problem of moral hazard, which is severe in a privatized banking system. In addition, for effective bank examination, supervision, and monitoring, it is essential to have a bank regulatory system that is sufficiently independent from political clout, along with a sound financial reporting system for transparency and reliability on asset quality and performance.

In the following section, we focus on the second and third factors (strategic investors, and foreign ownership) and how they affect the economy of South Korea in terms of financial resource allocation.

2. Experiences of South Korea

2.1 Legacy of South Korea's Government-Controlled Financial System

It is well-known that the government of South Korea heavily intervened in financial markets to strategically utilize financial resources for economic growth from the 1960s.[53] While it was necessary given the lack of capital

53 See (Kim 2007) for a nice summary regarding the role of finance for economic growth of South Korea.

and undeveloped financial markets, its side effects have emerged over time. The legacy of South Korea's government-controlled financial system during the development stage include low ability of loan screening and monitoring, low productivity and profitability, and reliance on interest income, which leads to low global competitiveness of financial sector. Figure 3-19 well summarizes the situation, showing the trends of firms' profitability, land-price-adjusted profitability, and average borrowing rate. Until the early 2000s, firms' profitability was lower than the average borrowing rates, suggesting the inefficient allocation of financial resources. Despite low profitability, banks had to lend because of explicit and implicit guidance of the government.

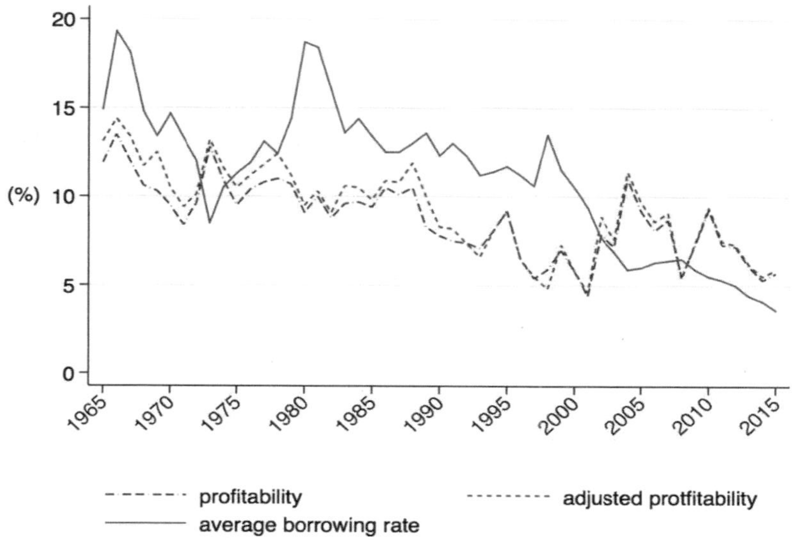

Source: Economic Statistics System (https://ecos.bok.or.kr), Bank of Korea

Figure 3-19 Firms' Profitability and Average Borrowing Rates

As the economy has reached the stage of take-off and its size has become too large to be dictated by the government, bank privatization has started. South Korea started bank privatization from 1972 (The Commerical Bank of Korea) and further privatized special banks such as Korea Exchange Bank (1989), Kookmin Bank (1995), and Housing & Commerical Bank (1997). Before 1997 Asian financial crisis, all banks were privatized except three national banks (Industrial Bank of Korea, Korea Development Bank, Korea EXIM bank). However, many banks became undercapitalized during the 1997 crisis and, through bailouts during the crisis, many banks were owned by the government. Since then, the government tried to re-privatize them and foreign investors have acquired domestic banks. As a result, the shares of foreign ownership in domestic banks are quite high. As of March 2016, the shares for the top 4 domestic banks are 65.6% (Shinhan), 68.3% (Kookmin), 64.8% (Hana), and 20.3% (Woori), respectively. The reason for Woori bank's low share is that the government is still the largest shareholder. That is, privatization has not been completed for Woori bank. Given the foreigners' share of Korean stock market as of 2006 is 31.8%, those numbers are unusually high.

What would be the consequences of high foreign ownership? We will examine two cases that affect financial resource allocation in South Korea. One is from high foreign ownership in domestic banks. The other is high shares of foreign investment in securities market. When the government decided to allow the takeover and acquisition by foreign investors during and after the crisis, it anticipated the introduction of advanced financial products and better screening and monitoring techniques, which would find financial constrained SMEs with good prospect and makes loans to them, contributing to an increase in business investment. Likewise, when the government allowed foreigners' investment in domestic equities and bonds, positive impacts on the economy through increased funding and monitoring would have been anticipated. While we do not have rigorous studies on the net effect of foreign ownership to the economy, we have experienced its negative effects: credit misallocation and outflow of national wealth. We will examine these two things in more detail and propose feasible policy options for not repeating the bad case of South Korea.

2.2 Negative Consequences of High Foreign Ownership

There are two types of foreign investors. One is strategic buyers, who tend to "buy and hold." The other is financial buyers, who tend to "buy low and sell high." When the government opened up the domestic capital market to foreign investors, it failed to fully anticipate the consequences resulting from both types of investment. We conjecture that, in case of South Korea, the distinctive consequences of foreign ownership in domestic banks are (1) undesirable credit allocation through increased foreign ownership of (previously state-owned) domestic banks, and (2) outflow of national wealth in the form of capital gains and dividends. There can be additional cases. And, of course, there must have been some benefits related to it. However, since our approach is to learn from "bad" examples, we focus on two "bad" cases, which are important to the Korean economy and, at the same time, which the Vietnamese economy should consider when it fully opens its capital markets and privatize domestic banks.

2.2.1 Undesirable Credit Allocation

As discussed above, what the government initially expected from foreign ownership of domestic banks is the best practices of banking in advanced economies. That is, foreign ownership could reduce financial frictions in financial markets and find good firms with limited funding. However, what was missing is the fact that foreign investors and institutions also seek higher risk-adjusted returns in their businesses. Rather than searching for and screening SMEs with good potentials, which is not an easy task, they tunneled financial resource to a relatively easy money-making source: mortgage loans

There are two kinds of costs involved in loan-making: selection cost and monitoring cost. The former is related to adverse selection and the latter is related to moral hazard. Selection cost is higher when screening is more difficult. Monitoring cost is higher when monitoring borrowers' action is more difficult. In case of mortgage loans, both costs are relatively lower. Household income and wealth, together with job status, provide sufficient information on the creditworthiness of mortgage loan applicants. Thus, selection cost is very low. And, since a house that the potential borrower will buy is used as collateral, a lender can just foreclose a mortgage by taking that house and reselling it in case the borrower defaults, implying that monitoring cost is not high at all. It is a natural consequence that the increased foreign ownership in domestic banks leads to an increase in mortgage loans.

Another mistake by the government made the situation worse. Since 1950s, the government has restricted loans to households and promoted loans to firms. However, it has started lifting the related regulations from the mid-90s and abolished them after the crisis. This decision is problematic because domestic banks did not equip themselves with proper technique of screening and monitoring firms.[54]

Combined with this deregulation on loans to households, increased foreign ownership has contributed to misallocation of financial resources. Figure 3-20 shows the relative shares of loans to large firms, SMEs, and household made by

54 See (Cho 2010) for a summary and evaluation on South Korea's experience of banking sector liberalization.

domestic banks. The share of large firms, who have better access to direct finance such as equities and bonds, has decreased far before the period of Asian financial crisis. The share of loans to households has suddenly increased from 1998, jumping from 18.2% in 1998 to 52.9% in 2002. Since then, it has been hovering around 50%, which is quite high. Meanwhile, the share of loans to SMEs, who have limited access to direct finance and rely more on bank loans, had decreased. It dropped from 18.8% in 1998 from 7.6% in 2002. As Figure 3-20 clearly shows, loans to SMEs (and part of loans to large firms) have replaced by loans to households. It is one consequence when the government loses its voice and foreign ownership have more rights to speak in the operation of domestic banks.[55]

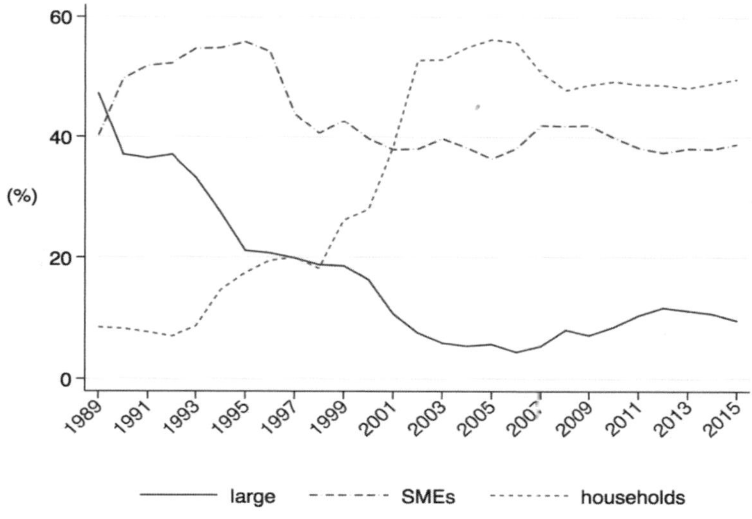

Source: Bank Statistics, Financial Supervisory Service (http://www.fss.or.kr)

Figure 3-20 Relative Shares of Domestic Bank Loans

55 We do not argue for government ownership itself. We emphasize that the government needs to deliberately consider the motives of foreign investors and the better usages of foreign capital. We also reject the approach based on the logic of good and evil.

The financial allocation heavily tilted toward mortgage loans result in a serious macroeconomic problem: severe household indebtedness. Household debt-to-disposable income ratio of South Korea as of 180% as of 2016. It was 143% in 2008 before rising to 180%, jumping 37 percentage points.[56] Given this high indebtedness, another problem is that too much of illiquid assets such as housing in household balance sheet. Figure 3-21 shows household portfolio composition by households' net worth and income quintile.[57] Net worth is defined as total assets minus total debts of households and home equity is defined as housing and other illiquid assets minus total debts. The most prominent characteristics is that household wealth is highly concentrated on illiquid assets such as housing and real estate. Regardless of income level, panel (a) shows that the share of financial assets is less than 20%. Panel (b) shows that even the richest 20% group concentrates more than 90% of their wealth on housing and other illiquid assets, holding only 5.7% of their wealth on financial assets.

Note that the fraction of financial assets on balance sheets increases as we move from top 20% to bottom 20% group. This pattern is in stark contrast to that of other countries, such as U.S. and Japan. According to (Park and Kim 2018), the poorest 20% group had $4 of home equity for every $1 of other assets in 2007 and the richest 20% were exactly the opposite, with $1 of home equity for every $4 of other assets, like money-market funds, stocks, and bonds. Considering that liquid assets can play a role of buffer stock to unexpected external shocks, too little liquid assets held by households can pose a threat to

56 Source: https://data.oecd.org/hha/household-debt.htm

57 The exposition on the figure comes from (Park and Kim 2018). Since KLIPS (Korean Labor & Income Panel Study) does not report the mortgage debt separately, home equity is defined as housing and other illiquid assets minus total debts. The sample is based on the household heads whose ages between 24 and 65. All variables are winsorized at 1% and 99%.

macroeconomic stability.[58] We examine the policy options in Section 5.

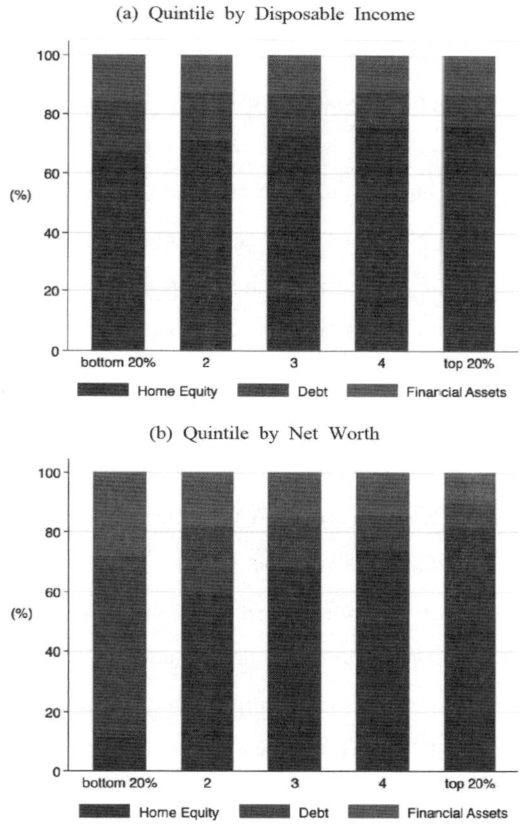

Source: (Park and Kim 2018)

Figure 3-21 Portfolio Composition, by Disposable Income and Net Worth, 2001-2014

58 See (Park 2017) for an empirical study on the macroeconomic implication of household debt in South Korea. He suggests that, even in a situation where high-income group holds a large amount of household debt, the macroeconomy can be susceptible to external shocks because of too little liquid assets held by this group.

2.2.2 Outflows of National Wealth[59]

After the 1997 crisis, South Korea has consistently experienced trade surpluses. During the period of 1997-2017, the accumulated amount of trade surpluses amounts to $692 billion. However, an increase in South Korea's net foreign assets is merely $303 billion. How can one explain this difference of $389 billion (= 692 billion – 303 billion)? It is because South Korea's net capital gain is negative. A negative net capital gain implies that return of foreigners' investment in domestic assets are higher than that of domestic residents' investment abroad. This relationship can be illustrated by the following identity:

$\Delta NIIP=CA+NCG+E$,

where $\Delta NIIP$ is a change in net international investment position (NIIP), CA is the current account, NCG is net capital gain, and E refers to errors and omissions. In case of South Korea, CA is far larger than $\Delta NIIP$ because of negative NCG, ignoring the small number of E.

Figure 3-22 shows the time-series of trade surpluses and changes in net international investment position (equivalent to changes in net foreign assets), as shares of GDP. Before 1997, trade surplus tends to move in tandem with a change in NIIP. After 1997, two time-series do not move together. It implies that, after 1997, the magnitude of net capital gain (NCG) becomes negative and larger. Different from the case of domestic stock investment in which a gain from one person is cancelled by a loss from another person, not affecting national income, a negative NCG is a loss of national income. Thus, a negative NCG is equivalent to outflows of national wealth. Based on a calculation by (Lee 2017), net capital losses relative to GDP increases from 0.2% to 2.3% after 1997.

59 The discussion in this section is based on chapter 4 and 5 in (Lee 2017). Refer to (Lee 2017) for more detailed explanation.

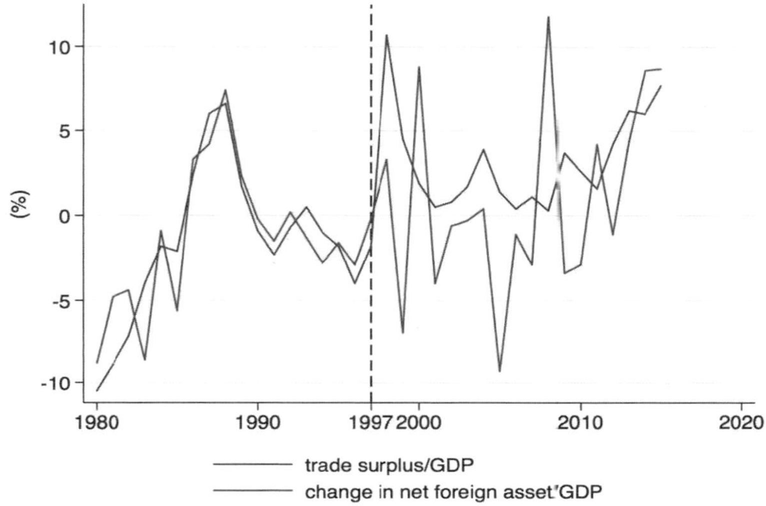

Source: Economic Statistics System (https://ecos.bok.or.kr), Bank of Korea

Figure 3-22 Changes in Net Foreign Assets and Trade Surpluses

How can foreign investors earn higher return? The main reason is that the prices of domestic assets held by foreign investors has risen more than those of foreign assets held by domestic investors. In addition to foreign investors' better skill of stock/bond picking, plummeted asset prices (including banks, buildings, equities, bonds, etc.) has contributed to foreign investors' outperformance. During and right after the crisis, some foreign investors purchased domestic assets and acquired shares in bargain and sold them high later. Other investors have held those shares and transmitted dividends to their countries.

Note that the part of net capital loss in ΔNIIP is inevitable for a country that does not have a key currency such as dollars. The relatively higher returns of foreign investors can be partially justified by the following arguments. First, the purchase and acquisition of foreign investors during and after the crisis was high risk-high return investments even to them. And, consequently, those investments have contributed to overcoming the crisis. Second, domestic investors' holding of foreign safe assets (for example, the central bank's purchase of US Treasury bonds to accumulate foreign reserves), which earns lower returns, can help prevent future crises. However, without the crisis, foreign investor could not have purchased domestic assets in such a bargain and would not have earned high returns.

2.3 Lessons to Be Learned

What can we learn from the experience of South Korea? Let along the wrong timing of deregulation related to loans to households, we need to consider the following:

(1) Fostering the competitiveness of domestic institutions should precede before allowing a full-scale CML or a large-scale foreign ownership.
(2) Macroprudential measures are essential.
(3) Promoting long-term investment is desirable in terms of stability and long-term growth potential.
(4) Reform in good times (and avoid fire sales)

In the following section, based on the discussion in Section 3 and 4, we examine the policy options worth considering for the stable long-term growth of the Vietnamese economy.

V. Policy Recommendation

We have identified several policy mistakes combined with external factors that led to the two major economic crises. Ideally speaking, if the government made the timing of deregulations right, paid more attention to the mismatches, and monitored their influences on other sectors, there would not have been such crises. In retrospect, those two crises could have been prevented or their impact could have been minimized. The common culprit of the two crises is the mismatches of maturity and currency during the process of opening the capital markets. Figure 3-23 well summarizes the key factors of our discussion and provides some clues on what to do in order not to repeat the same mistake. Figure 3-23 shows the volatility (measured by 12-month moving standard deviation) of components of net capital flows: net flows of direct investment, portfolio investment, bank loans. Remind that the main cause of maturity/currency mismatches was bank loans and the factor that aggravated the situations during the crises was sudden capital outflow, for which portfolio investment was largely responsible. Figure 3-23 shows that the volatility of bank loans and direct investment is quite high while that of direct investment is not.

In this regard, policy options should include at least measures of curbing volatility of capital flows, managing the structures of maturity and currency, and promoting long-term investment. In the following discussion, we introduce the available policy options that the

Vietnamese economy need to consider. Some of them are already implemented by South Korea and have been evaluated as successful.

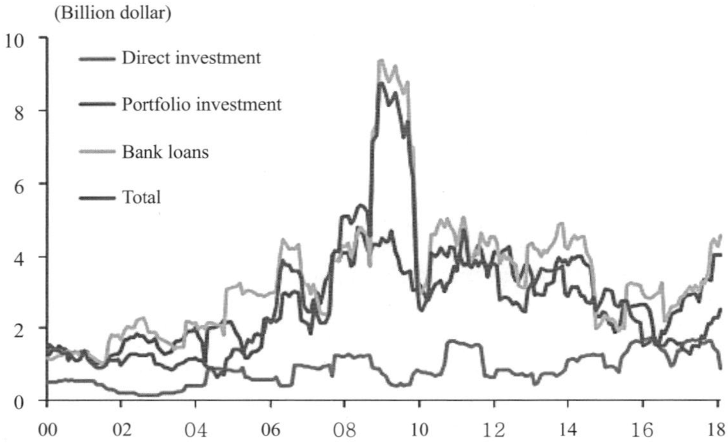

Source: Economic Statistics System (https://ecos.bok.or.kr), Bank of Korea

Figure 3-23 Volatility of Net Capital Flows

1. Macroprudential Policy

1.1 Macroprudential Measures for Capital Flows

1.1.1 Leverage Caps on FX Derivatives

In order to prevent speculative risk-taking and over-hedging, the government and the Bank of Korea have implemented the policy of leverage caps on FX derivatives from October 2010. FX derivatives include forward, swaps, NDF (non-deliverable forward), etc. Initially, the cap on FX position was set at 50% of bank capital for domestic banks and 250% for foreign bank branches. Later, to further suppress foreign borrowing, it was strengthened bylowering the cap at 40% and 200% in July 2011. The authority adjusts the levels of cap depending on macroeconomic conditions, as shown in Figure 3-24.

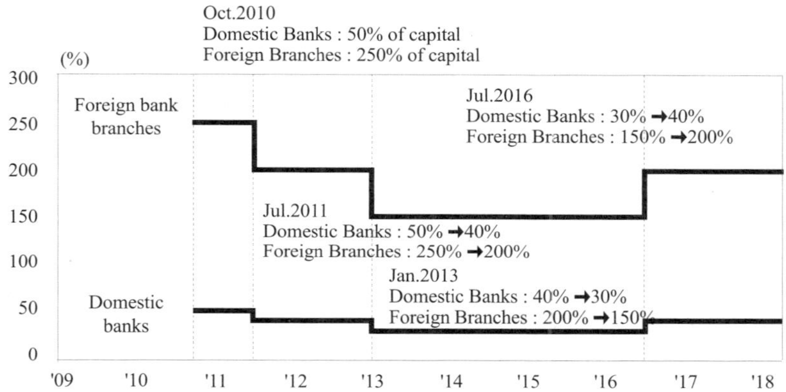

Source: Economic Statistics System (https://ecos.bok.or.kr), Bank of Korea

Figure 3-24 Leverage Caps on FX Derivative Positions

One advantage of this regulation is that it is not too restrictive to banks as it seems. Since the cap is defined as a ratio to the previous month's bank capital, banks can use more FX derivatives as long as they raise their own bank capital. In addition, since the cap is applied to net positions, it does not discourage the transaction of FX derivatives. In case a bank wants to buy more FX derivatives, it can do by doing more transactions in opposite directions. So far, this regulation has been evaluated as successful. As Figure 3-25 shows, the net positions of FX derivatives declined after the GFC and have stayed at low levels.

Source: Bank of Korea

Figure 3-25 Net Position of FX Derivatives

1.1.2 Macroprudential Stability Levy

Macroprudential stability levy was introduced in August 2011 in order to prevent excessive short-term FX borrowing by banks. It is imposed on non-core FX liabilities of banks and saved in a reserve fund for later use. Initially, the rate ranged from 0.02-0.2% and higher rates were applied to short-term financing. From July 2015, it is applied only to shortterm financing whose maturity is less than one year and the uniform rate is applied at 0.1%. Figure 3-26 and Figure 3-27 show that short-term FX liabilities are well managed. After 2011, the share of short-term FX liabilities held by foreign bank branches and its share to foreign reserves have been stabilized at low levels.

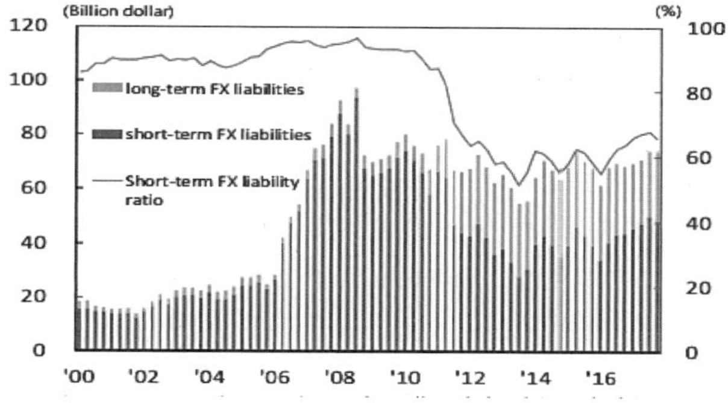

Source: Economic Statistics System (https://ecos.bok.or.kr), Bank of Korea

Figure 3-26 External Liabilities of Foreign Bank Branches

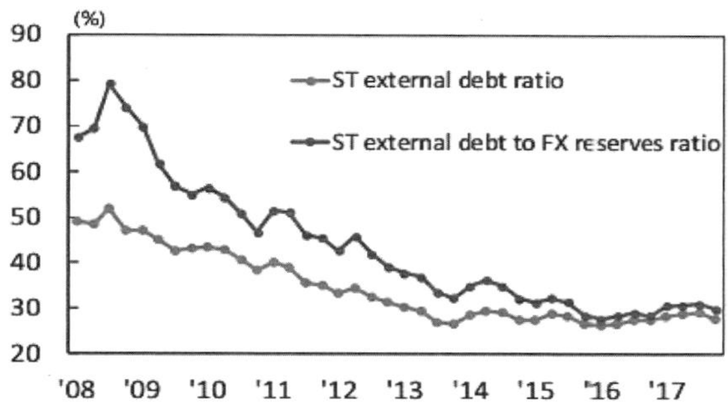

Source: Economic Statistics System (https://ecos.bok.or.kr), Bank of Korea

Figure 3-27 Short-term External Debt to Reserve Ratio

1.1.3 Taxation on Foreign Bond Investment

During the period of the GFC, a large amount of foreign capital flew out of South Korea. In May 2009, the government decided to exempt taxes on foreign bond investors' interest income and capital gains to prevent sudden capital outflows. As the economy has shown a strong recovery, capital inflows have sharply increased again, raising concerns on systemic risk. In response, taxes on foreign bond investment was reinstated in January 2011. Tax rates can be adjusted by the presidential decree in the event of financial market turmoil. This policy has been successful in reducing the volatility of foreign investors' bond investment by affecting the incentive to invest in domestic bonds.

1.2 Macroprudential Policy for Household Debt

It is reckoned that South Korea's household debt problem was largely originated from banks' switching to loans to households around 1997, as discussed in Section 4. Since then, rising housing prices and household debts are often cited as the major threat to the economy. In response, the government has implemented various macroprudential polices and South Korea is at the forefront of countries using macroprudential policy (IMF 2018). In South Korea, both LTV/DTI regulations have put brakes on housing prices and mortgage loans and are successful in reducing systemic risks.

1.2.1 LTV (Loan-to-Value)

LTV policy was introduced in 2002 and different LTV ratios have been applied depending on housing market conditions, regions and housing types. For example, a higher ratio is applied in overheated and speculative regions.

Figure 3-28 displays the changes in LTV regulation. One can see that the ratio was adjusted upward or downward several times. Currently, the ratio ranges from 30% to 70%.

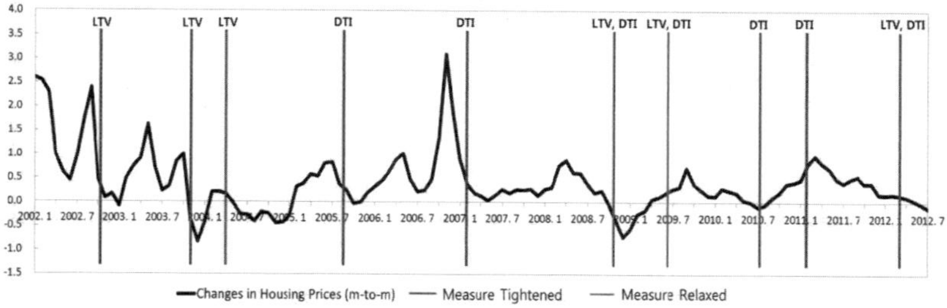

Source: Bank of Korea

Figure 3-28 Changes in LTV and DTI Regulation

1.2.2 DTI (Debt-to-Income)

DTI policy was introduced in 2015. It is applied only debtors living in Seoul and its neighboring metropolitan areas. As shown in Figure 3-28, DTI ratio have been adjusted several times depending housing market conditions.

Since January 2018, new DTI policy has been implemented. It is designed to better evaluate the repayment capacity of households and apply DTI ratios accordingly. In calculating ratios based on new policy, it also includes the principal of non-bank mortgage loans. The old DTI policy considered only bank-issued mortgage loans.

1.2.3 DSR (Debt Service Ratio)

A new index related to household debts will be implemented from October 2018. DSR, ratio of debt service to disposable income, is a better measure in measuring how much of debt burden is actually imposed on current consumption, compared to LTV and DTI. It will be used as a management indicator, not a regulatory index. It will be extended to non-banking sector in 2019.

2. Making the Most Effective Use of Foreign Capital

While foreign capital is essential for economic growth of emerging economies that lack sufficient capital, it exerts both positive and negative influences to the economy as we have observed in case of South Korea. As a way to minimize the negative effects of foreign capital, promoting FDI is desirable since it is not volatile like portfolio investment and it helps accumulate domestic capital stock. To entice FDI, it is important to make favorable market conditions to potential investors. It is important to entice greenfield type of FDI, rather than M&A type.[60] Using the panel data of 128 countries during the period of 1996-2014, (Lee et al. 2015) empirically analyze the determinants of FDI depending on FDI types and development stages. summarizes the main empirical finding of (Lee et al. 2015). Focusing on the categories of greenfield investment in emerging economies, which is relevant to Vietnam, let alone GDP growth rate, managing inflation and country risk at low levels, avoiding international investment disputes, and making more investment agreements are positively associated with an increase in greenfield investment.[61]

60 Also note that real estate investment is categorized as FDI.

61 This result needs to be interpreted carefully because it is about correlation, not causation.

Table 3-9 Determinants of FDI

	Investment type	
	Greenfield	M&A
Advanced economies	Real GDP per capita (+)	Inflation (−) Real exchange rate (−) Financial market development (+)
Emerging economies	GDP growth rate (+) inflation (−) country risk (−) investment agreement (+) international investment dispute (−)	real GDP per capita (+) GDP growth rate (−) population (+) real exchange rate (+) financial market development (+) country risk (−) investment agreement (−)

Source: (Lee et al. 2015)

FDI in the form of M&A can be beneficial through the economy of scale and scope. In addition, it can provide valuable opportunities by getting into the global production networks. However, as pointed out in 4, the authority should pay attention to the possible negative effects of high foreign ownership.

A tax regime for long-term investment can be an effective tool. However, its effect can differ depending on the target industry, development stages, and so on. (Wilson, Hubbard, and Slemrod 1993) and (Single and Kramer 1996) find that foreign investors value infrastructure and residential environments higher than tax rates. In addition, based on South Korea' experience, it might not be useful as expected as the economy grows. According to (Choi and Choi 2014), the amount of tax exemption for foreign investors has decreased from $745 million in 2011 to $106 million in 2017, implying that foreign investors do not consider tax exemption seriously and do not rely on it much.

VI. Conclusion

Through economic and political reforms initiated by Đổi Mới in 1986, Vietnam has turned itself from an underdeveloped country to a middle-income country of rapid economic growth. One of the key tasks facing Vietnam is to keep this momentum and to build the foundation for stable and sustainable growth. In this regard, we examine the experiences of South Korea in the area of financial markets and attempt to provide policy lessons that the Vietnamese may benefit in the future.

While South Korea has undergone an economic miracle, often called "Miracle on the Han River," there were two economic crises that stalled its solid economic growth: 1997 Asian crisis and 2008 Global Financial Crisis. One common cause for the two crises is the mismatches of maturity and currency. As our first topic, we examine various factors that led to those mismatches before 2008 Global Financial Crisis. Surprisingly, seemingly unrelated factors such as outstanding performance of shipping industry, bank size competition, deregulation on capital outflows, and so on are intertwined, leading to the unexpected outcome of maturity mismatch.

As our second topic, we examine the aftermath of opening domestic financial markets to foreign investors. As foreign ownership of domestic banks has increased, banks indulged in lending to households and reducing loans to SMEs. In addition, as foreign investors' returns on domestic assets are higher than domestic investors' returns on foreign assets, South Korea has experienced outflows of national wealth. While it is true that South Korea has benefitted from foreign capital, its negative impact could have been reduced with better policies.

In order not to repeat the same mistakes that took place during the two crises, we propose policy recommendations. They are preventive measures by nature. And some of them mainly aim to reduce the negative effect of short-term foreign capital and to entice long-term investment from abroad. We also discuss various macroprudential policies in terms of foreign capital flows and household debts, most of which have already been implemented in South Korea. The macroprudential measures discussed above are assessed to have been successful in reducing volatile short-term foreign currency funding, which has been blamed for the main cause of the previous two crises. According to (IMF 2012), these measures are effective in curbing reliance on short-term foreign currency funding, leverage and capital flow volatility. However, macroprudential policy should be coordinated with monetary policy and the authority needs to avoid "overcooking" that can lower market efficiency.

Last but not least, since all suggestions are devised based on South Korea' own experience, the Vietnamese authority should choose policy tools that reflect its own economic environments and historical context. Also, it is important to recognize that these issues are still insufficient to deal with sudden outflows of foreign portfolio investment in bad time.

CHAPTER FOUR:

ENHANCING THE INDUSTRY ECOSYSTEM IN VIETNAM

Yun Jeong Choi
Professor, School of Economics, Yonsei University

CHAPTER FOUR:

Enhancing the Industry Ecosystem in Vietnam

I. Introduction

Vietnam has made remarkable achievements, transforming from an agricultural economy to one of the most dynamic economies since Doi Moi. Vietnam became an attractive investment destination with great potential and brought foreign direct investment of US$ 35.88 billion in 2017. According to the World Bank, the average growth rate from 1986 to 2016 was 6.4%, peaking at 8.2% during the 1991-1995 period. The per capita gross domestic product (GDP) increased from US$ 239 in 1985 to US$ 2,185 in 2016. Exports totaled US$ 162 billion in 2016, and Vietnam ranked the 24th largest exporter in the world with the average growth rate of 18.6% during the 2010-2015 period.

However, the decreasing growth rates since 1995 and the stagnation during the 2011-2015 period called for the second round of Doi Moi. In the private sector, domestic firms have faced difficulties in terms of productivity, innovation, management skill, and financial access. The efficiency of large enterprises with more than 300 employees has been aggravated. The productivity of state-owned enterprises that account for a large proportion of the national economy also has been declining. In 2016, the Ministry of Planning and Investment and the World Bank group in the Vietnam 2035 report provided recommendations for overcoming Vietnam's current challenges and moving onto an advanced economy with industrialization and modernization.

As the first and foremost pillar of Vietnam 2035, it stated economic prosperity with environmental sustainability and emphasized further improvements in productivity and efficiency of the private sector and the public sector in Vietnam are imperative.

The primary reasons behind prevalent inefficiency are lack of competition and failure of the price mechanism, which led to the distortion of incentives and resource allocation. It restrained economic agents' motivation to enhance its competitiveness, productivity, and profitability and hindered economic development.

Insufficient competition and failure of the price mechanism have been mainly rooted in the preferential treatments of the state-owned enterprises (SOEs). SOEs have enjoyed favorable access to capital despite a lack of management capability and development strategy. The reckless expansion impeded its efficiency. The failure of many investment projects of SOEs including Vinashin and Vinalines has caused tremendous damage to Vietnam. Although the system to monitor SOEs was established, it has not been working well. The coordination efforts of SOE investments at the central government and provincial government levels were weak. Inefficient management, lack of transparency, and corporate governance under the strong influence of the State made SOEs unattractive to investors, and miss an opportunity to grow.

However, the negative impact of insufficient competition and malfunctioning markets was not limited to SOEs only. It also hampered the growth and competitiveness of private firms. The barrier to finance access for domestic private firms made it difficult for them to grow and expand.

Therefore, building a level playing field and promoting competition between firms is a starting point. For this, Vietnam needs to strengthen the institutions and systems to support fair competition. Based on the proper institutional foundation, the effective implementation of monitoring and evaluation systems for SOEs, the gradual changes of the corporate governance system of SOEs, and the privatization of SOEs would enhance the competitiveness of SOEs. The implementation of industrial policies based on the principles of a market economy would promote the competitiveness of both the private sector and the public sector.

To provide policy suggestions for enhancing Vietnam's industry ecosystem and industrial competitiveness, we investigate success and failure factors based on Korea's advancement experience and explore the possibility of applying them to Vietnam. Section 2 covers corporate governance system and privatization of SOEs, section 3 focuses on industrial policy and institutions in the private sector, and section 4 covers competition policy.

II. Enhancing the Competitiveness of State-Owned Enterprises

1. Vietnam's State-Owned Enterprise System and Equitization

1.1. Governance and Performance Evaluation

1.1.1. Related Laws and Governance

The improvement of the legal institutions and framework for the development and management of SOEs has been made gradually. The commercialization of SOEs and the dismantling of central bureaucratic controls were crucial steps in Vietnam's Doi Moi (Painter, 2003). Decree 217/1987/HDBT created the conditions for increased enterprise autonomy by dismantling some of the institutions of state subsidy and control (Huy and Nghia, 1996). The range of targets and controls was significantly reduced; the enterprise manager was given authority to manage day-to-day matters, including staff hiring and remuneration practices; the state was no longer to provide for inputs; transactions between enterprises were to be based on contracts; each enterprise was in theory free to buy and sell inputs and products on the open market although central price controls were retained for key products; and enterprises were to be self-financing through the retention of depreciation charges and the raising of funds from the state bank, which were to decide on loans on commercial banks (Painter, 2003). However, the change of the SOE management mechanism caused large numbers of SOEs to experience difficulties and suffer losses, which led to the dissolution or mergers of SOEs in the 1990s.

In 1994 and 1995, following the Prime Minister's Decision 90 and Decision 91, "General Corporations," successors to earlier "Union of Enterprises" established in 1978 were established to help the reorganization of SOEs. General corporations 91 are vertically organized ones with the minimum capital of 500 billion VND in key industrial areas and later became industrial groups with additional capital from the government. General corporations 90 are horizontally organized ones with the minimum capital of 1,000 billion VND.

The first institutional frameworks and legal status for the operation of SOEs were provided by the SOE Law enacted in 1995. SOEs were classified into three groups: independent enterprises, General Corporations, and member enterprises of General Corporations. SOEs obtained the right to decide their business on production, investment, and capital and were allowed to do business with SOEs and non-SOEs. However, the separation between ownership and management was not clear.

From the beginning of the 2000s, experimental policies that aimed at changing the relationship between the state and SOE groups were pursued actively. The Vietnam Communist Party decided to change the role of the state from the controller of SOEs to the owner of state capital (Ishida, 2013). The Resolution of the third Meeting of the Xth Central Committee of the Party in 2001 highlighted a further development of strategy on Corporatization. Aims and roles of Corporatization had been set, and several SOEs had been experimentally established.

One cornerstone was the revision of the Law of Enterprise in 2005, which became effective on 1 July 2006. Before this law, SOEs, private enterprise and foreign-owned enterprises were governed by the law on SOEs, the law on Private Enterprises, and the Law on Foreign Investment, respectively. However, after the revision in 2005, all types of enterprises operating in Vietnam have been regulated by the same law. It was for the first time in history since the start of Doi Moi. Moreover, private interests were allowed to have partial ownership in certain SOEs. Also, all SOEs were required to transform into joint-stock companies (shareholding companies) or into one-member limited liability companies with 100 % capital from the state between 1 July 2006 and 1 July 2010. SOEs were allowed to mobilize capital from different sources other than state capital and have independence in allocating profits or setting up legal funds (OECD, 2013).

Another critical step was the establishment of the State Capital Investment Corporation (SCIC) under Decisions No.151/2005/QD-TTg of the Prime Minister to improve the corporate governance and management of SOEs. It represents the state's ownership of several types of state-run corporations and equitized firms where the state retains an ownership share and manages state capital. It is also in charge of investing state capital into enterprises to utilize investments in the best way.

Since 2015, the Law on Enterprises of 2014 has been applied. It defined SOEs as enterprises of which the State holds 100%-charter capital while the old Law on Enterprises defined SOEs as enterprises more than 50% owned by the State. It also added Section IV titled SOEs that describes SOE organization structure, a board of members, an appointment of the president, board members, and director, and public information disclosure. The Law on the Management and Use of State Capital Invested in Production and Business 2014 specifies the power and responsibility of state representatives in enterprises with state ownership below 100% and regulates the management and investment of state capital.

In 2018, Decision No 09/NQ-CP on the establishment of the Commission on Management of State Capital in enterprises (CMSC) was signed by the Prime Minister of Vietnam. The Decision identifies the Commission as a representative of the owner of enterprises that the Vietnamese State is holding 100% charter capital. The Minister of Ministry of Planning and Investment and Minister of Ministry of Finance were appointed as two Deputy Commissioners by the Commissioner. The Commission is in charge of commanding the process of transferring state capital and assets in enterprises to the Commission.

1.1.2. Performance Evaluation System

Vietnam has a decentralized ownership model such that line ministries, state-owned corporations, and provincial governments exercise its ownership of SOEs. The Office of the Government and the central government govern the performance evaluation system of SOEs. At the same time, they cannot interfere in management decisions made by ministries, SOEs, or provincial governments.

The Ministry of Finance (MOF), based on its functional responsibilities and authorization, plays an essential role in monitoring and evaluating the performance of SOEs. The MOF issued a Circular No 158/2013/TT-BTC to guide the implementation of Decree No 61/2013/ND-CP, and Decree 71/2013/ND-CP on three types of firms: (i) entire financial monitoring for SOEs owned 100% by the State; (ii) partial financial monitoring for SOEs owned less than 100% and higher than 50% by the State; (iii) partial financial monitoring of firms owned by the State lower than 50%.

The performance evaluation system in Vietnam was comprehensively built from central to local governments. Ministries, SOEs, and provincial governments assign their own departments to monitor and evaluate the performance of SOEs or branches (Figure 4-1). Indeed, these departments or branches on behalf of their line office report the performance of SOEs to the Office of the Government. In other words, there is no independent evaluation team. The Office of the Government that receives the performance reports sends out the final decisions of the Prime Minister and the Deputy Prime Ministers.

Line ministries and government bodies have established the criteria of the system. There is a general framework issued by the central government. Ministries, SOEs, provincial governments based on the framework create their own sub-system to monitor and evaluate the performance of SOEs. Theoretically, the system must operate correctly. However, practically, the system does not meet the expectation of the government.

Moreover, according to Decree 81/2-15/ND-CP, some SOEs are required to not only submit annual and bi-annual audited financial statements to the line ministry and the Ministry of Planning and Investment but also publish them on their websites. However, according to the Ministry of Planning and Investment, at least 380 SOEs out of 620 SOEs (around 61%) that were required to publicize information did not comply fully as of 31 December 2016.

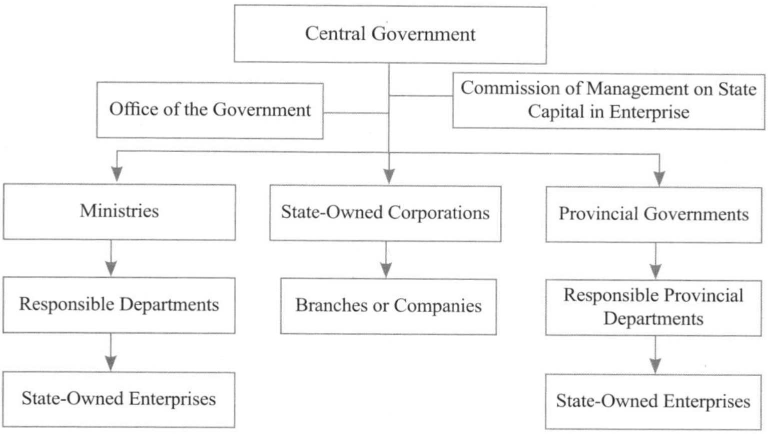

Figure 4-1 Structure of the SOE Performance Evaluation System in Vietnam

Recently, the Vietnam National Assembly has stepped on the monitoring and evaluation system. The supervision delegation of the Vietnam National Assembly has investigated the whole structure of the SOE performance evaluation system and supervised the management, use of state capital and assets, and equitization process of SOEs and implementation of government policies from 2011 to 2016.

1.2. Five Waves of Equitization[62]

In Vietnam, the equitization of SOEs is the diversification of ownership, which does not necessarily mean privatization. SOE equitization aims to reorganize SOEs by diversifying ownership, and hence to improve management, financial capacity, and technological innovation, which leads to the effectiveness and competitiveness of SOEs and ultimately would boost the competitiveness of the private sector and the economy.

<The first wave (06/1992 – 04/1996) of Volunteered Equitization>

In 1991, the Second Plenum of the Seventh Party Congress approved a proposal on "Equitization," that is, the transformation of SOEs into joint-stock companies. A pilot program was approved in the mid-1992, and efforts were made to speed it up a year later. Steps were taken to clarify both the principles and the practical details – for example, principles were laid down on the conditions under which enterprises should remain in state ownership, on how shares are sold, what proportion of shares was to be sold, who was eligible to buy them, and so on. In 1992, the Central Steering Committee for Enterprise Reform was set up. Line ministries and People's Committees at provincial and district levels were instructed to set up committees to develop divestiture plans, which were to be submitted to the Central Steering Committee for approval.

<The second wave (05/1996 – 05/1998) – Expansion of the Equitization Pilot Program>

By the end of 1997, under the "bottom-up process," only fifteen enterprises

62 This subchapter is based on Painter (2013).

had been converted to joint-stock companies. Obstacles included technical difficulties (for example, disagreements over the value of assets) and legal impediments (for example, contradictory statements in different decrees). As many targets for equitization were loss-making, there were no prospective buyers. Potential purchasers – who in most cases included managers and employees – saw the high risk of taking on ownership responsibilities since they would need to sacrifice many advantages that public ownership brought such as more clear title to land, easier access to loans, fringe benefits for employees, and security of employment.

<The third wave (06/1998 – 05/2002) – Acceleration of Equitization>

Various measures were adopted to speed up equitization in the second half of the 1990s. Each new measure attempted to clarify confusions and relax some of the criteria – for example, restrictions favoring employee and manager buy-outs and inhibiting individual share ownership. The issues included the way valuations were conducted to determine the sale price, treatment of redundant labor (compensation and retraining), and the proportion of shares (if any) available to foreign investors. Other forms of ownership and management structures were also devised to facilitate divestiture, such as contracting or leasing out of enterprises and transformation of SOEs into single-owner limited liability companies.

<The fourth wave (06/2002 – 02/2011) – Final call for Equitization>

The Ninth Party Congress in 2001 laid out an ambitious and expansive future role for the SOE sector: "providing necessary public utility goods and services for the demand of national defense and security, being the key force in boosting economic growth, and providing ground for the industrialization and modernization of the country with the socialist orientation." (Painter, 2003). Decision 58/2002/QD-TTg elaborated it and laid out a range of size and profitability criteria for either state retention or equitization. Large, strategic, profitable SOEs in key sectors (particularly those in General Corporations) would largely remain in state hands. The state would hold 100 percent ownership of SOEs in public interest categories, such as state monopolies in explosives, toxic chemicals, radioactive materials, and transmission of electricity; SOEs in businesses that maintain the essential needs for production, development, and enhancement of physical and spiritual living conditions of people in rural mountainous and remote areas"; SOEs in publishing, lottery and other areas decided by the Prime Minister; and lastly, SOEs in a range of specific public utility area.

In 2003, the new Law on SOEs addressed more clearly all the forms of SOEs, not only the wholly state-owned ones but also the multi-owner joint-stock companies or limited liability companies. The relationship between the government and enterprises was regulated and made more transparent. At the end of 2004, the government of Vietnam promulgated Decree No.187/2004/ND-CP on transforming SOEs into joint-stock companies, but with new stipulations. According to the decree, all SOEs, including both subsidiaries of SOCs and the corporation themselves, were subject to equitization so long as they were not required to be kept entirely under state ownership. Then, the Enterprise Law, passed by the National Assembly of Vietnam in November 2005, stipulated that from July 1, 2006, all SOEs would have to be transformed into shareholding or limited liability companies. It also created a common legal framework for all enterprises in Vietnam, regardless of the type of ownership and economic sector.

To further promote equitization, the government promulgated Decree

No.59/2011/ND-CP (July 18, 2011) on transferring SOEs with 100 percent state capital into joint-stock companies. The objective of this decree was to change those SOEs in which the state did not perceive the need to keep 100 percent of the capital into multi-owner businesses. The valuation of SEO equitization is determined by an independent third-party organization and approved by the state audit. The procedure of SOE equitization also became more transparent through the public auction by an independent third-party organization.

<The fifth wave (03/2011 to the present) – Restructuring of SOEs and Deadline of Equitization>

Several policies have been implemented to boost up the process of restructuring of SOEs. On May 25, 2017, the Prime Minister issued Decision 707/QD-TTg approving the master plan on “restructuring state-owned enterprises, focusing on state economic groups and corporations for the period from 2016 to 2020”. It assigns specific tasks to ministries, ministerial-level agencies, state agencies, provincial people's committees, state economic groups, and corporations in implementing the SOEs restructuring and equitization. Based on that, the Government has just issued Decree 126/2017/ND-CP on the equitization of SOEs, which is effective from 1/1/2018. According to Decree 126, many difficulties in the process of equitization of SOEs have been eliminated.

Moreover, the deadlines for equitization were set. According to Decision 991/TTg-DMDN of the Prime Minister, there would be 64 SOEs that have to be equitized in 2018. There are some big state corporations in the list, such as Mobifone Telecom, Electricity Corporation 1, Electricity Corporation 2, and Urban Infrastructure Development and Investment Corporation. There is a high expectation in the government. Additionally, there are 25 SOEs, who moved from the 2017 plan to 2018. In 2018, the government also planned to withdraw capital in 181 other SOEs. The state firms selling capital would have a substantial contribution to the government, such as Vietnam Petroleum with 24.86%, Vietnam Industrial Constructions Corporation with 46.75%, and Machinery Industry Corporation with 63.54%.

The Ministry of Finance has been playing an essential role in the equitization process of SOEs, which are managed by ministries and provinces. The MOF, with the relevant government agencies, participates in the joint appraisal of valuation of equitized SOEs, appraises their equitization plans, and provides feedback on the financial backlog of these enterprises before equitization. Additionally, the circulars related to the appraisal process mentioned above are all regulated by the MOF.

The Ministry of Finance is also drafting a Circular to guide the restructuring process of SOEs transforming to equitized enterprises. In the drafted Circular, the solution for the restructuring of SOEs is based on market principle where the owners of SOEs have active discussions to reach a final agreement with the Vietnam Debt Asset Trading Company (DATC) or Creditors.

1.3. Current Situations and Problems of State-Owned Enterprises

In 2000, Vietnam had 5,759 state-owned enterprises (SOEs-having more than 51% state-owned capital), which contributed 13.62% to the total number of Vietnam enterprises (Table 4-1). The SOEs number decreased to 2,835 and contributed only 6.4% to total in the country in 2015. Collaterally, there were 1,416 firms, in which the state still holds lower than 50% of capital. Meanwhile, the number of non-state and FDI enterprises grew up significantly in the last 15 years.

In general, SOEs focus mainly on some key sectors, which need to be controlled by the government or are not attractive to non-state/FDI enterprises. SOEs hold the core position in most important essential industries, such as oil and gas, electricity, coal and minerals, chemicals and fertilizers, mechanical engineering, and steel and shipbuilding.

Recently, the efficiency and competitiveness of state-owned enterprises raised and met the essential requirements for national defense and security. The effectiveness of some SOEs recently has been improved significantly. For example, Viettel Corporation reported its high rate of profit, 43.5%; Vietnam Rubber Group has a rate of 30.4%. Petrolimex Vietnam has contributed 147,941 billion VND to the State budget. According to the report, many SOEs have a rate of profit over ownership capital about 10% per year. Additionally, the average rate of profitability of SOEs is about 5.6% in the year of 2016, which is close to the average rate of FDI enterprises and much higher than non-SOEs with 1.9%.

However, the performance of SOEs does not meet the expectation given the allocated resources. The technology level of most SOEs is still low. There are some SOEs who have been loose in a long time. There is a significant waste of resources, especially in some sectors such as mining, natural resources, and minerals. Also, some serious violations of law and economic consequences occurred, which affected the reputation of SOEs and the government.

Table 4-1 Number of Enterprises by Type

type \ year	2000	2005	2010	2015	2016	2017
Total	42,288	112,952	279,360	442,485	505,008	561,064
SOEs	5,759	4,086	3,281	2,835	856	782
Non-State Enterprises	35,005	105,169	268,831	427,710	490,782	545,682
FDIs	1,525	3,697	7,248	11,940	13,370	14,600

Source: General Statistics Office =of Vietnam (2005; 2016;2017)

Table 4-2 Summary of Financial Situation and Operation of SOEs in 2016

Indicators \ SOEs	SOEs 100% charter capital (583 enterprises)	SOEs less 100% charter capital (273 enterprises)
Total assets	3,085,547	495,126
State Capital in enterprises	1,398,183	65,673
Revenue	1,515,821	423,250
Profit before tax	139,658	31,723
Total amount payable to the State budget	251,845	62,967

Source: Report of Supervision delegation of Vietnam National Assembly in 2018

According to the report of the National Assembly (2018), the performance of SOEs in the 2011-2016 period was not commensurate with their holding, and it has not promoted the leading role in the economy. Despite SOEs increasing in total assets and capital, the revenue, profit before tax and payment to the state budget saw a slow annual growth rate of 3% on average. The total liabilities in 2016 increased by 26% compared to 2011. In 2015, the profitability of SOEs was 2.1%, much lower than that of FDI enterprises of 5.5%. The investment efficiency of SOEs is also low compared to that of non-state enterprises and FDI enterprises. The velocity of the capital of SOEs in 2016 was only 0.41, which decreased significantly compared to those of the previous years. Besides, the capital velocity in SOEs is lowest among all types of enterprises. Private enterprises and FDI enterprises have a velocity of 0.74 and 1.01, respectively. The Incremental capital output ratio (ICOR) of SOEs in 2011-2016 was much higher than the two remaining ones. In 2016, it was 1.58 times compared to non-state enterprises, 1.86 times higher than FDI enterprises (Table 4-3). In addition, the ROE of the entire SOEs for 2011-2016 went down by 39%, and the ROA decreased by 30% (Table 4-4).

Other inadequacies are the wastefulness, the loss of land and property resources, the non-transparent formal tender status has not been effectively prevented, and the management of public assets is not tight. The inspection and handling of violations of the law on minerals by state management agencies have not been fully and thoroughly implemented to detect and handle in time. in the management and use of land of SOEs, there are still enterprises which do not put land into use, use the land for the wrong purpose, or to land encroachment. The information disclosure of SOEs is limited, not timely, and lacking transparency. The restructuring of losing SOEs and the recovery of the state capital from ineffective investment projects were slow. Generally, the transfer of state ownership of state capital to the State Capital Investment Corporation (SCIC) is slow with limited scope. Over ten years, the state-owned capital managed by SCIC is just about 1% of total state capital in enterprises, while the other 99% still managed by ministries and localities.

The main reason for these shortcomings is the inclined expanding of SOEs in many subsectors without development strategy. While they have poor management quality, they have the monopoly of many state corporations under the lack of government's control. On the other hand, many ministries do not want to leave their state capital at the hands of firms As a result, ministries and agencies do not act objectively in policymaking and reducing management effectiveness. The interference of ministries and agencies makes SOEs dependent on them and aggravating the weakness of SOEs.

Table 4-3 Incremental Capital Output ratio across Types of Enterprises

Type / Year	2011	2012	2013	2014	2015	2016
SOEs	9.03	8.00	10.02	12.12	9.17	9.75
Domestic non-SOEs	3.76	4.85	6.24	5.32	5.12	6.15
FDI	6.82	6.33	6.02	5.67	4.64	5.22

Source: Report of Supervision Delegation of the Vietnam National Assembly (2018)

Table 4-4 Summary of the Rate of Profit of SOE in 2012-2016 (Unit: %)

Year	2012	2013	2014	2015	2016
ROE	16.4	15.8	15.2	11.7	10.0
ROA	6.5	6.3	6.0	5.3	4.6

Source: Report of Supervision Delegation of the Vietnam National Assembly (2018)

2. Korea's Experience

2.1. Reform of the State-Owned Enterprises

2.1.1. Related Laws and Governance

In the 1960s and 1970s, SOEs played a critical role, especially in the financial, telecommunication, and electricity industries as a means of economic development strategy. Regarding the management of SOEs, the Government Invested Institutions Management Act introduced in 1973 prescribed a governance structure and procedures for budgeting and accounting of all the Government Invested Institutions (GIIs). The Economic Planning Board participated actively in the GII budgeting, and the line ministry had the authority of all the decisions regarding the operation of a GII.

In the 1980s, the inefficiency of SOEs was brought into the open along with the movement toward the privatization of SOEs. The Framework Act on the management of GIIs was enacted in 1983. It provided more flexible management of SOEs by separating the board of directors from the management and by allowing SOEs to compile and adjust its own budget. On the other hand, to resolve the principal-agent problem, the performance evaluation of SOEs was carried out for the first time in 1984. However, under the Act, SOEs were not able to be entirely free from the government's or the line ministry's tight control since the board of directors consist of the CEO, two government officials, one from the line ministry, the other from the Economic Planning Board, and outside experts.

In the 1990s, more changes were made to provide SOEs sufficient profit incentives and more autonomy. The Law on Management Structural Adjustment and Privatization of Public Enterprise in 1997 under the Kim Young Sam administration prescribed an Anglo-American style governance structure. It aimed to prevent the intervention of the government and to improve efficiency for four large commercial SOEs (KT&G, KGC, KT, and KHIC) before full privatization. The board of directors consisted of specialists and outside directors, excluding a director from the government. The CEO of an SOE was selected by the President's Recommendation Commission and was granted the autonomy of personnel, budget, and projects.

The Framework Act on the management of GIIs was also amended in 1997 under the Kim Dae Jung administration to further build up a responsible management system by introducing the CEO management contract system. Based on the performance of a CEO, incentives, and a dismissal of a CEO are determined. The management publication system and the minority shareholder protection system were also introduced to enhance the transparency of SOEs and public participation.

The Act on the Management of Public Institutions (AMPI) introduced in 2007 under the Roh Moo Hyun Administration formed a new legal basis by consolidating various legal systems and reformed the classification system of all public institutions. As of 2017, public institutions are classified into three groups: SOEs that have self- generating income more than 50% of gross income and the number of employees more than 50, quasi-government institutions with the number of employees more than 50, but other than SOEs, and other public institutions (Table 4-6).

Under Korea's current governance system of SOEs, the exercise of the state ownership function is carried out by the Ministry of Strategy and Finance (MOSF): from setting policy for ownership, approving strategy and/or coordinating policy with the line ministry of the corresponding SOE, appointing board members, overseeing SOEs' information disclosure practices to carrying out performance evaluation. The major strategies and targets are set up by the Office for Government Policy Coordination, Prime Minister's Secretariat. On the other hand, throughout a couple of revisions of the Management of Public Institution Act, the autonomy of the CEO of an SOE was strengthened with the transparent and expanded appointments of standing/non-standing directors and steering committee members.

Table 4-5 Changes in Korea's SOE related Laws and Systems

	Major Laws	System
1960s - 1970s	GII Management Act (1973)	- Authority of the line ministries & EPB's involvement of GII budgets - SOEs as a means of economic development
1980s	The Framework Act on the Management of GIIs (1983)	- Under the tight control of the line ministry - More flexible management than before - Privatization - Introduction of performance evaluation (1984)
1990s	The Law on Management Structural Adjustment & Privatization of Public Enterprise Amendment of The Framework Act on the Management of GIIs (1997)	- Introduction of the Anglo-American style governance for more flexible management - Introduction of the CEO management contract system
2000s	The Act on the Management of Public Institutions (2007)	- Ownership by the Ministry of Strategy and Finance & Major strategies & targets by the Office for Government Policy Coordination - Alio (All Public Information In-One) (2006) - The Public Institutions Management Committee (2007) - The Electronic-Integrated Public Service Evaluation System (2007)

Table 4-6 Classification of Public Institutions (as of 2017)

Category	Criteria	Number
SOEs	Self-generating income >50% of gross income & more than 50 employees & designated by the MOSF	35
Market-based	Self-generating income >85% of gross income & more than 50 employees	14
Quasi-market based	The rest	21
Quasi-Government Institutions	more than 50 employees & designated by the minister of MOSF	88
Fund-management Based	Institutions that manage funds or are entrusted with the management of funds	16
Commissioned-service based	The rest	72
Non-classified	Other public institutions	207
Total		330

Source: All Public Information In-One (www.alio.go.kr)

2.1.2. Performance Evaluation System

The performance evaluation of SOEs has been carried out since 1984. The current evaluation system is based on the Act of the Management of Public Institutions in 2007. Following the recommendation of OECD, the Public Institution Management Committee under the Ministry of Strategy and Finance (MOSF) has been established to unify the management of all the public institutions. The Committee consists of government officials and outside experts recommended by the minister of MOSF. It is responsible for personnel matters and performance evaluation as well as the establishment of public institutions. However, in the case of quasi-government institutions, both the committee and the line ministry maintain the supervisory authority together. Based on the performance evaluation conducted by the committee, MOSF decides the remuneration and bonus of CEOs as well as the appointment decision of CEOs.

Every year, SOEs are required to submit the report of the previous fiscal year to the minister of MOSF and the minister of the line ministry by March 20th, and the performance evaluation team carries out the evaluation by June 20th. The Public Institutions Policy Bureau, under MOSF that is in charge of the overall management of the evaluation system, organizes the performance evaluation team every year. The performance evaluation team consists of external civil experts such as professors, accountants, lawyers, and retired government officials. With some training courses, workshops, and on-site interviews with the staff at SOEs, it conducts evaluations annually on three levels: SOEs, CEOs, and auditors (OECD, 2016).

At the SOE level, internal management and core business are evaluated. At the auditor level, the evaluation is conducted in 3 areas: adequacy of audit activities and job performance, the results from the external evaluation, and the results of the evaluation on SOEs. At the CEO level, the performance of CEOs is evaluated in 2 areas: common tasks and performance tasks. The evaluation of performance tasks includes financial budget management, management of employee remuneration and employee benefits, medium-term, and long-term strategic tasks. There are two kinds of performance evaluation indicators used for financial performance and non-financial performance: qualitative indicators and quantitative indicators, as in Table 4-7. Based on the combined evaluation points, the grade is determined, ranging from excellent to very poor in 6 grades. For the efficiency improvement of the management, the evaluation results are used in four areas: personnel measures such as a dismissal of the CEO or standing directors, incentives for CEOs and employees, budget feedbacks, and management improvement such as consultation supports. For those institutions that report untruthfully, violate the guidelines, or do not provide the annual report, the law can take severe measures on personnel and budget matters.

Moreover, in 2012, to monitor and evaluate the financial soundness and performance of the public institutions, the government required the public institutions with assets of more than 2 trillion Korean won to report medium-term and long-term financial plans to the National Assembly.

Table 4-7 Performance Evaluation Indicators in Korea

	Quantitative indicators	Non-Quantitative indicators
Financial performance	Debt ratio, interest coverage rate, labor productivity, equity productivity, rate of value-added, return on assets	Risk management, budget transparency practices
Non-financial performance	Customer satisfaction survey result, degree of government policy achievement, degree of core business target achievement	Corporate social responsibility practices, gender equality policy, improvements in labor conditions, public disclosure of business information, management policy on contract workers

Source: OECD (2016). State-owned Enterprise in Asia: National Practices for Performance Evaluation and Management

2.1.3. Success and Failure Factors of Korea's SOE Reform

The most key success factors in improving SOE's efficiency and transparency are the effectiveness of the performance evaluation and public information disclosure. Its effectiveness resulted from the well-designed incentives: linkage between performance evaluation results and incentives, and linkage between a violation of public disclosure and penalties.

However, to enhance the SOE reform further, the independence and autonomy of the Public Institution Management Committee should be ensured. The Committee is under the significant influence of the Ministry of Strategy and Finance (MOSF). The government officials from MOSF and the relevant ministries of SOEs tend to be employed by SOEs. The connection between SOEs, government, and the Committee by ex-government officials would likely influence the decisions of the Committee. The continuous intervention of the government in the appointment of CEOs and management of SOEs is the key failure factors of Korea's SOE reform that hinders the improvement of SOEs.

Therefore, Korea needs to improve the governance of SOEs by reducing the influence of the government. The autonomous management should be guaranteed to accelerate the efficiency and accountability of SOEs. The details of success and failure factors are discussed below.

(1) Effective Linkage between Performance Evaluation and Incentives

The effectiveness of the performance evaluation system in improving SOEs' efficiency and accountability depends on how its results can be used as incentives for related SOEs and employees.

The Minister of Strategy and Finance can recommend the dismissal of CEO or standing directors of institutions if they receive the lowest grade in the performance evaluation over two years. Regarding the remunerations, CEOs of SOEs can receive bonuses between 0 and 120% of their annual salary, and employees can receive bonuses between 0 and 250% of their monthly salary. Moreover, SOEs that receive the highest grade may increase their budget by 1 percent, while those that receive the lowest grade are required to decrease their budget by 1 percent.

(2) Adoption of Information Technology for Public Information Disclosure and Performance Evaluation

Public information disclosure and performance evaluation improve the efficiency and transparency of SOEs, which has been more emphasized after the financial crisis in 1997. The 'Alio' System (All Public Information In-One, www. alio.go.kr) is the consolidated publication system that includes all the information regarding SOEs, such as SOE's overall status, operation, management performance, internal and external evaluation, and announcement. The AMPI in 2007 further required corresponding SOEs to publish their information such as annual reports, financial reports, sustainability report, and performance evaluation results on their websites.

Moreover, the government launched the electronic-Integrated Public Service Evaluation System (e-IPSES) in 2007 so that each agency can integrate performance evaluation information in real-time. This system greatly benefited both evaluators and SEOs by improving efficiency and accuracy.

(3) Government Intervention in the Governance and Management of SOEs

Korea has a centralized ownership of SOEs. The Ministry of Strategy and Finance (MOSF) exercises ownership function. It reviews financial statements of SOEs, approves strategies, appoints board members, and evaluates performance, and decides dividend policy. Meanwhile, each line ministry makes industrial policy for the corresponding SOE and regulates them.

Under the MOSF, the Public Institutions Management Committee (PIMC) established in 2007 deliberates and resolves the matters regarding the designation of public institutions, management, CEO appointment, evaluation and monitoring of SOEs.

Therefore, the independence and autonomy of the PIMC should be ensured for the independent and autonomous management of SOEs. However, despite some changes toward more autonomous and flexible management, the influence and intervention of the line ministry and the MOSF on SOEs have continued through the PIMC.

Since the PIMC is composed of government members and private sector members and chaired by the minister of MOSF, it has a structural limitation that is not free from the influence of the government. Most official decisions of the Committee including the COE appointment and large size investments are highly likely to be made or influenced by the MOSF bureaucrats who prepared them (Nam, 2013).

In addition, the Act on the Management of Public Institutions in 2007 prescribes that the board of directors of SOEs is composed of a majority of non-standing (outside) directors and a minority of standing directors from line ministries and MOSF. Having most directors being outside directors and the chairperson of the board being a non-standing director helps the enhancement for the independence and the autonomy of the board. However, half of the executive recommendation committee that recommends non-standing directors are the board members appointed by MOSF. Again, SOEs are not free from the influence of the government.

2.2. Privatization of the State-Owned Enterprises

2.2.1. Five Waves of Privatization

Korea had only 36 enterprises owned by the government in the late 1950s since the government sold many confiscated properties from the Japanese occupation to private firms and individuals (KSP, 2013).

In the first phase (1963-1978), the Park Chung Hee government privatized 12 SOEs, including a few large-scale SOEs such as the Korean Machinery Industries Corporation, Korea Express Corporation, Korean Airline Corporation, and Korea Shipbuilding Corporation, which were considered as successful privatization.

In the second phase (1979-1986), the Chun Doo Hwan government privatized four nationwide commercial banks through competitive open bids to increase the banking sector's autonomy and improve transparency and efficiency in addition to many other SOEs. However, the shareholding limits were set at 5% for corporations and 5,000 shares for individuals. Besides, a single shareholder whose limit was set at 8% after the listing could not participate in management while the government had its continuous involvement and de facto control. So, the privatization of four commercial banks has been evaluated as unsuccessful privatization.

In the third phase (1987-1992), the Ro Tae Woo government launched systematic and full-fledged privatization by forming the SOE privatization promotion committee but ended in the partial privatization of only 3 SOEs, far fewer than planned. Blue-chip SOEs such as Pohang Iron and Steel (POSCO), Korea Electric Power Corporation (KEPCO), and Kookmin Bank (KEB) were partially privatized through either public tender offerings or People's Share Program. However, by placing a priority on the government revenue, and the formation of the middle class, the efficiency improvement of SOEs was neglected. The Committee the large supply of stocks under the prohibition of foreign equity participation caused a downturn in the Korean stock market.

In the fourth phase (1993-1996), the Kim Young Sam government pursued neoliberal economic policy and claiming a small-government scheme. A project of privatizing 58 SOEs and restructuring 11 SOEs accomplished the privatization of only 22 SOEs.

In the fifth phase (1997-2002), the Kim Dae Jung administration had more SOEs privatized than planned under the Implementation Committee for the Privatization of SOEs. The Committee took charge of all the matters from the formulating the action plan, monitoring to implementing the privatization. The government's financial needs to recover financial institutions after the financial crisis in 1997 propelled the privatization. That is, to some degree, the external shock of the IMF crisis was a drive for privatization. However, the momentum was lost in the later period of the Kim Dae Jung administration along with the strikes of the labor unions.

Since then, the government has not been able to pursue privatization. The Roh Moo Hyun administration had either postponed or stopped the privatization, which is considered as one of the Ro Moo Hyun administration's policy failures. Instead, the reform of the governance structure has started to be recognized as a tool for achieving the efficiency of public institutions. The Lee Myung Bak administration (2008-2012) planned to revive privatization under his policy of the Advancement of Public Enterprises but failed without obtaining ideological supports after the financial crisis in 2008. It ended up selling only seven subsidiaries of SOEs.

2.2.2. Success and Failure Factor of Korea's Privatization

The privatization of SOEs has always been considered as one of the important economic policies in every administration in Korea. Its purpose has changed over stages of economic development, political ideology, and inside and outside socioeconomic environment. In the 1980s, the Korean government promoted the privatization to supplement its financial resources. In the 1990s, the improvement of efficiency and competitiveness of SOEs were pursued through privatization. In the late 1990s, the government needed the privatization to raise capital for corporate and financial restructuring. On the other hand, in recent days, the focus has been more on the improvement of corporate governance.

The SOE privatization during the Kim Dae Jung administration (1997-2002) can be considered quite successful relative to that of other administrations. The independent committee backed by the government's strong drive carried out the successful privatization of SOEs. Eight out of eleven SOEs in the privatization plan were privatized, which helped the Korean government to secure financial revenues and overcome the Asian financial crisis. Moreover, most privatized public firms improved their management, efficiency, and profitability, which led to the improvement of firm value.

Another success factor was to create a competitive environment for SOEs before and after its privatization so that privatized SOEs can have the capability to compete in the market, and neither privatized SOEs nor private firms are subject to unfair competition and abuse of monopoly power.

However, there have been many failed privatization attempts. Resistance from stakeholders and labor unions in SOEs, opposition from the public, and privatization policy with lack of consistency have brought almost fifteen years of privatization vacancy. Another failure factor is the continuous government intervention in SOEs that decreases the capability of SOEs and hence lowers the interests of investors. For instance, the failure of the privatization of four banks in the 1980s was due to government intervention in the appointments of CEOs and management and made the financial sectors weak.

In the following, we discuss what the major factors were behind the success and failure of the privatization in Korea, taking examples mostly from the Kim Dae Jung administration.

(1) Government's Strong Drive with an Independent and Competent Committee

The OECD guidelines suggested that the firm will of the leader and the government is necessary for successful privatization. An independent, competent, and well-resourced committee that can support and carry out privatization is essential as well. The independence of the committee free from the relevant ministry of SOEs is critical because if the privatization conflicts with their interests, related public officials may try to avoid or delay privatization.

Under the Kim Dae Jung administration, the Implementation Committee for the Privatization of SOEs was launched pursuant to Presidential Directive No 71. The committee developed a privatization program for each SOE in the consultation with the Ministry of Finance and Economics.

It also monitored and supervised the privatization process, dealt with matters related to all relevant laws, decrees and regulations, and took charge of all other issues relating to the implementation of privatization (Kim and Kim, 2001). The implementation task force team for the privatization of each SOE was also established under the line ministry and required to submit a monthly progress report to the committee. Organizing the independent committee under the Ministry of Planning and Budget increased the chance of successful privatization and the inclusion of civilian experts strengthened the expertise of the committee.

Advance announcement of the privatization plan and systematic preparation showed a strong will of continuation of the privatization in the long term, not only mitigates political influences.

The Ministry of Planning and Budget under the Kim Dae Jung administration announced the privatization and restructuring plan of SOEs in 1998 and classified public enterprises into three groups. The first group included SOEs which are the privatization target. The second group was planned for sequential privatization. Detailed and thorough privatization process and method were prepared, and necessary legal arrangements were taken in advance. Large SOEs in the network industry, which were considered as impossible to privatize, were included for privatization. The last group was prescribed internal restructuring or liquidation.

Moreover, precise information on privatization was offered by the country leader, and the government institutions, opinions from stakeholders were actively collected, and incentives or countermeasures were continuously provided for persuasions. Those multi-directional efforts helped stakeholders and people understanding the benefits of privatization and reduced the opposition and political influences from stakeholders.

(2) The Establishment of Institutions and Improvement of SOEs to Foster a Competitive Environment and Competition

The competition of privatized public institutions and private firms on a level playing field makes privatized public institutions more efficient and competitive, which is one of the primary purposes of the privatization of SOEs. To achieve this, the Kim Dae Jung administration took a couple of measures prior to the privatization.

First, related laws and regulations were modified or established to create a competitive environment.

In the case of the privatization of Korea Telecom (KT), the related laws were amended so that other operators could use KT's monopolized network, and a private firm could enter all the telecom markets. The government attempted to foster a competitive environment in the telecommunication industry by introducing competitors. Indeed, prior to the privatization of KT, two private companies, LG Dacom and SK Telecom, were competing with

KT in terms of product and/or service while they shared the network. It took about eight years to have competitors in all the telecommunication markets: LG Dacom in the international phone service in 1991, LG Dacom in the local distance phone service in 1996, and SK Telecom in the local phone service in 1999. The privatization of KT was completed in 2002.

In the case of the privatization of Korea Electric Power Corporation (KEPCO), the laws and the regulations related to the electric power industry were introduced and/or amended to prepare its split-off. Following the establishment of laws, the government divided the power generation sector into six subsidiaries so that they compete internally. The Korea Power Exchange (KPX) was established as a separate corporation to take charge of the operation of Korea's electricity market and the power system. The Electricity Commission was also established as a regulatory authority within the Ministry of Commerce, Industry, and Energy (MCIE) to implement the restructuring of KEPCO and supervise the competition system.

Second, the restructuring of SOEs was carried out. Many subsidiaries of SOEs were either privatized with the mother company, independently privatized, consolidated with the other company, or liquidated. By the end of the Kim Dae Jung administration, 8 of 11 targeted SOEs were privatized, and more than 85% of targeted subsidiaries of SOEs were reformed (Park and Park, 2011). Restructuring improved efficiency and competitively of SOEs, which led to an increase in the market value of SOEs and hence the government's revenue from the privatization.

(3) Appropriate Method and Timing of Privatization

The appropriate process and timing of privatization should be chosen by considering domestic and foreign market conditions to maximize the outcomes of the privatization, i.e., fostering a competitive environment, improving the efficiency of SOEs, increasing the government's financial resources. Various methods and strategies such as the issuance of convertible bonds or depositary receipts, divestiture of a division or a subsidiary, and block deal should be utilized as well.

Many countries have employed a partial or tranche-wise sell-off approach, especially for large SOEs in the network and utility industries, as they could not have been sold in one transaction without triggering a hefty price discount (OECD, 2009). So, the privatization of large SOEs tends to take many years.

For instance, the oversupply of POSCO stocks in 1988 and of KEPCO stocks in 1989 in Korea caused the deterioration of the Korean stock market when the government share of POSCO decreased from 71.4% to 35% and that of KEPCO decreased by 21% (Table 4-8). In 1990 and 1991, Korea Telecom (KT) that was the second-largest SOEs in terms of assets with high profitability attempted to privatize by offering the People's share program. However, due to the bad stock market, it failed. After that, KT had been sequentially privatized considering the relatively small size of the stock market in Korea at that time. Its full privatization was completed in 2002 (Table 4-9).

(4) Abolishment of Eligibility Restriction or Equity Restriction

The Foreign Investment Promotion Act (FIPA) is the law on foreign investment in Korea regarding FDI registration procedure, tax incentives and government supports, etc. More liberalization has attracted more FDI. Restrictions on foreign ownership of equity were abolished so that foreign investors could acquire as much as 100% of a company except 30 industrial sectors.

Simplified procedures for mergers and acquisitions and allow foreign investment companies to acquire land without limitations on its size and use of land freely.

(5) Creation of Public Consensus

One of the severe obstacles to privatization is the opposition from the stakeholders that include public employees in the line ministry, politicians, unions, consumers, etc. Labor unions and workers oppose privatization in case they think it threatens job security and payment. Consumers oppose privatization if they believe it would increase prices or costs that they need to pay for privatized firms that operate for profits. Some oppose privatization for the dilution of national assets. Others worry about the dominance of Chaebols and criticize Chaebols' acquisitions of privatized firms. All those oppositions set back the privatization plans of the government, and Korea has had more than fifteen years of privatization vacancy.

There are two ways to overcome this. First, more precise information on privatization offered by the country leader or related field experts would make people understood the benefits of privatization to society, which makes the opposition from specific shareholders undermined. The transparent process of privatization, as well as its purpose and possible outcomes, would bring trust in the government's determination toward privatization. Second, incentives or countermeasures can be provided to stakeholders. An independent regulatory body to monitor the price of privatized firms would be established, such as the Office of Telecommunication in the privatization of the telecommunication industry of the United Kingdom.

Table 4-8 Privatization of Pohang Iron and Steel Company (POSCO)

Year	Government		Foreign	The rest	Methods of privatization
	MOF	KDB			
1987	33.4	38.0	0.0	28.6	
1988	20.0	15.0	0.0	65.0	- Listed in the stock market in 1988 - Employees' buy-out 10% - The People's share program 27.3% - Commercial banks
1996	19.6	14.1	15.3	51.1	- Foreign share allowed from 1992 - Listed in the NYSE in 1994
1997	19.6	14.1	25.1	41.3	
1998	0.0	21.1	38.1	40.8	- Government Announcement of Privatization - Sales of public share to domestic and foreign investors (maximum of 3% per each investor) - Issue of the 1st global depositary receipts on the NYSE and the LSE ('98.12)
1999	0.0	10.0	43.0	47.1	- Issue of the 2nd global depositary receipts
2000	0.0	0.0	48.9	51.1	- abolishment of the ownership limitation on foreign investors and each individual investor at the end of 2001 - introduction of the professional management system
2001	0.0	0.0	62.0	38.0	
2018	0.0	0.0	54.8	45.2	Worlds' most competitive steel maker by World Steel Dynamics for 9 years since 2010 (as of August 2018)

Source: Nice Information Service Database (KISLINE)

Table 4-9 Privatization and Shares of Korea Telecom (KT)

Share / Year	Government	Foreign	The rest	Methods of privatization
1990	100.0	0.0	0.0	- the 1st People's share program failed
1991	100.0	0.0	0.0	- the 2nd People's share program failed
1993	71.2	0.0	28.8	- aimed to sell 49%, but end up selling 28.8%
1998	71.2	0.03	28.8	Full, but gradual Privatization determined
1999	59.0	18.7	22.3	Issue of the global depositary receipts (14.5%)
2000	59.0	19.4	21.6	Amendment of the Telecommunication Business Act & Abolishment of the Korea Telecommunications Corporation Act
2001	40.2	37.2	22.6	-Third-party sale by auction (1.1%) - Increase the limit of foreign ownership from 33% to 49% by the amended Telecommunication Business Act - Issue of the global depositary receipts (17.8%) - Issue of global EB·BW (11.8%)
2002	0.0	41.7	58.3	- Public offerings (28.4%) and completion of privatization - Strengthening the authority of the board by the amendment of the articles of incorporation
2018	0.0	49.0	51.0	- Foreign ownership limited to 49 percent

Source: Nice Information Service database (KISLINE)

3. Policy Suggestions for Vietnam

The influence of SOEs on the economy is strong, and hence the reform of SOEs, if it is successful, would have far-reaching consequences. Depending on the development stage as well as industry characteristics, each country may choose a different strategy for an SOE to improve the competitiveness and efficiency of SOEs. One is the privatization of SOEs, and the other is the internal reform of SOEs while keeping them as SOEs. Therefore, in the following, we suggest how to bring the success of the privatization of SOEs and the improvement of SOEs' efficiency.

(1) Creation of a Level Playing Field and Fair Competition

Pressure from competition improves the efficiency of both SOEs and privatized enterprises. Therefore, fostering competition and ensuring a level playing field is necessary to achieve even before discussing whether to equitize an SOE or not. Regardless of their legal status, SOEs, privatized enterprises, or private enterprises, the creation of a level playing field improves firm efficiency and market efficiency.

First, an appropriate supervisory and regulatory framework for SOEs and equitized enterprises should be established in place so that they cannot abuse a position of monopoly and hurt other competitors, i.e., private enterprises and potential entrants.

Like SOEs in other countries, SOEs in Vietnam have received substantial benefits such as easier access to land and capital and preferential regulatory treatment and enjoyed a monopoly position in many sectors. So even after equitization, they would be likely to maintain a monopoly position where other domestic firms are still small and medium-sized. Therefore, regulation should be in place before equitization to ensure competitive neutrality in the market. SOEs and equitized SOEs should be subject to the same rule and tax policies as domestic private enterprises. They also should not have preferential access to government contracts, resources, and financing any longer.

Those arrangements should not be affected by the political influence and corruption between stakeholders and SOEs.

Second, introducing competition into the market is an alternative way to foster competition, so that SOEs or an equitized enterprise can compete with other private enterprises like in the case that the entries of other operators were allowed before the privatization of KT in the telecommunication market. For this, the regulation or institution should be established to make the primary resource of the business be shared by private enterprises, either potential entrant or incumbent.

(2) Government's Strong Drive with an Independent Committee for Privatization

The independent committee free from related ministries and SOEs should lead the equitization from the planning stage because it can accelerate the privatization and the reform of SOEs by reducing complications and delays that arise from the conflicting interests of related ministries and SOEs that fear of losing power.

The Vietnam government and the Prime Minister have shown a firm resolve for the equitization. In Feb 2018, the Vietnam government set up the Committee for State Capital Management at a ministerial level to oversee the government assets of 21 large state-owned groups and corporations, which was the right direction. The Committee will also govern the State Capital Investment Corporation (SCIC) that has been managed by the Ministry of Finance. According to the Ministry of Planning and Investment, the combined state capital at the 21 corporations is around US$ 220 billion worth, equivalent to 50 percent of total capital owned by the State at State-owned enterprise.

The Vietnam government expects the Committee to control the state capital effectively and transparently and boost the equitization. The Committee will be responsible for reviewing corporations' business activities and investments following the plan and implementation of the tasks and continuing to direct and promote the arrangement, equitization and divestment of state capital in enterprises. More importantly, it will chair and coordinate with relevant ministries and agencies to review and amend the legal documents related to corporate governance to focus on the process of reform and restructuring SOEs. These solutions are highly innovative to bring SOEs to become one of the spearheads of the economy.

To achieve the success of privatization and the reform of SOEs, the Committee plays a paramount role in preparing step-by-step goals and selecting specific action plans in the long term.

In the first place, those specific action plans backed up by human resources and financial resource, should be established in detail. The plan on the methods of privatization should be prepared, and necessary legal arrangements should be taken in advance. Therefore, organizing task forces for each SOE and making them work effectively would be critical.

Secondly, all the process should be carried out transparently and effectively while continuous coordination and persuasion would be needed between the Committee, related ministries, and other stakeholders. This will bring trust as well as political support from the public for the Committee and the country leader.

Last but not least, to have successful implementations, the firm determination of the country leader and the Committee with full authority are necessary conditions.

(3) Selection of the Right Method, Mechanism, and Timing for Privatization

Systematic and detailed preparations for privatization is essential. It promotes the efficiency of SOEs and the economic growth of the nation. It also helps to attract more investors and obtain more substantial revenues for the government.

First, since each method has some advantages and disadvantages, the right one should be selected at the right timing after considering the characteristics of an SOE and industry, the primal purpose of privatization and the economic conditions of a nation.

Second, privatization timing is crucial since it has enormous impacts on the economy and the outcomes of the following privatization. It should not be hastened just for the sake of completing the deal. It should be privatized considering the interests of investors.

Third, once the method of privatization is selected, the right mechanism should be designed to attract more buyers or bidders. For instance, in the case of Sabeco auction, while the privatization was expected, the window of time for investors to prepare for bidding was too short, and there was only one round in the auction with only one bidder. Auctions should allow enough window of time to make it more competitive by attracting more bidders and hence maximize government revenue. Cumbersome requirements such as bidder prequalification and restrictions on the form of payment should be reduced not to prevent bidders' participation. Other conditions, such as restrictions on foreign direct investment, should also be reduced. Instead of having restrictions on FDI, mechanisms to maintain a right of veto in strategic decisions, i.e., golden shares, can be utilized.

Forth, the announcement of the schedule of equitization should be made, which provides predictability to both relevant enterprises and investors preparing for privatization. Moreover, Transparent procedure and correct information disclosure should be arranged. Full preparatory work in depth should be carried out to maximize the benefits of privatization.

(4) Improvement of the Performance Evaluation System of SOEs

The performance evaluation of SOEs improves transparency and efficiency. While providing more autonomy to SOEs, the government should improve the current performance evaluation system of SOEs and provide performance-based incentives to reduce the principal-agent problem.

First, there should be a coherent governing structure of the performance evaluation system. Currently, too many line ministries monitor and evaluate SOEs separately in Vietnam. The evaluation of SOEs is mostly based on a self-evaluation of SOEs. While line ministries may do monitor and regulate SOEs, it would be more coherent and effective for one organization to evaluate all the SOEs. In addition, the responsibility and rights of the organization that assesses SOEs should be precisely defined. For instance, in Korea, the Committee for Management of Public Institutions under the MOSF governs the performance evaluation of SOEs.

Second, incentives for SOEs should be linked with evaluation results. Performance-based incentives may include from the bonuses on the top of their annual salary to the consecutive appointments or dismissal of a CEO. Without incentives or penalties, the system stays only in paper.

Third, SOEs should be required to provide accurate and sufficient information for performance evaluation. For insufficient or distorted information and/or violation of the guidelines, penalty should be imposed. This kind of feedback mechanism helps SOEs improve responsibility and efficiency.

Forth, another way of monitoring and evaluating the performance of SOEs would be the one that brings the close attention of the public, the media, and the government by making SOEs present a report of its plan and performance in the open space, like the way that big SOEs in Korea submit a report to the

National Assembly.

Fifth, for the effectiveness of the performance evaluation and incentive system, SOEs should take it seriously. Therefore, it should be based on transparent and rigorous performance evaluation and firm implementation.

Outside experts that can provide precise evaluation objectively should be involved in the performance evaluation process. Further, the independence of the performance evaluation from SOEs and interest groups should be protected. These will improve the quality of performance evaluation. In addition, the government's strong will and firm implementation should be accompanied.

(5) Enforcement of the Public Information Disclosure System

The scrutiny of the public and potential investors through a public information disclosure system helps SOEs improve the efficiency of resource allocation and precipitate innovation. The essential items to disclose should include information on the operation, management, evaluation, and financial information of a SOEs. Many of items should be regularly published with some occasional disclosure items for persistent checkups. The number of the disclosed items and the number of SOEs required to disclose information would likely increase as the system becomes mature. Nevertheless, since the initial success is critical for the public and potential investors, it should include the major SOEs and the key items, even in the early stage of the system.

The participation of SOEs should be mandatory for the system to be effective. SOEs in Vietnam have the disclosure responsibility in accordance with Degree 81. However, around one-third of SOEs disclose information according to the survey of CIEM. Without penalty on non-compliance, it would not work. Therefore, the penalty such as warning or public announcement should be established.

Furthermore, the convenience of having the information of all the SOEs in one system would bring more interests and attention of potential investors by reducing uncertainty over performance and fair value of SOEs, which may increase the revenue in case of privatization. Having all the information in one system also makes it easier to compare and analyze SOEs, which would help the reform or restructuring of SOEs.

(6) Improvement of the Corporate Governance of SOEs

The separation of ownership and management should be enforced. In Korea, especially for the market-based SOEs, the autonomy of management is given at the level of large private corporations. The management autonomy reduces potential investors' fear of government intervention and helps to attract investors in case of privatization.

The changes in corporate governance are not easy to achieve in the short term. Since the late 1990s, Korea had made many efforts and introduced systems from developed countries for the separation of ownership and management. However, the changes and outcomes have not met the expectation of the public due to the different cultures and different histories and stages of economic development. Therefore, the followings are the suggestions that Vietnam may take to make a gradual change in the long-term, not at this moment. Moreover, the corporate governance changes for autonomous management should be accompanied by the monitoring and evaluation system, such as the performance evaluation system that reduces the principal-agent problem.

First, the separation of management from ownership can be made in two ways: the appointment system of board members and the involvement of outside experts. Under the current situation of Vietnam, the establishing authority appoints CEOs of SOEs and board of management, and hence the autonomy of SOEs free from the political influence and the line ministry is difficult to achieve. So, the appointment system of the board members should be revised so that the authority or line ministry may recommend candidates for board members, but the CEOs of SOEs have the power to appoint its board members.

Second, Vietnam should increase the proportion of outside experts free from the authority or line ministries to enhance the autonomy of SOEs. In addition, it is necessary that the board members should be recommended and selected based on their capability, not on their connection with the authority/line ministries or other interest groups.

Third, the appointment of the CEOs by the establishing authority should be objective and transparent. It also should be based on the management experiences and capability of a CEO candidate, not on the political relationship. The active involvement of outside experts in the CEO appointment committee would make the appointment system transparent and credible.

III. Enhancing the Industrial Competitiveness

1. Vietnam's Industrial Competitiveness

1.1. Vietnam's Industrial Policy

Vietnam has undertaken industrialization and modernization with various economic development policies since Doi Moi in 1986. In the 1990s, sectors such as heavy industry, natural resource-based industries, manufacturing industries, and export-oriented industries were prioritized under the protection of the government through tariff and non-tariff instruments.

In the early 2000s, the government continued sector-specific policies such as incentives and supports for garment and textile industries to accelerate the development of these industries and to lay out the foundation of the national industry, which was quite successful. Trade liberalization and trade agreements with key trading partners have opened vast market opportunities for Vietnam's export products. The environment for investment has been improved favorably for both FDI and the private sector. According to MOIT, Vietnam's export growth developed faster than GDP growth and global export growth. Besides, the state-owned enterprises were equitized on a large scale. It led to the emergence of a series of independent companies that operate more efficiently than before.

In 2007, the Government issued Decision 55/2007/ QD-TTg approving the list of priority and key industries until 2010, vision to 2020, and incentive policies for development. Three key industries were identified: (1) mechanical manufacturing, including automobiles, shipbuilding, agricultural machines, and mechatronics, (2) electronics, telecommunications and information technology, and (3) products from new technologies, including new energy, renewable energy, software industry, and digital industries. In addition, seven priority industries were indicated: textiles and garment, leather and footwear, plastic, agro-forestry and fishery processing, aluminum bauxite processing, steel, and chemicals. However, the policy for these priority and key sectors was as general as adequate allocation of land for investment, and support for trade promotion. In addition, the difference between priority and key industries is still a controversial issue.

In 2011, the government also issued the Decision 12/2011/QD-TTg to encourage the development of the supporting industries for six sectors, including mechanical manufacturing, electronics and informatics, automobile assembly, textiles, footwear, and hi-tech industries. However, the incentives for above supporting industries, such as import tax exemption, and corporate income tax, were as general as for SMEs. In addition, article 4 in Decision 12 indicated that a specific incentive for investment projects would be proposed by an investor and approved by a state council. Due to this complicated mechanism, few enterprises received incentives under Decision 12. As a result, in 2015, the Government has promulgated Decree 111 on the development of supporting industries stipulating that the sector has the highest incentives (as for high technology products). In addition, in 2016, the national program development (Decision 68) of supporting industries has been built, which will be implemented from 2018 under the government fund to enhance the sectoral capability focusing on the domestic manufacturing SMEs.

On the other hand, joining the WTO has brought significant changes. During the WTO negotiations from 2006 to 2013, Vietnam has had to amend several laws and regulations to comply with WTO commitments. A series of incentives for development industries, such as export incentives for garment and footwear, have been removed. This left Vietnamese companies facing many difficulties and challenges from their competitors since their export scale is small, and export turnover per capita is lower than the world average.

However, Vietnam's industrial policies, which have been in a top-down manner and involved by many relevant ministries and provinces, have not met their goal of industrialization and modernization fully. One of the reasons is that many industrial policies are developed and implemented without specific action plans and supports. Resource allocation, implementing agencies, implementation methodology, timing schedules, and expected outcomes are not well-prepared. Therefore, most policies lay only "in a paper" and do not have much impacts on the business community as well as society. In addition, the state-management agencies and civil servants that often have not enough practicality of industry and enterprises do not reach to enterprises, especially to small and medium enterprises, and to the businesses in remote areas, and to start-up enterprises. These lead to the lack of the participation of enterprises. At the same time, it is difficult for weak business associations to represent the updated voice of their members. Moreover, without specific action plans, it is very challenging to monitor and evaluate policy performance, draw experience, and propose changes for the next term and policy adjustment.

1.2. Vietnam's Industry Structure and Firm Performance

The transformation from a centrally planned to a socialist-oriented market economy since Doi Moi policy in 1986 brought quite a successful industrial development to Vietnam. According to the World Bank, Vietnam's industrial value-added and the manufacturing value-added grew at an average annual rate of 7.7 percent and 8.2 percent, respectively, during the period of 1986 to 2016.

The structure of the economy experienced a dramatic change. From the late 1980s to recent years, the share of agriculture in GDP dropped from more than 40 percent to below 20 percent. At the same time, that of the industry in GDP including mining, manufacturing, construction, and utilities increased from less than 25 percent to more than 35 percent, and that of service in GDP increased from less than 5 percent to more than 40 percent.

In terms of industrial output share by the ownership, the private sector (both the non-state sector and the foreign direct investment sector) dominates the state sector. Before 1995, the state sector had contributed more than 50 percent and currently less than 17 percent of the industrial output. The FDI sector has the largest share close to 50 percent, which implies that much of Vietnam's industrial growth has come from the FDI sector, especially in the manufacturing sector. The FDI sector also had sustained a high industrial output growth rate of nearly 23 percent, as twice high as the other two sectors, in the 1990s. However, since the 2000s, the non-state sector led by domestic private enterprises has shown high industrial output growth of around 20 percent compared to 16.7 percent of the FDI sector and 8.8 percent of the state sector (Tu-Anh Vu-hanh, 2017).

The number of enterprises increased significantly by 17.2 percent per annum from 2000 to 2015, and by 11.1 percent from 2010 to 2015 (Table 4-12). The manufacturing firms contributed about less than 30% of all enterprises and had a slower increasing annual growth rate of 8.6% from 2010 to 2015. While the percentage of the manufacturing sector in terms of the number of enterprises decreased from 33.06% in 2010 to 30.27% in 2015, the capital went up evenly from 2010 to 2015 with the annual growth rate of 17.8% and the growth rate of net turnover and profit before taxes of manufacturing sector reached 19.1 % and 9.9%, respectively (Table 4-13). Meanwhile, the service sector has the highest number of enterprises. Overall, the increase in the number of enterprises has brought about significant economic benefits: per capita income per annum has increased from US $ 471 in 2003 to US $ 2,300 in 2016.

According to MPI (2017), Vietnam has 535,920 active enterprises, of which about 95% is small and medium-sized enterprises (SMEs). Recently, 98.74% of local private firms are SMEs, and 79.43% of FDI firms in Vietnam are SMEs, while 58.17% of SOEs are SMEs. More than 400,000 SMEs operating in Vietnam employ 51% of workers and contribute over 40% of GDP.

However, as of 2015, SMEs' total revenue of VND 6,774 trillion was equal to 80% of large enterprises and SMEs' net revenue accounted only for 44.45% of the total net revenue. Especially, the average revenue of large enterprises increased significantly from VND 756.3 billion in 2011 to VND 937.3 billion in 2015. In terms of the average profit, SMEs earn only VND 150 million while large enterprises earn VND 1,133 billion. This partly reflects SMEs' capacity of management, especially that the cost management of SMEs, is feeble.

In addition, the average capital for large enterprises was VND 1,549 billion, which is 70 times that of SMEs reaching only VND 22.21 billion. The fixed asset and average long-term investment of small enterprises were VND 7.79 billion, equivalent to nearly 1% of a large enterprise. This reflects that SMEs ' capability is very limited that they use most of their capital to short-term investment and liquidity.

Vietnam industry and firm growth heavily rely primarily on foreign direct investment (FDI), cheap labor cost with low skills, and natural resources exploitation. According to the World Bank (2017), Vietnam firms need to improve productivity, innovation, management skill, and finance access. Productivity and efficiency are low both in the private sector and in the public sector. The links between FDI or leading companies and the SME sector in Vietnam are very weak due to the limited capacity of domestic firms, it is difficult to accelerate spillover effects via technology transfer. Generally, the manufacturing industry is less competitive even in the domestic market. Vietnamese enterprises are also marginalized due to poor management skills. Finally, access to finance appears to be a compelling concern for new businesses and firms who want to make a breakthrough to become a supplier for FDIs.

Table 4-10 Key Economic Growth Indicators (Unit: %)

Growth \ Year	1986-1995	1996-2005	2006-2015	2016
GDP per capita growth	4.3	5.7	5.0	5.1
Industry value-added growth	8.4	9.7	5.1	7.6
Export of goods and services growth	18.8	19.4	10.9	13.9

Source: World Bank

Table 4-11 Industrial Output Share by Ownership

Firm \ Year	1986-1990	1991-1995	1996-2000	2001-2005	2006-2010	2011-2013
State	55.4	55.0	43.3	28.9	19.5	9.0
Non-state	43.1	28.3	23.1	28.4	36.7	34.8
FDI	1.4	16.7	33.6	42.8	43.8	56.2

Source: Vu-Thanh (2017) and the authors' calculation.

Table 4-12 Number of Enterprises (Unit: Enterprise, as of Annual 31 December)

Industry \ Year	2000	2005	2010	2011	2012	2013	2014	2015
Total	42,288	112,950	279,360	324,691	346,777	373,213	402,326	442,485
Manufacturing	10,849	36,057	92,357	101,288	102,502	113,043	120,953	133,966

Source: General Statistics Office of Vietnam (2007; 2013;2016;2017)

Table 4-13 Indicators on Vietnam Manufacturing Enterprise (Unit: Billion VND)

Indicator \ Year	1990	1995	2000	2005	2010	2015
Annual average capital	16,633	127,364	363,222	1,093,017	12,128,268	23,620,283
Value of fixed asset & long-term investment	14,187	88,327	220,804	407,911	4,685,942	10,466,760
Net turnover	NA	NA	NA	800,347	7,858,209	15,241,182
Profit before taxes	NA	NA	NA	40,827	356,301	552,747
Profit rate (%)	NA	NA	2.6	5.1	4.53	3.62

Source: General Statistics Office of Vietnam (2007; 2013;2016;2017)

2. Korea's Experience

Korea achieved a miraculous economic development from the ashes of the Korean War. It became the 11th largest economy in terms of GDP with have international brands such as Samsung and Hyundai. According to IMF, per capita GDP increased from less than $100 in 1960 and $1,704 in 1980 to $29,891 in 2017. As of 2015, the 30 largest conglomerates account for 39.4% of value-added and 40.2% of total sales.

Korea's current industrial ecosystem, as well as the success of the Han River, have resulted mainly from Korea's industrial policies. So, in this section, Korea's five-year economic development plans and SME supporting policies are investigated, and its characteristics and outcomes are evaluated.

2.1. Korea's Experience to Boost the Industrial Competitiveness

2.1.1. Korea's Industrial Policy

The Korean government implemented seven rounds of the five-year economic development plan from 1962 to 1996 to promote industrialization and growth for international competitiveness (Table 4-14). The first and second plans (1962-1966, 1967-1971) aimed to modernize the industry structure and establish the foundation for a self-sustaining economy. Export-oriented industrialization was pursued to improve the international balance of payments. The focus of industrialization was the light industries such as textiles and clothing that Korea had comparative advantages with cheap labor. From the late 1960s, several laws were enacted to promote the heavy chemical industries.

The third and fourth plans (1972-1976, 1977-1981) aimed to establish an independent (economic) development structure and to foster the heavy chemical industries. Six industries, including the iron and steel, nonferrous metal, machinery, shipbuilding, electronics, and chemical industries, were selected industries in the fourth plan because they have high forward and backward linkage effects with high-skill labor intensity.

In the 1980s, some significant shifts were made in the industrial policy. First, the government sought the change from government-oriented to market-oriented development. It was a shift from the industrial policy to corporate governance and competition policy (Lim, 2012). The Monopoly Regulation and Fair Trade Act was enacted in 1980. Moreover, instead of direct and selective supports, indirect and general supports were provided neutrally across sectors. Second, a series of Industrial Rationalization was implemented to resolve overcapacity and low profitability of the heavy and chemical industries that resulted from the HCI drive in the 1970s. Industrial restructuring programs were also carried out in the shipbuilding industry. To coordinate investments and help distressed firms, tax benefits, and financial supports were given to merging firms. Third, it began to emphasize the importance of research and development and provide function-oriented support for R&D instead of sector-oriented support such as the HCI Drive (Lee et al., 1989; Mah, 2007). Tax incentives were provided for the private sectors' R&D. Third, it started to pay attention to small and medium enterprises, especially after Korea's democratization in 1987. It strengthened support by utilizing SME specific policy instruments.

The fifth plan (1982-1986)'s aim expanded from the economic development to the development of overall society, economy, and culture. Its name changed to the Economic and Social Development Plan. The fifth plan pursued economic stability and balanced development, and the sixth plan (1987-1991) aimed at the advancement of the economy and the improvement of people's welfare.

In the 1990s, the industrial policy promoted the information technology industry and the high-tech industry as new sources of growth. The need for the transformation toward high value-added industries and high growth industries put continuous emphasis on the development of SMEs. Moreover, after the financial crisis in 1998, the government propelled the knowledge-based economy.

The seventh plan (1992-1996), called 'New Economy Plan,' tried to transform to market-led growth and proposed ten policy tasks to solve to strengthen the industrial competitiveness, improve equity and balanced development, and promote globalization and autonomy and lay the foundation of the unification, instead of setting the policy direction. After the financial crisis in 1997, the Kim Dae-Jung administration (1998-2003) pushed globalization and financial liberalization, which continued from the previous Kim Young Sam administration.

In the 2000s, the search for exploring new growth engine industries became more and more critical with innovation (Koo, 2013). As a national development strategy, the Roh Moo Hyun administration (2003-2C08) pursued balanced growth and developed the regional innovation networks of the industry-university-research institution with the regional clusters of SMEs in the technology-intensive sectors (Koo, 2013). The Lee Myung Bak administration (2008-2012) pursued the green growth strategy focusing on energy and environmental issues.

Table 4-14 Overview of Korea's Industrial Policy

Period	1962	1972	1982	1992	2000	2010~
Regime	Government-led			Market-led		
5-year Plan	1st & 2nd	3rd & 4th	5th &6th	7th	-	-
Focus / Priority	Light Industry	Heavy & Chemical Industry	Economic Stabilization	Globalization IT industry	New growth Engine & Innovation	Green Growth

2.1.2. Development of SMEs and Related Policies

The Korean government established the two major independent organizations to support SMEs: the Small and Medium Business Corporation (SBC) in 1979 and The Small and Medium Business Administration (SMBA) in 1996. The Small and Medium Business Administration (SMBA) expanded into the Ministry of SMEs and Startups in 2017. The central role of SMBA and SBC has been to supply loans and funds to SMEs that are lack of collateral and are avoided by private banks. However, in recent days, the needs of SMEs have been diversified as their business scopes get diverse, and their markets expand to the global markets. The assistance programs of MSS and SBC have been diversified and customized to meet SMEs' needs.

The role and status of SMEs and the corresponding SME policies have changed during the economic development of Korea. In the 1960s and early 1970s, SMEs were not the target of the Korean government-led industry policy since the government focused on the development of large companies and SOEs in the network and utility industries. However, in the late 1970s, the government started to provide supports for SMEs' facility investment and productivity. In 1976, the Korea Credit Guarantee Fund (KODIT) was founded to provide credit guarantees for the liabilities of promising SMEs that lack tangible collateral. As SMEs started to grow and expand by supporting the production of large firms in the heavy and chemical industries, the Law to promote SMEs was enacted in 1978 to promote and accelerate the modernization of SMEs. In 1979, the Small and Medium Business Corporation (SBC) was established to provide SME financing. It provides customized funds and financial assistance for SMEs according to the growth cycle of a firm, consulting programs for customized solutions, human resource development programs, and export marketing programs.

In the 1980s, the government protected SMEs' especially in light industries such as textile and garment, to cultivate SMEs. The proportion of SMEs in the industry has continued to increase. In the 1990s, the Small and Medium Business Administration (SMBA) was established in 1996 to promote the development of SMEs. However, Korea's past industrial policies focusing on selected industries and chaebols did not narrow the gap between large firms and SMEs in terms of capability and performance.

The financial crisis in 1997 took a heavy toll on SMEs, not only on large firms. The number of SME bankruptcies in 1997 reached 22,800, almost double of that in 1996 (Gregory et al. 2002). SMEs had to go through the restructuring process to increase productivity. In 1997, the Venture Act was established.

In the 2000s, the government promoted technology and knowledge-based innovative SMEs' and the number of innovative SMEs in 2006 increased by more than twofold compared to that in 2003 (Sung et al., 2016). Sales and job creation of innovative SMEs were 3.2 times and 2.6 times higher than those for general SMEs (Kim, 2007). In recent years, the government has promoted a win-win growth strategy to foster a business-friendly ecosystem for SMEs. The Korea Commission for Corporate Partnership (KCCP) was established in 2010 to draw consensus of the private sector for the conflicts between large enterprises and small and medium-sized enterprises and spread the culture of mutual growth.

In summary, Korea's SME policies have changed from financing supports to diversified supports for SMEs, from SME protection to fair competition between SMEs and LEs, and from direct assistance to the creation of SME friendly ecosystem.

As of 2015, according to the MSS, SMEs accounted for more than 99.9% of the establishments and 90.2% of employment in Korea. The share of SMEs in export was 20.1%. The shares in terms of sales and operating income were 53.9% and 58.1%, respectively. They contribute to 31.6% of the value-added of the manufacturing sector and 59.3% of the value-added of the service sector.

In Korea, one of the most critical barriers that SMEs face has been access to finance, which would be the same for SMEs in other developing countries. According to the Korea Federation of SMEs (KBIZ)' survey, 79% of SMEs funding is bank loans, 15.1% is policy loans, and the rests are corporate bonds and others in 2015. As for the borrowing of financial institutions, mortgage was the most common condition (46.0%), followed by pure credit (22.4%) and credit guarantee (16.6%). Higher lending rates were the number one reason for SMEs' financing difficulty, followed by difficult loan examination and excessive collateral demand. The average borrowing rate of interest rates for SMEs is around 4.2% compared to 3.51% of large firms, and the financial expenses to sales of SMEs is 1.56%, compared to 0.78% of large firms. According to the BOK, the debt ratios of SMEs were 223% in 1985, rising to 305% in 1997 during the Asian financial crisis, but decreasing to below 200 since 2000. As of 2015, the debt ratio is of SMEs is 152.1%. While it has been improving, it is still much higher than that of large firms, which is 105.4%.

Table 4-15 Overview of SME Policy and Institutions

Period	1962	1972	1982	1992	2000	2010~
5-year Plan	1st & 2nd	3rd & 4th	5th &6th	7th	-	-
SME Policy and Institutions	Basic Law(1966) Credit Guarantee Law(1967)	KODIT (1977) SBC(1979)	KOTEC (1989)	Venture Act(1997) Fast-Track Restructuring program	KOREG (2000) KVIC (2005)	KCCP (2010) for win-win growth

2.1.3. Korea's SME Financing Supporting System

The Korean government has implemented SME financing policies to solve SMEs' barriers in access to financial resources and to create an SME business-friendly environment. The key players for the SME policy financings are the Small and Medium Business Corporation (SBC), the Bank of Korea (BOK) as well as the Industrial Bank of Korea (IBK). Moreover, there are three Credit Guarantee systems (Figure 4-2).

The SBC directly provides direct loans, promotion funds, and credit guarantees to SMEs and startups. On the other hand, the BOK employs two indirect mechanisms to support SME financing: Commercial bank's obligatory SME loan ratio system and total limit loan system (or the aggregate credit ceiling system). As of 2018, the minimum SME loan ratio is 45% at commercial banks, 60% at provincial banks, and 35% at domestic branches of foreign banks. The BOK encourages commercial banks to lend loans more than an established ratio of loans to SMEs. When a bank violates this recommended SME loan ratio, there is no penalty. However, the bank which follows it can get the compensation in the total limit loan by having the interest rate less than the banks' loan rate. On the other hand, the IBK that was established as a Small and Medium-sized Business Bank in 1961 is a government-funded financial institution, playing a leading role in supporting SMEs. As of 2016, the IBK provides 77.5% of its total loans to SME, and its market share of SME loans is the highest as 22.6%.

The public credit guarantee systems provide guarantees for SMEs to obtain loans from the banks or receive the SME policy funding. Its funds come from the government, financial institutions, and the private sector. The Korea Credit Guarantee Fund (KODIT) established in 1976 extends credit guarantees for liabilities of promising SMEs with lack of tangible collateral such as non-technology-oriented SMEs, startup firms, exporting firms and green-growth firms, and also provides credit insurance from 1997 to prevent SME's chained bankruptcies caused by nonpayment of buyers. The Korea Technology Finance Corporation (KOTEC) founded in 1989 serves technology-oriented SMEs, venture firms, Inno-Biz, and green firms for technology guarantee and technology appraisal. The Korea Federation of Credit Guarantee Foundations (KOREG) established in 2000 provides credit guarantee assistance for regional SMEs. The guarantee programs are customized for each purpose and revised for the customer-friendly system.

To obtaining a credit guarantee service, a firm must submit an application to one of the guarantee agencies. Then the agency inspects and evaluates the applicant's facilities, production capabilities, and operations, and credit status, etc. When the application is approved, a firm receives a guarantee certificate to submit to banks for loans.

The amount of credit guarantee issued to SMEs by KIBO, KODIT, and KOREG has been increasing from 56,476 billion Korean won in 2010 to 61,916 billion Korean won in 2015. The amount of credit insurance issued to SMEs by KODIT in 2015 was 17, 989 billion Korean won, which increased from 5,966 billion Korean own in 2010. In addition, the Korea Trade Insurance Corporation (K-SURE) provides export credit and export insurance to SME exporters.

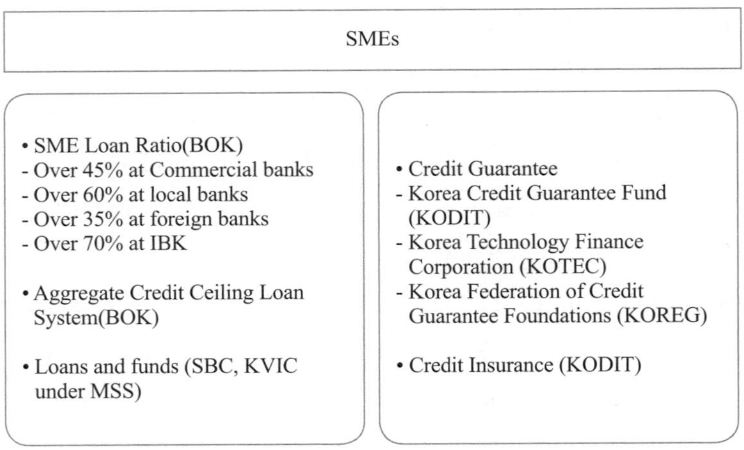

Figure 4-2 SME Financing Policy and Institutions in Korea

2.1.4. Success and Failure Factors for the Industrial Competitiveness

This sub-section investigates the success factors that have shaped the industrial competitiveness of Korea as well as the failure factors that could have been avoided in Korea's development experience.

The key success factors include the comprehensive export-oriented industrial policy under the strong control tower and the synchronized support of political leaders, private sectors, and the people. Most importantly, it was not state-owned enterprises, but private firms that developed and upgraded the industrial competitiveness. The government attempted to foster a competitive environment by allowing multiple firms to compete to avoid the abuse of monopoly power instead of involving directly through state-owned enterprises. This made Korea achieve international competitiveness.

However, the industrial policy involves government intervention. Failure rises from the government support and protection with a lack of market principles that result in overinvestment, inefficiency, and moral hazard of firms. In Korea, epower was more and more concentrated on a few firms, and the dependence of the economy on Chaebols increased. This also ended up with the widened gap between big firms and SMEs, which hindered further advancement. To this extent, the Korean government's competition policy to promote competition and market discipline was not enough to overcome government failure. More details are discussed below.

(1) Comprehensive Industrial Policy under the Strong Control Tower

The Economic Planning Board (EPB) took charge of designing the five-year economic development plan, overseeing the government budget allocation, and attracting foreign capital from 1961 to 1994 (MSF, 2014). It consisted of four bureaus: Overall Planning Bureau, Budget Bureau, Material Resource Mobilization Planning Bureau, and Bureau of Statistics.

Since it was newly organized in 1961 and separate from the ministries, it had fewer interest conflicts. Moreover, in 1964, the minister of the EPB was given the deputy prime minister, ranking higher than other ministers, which strengthened the authority of the EPB. With the strong power and capacity, the EBP coordinated and adjudicated policies that were drafted from the planning groups. Those planning groups consisted of related ministry government officials, academics, and experts of public and private organizations.

The EPB also held a monthly economic briefing meeting presided by the president. For instance, President Park Jung Hee seldom missed the meetings. These monthly meetings were very critical in that various important issues were shared by relevant ministries and measures to resolve problems, and obstacles were suggested or taken. With financial resources and measures, the EPB implemented economic policies effectively and efficiently and helped the nation achieve high growth.

Under the strong control of the Economic Planning Board, Korea had five-year economic development plans that were forward industrial policies envisioning the future of the world's top competitiveness. The Korean government accelerated the transformation of the industry structure through the plans. It was such an integrated and systematic industrial policy that include specific goals, clear targets, detailed action plans, and full and well-rounded support.

First, the goal of each plan had been chosen by considering Korea's development stage and income level in the long-term.

Clear and quantitative targets such as growth rate and exports were chosen so that every participant can agree and follow. For instance, the third and fourth five-year plans had promoted six heavy and chemical industries. The committee for the promotion of the heavy and chemical industry was established, and the yearly goal of the production volume, budget, and investment for each sector was set in detail.

Second, since Korea had limited resources and faced market failures with underdevelopment institutions everywhere at the early stage of economic development, an 'industry targeting policy' was implemented. Target industries changed over the stages of economic development.

Third, the government provided full supports for firms through detail and coherent action plans and resources so that firms could boost competitiveness and achieve the goals of the economic development plans. The laws that enabled the government to select specific industries and implement supporting policies had been enacted. For instance, in the 1970s, the promotion law for each heavy chemical industry was enacted, and the regulation on entry provided monopoly rights to selected firms in selected industries.

Moreover, supports through revisions of income and corporate taxes, debt guarantee system for foreign loans, and human resource training were implemented for firms to build up the foundation. Export subsidies and substantial concessions linked to exports were put in place to achieve the nation's export targets (OECD, 2012). However, most of all, those supports, and benefits were given to industries and firms of high performance.

(2) Selection and Development of Industries

The Korean government aimed to achieve international competitiveness and implemented an "industry targeting policy" at the early stage of economic development.

Over the stages of economic development, the light industry in the 1960s, heavy and chemical industries in the 1970s, and the information technology in the second half of the 1980s have been selected as target industries. Industrial clusters also have been developed following the industrial policies: the first industrial cluster specialized in textiles and apparels in the 1960s, several industrial clusters in the 1970s for the heavy and chemical industry drive, high-tech and science industrial clusters in the 1990s with the development of the IT industry, high-tech industry clusters and regional innovation clusters in the 2000s for the balanced growth. Those industrial clusters where related suppliers and institutions are concentrated provided efficiency and synergy that have been a driving force of economic development.

Target industries were chosen by considering its comparative advantage, efficiency, profitability, and impacts on the economy and structural transformation during industrial development. Only a small group of industries were chosen as the target industries at each stage. Once selected industries were fostered, other industries were chosen for the next stage development target.

In the 1960s, the light industries such as textiles and clothing were selected since Korea had comparative advantages with cheap labor. In the 1970s, six heavy chemical industries including the iron and steel, nonferrous metal, machinery, shipbuilding, electronics, and chemical industries were chosen because the Korean government and President Park Jung Hee realized the limitation of the light industries in promoting exports and were convinced that for the success of the export-led industrialization, the industry restructuring with heavy chemical industries was necessary. In addition, those industries have high forward and backward linkage effect with high-skill labor intensity. At the same time, Korea needed the security of defense since the U.S. was considering the withdrawal of US troops from Korea.

However, whichever industry were chosen, the most success factors were the government's export-oriented industrial policy that let private firms achieve the industrial and international competitiveness, not through the state-owned enterprises. Moreover, the government's competition policy created the competitive environment of private firms.

For example, Korea's automotive industry that was one of the target industries has exported its national cars, i.e., fully Korean-made cars, and ranked as the sixth-largest motor vehicle producer in 2017.

Compared to other countries that make knockdown production of foreign models but fail to produce its national car, Korea's automotive industry achieved international competitiveness. The first key success factor is that the Korean government aimed to develop the automotive industry as an export-oriented industry and to produce its national car for exports since the domestic market was too small to achieve economies of scale. The second factor is that it was carried out by not a state-owned enterprise, but private firm. The government instead built the competitive industry structure and promoted the competition of big three to four private firms to prevent the harmful effects of the monopolist. It is quite the opposite of Malaysia's case that carried the development of the automotive industry through a state-owned enterprise and is still protecting the government-linked and loss-making automotive enterprises. Malaysia ended up as a captive of the regionalized Japanese Keiretsu system (Wad and Govindaraju, 2011). The third factor is the skilled workforce. Korean workers had experience from assembly and car restoration since the Japanese colonization period and training from Japanese car companies in the 1960s. Moreover, the automotive companies have founded research institutes and fostered workforce through education and training programs domestically and internationally. The skilled workforce is one of the most important factors for the advanced and innovative economy studied in the first year of the DEEP project.

(3) Close Public-Private Collaboration and Synchronization of Mutual Interests

Public-private consultations and cooperation have taken place in the forms of various councils, sectoral round tables, workshops and seminars, with the active participation of outside experts from the private sector, research institutes, and academics. Close collaboration goes back to the early days of the economic development plans and has expanded ever since.

The participation of civilian experts has increased over time across all the 4-stage sequence of the five-year economic development plan process: choosing goals & writing guideline based on the vision, preparing sub-goals, targets, and action plans, extensive coordination and plan confirmation.

While only a small number of people and related ministries prepared the first five-year economic development plan (1962-1966), the involvement of outside experts expanded from the second plan (1967-1971). Related ministries, as well as domestic and foreign experts, participated from the goal planning stage, not from the action plan stage. In the third plan (1972-1976), the role of the Economic Planning Board has gradually been transferred to related ministries in setting up targets and action plans.

In the fourth plan (1977-1981), more experts participated in the goal and guideline setting stage and subsequent stages. In the 22 planning groups for the divisional plans, 33.2 % of the members were from the public institutions such as KDI, BOK, and research institutes, and 15.7% were civilians from universities, corporations and associations and 51% were government officials (Eom and Bae, 2014). At the completion stage of the planning, the Korea Development Institute (KDI), a government research institute, organized the Economic Policy Council (EPC) that consisted of 10 subcommittees and included experts from academia, industry, finance sector, labor organization, media, and others to collect their opinions.

In the fifth plan (1982-1986), the EPC played a role in the stages of establishing the guideline and coordinating the plan. In the sixth plan (1987-1991), outside experts outnumbered the government officials. Further, the regional economic policy council was held for regional coordination. In the seventh plan to propose the directions for the improvement of a socioeconomic system, the role of research institutes and experts became more vital as they drafted some of the action plan drafts.

On the other hand, the monthly enlarged export promotion meetings from 1965 to 1994 held by the Ministry of Commerce and Industry were also the institutionalized framework that public and private could share the information and voice their opinions. Its golden days were from 1968 to 1977 when it was chaired by the president and held almost every month. It had the role of monitoring and evaluating the progress of export promotion and provided ways to mitigate or resolve the obstacles of the private sectors in the implementation of the industrial policy. The Office of Planning and Coordination Policy under the Prime Minister operated the formal evaluation system called the Program Assessment System from 1961.

Public-private exchange of information and collaboration took place in preparation for the meeting. Government officials met many civil servants, civilian experts, and the private sector to understand the current situation and come up with measures to take. Furthermore, in the meeting, not only government officials and experts of public organization, but also the private sector, experts of private organizations, and journalists attended the meetings.

The government listened to the voices of business people. The goals of the government and the benefits of businesses were synchronized during the process of drawing up the plan (Jones and Sakong, 1980; Choi, 2008). The process of elaborating goals for industrial promotion was a process of adjustment between the mutual interests of the government and business (Eom and Bae, 2014).

(4) Firm and Persistent Will of Political Leaders

The will of the president has been one of the most important things in Korea's industrialization. The strong will and power of the government were essential and valuable, especially in the early stage of industrialization. The most representative example is the case of President Park Jung Hee that emphasized the export-oriented economic growth with the slogan of "Export Number One." The president presided almost all the monthly export promotion meetings (EPM) that the Minister of Commerce and Industry and the Minister of Foreign Affairs gave a progress report on export and overseas market conditions related to exports, respectively.

The presence and speech of the president showed his strong interests and the will on export promotion and economic growth. Therefore, these meetings not only monitored and assessed the progress of the industrial policy implementation but also provided opportunities to receive attention from top leadership. Moreover, it was a window to seek a solution for obstacles and problems.

(5) Government Subsidies, Overinvestment, and Industrial Rationalization

Through the HCI drive, Korea had developed and upgraded several key industries and firms from being assemblers to be advanced and innovative producers. However, it also had pitfalls. The government support and protection had brought overinvest and inefficient resource allocation.

During the HCI drive period, the average rate of return was lower in the HCI sectors than in otheres (Yoo, 1989). While it might indicate overinvestment in those sectors, firms and investors nevertheless made investments, and even new entry occurred because available subsidies compensated them for the low returns (Graham, 2003). In the targeted industries during the HCI drive period, a sizable number of attempted entries that followed the government's subsidies went bankruptcies or created unsounded firms (Graham, 2003). It resulted in producing too many look-alike firms without competitive capability, while subsidies flowing into the industry kept growing. Due to inefficient resource allocation, production costs increased, and efficiency decreased.

In the 1980s, a series of industrial rationalization and industrial restructuring in the heavy and chemical industries were carried out. The government set the industrial rationalization criteria, and firms going through rationalization according to those criteria received tax reductions or exemptions. Until 1988, 70 firms were classified as firms necessitating rationalization. Among them, 67 firms were disposed of through government-led M&As, two firms went through a reorganization process, and one firm was liquidated (Jwa, 2001). Further, to stop the overcapacity and distress problems, the government also blocked the entry of a new firm.

However, the industrial rationalization has been criticized for its limited success because the targets of industrial rationalization were chosen by the government, not through market disciplines, and the government failed to monitor the results of corporate asset disposals (Sakong and Koh, 2010).

(6) Chaebols and Widened Gap in Economic Power

Regarding the success of Korea's economic development, the role of Chaebols cannot be missed. Chaebols have helped Korea becoming the 11th largest economy by GDP as of 2017, with international brands such as Samsung, Hyundai, LG, and SK. Chaebols have formed and grown along with Korea's industrial policy.

In the 1960s and 1970s, Chaebols were viewed by the government decision-makers as an attractive means to achieve the goal of economic growth (Kang, 1996). As the Korean government's industrial policy aimed to foster the heavy and chemical industry that requires economies of scale with large investments, it had no choice but to concentrate its scarce resources on a few firms with the potential. Therefore, it provided direct supports such as preferential tax rates and interest rates, and investment licenses to Chaebols in the industries such as the electronics, automobile, and shipbuilding industries while it monitored chaebols' performance. Chaebols also acquired some SOEs since they had a bigger pocket than non-chaebols.

Those industries were protected from domestic competition and imports, as the government considered too much competition might hinder Korean firms from achieving international competitiveness. Chaebols enjoyed high monopoly or oligopoly rents and, in return, had close cooperation with the government in achieving the government's goal, economic growth, and export promotion. With all those benefits, Chaebol grew bigger.

In the 1980s, a series of industrial rationalization and industrial restructuring in the heavy and chemical industries strengthened Chaebols further since they were the only ones that had financial resources to acquire distressed firms. To stop the overcapacity and distress problems, the government also blocked the entry of a new firm. These industrial policies from the 1960s to 1980s, which had the concentration of resource allocation and the protection of selected industries, formed and strengthened chaebols in Korea.

While Korea achieved astonishing economic development and some Korean Chaebols achieved the number one international competitiveness, it had drawbacks. Unreasonable standards in assessing sectors and firms for rationalization and failure in monitoring the results of corporate asset disposal resulted in partial success of industrial rationalization (Sakong and Koh, 2010). Moreover, until the present, the Korean economy has a high dependence on Chaebols with concentrated industry structure and a wide gap between small and medium enterprises and Chaebols.

In the 1990s, the government's industry policy changed from direct intervention to indirect and functional supports as the economy became larger and complex. The reliance of the government on the private sectors and the trend of globalization and liberalization further strengthened the power of Chaebols. Chaebols established the empire with reckless business diversification and short-term foreign borrowings in the lack of financial supervision and regulations. However, the investment boom of Chaebols stopped when the Asian financial crisis hit Korea in 1997.

Among many causes of the financial crisis in Korea, the highly leveraged and vulnerable financial structure of Korean firms was a significant one, which resulted from the government's 'Too-big-to-fail' policy, premature financial market liberalization, and lack of supervision on excessive debts. To overcome the financial crisis and prevent further crisis, the Korean government abandoned the large firms favoring policies and aimed to improve the institutional environment for fostering competition and prudential supervision.

(7) Complicated and Overlapping Supports for SMEs

To inspire entrepreneurship and expand a vigorous startup climate, the MSS operates many programs and centers such as startup centers, business incubators, home-startup program. It also manages entrepreneurship graduate schools and BizCool programs targeting elementary to high school students. Further, to enhance SMEs' capacity and promote SMEs' globalization, the MSS also operates export support centers at regional offices and provides one-stop supports through the cooperation with SBC, Korea Trade-Investment Promotion Agency (KOTA) and other government organizations.

To foster SMEs' technologies and innovation, the MSS carries out a program to discover and develop technologically innovative SMEs, supports technological development through the cooperation of industry, academia, and research institutes, and supports the protection of SME technologies. It also fosters technical and skilled workforce with three technical high schools to provide and match innovative SMEs' needs.

The number of SMEs has been increasing from 2,670,625 in 1996 to 3,601,276 in 2015. Innovative SMEs increased from 30,260 in 2008 to 51,322 in 2016. More than two-thirds of innovative SMEs are venture firms where more than 70% of venture firms are in the manufacturing sector.

However, for both financing and non-financing supports, the current SME supporting systems are too complicated to hinder SMEs' access and utilization. Some support programs and functions are overlapping across many supporting organizations, and some functions are too fragmented at central and local levels. The same phenomena of investors getting into the market for supports that happened during the HCI drive period in the 1980s exist. These weaknesses reduce the effectiveness and efficiency of SME policies significantly. So, the systems and procedures must be simplified. Overlapping functions and organizations must be rearranged and reorganized.

2.2. Policy Suggestions for Vietnam

Korea has been well known for its continuing efforts to pursue e-Government as a crucial means to make its government more competitive. The Kim Dae Jung administration had put the implementation of e-Government as a major national priority in the 2000s. It concentrated on 11 major tasks for e-Government (2001–2002), and the Roh Moo Hyun administration initiated 31 major tasks for the e-Government roadmap (2003–2007).

The government's intervention and industry policy can contribute to overcoming market failure that results from information asymmetry, externality, coordination problems, and absence of markets and institutions, and enhancing the nation's industrial competitiveness.

However, the government should adopt the right industrial policies that have the appropriateness of goals and effectiveness. Therefore, the followings are the recommendations for Vietnam to achieve the success of the industrial policy.

(1) Comprehensive Industrial Policy

The Vietnam government needs to establish a comprehensive industrial policy that includes detail action plans and supports.

First, it should choose the goal and the target of the industrial policy by considering Vietnam's comparative advantage and development stage while having a long-term vision of international competitiveness. Industry targeting strategies may be adopted due to scarce resources, but the choice should be made wisely considering the global context and Vietnam's context. Moreover, clear targets such as exports and growth rates should be provided so that the effectiveness and performance of the industrial policy can be evaluated. The evaluation of the success or failure of the industrial policy can be used for determining supports and incentives, which have feedback effects and learning effects for the on-going industrial policy and the following industrial policy.

Second, as having a vision and/or a target is not enough, the government needs to provide supports so that the private sector can achieve the capacity to grow and compete domestically and internationally. Those supports include institutional arrangement, human resource development, and infrastructure. Korea has established appropriate institutions and laws prior to implementing industrial policies. In addition, supports such as public-private consultation, performance-based incentives, insurance, export credit, and project financing are still valid and should be fully utilized under the WTO regulation, while much direct financial support in the old days is not allowed.

At the same, those supports should be provided based on market principle, not by preferential treatment for some favored groups. Otherwise, firms that received benefits and supports cannot develop competitiveness and would fail in the market. This is a waste of resources and damage to the country, even stealing other firms' opportunities. The government should make sure that the government investment should be profitable, and supports cannot continue forever, which also should be recognized by firms. Therefore, it should be implemented with market principle and transparency that everybody can have trust in the system.

Third, targets, action plans, and supports should be coordinated and established with the collaboration of related ministries and regional governments. Otherwise, not only overinvestment or a waste of resources occurs in industrial policy targeted industries, but also a distortion of other markets would bring another market failure. For instance, industrial clusters need detail plans and cooperation between the central and regional governments. Moreover, the participation of the private sectors, outside experts, and the public are also necessary since they have more information on investment opportunity and challenges. Collaboration from the initial stage of the industrial policy helps the allocation of resources to be efficient under the constraint of limited human and financial resources. When the rationale and importance of the industrial policy are shared, it can obtain support from the private sector and the public, which expedites the success of the industrial policy.

Fourth, action plans and supporting systems should be simple, efficient, and customized. Vietnamese firms do not utilize many supports because of lengthy administrative procedures and lack of transparency, and corruption. So, it should be simple, straightforward, and transparent. Moreover, step-by-step customized policies are needed based on the development stages of the targets.

(2) Institutions and Top Leadership to Support Industrial Policy

For the industrial policy to work, the planning institution with the powerful autonomy that formulates and carries forward the plans following the strong will of the political leaders is needed. Like the Economic Planning Board (EPB) in the 1960s and 1970s in Korea that had the powerful autonomy over other ministries, the institution should be free from the interests of the ministries and the SOEs and be able to focus on Vietnam's future vision.

At the same time, having a plan is not enough. The institution should be able to monitor and evaluate the progress of the industrial policy. For this, the capability of the statistical office should be strengthened to provide the market situation and measure the impacts of the industrial policy. Regular monitoring and evaluation help the planning board improve the action plans and supporting systems. It also helps the planning board devise functional incentives based on performance in the markets, which promotes competition.

Korea's monthly export promotion meetings attended by the president, ministers, and the private sector from 1965 to 1994 had a role of monitoring and evaluating the progress of export promotion. It also provided ways to mitigate or resolve the obstacles of the private sectors in the implementation of the industrial policy. The Office of Planning and Coordination Policy under the Prime Minister operated the formal evaluation system called the Program Assessment System from 1961.

Last, but not least, the firm will of the political leaders is necessary for the success of the industrial policy.

(3) Institutions to Foster SMEs

Considering the considerable influence of SMEs on the Vietnamese economy, the independent institution for SMEs, such as Korea's Ministry of SMEs and Startups, needs to be established so that it can set more comprehensive policies and measures on SMEs. Moreover, for SMEs to increase investment and raise their competitiveness, barrier for access to financial resources should be reduced. So, supporting institutions and financial resources to implement SME policies are needed, such as Korea's SMBA and SBC. At the same time, to provide loans and financial assistance to SMEs that do not have collateral, the credit guarantee program should be established. Independent institutions for policy plan, policy implementation, financial assistance fund, and credit evaluation can dedicate itself to specific jobs with more expertise. On the other hand, it should be cautious to have too many independent institutions because it may result in overlapping supports and overinvestment.

(4) Public-Private Collaboration

Public-private collaboration helps overcome information asymmetry, which allows the government to use the right industrial policy and come up with appropriate measures and actions and hence increase efficiency. As economic development becomes mature and advanced, more cooperation is needed. The government should listen to the voices of Vietnam's business people and utilize all the possible outside expertise. The synchronization of the public-private sector goals and benefits is the most powerful drive for the success of the industrial policy.

Therefore, the government should facilitate public-private collaboration at various stages of planning, implementing and evaluating the industrial policy.

(5) The Level Playing Field

The government should establish the level playing field that big firms and SMEs compete by the same set of rules. Competition neutrality that state-owned enterprises and private businesses compete on the level playing field should also be ensured. For the long-term socioeconomic growth, the hindrance of SOEs and big firms should be prevented.

Korea's big firm favoring policies and industry targeting policies to boost the nation's competitiveness produced international brands such as Samsung and Hyundai. However, it came at the price of competitive discipline and regulatory oversight. Those Chaebols are not free from the object of blame as the cause of stifled growth of SMEs and startups and weakening competitiveness. However, the reform of Chaebols has not been easy due to the close relationship between Chaebols and politicians and the enormous influence of Chaebols on the economy.

Therefore, comprehensive industrial policy should be accompanied by competition policy. Allocation of the resources should be based on the market mechanism and competition. Moreover, corruption between individual firms and politicians should always be kept away.

IV. Fostering a Level Playing Field and Fair Competition

1. Vietnam's Competition Law and Institutions

Since the Sixth Party Congress and the Doi Moi policy in 1986, the State of Vietnam has gradually built up and perfected the institution in defining the economic function of the state. The change from a state-controlled to a market-oriented economy required the competition law. Since Vietnam became an official member of ASEAN in 1995 and WTO in 2007, there have been increasing demands and pressures from the world for building up a level playing field in Vietnam where all business entities compete under the same set of rue. Moreover, as the industries under the state monopoly have sought competition and opened its door to domestic private firms as well as foreign firms, it became necessary for Vietnam to establish legal regulation and institutions for a competitive environment.

In the late 1980s and 1990s, the Vietnamese government started building blocks for market development and setting the rules of the game for investors and enterprises (Pham, 2006). On the mobilization of investment capital, the State has promulgated legal documents on investment and business, such as the Foreign Investment Law, Corporate Law, and the Private Enterprise Law.

However, it was not until 1 July 2005 when the Competition Law of Vietnam passed by the National Assembly of Vietnam in 2004 came into effect. The Vietnam Government established the Vietnam Competition Administrative Department (currently, Vietnam Competition Authority, VCA) under the Ministry of Commerce (now the Ministry of Trade and Industry) in 2006 under the Competition Law. The Vietnam Competition Council (VCC), an independent adjudicative body that consists of eleven to fifteen members appointed by the Prime minister at the recommendation of the Ministry of Trade was established to decide anti-competitive behaviors after the investigation of the VCA.

The current Competition Law has designed with three main objectives: i) control of practices that restrict competition or actions that may lead to restriction of competition, especially when opening the market; ii) safeguarding the legitimate business rights of enterprises against acts of unfair competition; iii) ensuring a fair competitive environment for businesses.

In brief Vietnam has a short history of implementing competition policy and still is in the early stage. Besides, it faces lots of challenges under the legacies of the state-controlled economy. However, the effective implementation of competition policy is essential to build up the foundation for economic prosperity, and hence, Vietnam needs to strengthen the institutions and enforcement.

2. Korea's Experience

2.1. Korea Fair Trade Commission and Competition Policy

Competition policy in Korea grew out of an environment of state-led growth and Chaebol structures and practices inherited from that period (OECD, 2000).

In the 1960s and 1970s, competition law enforcement was weak, and regulations were often the ones that contradicted competition policy. The Korean government had intervened markets, and allocated limited resources to target industries and/or selected firms by providing financial and tax incentives and setting entry barriers. Such a government's intervention created and solidified the monopolistic or oligopolistic market structure. Also, Chaebols, Korea's family-owned conglomerates, were formed and the concentration of economic power on Chaebols was accelerated. The government tried to establish a competition authority many times, but with strong opposition from businesses and interest groups, failed.

However, in 1980, the Monopoly Regulation and Fair Trade Act of Korea (MRFTA) was enacted to regulate the improper market-dominating behavior of chaebols and pursue a more balanced economic development. In 1981, the Fair Trade Office (currently, KFTC) was finally established within the Economic Planning Board (EPB). However, Chaebols kept expanding recklessly through cross-shareholdings and cross-debt guarantees. So, in 1986, the MRFTA had a new chapter called "regulation of economic concentration" regarding enterprise groups' limitation on cross-shareholdings, debt guarantees, and mutual investment.

The turning point for competition policy came as the Asian financial crisis in 1997 hit Korea so hard, and the whole country went through restructuring. The Asian financial crisis pushed the Korean government to carry out deregulation and SOE privatization aggressively. The KFTC involved in the privatization process actively; it formed an internal task force and reported its results to the Implementation Committee for the Privatization of SOEs during the Kim Dae Jung administration. Such an environment empowered the KFTC. It became an independent central administrative authority in 1995, and the chairman of the KFTC was promoted to the level of a minister in 1996.

Since the 2000s, the KFTC has been powerful as a competition policy enforcer and competition advocate. As a policy enforcer, it handles cases regarding competition restriction, consumer rights protection, subcontract, and international cooperation. As a competition advocate, the KFTC has carried out the Clean Market Project (CMP) to suggest the measures to mitigate the anti-competitive effect in selected monopolistic or oligopolistic markets since 1999 and published the market structure study report jointly with the KDI since 2008 that analyze the fundamental sources of market distortions and develop measures to counteract these elements.

2.2. Success and Failure Factors of Korea's Competition Policy

The key success factor of competition policy in Korea is the competence of the KFTC to advocate competition through the timely participation of the KFTC in the regulatory procedure and privatization process. It was made possible by the legal supports of the MRFTA, the government, and the political leader.

However, the KFTC's broad coverage of social goals and too much focus on a balanced economy have been controversial issues. Overlooking the price mechanism in markets, instead of safeguarding the well-functioning markets, is likely to result in the distortion of resource allocation and inefficiency.

(1) KFTC's Competition Advocacy: Active Participation in the Public Agencies' Legislative and Regulatory Procedures as a Market Creator

The KFTC participates in the government decision-making process actively in a timely manner. The MRFTA requires and protects the involvement of the KFTC through the prior statutory consultation system in the legislative and regulatory process relating to restrictions on competition. The chairman of the KFTC is also present in the State Council and the Regulatory Reform Committee. The institutional arrangements protecting the authority and role of the KFTC are as follows.

First, the prior statutory consultation system in Article 63 of the MRFTA imposes obligations on the head of a relevant administrative agency to seek consultation with the KFTC or to give prior notice to the KFTC when a statue that contains competition–restricting provisions is enacted or amended. While the KFTC's opinion has the legal force of a recommendation, a substantial number of the KFTC's opinions have had an impact on the adoption of the final regulation (Hong, 2014). According to the KFTC, an average of 60 requests for consultations have been filed each year since 2004, out of which approximately 40 opinions have been resented thereon. The ratio of options reflected in relevant cases to opinions presented reaches an average of 80% and tends to be on a gradual rise. The substantial increase in the ratio has been observed as the KFTC became an independent central administrative authority, and the chairman of the KFTC was promoted to the level of a minister.

Second, Article 38 of the MRFTA provides the chairman of the KFTC a right to attend and make an opinion in the State Council that discusses and resolves relevant policies, although not an official member of the State Council.

Third, the chairman of the KFTC is an official member of the Regulatory Reform Committee under the President that was established in 1998 to enacts regulatory reform tasks, evaluate and reform regulations. Regarding new and reinforced regulations, the Committee examines the Regulatory Impact Analysis (RIA) that the head of the central administrative agency should submit under the Framework Act on Administrative Regulation. The KFTC performs the Competition Impact Assessment as a part of the RIA that includes a part regarding related competition restriction issues(Hong, 2014). In addition, the Task Force for Reformation of Competition-restricting Regulations has been working since 2000 as an internal organization of the KFTC.

Fourth, Article 3 of MRFTA also requires the KFTC to establish and implement action plans to promote competition in markets where monopoly or oligopoly situations have continued over an extended period. Most monopolistic or oligopolistic industries are those industries created by the Korean government-led economic development. The KFTC has surveyed market structure and published the market structure study report jointly with the Korea Development Institute since 2008 to suggest measures to counteract the causes and/or sources of market distortion. The role of the KFTC has become much stronger and more active in the 1980s and 1990s since the KFTC started to involve in the privatization and deregulation as a task force

In short, the MRFTA provides a legal basis for the KFTA to advocate competition and the independence of the KFTC. It has strengthened the power of the KFTC in making its opinion, and has made its competition-advocating voice timely and effectively reflected in the legislation and regulations.

(2) MRFTA and KFTC to promote Fair and Free Competition

Korea's competition policy encourages fair and free competition for balanced development as stated by Article 1 of MRFTA by preventing business entities from abusing their market-dominant positions and any excessive concentration of the economic power and by regulating illegal cartel conduct and unfair trade practices. Free competition means competitive industrial structure without an excess concentration of economic powers and entry barriers, while fair competition means all economic players being on an equal footing regardless of a public corporation or Chaebol. The pursuit of balanced development is a basis for the KFTC's restraining concentration of economic power of large enterprises and securing a competitive environment for SMEs.

These aims of Korea's competition policy have been heavily influenced by the historical background of the government-led economic development and the creation of Chaebol. Chaebols enjoyed complete supports from the government as the tools for economic success. The phrase Too big to fail," has been guaranteed by the protection of the government. Chaebols' reckless expansion and anti-competitive behavior were overlooked but have taken a heavy toll on Korea in recent days.

So, the MRFTA spares one chapter on Chaebols, which is quite unique compared to other OECD countries. Regulations address Chaebols' corporate governance and finance issues with the terms on limitation of debt guarantee and mutual investment, prohibition on circular shareholding and debt guarantees for affiliates, and resolutions by a board of directors. Meanwhile, Chaebols' anti-competitive behaviors would be subject to the abuse of market power dominance as they are likely to have a market-dominant position. Some regulations, such as cross-shareholding and limit to debt guarantees, have been successfully enforced. Recently, the KFTC has been working on unfair assistance and internal dealing, which has been mostly abused for the profit and inheritance of family members of Chaebols'.

On the other hand, some of Korea's competition policies aim to protect the interests of small and medium-sized enterprises. The MRFTA provides exemptions on SMEs' restrictive agreements and cooperatives if it is for the improvement of the competitiveness of SMEs. In addition, a large company is allowed to enter in a particular business area where SMEs occupy 2/3 or more of the whole market share. The issues regarding large enterprises and SMEs are dealt not only in the policy regarding abuse of market dominance but also in the policy regarding subcontracting.

It has been necessary since the government needs to protect the exploitation of large enterprises such as Chaebols. In addition, shared growth has been emphasized in recent days, and improving the relationship between large enterprises and SMEs has been one of the top priorities as the government recognizes the gap between LEs and SMEs as causes of the hinderance to further economic growth and social cohesion.

However, the SME protection policy in the area of competition policy has been controversial since it often conflicts with promoting economic efficiency and consumer welfare.

3. Policy Suggestions for Vietnam

Developing countries may be tempted to adopt the Korean model of industrial policy, i.e., government-led economic development with resource concentration on selected industries and enterprises. However, it should be noted that while Korea's industrial policy having achieved Han River's miracle in such a short period, the government interventions that restricted competition also led to resource distortion and market failure, which decreased industrial competitiveness. For instance, while Chaebols' contribution to Korea's economic development should be acknowledged, we should not overlook the negative impacts of abuse of its market-dominant power on society and the economy. The temptation to blind ourselves to the danger of anti-competitive behavior for the early success of economic development would likely bring more severe damage to the whole economy eventually. On the other hand, too much focus on a balanced economy, ignoring the function of a market is not the right direction, either. Competition policy, as well as industrial policy, should make efforts to promote competition, not to protect competitors.

Moreover, we should note that some Korean public enterprises exempted from competition policy and enjoying a monopoly position are still quite behind in terms of competitiveness and efficiency.

(1) Legal Framework for Competitive Neutrality and a Level Playing Field

The legal framework for competitive neutrality that state-owned and private businesses compete on a level playing field should be established. It is a concomitant requirement for market-based reform as it is essential to use resources effectively. Such law aims at limiting unnecessary interventions or abuses of power in the marketplace by the State or by private sector enterprises that adversely affect economic efficiency and consumer welfare (Pham, 2006).

Its promulgation would enhance the awareness of SOEs, private firms, and the public on the level playing field by defining the obligation mandates clearly. Related laws on competitive neutrality from the tax, credit, land. should be revised especially along with the reform of SOEs since SOEs in Vietnam have received preferential treatments from the government, building entry barriers and hurting the competition in some industries. The concentration of economic power and rent-seeking behavior should be monitored to the extent of competitive neutrality. The prohibition of anti-competitive practices by dominant firms and provisions for equal opportunity strengthen the economy and social cohesion.

However, for competition policy to be effective, strong enforcement should be followed. The continuation of discriminatory treatment and exemption from the competition law on SOEs would hurt the settlement of competition policies, which would hamper economic efficiency and public welfare. Therefore, top leaders' firm determination to enhance competition neutrality and political supports should be accompanied for strong enforcement and sanction.

(2) Competition Agency's Active and Timely Involvement in the Privatization and Reform of SOEs

Integrating competition principles into the regulation and legislation should be carried out in the early stage and before the privatization of SOEs as much as possible in order to reduce the possibility of distortion and market failure. Therefore, to enable the competition agency to involve actively and timely in the regulation process, the competition law should impose the competition agency the rights and obligations to do so. Moreover, the competition agency should be able to implement it, that is, no policy-practice gap, which leads to the following requirements.

(3) Independence of the Competition Authority

The full authority of the competition agency should be established for the enforcement of the competition laws and its effectiveness.

First, the independence of the Vietnam Competition Authority (VCA) from the Ministry of Trade and Industry would help the enhancement of its autonomy. Otherwise, we cannot say that the VCA would be entirely free from the influence of ministries.

Moreover, while the Vietnam Competition Council (VCC) is an independent adjudicative body, the members recommended by the Ministry of Trade and Industry and appointed by the Prime Minister represent many ministries. Therefore, it is difficult to be free from the influence of many ministries that have ownership of various SOEs. When those SOEs that have much influence in Vietnam are subject to the competition law, the conflicts of interests would be likely to rise.

For instance, Korea's Fair Trade Commission is an independent organization at a ministerial-level under the authority of the Prime Minister that formulates, administers competition policies and adjudicate anti-competitive cases. Its committee that makes decisions on competition and consumer protection issues consists of the chairperson and the vice-chairperson recommended by the Prime Minister and appointed by the President, while the other seven commissioners are recommended by the chairperson and appointed by the President. Among seven commissioners, three standing commissioners are from the inside of the KFTC, and four non-standing commissioners are from outside experts. Therefore, selecting members of VCC from VCA and outside experts would be a way of achieving the independence of VCC.

In addition, promoting the competition authority to a ministerial-level would empower it. Since line ministries that have ownersheip of SOEs are likely to have power and influence over the regulation for related SOEs, there could be cases that the VCA could not reach. However, those regulations conflicting competition should be reduced. In the case of KFTC, its opinions on regulatory and legislative processes have been appreciated, accepted and/or implemented more after the KFTC became an independent central administrative authority and the chairman of the KFTC was promoted to the level of a minister. That is, integrating competition policy into the general policy framework for regulation has been quite successful.

Second, the integration of VCA and VCC would be considered to create a synergy effect like the KFTC having a committee, the decision-making body, and a secretariat, a working body. Currently, VCC makes decisions on anti-competitive cases that VCA investigates. Having VCA and VCC under one umbrella would use human resource more efficiently and speed up the process. However, the integration of VCA and VCC is the next step to consider only after the independence of VCA is achieved.

(4) Enhancement of the Competition Agency's Expertise

The VCA handles not only competition matters, but also consumer protection and trade remedies, which requires vast amounts of work with expertise due to complex issues and procedures. However, the competition authority in Vietnam has a short history, and less expertise and budget relative to the ones in other developed countries. While it is inevitable to face growing anti-competitive matters, the enforcement of the VCA seems not catching up with it. The anti-competitive cases that the VCA dealt with have been growing very slowly, but the numbers of initial investigation and subsequent supplementary investigation are minimal. So, the VCA needs to continue the cooperation with other competition agencies to enhance its expertise.

V. Conclusion

This chapter attempts to provide directions and policy suggestions to enhance Vietnam's industry ecosystem by examining the institutions and policies of Vietnam and Korea. The success and failures from Korea's experience are examined to shed light on what and how Vietnam should reform for its advancement.

Both Vietnam and Korea have a history of government-led economic development. With limited resources, preferential treatments have been provided to a small group of firms and industries. Although some successes have been achieved, it came at the price of competitive discipline and regulatory oversight, which have brought inefficiency of some SOEs and private firms, significant loss to the economy from a failure of SOEs, lack of international competitiveness, and s widened gap between firms.

In the long term, competitive discipline is one of the essential elements to improve the industry ecosystem and the competitiveness of enterprises one step further since pressure from competition improves the efficiency of enterprises and makes policies work. Therefore, fostering competition and ensuring a level playing field is necessary to facilitate the virtuous cycles of Vietnam's economic advancement. This gives us the highest priority in the following policy suggestions.

First, the Vietnam government should strengthen the institutions and systems to support competitive neutrality and a level playing field. Vietnam needs to make it work by changing the culture. All types of firms should acknowledge and follow market principle, and the government should protect the functionality of a market and competition. Every player should get out of preferential treatment or favoritism in the past and acknowledge that supports cannot continue forever. This will pull up the motivation of players on the field to the maximum for the best. The competition authority with the right and obligation, and also with the capability to implement competition policies should be protected and strengthened by the law, the government, and the leader.

Second, the privatization and the internal reform of SOEs are two ways of promoting competition and enhancing efficiency. For its success, the independent authority should carry out well-prepared and detailed action plans with the full support of the country leader and people. Moreover, either privatization or internal reform, incentives and benefits should be allocated by competition and performance following market principle under the transparent system. The current performance evaluation system and information public disclosure system should be linked with incentives and penalties for them to work.

Third, the government should coordinate the industrial policy and the competition policy well, so that they should not contradict each other. The government's intervention and industry policy should be used to overcome market failure and enhance the nation’s industrial competitiveness, not for favoring some groups. Getting industrial policy right at the right timing is important. So close public-private collaboration and synchronization should be facilitated to utilize expertise from the formation of the policy. It would also bring the public-private cooperation and active participation of the private sector in achieving the nation’s goal. However, most of all, detailed action plans should be prepared under strong leadership.

CHAPTER FIVE:

SUSTAINABLE WELFARE FOR LABOR MARKET: LABOR FLEXIBILITY AND EMPLOYMENT PROTECTION

Ji Young Park

Ph.D, Department of Economics, Yonsei University Graduate School

CHAPTER FIVE:

Sustainable Welfare for Labor Market: Labor Flexibility and Employment Protection

I. Introduction

1. Overview

The relationship between South Korea and Vietnam has been maintained historically and economically. Since the normalization of diplomatic relations between the two countries in 1992, South Korea's foreign direct investment (FDI) towards Vietnam has increased drastically. Vietnam is recorded as Korea's second largest manufacturing investment destination and receives the largest share of its total FDI inflows from South Korea (Kwak et al. 2014). As such, both countries have formed an intimate and special relationship; especially the economic one is expected to increase more in the near future.

Vietnam is now entering upon a new phase of middle-income country, escaping from the poorest one (BMI, 2016). Besides large Korean companies such as Samsung and LG, many global multinational companies and small and medium enterprises (SMEs) rushed to invest in Vietnam during the 2000s. While developing its economy via catch-up strategy based upon FDI and exports, however, Vietnam's national competitiveness is ranked 55 among 137 countries (GCR, 2017). In spite of its young workforce with high growth potential, uneducated workforce and government repression against labor groups are major threats to continuous economic growth (Vietnam 2035).

Vietnam has maintained its wage level lower than the market equilibrium and controlled labor union to suppress labor dispute (Kwak et al. 2014). The primary reason for such control was to maintain abundant cheap workforce so as to retain the national competitiveness in the period of export-oriented industrialization. Another reason for labor repression was derived from the prevalent logic among the middle-income countries, which labor dispute negatively affects production.

Southeast Asian countries have met a turning point after the 2000s. Recently they are preventing further labor disputes by enacting new labor laws for protecting workers' rights and increasing the minimum wage. Vietnam is also enacting, amending and modernizing labor-related laws along with its transformation towards a market economy system and rapid socioeconomic change. The Vietnamese government's efforts vary from improving its low labor productivity to developing human resource via higher education and vocational training.

In 2016, the World Bank Group and Ministry of Planning and Investment of Vietnam co-wrote a report, *Vietnam 2035: Toward Prosperity, Creativity, Equity, and Democracy*, for the future vision and strategy of the Vietnamese government. This report mainly emphasizes the concept of labor flexibility in the section of labor market policy. Labor flexibility suggests balancing between labor productivity and workers' demand toward employment. The essence of labor market reform for fulfilling labor flexibility is to ensure job security.

To increase labor market flexibility and to achieve long-term growth, Vietnam should rationalize the existing regulations. First, Vietnam should gradually expand the coverage of unemployment insurance and active labor market program in order for increased flexibility of regulated labor market to accompany workers' security. Active labor market policy including well-designed unemployment insurance and public employment service can contribute to enhancing labor market efficiency and labor welfare. At the same time, the influences of labor market intervention exerted upon important social protection and finance should be identified. To do this, the government authorities should closely examine the fiscal impact of expanding unemployment insurance. In this chapter, a set of options to monitor labor environment and taxation, which would be a source of larger aspects of social security and ALMP, are sought and presented.

2. Research Questions

Nowadays, Vietnam is changing its legislation according to its rapid economic development and change of social/labor environment. Especially the laws of employment and labor were largely reformed in 2012 than that of any another field; labor law and labor union law in 2012, social security law and vocational education law in 2014. Employment law in 2013 and labor safety sanitation law in 2015 was newly enacted. Lower statute including enforcement ordinance and regulations were enacted, amended, and remain to be issued until now. Issues surrounding current labor law revision contain modification or supplementation of articles related to labor condition and labor-management relation, a core of which are contract termination, overtime work hours, retirement age, labor union establishment and so on.

Labor market regulations are composed of the minimum wage, employment protection, and labor-management relations. Especially, the minimum wage is to guarantee a basic standard of living of workers. The amendment of

Vietnamese labor law in 2012 stipulated that minimum wage is a means of living support as well as demand for the simplest job performance under normal labor condition. It is known that minimum wage law affects 22% of Vietnamese workers getting "formal" wages (those who made job contract required by the labor law). Minimum wage is the basis for calculating the total wage of government officials and other public sector workers. Current minimum wage is one of the four stages, set by the national government. Another one, known as standard or basic wage, is still applied to public officials. However, how the change of minimum wage influences employment is theoretically uncertain.

Without strict execution of the system, an employee can unofficially employ workers without any contract to avoid minimum wage restriction if the minimum wage exceeds labor productivity. According to economic theory, the effect of increasing minimum wage is changing the regular employment to irregular one, in the case of the perfectly competitive labor market where official minimum wage law and unofficial sectors are applied. In reality, however, the labor market is not completely competitive, especially because big corporations can exercise market power. Thus the effect of minimum wage is less clear.

According to efficiency wage theory, workers getting paid are inclined to work harder with higher productivity and thus are less inclined to change jobs. Since the market authority or efficiency wage is in effect, minimum wage change hardly affects employment. Under the status quo, Vietnamese labor law focuses primarily on protecting and supporting worker and its enactment/amendment on strengthening or establishing the regulation than mitigating it.

Hence, this research tries to delve into how to deal with Vietnamese labor market structure and increase labor productivity in the context of analyzing the status quo and solution of the labor market. This research examines the appropriate level of employment protection and its desirable direction of transformation.

In the 1980s, South Korea preferred economic growth with pro-business policies and suppressed individual workers. This oppression policy accumulated labor unions' complaints and erupted more rigorously with democratization in 1987. Vietnam, a transition country into the market economy undergoing the process of modernization, should be careful not to repeat the failure of the Korean government in balancing management-labor relations.

Furthermore, we plan to seek employment protection model appropriate for Vietnam in comparison to South Korea's case and propose an employment protection model and labor market policies in the labor market.

II. Conceptual Framework

1. An Overview

Labor flexibility indicates how well the variables decided in the labor market including wage and employment reflect the supply and demand factors of the market. It is influenced by several institutions surrounding labor market, which entails such systems as law (articles), collective agreement (the power of labor union) as well as custom, practice, ceremony, and so on[63].

---

63 Enhancing labor market flexibility aims to easing labor market inequality by alleviating legal systems about labor condition and labor-management relation; it is largely divided into quantitative and functional flexibility. The quantitative one is again divided into external, internal and wage; while external and internal flexibility are related to number of workers and working hours, wage flexibility the extent of wage gap between workers.

In view of the rising labor productivity and the lowest labor costs, labor demand and supply is an effective way of responding to the employment crisis caused by the labor market. Labor flexibility does not abolish anti-market regulation, but stimulates labor demand, promotes market-friendly rules and labor supply. Specifically, abolishing anti-market government regulation has the effect of increasing the labor demand. Education system producing talented people makes technological innovation through research and development easier and increases labor demand through improvement of labor quality.

Vietnamese labor environment reflects national policy stance for strengthening labor rights, improving labor condition and economic development. Following changes are the signal of emphasizing labor-management autonomy over government authority: legalizing labor organization (apart from labor union) in the company unit, strengthening the status and role of labor organization and labor union, enhancing laborers' rights, expanding dialogue and cooperation between labor and management. As noted in Vietnam 2035, labor flexibility is important for Vietnam's sustainable growth.

Awareness of labor flexibility and direction of its policy have varied according to the economic situation of the time. Vietnamese labor law was established in 1995, and has been amended five times: 2002, 2006, 2007 and 2012, 2017. Labor law pertains to overtime work hours, labor contract, and minimum wage, extension of retirement age, labor union and organizations, defining Vietnamese labor relations.

Labor legislation in Vietnam is a legal provision[64] that applies to working relationships between employers and workers, that is, social relations that arise

64 Vietnamese Labor Law Article 3 Section 6.

in connection with the payment of employment and wages between workers and employers.

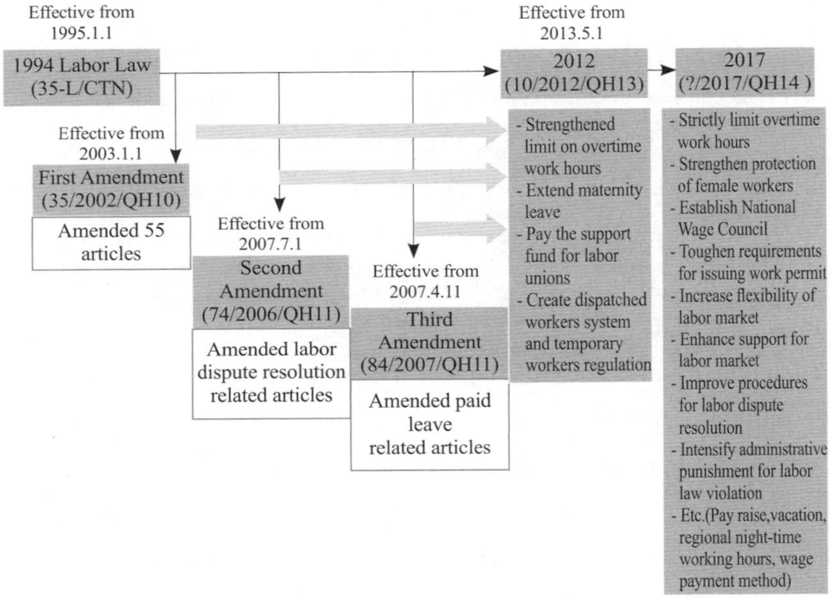

Figure 5-1 Labor Market Policy in Current Standing Vietnam

The policy was focused on eliminating regulation and rigidity in the labor market, such as disparity in labor supply and demand, rigid wage structure, and discrimination against certain classes. The first concern was the rigidity of the labor market caused by the expansion of welfare systems in major European countries. It has been pointed out that the minimum wage legislation distorts the efficient allocation of the production factors, the high unemployment benefit reduces the motivation for labor, and the employment protection regulations and high non-wage costs are the factors that inhibit the recruitment of enterprises.

2. Concepts of labor flexibility

2.1. Degree of labor flexibility

Bonoli(2003) is a noteworthy study regarding combination of employment protection and social protection. Assuming that labor law regulations, collective bargaining, and public income transfer systems are functionally similar in the sense that they are the means to provide economic security of wage workers in capitalist societies, he explains the cause of national difference depending on their respective focus among the three institutions. As for the three systems he dealt with, labor law regulations and collective bargaining can be categorized under institutions for the protection of employment.

Bonoli(2003) uses the term "functional equivalents" in the sense that the three schemes above are the mechanisms to protect the economic security of wage workers. Although this may not be what he intended, this concept implicitly suggests alternative or marital relations between employment protection and social protection. It implies that employment protection system and social protection system together should reach a certain level, providing a logical basis for the discussion of flexicurity. But as generally known, some countries have strong employment protection and social protection, while others not. This is the point where we are provided with limited implications while gaining some implications in Bonoli's analytical framework.

Over time, the significance and role of business have gradually changed. Amable discusses two forms of social security system: labor market system and income redistribution system (Amable, 2008; Amable & Gatti, 2004). By accepting the concept of 'Varieties of Capitalism', which distinguishes between the Coordinated Market Economies (CMEs) and the Liberal Market Economies

(LMEs) and applying the concept of 'institutional complementarity' following Hall & Soskise (2001), he presented five types of social models similar to the welfare state typology.

Neoliberal or market-based models emphasize competition in the product market, which leads to flexibility in employment. Social protection is underdeveloped and there are few incentives for enterprise specific technologies. The level of employment protection and social protection are both low.

Social-democratic model utilizes human resource investments such as training, not simply depending on dismissal or market adaptation, despite the fact that external competition acts as a pressure on labor flexibility. Following are its characteristics: high level of active labor market policy, coordinated wage negotiation system, moderate level of employment protection and high level of social protection.

Table 5-1 Combination Model of Labor Market System and Income Distribution System: Amable

	Employment Protection	Social Protection
Neoliberal model	-	-
Social-democratic model	Dualization	Medium
Continental European model	Medium	+
Southern European model	+	-
Asian model	Consequential Protection	?

Source: Amable, Bruno(2008), "Structural reforms in Europe and the (in) coherence of institutions," CEPREMAP Docweb No. 0809

Continental European model features high level system has been in operation; solidarity wage and retraining policies have be of employment protection and can be characterized as a lower level of welfare state. Adjusted wage bargaining en developed but not to the level of social-democratic models. In this model, productivity of the economy stems from 'labor-shedding' of vulnerable workers, substituted by social protection schemes such as early retirement pensions or long-term parental leave.

South European model is characterized by strong employment protection and weak social protection. Employment protection was possible because of the relatively weak competition in the product market, but the pressure on this part of the labor market has led to a dual structure of labor market due to intensified competition.

Asian model is a capitalist model based on the cooperation between the state and large corporations. Protection for workers is not institutionalized but consequential protection.

Eichhorst & Konle-Seidl(2005) and Eichhorst & Hemerijck(2010) have exemplified similar social models. These studies explicated three factors affecting economic actors responding to structural changes and economic crises: employment protection regulations (EPL), unemployment benefits, active labor market policies(ALMP); they also categorized how such policies are applied by type of welfare state. Eichhorst & Hemerijck(2010) concluded that the common direction of policy in European countries converged mainly on activation, and that it is difficult to note any radical changes except in the case of UK.

In other words, there has been a change in the degree to which a strong activation policy is added rather than employment protection being retreated and social income guarantee being strengthened.

2.2. Different models of labor flexibility

There cannot be an ideal economic system that satisfies everything. A problem of choice always exists that if you get one, you have to give up the other one.

Employment protection and social protection are in conflict. In the neoliberal national model, for example, the unemployment rate (especially the structural unemployment rate) is small while employment protection is weak.

Overemphasizing employment protection in the labor market creates problems of limiting the creation of new jobs and increasing the number of non-regular workers.

Emphasizing social employment may increase social spending-to-GDP. In terms of unemployment, the proportion of cash benefits and spending on active labor market policies will increase.

Employment protection	Social protection
• New employment creation constraints • Increase in temporary employment	• GDP vs Social Spending • Unemployment-related cash benefits • Proportion of spending on active labor market policies

Figure 5-2 Characteristics of Employment Protection and Social Protection

Since there is a trade-off between employment protection and social protection, Vietnam need institutional improvement to create jobs and increase labor flexibility The best employment protection measures are job creation. Job enables self-reliance, self-help, self-sustain, making dependence on the government unnecessary.

Flexicurity signifies labor market policy that combines four elements: labor market flexibility, social safety net guaranteeing workers' livelihood security, skills training, and job information provision (flexibility + stability + training + job placement). By analogy, unemployed workers are taught how to catch fish instead of just eating it, so that they could get jobs again in the labor market, solving poverty by themselves.

3. Issues for labor flexibility in Vietnam

3.1. Economic development stage: becoming middle powers

Vietnam's current labor market policies have evolved in the context of its long and ongoing transition from a mainly planned to a modern, market-led economy with a fast-growing middle class(Vietnam 2035).

Vietnman GDP growth (annual %)	1985-93	1994-2003	2004-2011	2012-2017
	~5.6%	~7.3%	~6.6%	~5.9%

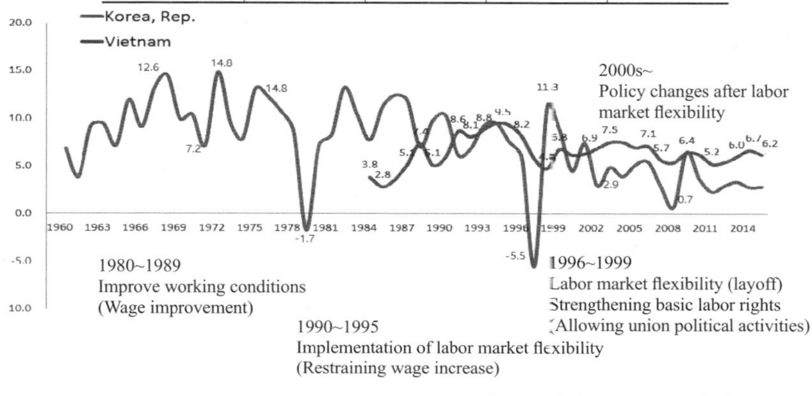

Source: World Economic Outlook Database.

Figure 5-3 Economic Development Stages in Vietnam and South Korea

Vietnam had 5.6% of annual growth rate from 1985 to 1993; 7.3 percent from 1994 to 2003, 6.6 percent from 2004 to 2011, 5.9 percent from 2012 to 2017. It is necessary to clarify the reasons for this slowdown tendency of the growth rate.

3.2. Enterprises' labor structure status: the absence of the middle management

The variation in the level of employment protection among countries is due to the diversity of economic systems and flagship industries each country aims for According to the economic system that Vietnam is aiming at, employment protection level should change.

The characteristic of the labor market structure in Vietnam is the overwhelming number of unskilled workers compared to skilled workers. Skilled workers, composed of (1) executives, (2) engineers and professionals, and (3) technical and office workers, account for 15 to 20 percent of the total, while unskilled workers, most of whom are women, constitute 80 to 85 percent of the total(Schmillen, Daniel and Truman 2016).

(1) Due to the nature of Vietnam, which has a lot of foreign direct investment, most executives are foreigners dispatched from the headquarters to manage subsidiaries.

(2) and (3) Professional and technical personnel, such as engineers, accountants and legal advisors (experienced operators in positions to manage and supervise production lines) and office staffs tend to be filled by Vietnamese citizens.

(3) Production line operators, without professional training, perform simple and repetitive tasks.

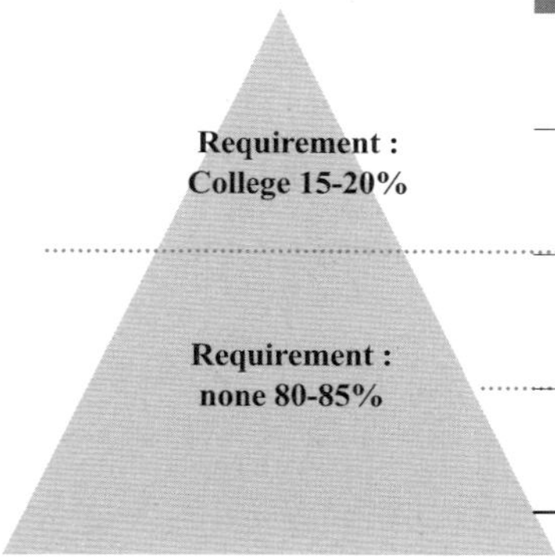

Type	Foreign nationals dominance
Engineers, professional office staff	Engineers: Male dominated: no particular gender trend
Technical workers office staff	Technical workers: experienced line operators: no particular qender trend
	vacancy
Line operators	Women dominate this category. Unskilled tasks

Source: Schmillen, Daniel and Truman 2016

Figure 5-4 Enterprises' Labor Structure Status

3.3. Issues for labor flexibility

3.3.1. Skill Training

According to the survey on labor in 2016, there is only 20.9 % of total labor force (11.3 mln in 54.4 total labor force) have the skill (i.e with vocational or higher education). The 80% of labor force with no skill and are mostly self-employed or working in the household economy.

Even though, among skilled labor force, there is an unusual structure among different skill levels as the University and higher account for the biggest share (9,2%) while the there very low proportion of vocational and professional education. (See Table 5-2). As a result, there is a wide gap between real needs of the economy and the education and training system in Vietnam.

Employers are not happy with the current skills level of workers and they are not filling the gap themselves. A World Bank survey that asks employers about the skill level of employees. Nearly half of firms surveyed felt that the TVET and the general education systems do not meet skills needs of their workplace. The skills shortage is even more pronounced among international firms, which may be seen as a proxy for the more dynamic, modernizing firms.

Table 5-2 Skill Level of Labor Force

Skill level	100,0
No skill	79,1
Vocational	5,0
Professional education	3,9
Diplome	2,8
University and higher	9,2

Source: GSO, 2017

But an employer is not filling skills gaps, either. The WB Enterprise survey finds that nearly all firms lament a lack of a range of skills – for example, 75% of d-EAP employers have a difficult time finding leadership or management skills and 58 percent cannot find the interpersonal skills that are needed for the jobs. But very few firms train in the skills that are missing. Instead, firm training focuses on job-specific training. (Cunningham, 2017 Vietnam future jobs.)

3.3.2. Residence permit, recruitment system:

Vietnam government use the residence permit system, which affects the labor mobility as residence permit is also a permit for children schooling and other public services. Recruitment system also links to the residence permit in many cities and provinces. This system might create a big barrier for the labor movement, especially in the long-term. In addition, the housing, health, and educational services are underdeveloped and structured in such a way to prevent migration between areas.

3.3.3. Wage- productivity linkage

There was a weak wage – productivity linkage especially in public sector. In many big corporations, the wage is still mostly linked with by seniority and education degree rather than to real productivity. The disparity between contract and non-contract workers, as well as between state and private sectors also affect the competitiveness in labor markets, which prevent a better linkage. In addition, a relative high proportion of special subsidies in wage structure (> 50%) is another negative factor in this respect as it does not link directly the wage with productivity[65]. On another side, the lack in competitiveness in job market as well as recruitment system also negatively affect the wage-productivity linkage as it is not linked closely to the position requirements[66]

3.3.4. Social protection

While the public sector employees are relatively better protected, there is a need to widen insurance coverage especially for the people who are self-employed and in the household sector, which accounts for more than 80% of total labor force. This is important since it facilitates the labor movement between sectors. In Viet Nam, the government prepares a Master Plan for the

65 https://laodong.vn/xa-hoi/tra-luong-theo-nang-suat-lao-dong-han-che-tu-duy-bang-cap-592622.ldo

66 Dinh Ngoc Giang (2017) . "Công tác tuyển dụng, đào tạo cán bộ, công chức, viên chức hiện nay", Lý luận chính trị số 8-2016.

Social Insurance Reform (MPSIR) by 2035, which can be viewed as a guide for future policy reforms. In the next 3 years, the plan target up to 50% of the total labor force will participate in both voluntary and involuntary schemes of social insurance.

3.3.5. National Funds: promoting the loans from National Fund for Employment

As the credit supports for stimulating employment, the Vietnamese government has run the National Fund to lend people with the aim of creating jobs and business. The fund, subject to young groups, female labors, disabled people, ethnic minorities, helped to create 110,000 jobs in 2017. Besides, the government executes actions in the Targeted Program on Vocational Training – Employment – Labor Safety and Sanitation during 2016 – 2020; promoting the loans from National Fund for Employment; focusing on improving the employment quality towards sustainable productivity. It also enhances information, forecasts and connects labor demand and supply, performs activities related to employment service, and develops the national database on the labor market to manage and circulate labor market.

3.3.6. Informal Labor

The movement of people and jobs from rural villages to urban centers due to the process of urbanization derived the shifts of employment away from agriculture toward manufacturing and services, from household enterprises toward registered and regulated business. In spite of this massive change, Vietnam does still boast a vibrant ecosystem of economic relationships on the urban streets, where family-run businesses and hawkers earn their living unbothered by economic authorities. Its informal sector takes responsibility for millions of jobs created during economic transition. Not considering this sector in Vietnamese growth policies would be a major shortcoming.

3.3.7 Funding for Job Creation and Employment Welfare: Taxing the Underground Economy

Underground economy means all 'negative economic activities' that are not caught by the official statistics of the government. The scope of the underground economy ranges from housework to illegal economic activities. Daily and non-institutional labor markets are also the cause of underground economy. Various methods have been used to estimate the size of the underground economy, but the actual size of the underground economy cannot be verified. Rather than estimating the absolute size of the underground economy, it is desirable to focus on its trends and causes for changes. The approximate size of Vietnamese underground economy accounts for 25 to 30 percent of GDP and involves around 57 percent of the country's total workforce. Policy efforts are needed to bring out into the open the underground economy and to make the taxation indices more transparent to solve the chronic deficit problem secure welfare resources for effectiveness of job creation policy. Labor costs in public sector should also be reduced through public service personnel reduction and privatization, meanwhile, measures need to be taken to give them better treatment.

Ⅲ. Labor Market Policy in Vietnam: Labor flexibility

1. Current Standing in Labor Market Policy

1.1. About working hours and rest hours

In Vietnam, laborers work 8 hours/01 day/ 48 hours/01 week. Breaking time is 30 minutes. This shall be included in the working hours.

Overtime: The overtime hours shall be to a maximum of four hours per day, and 200 hours per year. About weekly break, employees are off work Sunday or Saturday and Sunday. For annual break, he employee who has completed one year i.e. 12 months' service in the company shall be entitled to an annual leave of 12 days with full pay.

For an employee who has completed more than five years of service in the company, there shall be a proportionate increase of one day holiday for every five years of service. The employee with less than 12 months' service also shall be entitled to an annual leave but the number of days shall correspond with the length of his/her employment.

The maximum working hours are eight hours per day or 48 hours per week for normal working conditions. Daily working hours must be reduced by one or two hours for employees subject to extremely heavy, dangerous, or toxic working conditions. Employees must take a rest period of a minimum of 24 consecutive hours per week. There are also various compulsory daily and weekly rest periods and breaks that must be observed.

To revise the terms provided by the Labor Code, which are about normal working hours and break time in order to achieve practical agreed interpretation of them.

To learn and revise the relevant principles to increase the maximum overtime, and terminate the principles of monthly maximum overtime while maintain the principles of daily and yearly maximum overtime.

1.2. Strengthen regulations on foreign working permission and visa schemes

Firstly, about the current legal base on foreign working permission and visa schemes, according to the Point d Item 1 Article 169 in the Labour Code, the foreigners are required to have working permission prior to entering Vietnam for their employment. Pursuant to the working permission that is granted by the security agencies in charge of granting visa or Temporary Resident Card, as stipulated in the Point c Item 4 Article 10 in the Law on entry, exist, transit, and residence of foreigners in Vietnam. The time duration of the visa shall not exceed the time specified in the granted working permission.

Secondly, about the application of the regulations in practice, as reflected from localities, foreigners working in enterprises of Vietnam often obtain the visa type "DN" for 3 months without working permission (that means they got entry permission into Vietnam while they do not have working permission). Within 3 working months, enterprises will supplement documents for requesting the working permission, then, their laborers will obtain the visa type "LĐ". While it is regulated in the Item 1 Article Điều 7 in this Law that no changes in purpose of entry are permitted. This implies a certain quantity of foreign workers enter Vietnam for short stay without having working permission, which challenges the administration and granting working permission for employees. At the moment, visa granting agencies have just provided the turns of entry into Vietnam under the visa types ("DN", "LV" and

"ĐT") meanwhile the number of foreigners, who obtained these visa types, have not yet been specified.

For an example with South Korean citizens in 2016: there were more than 100,000 turns of entry into Vietnam for working purpose. In which, the number of entries through visa type "DN" was more than 30,000 and the number of entries under visa type "LĐ" was more than 17,000 turns. In 2017, there was more than 141,000 of entries into Vietnam for working purposes. Of which, entries under visa type "DN" was more than 86,000 and "LĐ" was more than 55,000 of turns of entry over the total of approximately 20,000 work permission granted to the South Korean citizens.

2. Public sector

Before 1990 the public sector in Viet Nam traditionally account for the largest part of total employment. Since then, the private sector expanded very fast. For the last 15 years, the Vietnamese government launch privatisation, as a result of which many state-owned enterprises have been equitized. The growth rate of labour force in the private sector was almost double of that of public sector. For the last 10 years from 2007, for example, labor force in public sector increased only 5% compared with 25% growth rate of the private sector (See table 5-3) A large part of labor force in Vietnam are working in the agricultural sector, with low productivity and high risk. Although the official number of unemployment is only 1,1 mln, many people especially in the rural areas are under-employed, i.e. many job are shared among a number of people, especially simple job which require no special skills and training. Even within the agricultural sector, the distribution of labor force over the country is not efficient since there are many factors prevent the labor movement. These factors include system of resident permit as well as lack of basic social services especially the lack of adequate housing and residential areas. For the last 5 years, however job stability was improved markedly as wage labour account for 75.7% compared with 40,0% about 5 years ago (2011)[67].

Table 5-3 Annual Employed Population at 15 years of age and above Types of Ownership by Items, Year and Types of Ownership

		Total	State	Non-state	Foreign investment sector
Total (Thousands)	2000	37075.3	4358.2	32358.6	358.5
	2001	38180.1	4474.4	33356.6	349.1
	2002	39275.9	4633.5	34216.5	425.9
	2003	40403.9	4919.1	34731.5	753.3
	2004	41578.8	5031	35633	914.8
	2005	42774.9	4967.4	36694.7	1112.8
	2006	43980.3	4916	37742.3	1322
	2007	45208	4988.4	38657.4	1562.2
	2008	46460.8	5059.3	39707.1	1694.4
	2009	47743.6	5040.6	41178.4	1524.6
	2010	49048.5	5107.4	42214.6	1726.5
	2011	50352	5250.6	43401.3	1700.1
	2012	51422.4	5353.7	44365.4	1703.3
	2013	52207.8	5330.4	45091.7	1785.7
	2014	52744.5	5473.5	45214.4	2056.6
	2015	52840	5185.9	45450.9	2203.2
	2016	53302.8	5234.2	45741.4	2327.2

Source: GSO, 2017

Currently, among total labour force of more than 53 mln, the public sector acounts for just 9,8%. As usual, this figure for urban areas is much higher than for the rural areas (18 % compared with 6% in rural areas). Consistently, in the rural areas, more than 80% of labor force is in the household sector (See Table 5-4)

67 Data Source: General Statistical Office, 2017. Báo cáo điều tra lao động việc làm 2016 (Survey report on labor and employment 2016), Ha Noi.

Table 5-4 Labor Structure by Economic Sectors (15 years and older)

Sector	Total			Urban			Rural		
	General	Male	Female	General	Male	Female	General	Male	Female
	100	100	100	100	100	100	100	100	100
Household	73,7	74,3	73,1	55	54,4	55,7	82,4	83,6	81,2
Collective	0,2	0,3	0,1	0,1	0,2	0,1	0,2	0,3	0,1
Private	11,9	12,8	11	21,1	23,2	18,8	7,7	7,9	7,4
Public	*9,8*	*9,9*	*9,7*	*18*	*18,2*	*17,7*	*6*	*6*	*6*
Foreign	4,4	2,8	6,1	5,8	4	7,7	3,7	2,2	5,3

Source: GSO, 2017

Despite general perception about lower productivity in the public sector, the average wage in public sector is also among the highest during 2016, with 5.66 mln VND (about 270 USD / month). The survey, however shows the steady faster rate of wage growth in the foreign investment sector. By the end of 2016, the average wage in foreign sector is much higher than that in public and other private sector. This also confirms the higher efficiency of foreign sector in general as concluded by many studies. (See Table 5-5)

Table 5-5 Monthly Average Wage by Economic Sectors (Million VND)

Sector	Quarter 2/2016			Quarter 3/2016			Quarter 4/2016		
	General	Male	Female	General	Male	Female	General	Male	Female
	4.845	5.098	4.496	4.933	5.191	4.578	5.080	5.245	4.855
Household	3.760	4.100	2.926	3.856	4.199	3.029	3.914	4.244	3.117
Collective	3.552	3.551	3.557	3.211	3.151	3.420	3.703	3.832	3.066
Private	5.392	5.846	4.829	5.497	5.950	4.938	5.580	6.035	5.041
Public	*5.663*	*6.073*	*5.215*	*5.715*	*6.118*	*5.275*	*5.823*	*6.220*	*5.403*
Foreign	5.513	6.218	5.192	5.557	6.192	5.236	6.364	6.326	6.384

Source: GSO, 2017

Concerning working hours, the public sector has almost the lowest working hour per week, about 44 hours, which is not much higher than the household sector. (See Table 5-6)

Table 5-6 Weekly Average Working Hours by Economic Sectors

Sector	Quarter 2/2016			Quarter 3/2016			Quarter 4/2016		
	General	Male	Female	General	Male	Female	General	Male	Female
	45	46,2	43,7	44,9	46	43,6	44,7	46	43,4
Household	43,8	45,4	42,2	43,7	45,1	42,1	43,5	45,1	41,8
Collective	48,2	49,2	44,9	49	49,9	45,8	49	49,6	46,6
Private	50,2	50,6	49,7	50,1	50,5	49,6	50	50,5	49,5
Public	*44,1*	*44,7*	*43,4*	*44*	*44,7*	*43,3*	*44*	*44,6*	*43,3*
Foreign	51,5	52,1	51,3	51,1	51,3	51	51,5	51,8	51,3

Source: GSO, 2017[68]

Among 41,2 mln wage workers, there are 58.8% have a contract, the rest either have no contract (7.8%) or only a verbal contract (33.5 %). Moreover, among wage workers, 79% do not have social insurance, 80% without health insurance. 25% in domestic firms do not receive health insurance. (GSO, 2017). The non-contract workers still accounts for a quite large part, 41,2 % of total wage workers.

Notably, unemployment rate among youth (15-24 years old) is quite high, 48,9%, which is almost 6 times higher than that of 25 years or older.

68 General Statistical Office, 2017. Báo cáo điều tra lao động việc làm Quý I- 2017 (Survey report on labor and employment , The first quarter 2017), Ha Noi.

Table 5-7 Labor Structure by Job Position, 2009-2016 (Unit: %)

Job position	2009		2012		2016	
	Total	female	Total	female	Total	female
Total	100,0	48,7	100,0	48,5	100,0	48,5
Employer	4,8	32,6	2,7	30,2	2,8	31,6
Self employed	44,6	51,1	45,1	49,5	39,9	49,0
Household	16,9	64,1	17,5	64,2	16,1	66,6
Wage workers	33,4	40,1	34,7	40,6	41,2	42,1
Cooperative	0,1	29,5	0,0	50,2	0,0	41,7

Source: GSO, 2017

3. Private sector

The renovation of economic and social base since 1986 in Vietnam had completely contributed to the dramatic change in labor market for the domestic economy. By adopting the market economy mechanism, it was witnessed of a continuous shift of labor market structure, in which the non-state sector has been dominated the state-sector regarding to the number of labor. However, this shift does not convey an efficient move for the labor market, since the divergence in wages and productivity have been existed amongst different ownership sectors (state, non-state, FDI).

The flexibility of labor market would firstly be embodied in the movement of labor market's structure, and this has been likely in line with the market economy adoption in the country. Table 5-8 shows the how the labor market has been distributed amongst different ownership sectors in the domestic economy since 2000. The information confirms that private sector has been dominated state sector over the years (2000-2016).

The average share of non-state sector and FDI was totally occupied 89 % of total annual employed population at 15 years of age and above as compared to 11 % of state sector over the period. The non-state sector (comprising of private companies, cooperatives, own account workers, household business) has played as the largest force as regarding to the share of labor market in Vietnam with its share of 86.2 % in averaged; and that it's share is roughly stable through the time points since 2000.

This flexibility is likely clear as seen by the change of the shares in the other two sectors. Labor market has informed a slight reduction of the number of labors employed for the state sector from 11.7 % in 2000 to 9.8 % in 2016. On the other hand, FDI sector showed a significant increase of share in the labor market with from only 1% in 2000 to 4.4% in 2016.

In averaged number, over the period 2000-2016, Non – state sector had employed 39,750 thousands labors, while that of State and FDI were 5019 and 1384 thousands labors, respectively.

A striking feature of labor market in Vietnam, which is considered as one of the barriers to the labor market's development, is the performance of informal labor force. The informal force is defined as the unregistered business/labor service to the authority both in state and local governments. By law of business in Vietnam, the state has allowed various kinds of business in line with the different ownerships. In which, some of business kinds do not need to register their internal labor source to the authority (without a labor contract), such as self-employed/household business, unpaid families or even cooperatives. Those labors in this informal sector, therefore are regard to as the non-wage workers. Specifically, these labors/workers are mostly belonging to the non-state sector. On the other hand, wage workers are those working in business kinds that are required to register labor source to the state by law, and firmly committing to the labor contract based.

Informal labor force (as referring to the non-wage labor force in non-state sector) appears as the largest driver of the labor market with regard to the number of labors. The domination of this force is displayed in the Table 5-8. This sector occupies a substantial share in total labor force, for instance from about 67% in 2009 and slowdowns to 59% in 2016. In parallel, there is a shift of labors to the formal sector in the period as with 33.4 % in 2009 rising to 41.2% in 2016.

In terms of wage worker (as defining to the formal sectors), we could see the domination of the private sector (non-state and FDI) in the formal market of labor as witnessing the Table 5-8. Number of labors are employed in these sectors grows from roughly 11 million in 2009 to 16.7 million in 2016, whist that number of state sector has a slow rise from 5.04 to 5.23 million in the same time points.

The dominant of informal labors would suggest an inappropriate job structure for Vietnam in the transition process. A critical evidence can be addressed from the published report on Vietnam Labor Force Survey - VLFS (2015) regarding to the employment distribution amongst business types. It is acknowledged that the job structure has dramatically shifted from industries (agriculture, forest, and fishery) with low productivity to those with higher productivity (manufacture). However, a large number of jobs have been employed in the traditional forms of work, recently. The VLFS (2015) reveals that the traditional forms of work occupied about 76 % of total jobs employed in this year, and such forms include family farming, non-farm household enterprise, and wage employment without a contract (see the chart bellows).

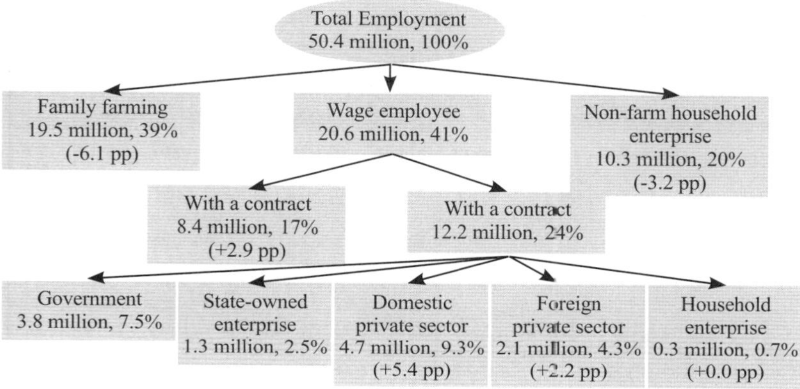

Source: As cited from Vietnam's Future Jobs, Dr. Wendy Cunningham, Head of Consultant Team, World Bank (2017)

Figure 5-5 Distribution of Job Employed amongst Different Forms of Work, Vietnam Labor Force Survey 2015

The trend of movement in labor market since "Doi Moi" in 1986, especially after the ASEAN joining (1995), APEC joining (1998) and WTO membership has significantly revealed the flexibility in this market in Vietnam with the direction of increasingly shifting labor from the state sector to non-state sector.

Table 5-8 Annual Employed Population at 15 years of age and above by Status in Employment by Status in Employment and Year

	2009	2010	2011	2012	2013	2014	2015	2016
TOTAL	47744	49049	50352	51422	52208	52745	52840	52840
Wage worker (total)	15981	16573	17432	17862	18189	18801	20773	21958
Wage worker – State	5041	5107	5251	5354	5330	5474	5186	5234
Wage worker - N.State	10940	11465	12181	12508	12858	13328	15587	16724
Employer	2286	1687	1455	1387	1300	1103	1533	1510
Own account worker	21358	21243	22104	23175	23746	21534	21447	21251
Unpaid family worker	8063	9524	9351	8982	8964	11299	9075	8557
Member of cooperative	56	22	11	16	9	8	12	26
Non- Wage worker	31763	32476	32920	33560	34019	33943	32067	31344
Non- Wage worker (%)	66.53	66.21	65.38	65.26	65.16	64.35	60.69	58.80
Wage worker (%)	33.47	33.79	34.62	34.74	34.84	35.65	39.31	41.20

Source: GSO, 2017 calculate and updated by the authors

It is worth noting to incorporate the surge of non-state and FDI sectors (i.e private sectors) with their investment and economies of scales. Vietnam is not an exception of a emerging economy in the region as the domestic economy needs to get a large scale of capital accumulation in it's development era. The Table 5-9 informs a relatively positive trend in the performance of social investment structure since 1995. Non-state sectors and FDI sector have more powerful role in creating a large share of social investment during the period of 1995-2016, when they total just 58 % of total social investment but this raises to about 63% in 2016. However, the data also confirms that the state-sector seems to be a dominate investor through the whole period.

Table 5-9 Investment by Types of Ownership (share, %)

Years	Total	State	Non-State	Foreign invested sector
1995	100	42	27.6	30.4
1996	100	49.1	24.9	26
1997	100	49.4	22.6	28
1998	100	55.5	23.7	20.8
1999	100	58.7	24	17.3
2000	100	59.1	22.9	18
2001	100	59.8	22.6	17.6
2002	100	57.3	25.3	17.4
2003	100	52.9	31.1	16
2004	100	48.1	37.7	14.2
2005	100	47.1	38	14.9
2006	100	45.7	38.1	16.2
2007	100	37.2	38.5	24.3
2008	100	33.9	35.2	30.9
2009	100	40.5	33.9	25.6
2010	100	38.1	36.1	25.8
2011	100	37	38.5	24.5
2012	100	40.3	38.1	21.6
2013	100	40.4	37.7	21.9
2014	100	39.9	38.4	21.7
2015	100	38	38.7	23.3
2016	100	37.6	39	23.4

Source: GSO, 2017

The contribution of non-state sector and FDI to the GDP (Gross Domestic Products) has positively significant. The Table 5-10 addresses the performance of these sectors (as going with the flexibility of labor market) as with their shares in GDP of Vietnam. Totally, the two sectors make up 62 % of GDP in 2005 and/or in 2016 as compared to 38% and 29% of the state sector in the same time points. Outside the state sector, the household business (as informed of mostly without labor contract/informal sector) interestingly keeps it's largest share over the years as comparing to the shares of private and FDI (as informed as mostly of contract labor based/formal sector).

Table 5-10 Gross Domestic Product at Current Prices by Types of Ownership by Types of Ownership, Items and Year (share, %)

	2005	2006	2007	2008	2009	2010	2011	2012	2013	2014	2015	2016
Total	100	100	100	100	100	100	100	100	100	100	100	100
State	37.62	36.69	35.35	35.07	34.72	29.34	29.01	29.39	29.01	28.73	28.69	28.81
Non- State	47.22	47.24	47.69	47.5	47.97	42.96	43.87	44.62	43.52	43.33	43.22	42.56
Collective	6.65	6.39	6.1	5.91	5.8	3.99	3.98	4	4.03	4.04	4.01	3.92
Private	8.51	8.98	9.69	10.23	10.46	6.9	7.34	7.97	7.78	7.79	7.88	8.21
Household	32.06	31.87	31.9	31.36	31.71	32.07	32.55	32.65	31.71	31.5	31.33	30.43
Foreign investment sector	15.16	16.07	16.96	17.43	17.31	15.15	15.66	16.04	17.36	17.89	18.07	18.59

Non- State = Collective + Private + Household

Source: GSO, 2017

3.1.1 Wages and Productivity - Current trend

The surge of labors demanded by non-state sectors and FDI since 1986 does not likely go in hand with the rise in income/salary levels for these ownership sectors. The sluggish of average wage over the years could be attribute to the slow improvement of basis salaries and interaction of labor demand and labor supply (as the businessman seems to depress the salary level to minimize production/business costs). With current data available with respect to the wages, one could see that labor market in Vietnam has shown a significant divergence amongst different ownership participants in the domestic economy, recently.

Regarding to the private sectors, labors/workers in FDI enterprises have much better monthly wage level as compared to those in non-state sector, in average number (see Table 5-11). Average wages in non-state sector is remarkably stable for the last three quarters of 2017 and fourth quarter of 2016, whereas there has a down trend for the FDI sector in the same period. However, current data indicates a convergence in monthly rates for labors working in state sector and FDI sectors for these quarters. It could be stated that the well-being's labors (as measuring by the average monthly earnings of wage) of non-state enterprises are left behind the other two sectors as years to come (see the detail in Table 5-11 for trend of this divergence).

It is also noticeable that there exists an inequality in monthly wage levels as regrading to gender. The information reveals the fact that male workers are monthly paid substantially higher that female workers, and that is true for not only by state sector but also for non-state and FDI sectors for the last quarters of 2016-2017. The gap is seriously widening for the non-state sector.

Regionally, private sectors has also been encountered as with a huge divergence in average earnings as we could see the difference from urban and rural division through the quarters (see Table 5-11). For both of non-state and FDI sectors, workers in urban area have significantly higher compensations than those in rural area. The Vietnamese government has tabulated the basic salary time to time in the manner that the level of these salaries would depend on the level of economic development in different areas within the economy; and basic salary can be divided into ordinal levels from low to high in line with economic development levels. As required by law that the employee has to pay their labors with wage of at least equal to basis salary, the ladder of basic salaries system might be one of the causes to produce the gap in average monthly earnings of wage between urban and rural areas.

Table 5-11 Average Monthly Earnings of Wage workers aged 15 and over by Sex, Urban/Rural, Employment Status (in thousand VND)

	Q4/2016			Q1/2017			Q2/2017			Q2/2017		
	Total	M	F	Total	M	F	Total	M	F	Total	M	F
Total	5080	5245	4855	5507	5715	5225	5202	5482	4821	5364	5632	4999
1 State	5823	6220	5403	6443	6882	5965	5996	6394	5569	6154	6505	5781
2 Non-state	4612	4879	4141	4923	5184	4464	4801	5116	4238	4963	5277	4401
3 FDI	6364	6326	6384	6869	7724	6446	5888	6666	5507	6052	6794	5684
URBAN	6031	6262	5749	6587	6950	6145	6084	6497	5577	6200	6625	5687
1 State	6502	7056	5900	7336	7947	6674	6693	7268	6074	6841	7391	6249
2 Non-state	5468	5836	4931	5966	6283	5499	5691	6053	5146	5774	6172	5195
3 FDI	7928	7010	8467	7804	8724	7243	6484	7329	5976	6744	7605	6236
RURAL	4309	4490	4035	4661	4822	4425	4534	4771	4185	4719	4932	4401
1 State	4880	5021	4738	5206	5414	4979	5047	5203	4881	5222	5289	5152
2 Non-state	4029	4300	3478	4244	4543	3649	4242	4585	3555	4434	4763	3761
3 FDI	5197	5730	4951	6235	6865	5966	5492	6111	5230	5611	6168	5365

Note: It is not included those people aged 15 and over who were currently not residing in Vietnam (not regarded as the respondent for individual questionnaire) Source: GSO, 2017

Regarding to the productivity, the transitional economy in Vietnam points out an alarming trend for the private sector against state sector. As addressing above, the share of private sector (in non-state enterprises, household enterprises, FDI enterprises, cooperatives) is significantly higher than that of state sector in the employment structure over the years, however most of forms in private sector (non-state enterprises, household enterprises, cooperatives) has performed a very low productivity and low wage earnings as compared to the state sector. This gap seems to be wider for the year to come.

It is evidenced that amongst the forms of non-state enterprises, private enterprises stood in the bottom as regarding to the labor productivity for the period 2011-2014 ("Alarming of labor productivity in non-state enterprises", Nguyen Van Thuat, Review of Investment& Security, 2017).

IV. Experiences of South Korea

1. Brief history on labor market policy

1.1. 1960~1986: Sprouting Period and Developing Period

In the 1960s, the growth strategy of South Korea based on government-led economic development policies could be characterized as an export-dependent model based on cheap labor(MOEL 2006;2008, Kim, 2005).

The beginning of South Korea's economic development was from 1962, which has made great strides through the first five-year economic development plan. In the 1960s, the government primarily supported export industries and large corporations while aggressively transforming growth strategies from export-oriented to export-led policies(MOEL 2008, Park et al. 2016). As the five-year economic development plan achieved goal higher than expected, it has become a keystone for economic sectors.

Growth was achieved through the introduction of foreign investment and exports, but low wages were inevitable. Thus, so-called the Miracle of the Han River as a basic setting for the growth strategy was a mixture of light and shade. In other words, the economic performance was made possible by the sweat and sacrifice of workers who had to endure a harsh environment. In this period, the labor force needed for economic development was supplied in a timely manner to raise the price competitiveness, and at the same time to raise the quality of export goods by cultivating excellent functional manpower(Kim, 2005, Park et al. 2016). In this consequence, labor administration was forced to concentrate on supplementary or complementary roles to support the nationwide economic growth policies, while its essential functions such as protection of labor rights were shrunk and dwarfed.

One of the characteristics of the labor movement in the 1960s was that it was difficult for workers to fulfill their demands. What is more, corporate labor control measures were gradually matured and intensified, while the government's labor restraint policy has also been strengthened. As it enters the late 1960s, the nature of workers' resistance movement was limited to extreme struggle for the right to survival. This phenomenon is indicative of the explosive and violent nature of the lower-class labor movement in the 1970s. In addition to economic ones, political struggles were difficult to achieve due to strengthened objective constraints, weakened bargaining power and support from existing workers, and last but not least, lack of solidarity(MOEL 2008).

In the 1970s, a structural vicious cycle of inflation and widening deficit of the international balance of payments coincided. In addition, as social and economic contradictions in the development process continued due to the overall recession of the world economy, slowing of employment growth, problems of insolvent corporations, and bribery bonds, the government issued an emergency financial order on August 3, 1972(PRL).

From 1960 to 1972, the rate of population turnover exceeded 3% and the labor market turnover rate exceeded 8% due to steady economic growth(large surplus labor force) and rapid economic growth of 7.1% per annum. In the 1980s, the average annual population growth rate was 240,000 (annual growth rate of 7%). (See Table 5-12)

Table 5-12 Trend of Economically Active Population (Unit: thousand persons,%)

Years	working age population	labor force	employed	Unemployed
1963	14,551	8,230	7,563	667 (8.1%)
1972	18,819	10,865	10,379	486 (4.5%)
1973	19,490	11,389	10,942	447 (3.9%)
1979	23,787	14,142	13,602	540 (3.8%)
1980	24,463	14,431	13,683	748 (5.2%)
1986	28,225	16,116	15,505	611 (3.8%)

Source: MOEL, 2006.

The changes of labor policy in the period of the Park Chung Hee regime, from May 1961 to October 1979, can be divided into two stages. During the primary stage, from 1962 until the declaration of the state of emergency in late 1971, the constitution was revised in full, and the Labor Relations Act was revised, the Labor Office was newly established, and laws related to individual labor relations, labor market, and social welfare were improved. The secondary stage began at the end of 1971 and lasted until 1979 when labor policies changed drastically according to the National Emergency Declaration and the Restoration of the Constitution. The Labor Union Act, the Labor Disputes Adjustment Act, and the Labor Relations Commission Act were amended to expand the scope of public service projects and administrative intervention in labor relations was strengthened(PRL).

From the mid-1970s, the structure of export industry centered on the light industry has changed rapidly to that centered on heavy industry(Park et al. 2016). The linkage between Korean economy and the global economic system has been strengthened gradually, and the growing foreign debt has increased pressure on the repayment of principal and interest, causing the government to focus on the attraction of direct investment, which lessens burden for repayment of principal in terms of foreign investment(MOEL 2006, 2008).

During the Chun Doo Hwan regime, from December 1979 to October 1987, the government actively intervened throughout the labor union. In particular, military authority tried to oppress the labor movement through the purification policy on the labor system and the revision of the labor-related laws. The labor-related laws, such as the Labor Union Act, the Labor Union Council Act, were revised or enacted, the Labor Policy Council was established as an organization to control the labor movement, and the Labor Office was promoted to the Ministry of Labor to strengthen labor administration. Due to these repressive labor policies of the military power, the labor movement in Korea was stagnant until the appeasement phase in 1983. After the phase, the labor groups and related organizations pushed for the revision of the Labor Relations Act, and the labor movement was revitalized with the enactment of the Minimum Wage Act. After the 1987 labor struggle, the government began to formulate new labor control strategies and amended the "Trade Union Act", "Labor Relations Adjustment Act" and "Labor-Management Council Act" (PRL).

During the 1960s to 1980s, economic conditions and labor-management relations were characterized by complaints accumulated during a high-growth period, poor working conditions, low wage problems caused by low wages, and insufficient labor policies. In this period, the government revised the collective Labor Relations Act, rather than rationally responding to changes in the labor movement and union members' dissatisfaction, thereby compromising the institutional influence of collective bargaining through the labor-management council system(MOEL 2006;2008, Kim, 2005).

However, at this time, disputes have begun to be intensified surrounding some large corporations, and the labor disputes have become politicized beyond the level of labor issues, such as being linked and diffused to regional movements. The accumulated complaints of the workers and the growth of labor movements in the field played a multiplicative role in the labor disputes of the next period(MOEL 2006;2008, PRL).

Over the past 40 years, the status of union organizations and the number of union members has shown distinct characteristics over time.

In the first period (1963 ~ 1979), the number of union members increased from 220,000 in 1963 to 1.9 million in 1979. In the second period (1980 ~ 1986), the number of union members decreased by 140,000 in 1980 due to the forced dissolution of industrial union regional branches and forced labor unionization by companies.

The third period (1987 ~ 1989), the labor union movement was activated in 1987, and the labor union movement was activated. From 1.40 million in 1986 to 1. 127 million in 1987, 1.71 million in 1988 and 1.93 million in the 1989 Year.

In the fourth period (1990 ~ 1998), the number of union members decreased to 1.40 million in 1998, peaking at 1.93 million in 1989. The fifth period (since 1999) is the period of stagnation when the number of union members who have decreased throughout the 1990s has increased temporarily. In 2003 ~ 2005, the number of union members was between 151,000 and 50,000. In 2007, the number of union members was between 173,000 and 80,000. (See Table 5-13)

Table 5-13 Number of Members and Organization Rate (Unit: thousand persons,%)

Years	Number of workers			Number of labor union			union density			Female ratio	
	Total	Man	Female	Total	Man	Female	Total	Man	Female	Workers	labor union
1963	2,383	1,810	574	224	174	50	9.4	9.6	8.7	24.1	22.3
1964	2,363	1,813	550	272	211	60	11.5	11.6	10.9	23.3	22.1
1965	2,609	2,014	594	302	235	66	11.6	11.7	11.1	22.8	21.9
1966	2,780	2,128	652	327	251	76	11.8	11.8	11.7	23.5	23.2
1967	3,040	2,310	729	378	287	91	12.4	12.4	12.5	24	24.1
1968	3,400	2,520	880	413	310	103	12.1	12.3	11.7	25.9	24.9
1969	3,547	2,582	965	445	333	111	12.5	12.9	11.5	27.2	25
1970	3,746	2,737	1,006	473	358	115	12.6	13.1	11.5	26.9	24.4
1971	3,923	2,879	1,045	497	373	125	12.7	12.9	11.9	26.6	25.1
1972	4,005	2,957	1,047	515	381	134	12.9	12.9	12.8	26.1	26.1
1973	4,153	3,008	1,145	548	392	156	13.2	13	13.6	27.6	28.5
1974	4,444	3,252	1,192	656	463	193	14.8	14.2	16.2	26.8	29.4
1975	4,751	3,499	1,252	750	509	241	15.8	14.5	19.3	26.4	32.2
1976	5,140	3,670	1,470	846	559	286	16.5	15.2	19.5	28.6	33.8
1977	5,714	4,074	1,640	955	635	320	16.7	15.6	19.5	28.7	33.5
1978	6,242	4,373	1,869	1,055	697	358	16.9	15.9	19.1	29.9	33.9
1979	6,479	4,467	2,012	1,088	724	364	16.8	16.2	18.1	31.1	33.5
1980	6,464	4,415	2,049	948	600	348	14.7	13.6	17	31.7	36.7
1981	6,605	4,522	2,082	967	628	338	14.6	13.9	16.3	31.5	35
1982	6,839	4,598	2,241	984	633	351	14.4	13.8	15.7	32.8	35.7
1983	7,170	4,749	2,421	1,010	673	336	14.1	14.2	13.9	33.8	33.3
1984	7,631	5,080	2,551	1,011	684	327	13.2	13.5	12.8	33.4	32.4
1985	8,104	5,295	2,809	1,004	692	312	12.4	13.1	11.1	34.7	31.1
1986	8,433	5,471	2,962	1,036	725	311	12.3	13.2	10.5	35.1	30.1
1987	9,191	5,872	3,318	1,267	900	367	13.8	15.3	11.1	36.1	29
1988	9,610	6,143	3,467	1,707	1,232	475	17.8	20.1	13.7	36.1	27.8
1989	10,390	6,440	3,950	1,932	1,402	530	18.6	21.8	13.4	38	27.4
1990	10,950	6,759	4,190	1,887	1,385	502	17.2	20.5	12	38.3	26.6
1991	11,699	7,260	4,438	1,803	1,342	462	15.4	18.5	10.4	37.9	25.6
1992	11,910	7,404	4,507	1,735	1,324	411	14.6	17.9	9.1	37.8	23.7

1993	11,944	7,427	4,516	1,667	1,276	392	14	17.2	8.7	37.8	23.5
1994	12,479	7,724	4,755	1,659	1,286	373	13.3	16.6	7.9	38.1	22.5
1995	12,899	7,975	4,924	1,615	1,254	361	12.5	15.7	7.3	38.2	22.3
1996	13,200	8,104	5,096	1,599	1,260	339	12.1	15.5	6.6	38.6	21.2
1997	13,404	8,145	5,259	1,484	1,194	290	11.1	14.7	5.5	39.2	19.5
1998	12,296	7,551	4,745	1,402	1,148	254	11.4	15.2	5.3	38.6	18.1
1999	12,663	7,639	5,025	1,481	1,173	307	11.7	15.4	6.1	39.7	20.8
2000	13,360	7,963	5,397	1,527	1,221	306	11.4	15.3	5.7	40.4	20
2001	13,659	8,050	5,609	1,569	1,263	305	11.5	15.7	5.4	41.1	19.5
2002	14,181	8,325	5,857	1,538	1,306	300	10.8	15.7	5.1	41.3	19.5
2003	14,402	8,432	5,970	1,550	1,223	327	10.8	14.5	5.5	41.5	21.1
2004	14,894	8,657	6,237	1,537	1,212	325	10.3	14	5.2	41.9	21.1
2005	15,185	8,794	6,391	1,506	1,183	324	9.9	13.4	5.1	42.1	21.5

Source: Statistics Korea, 'Economically Active Population Survey', Ministry of Employment and Labor 'Status of Labor Union'.

1.2. 1987~1997: Advancing Period

The 1980s was a time when structural problems formed and accumulated in the process of high economic growth during the 1960s and 1970s acutely came to the fore(MOEL 2006;2008, Kim, 2005). In particular, 1987 was the year of the largest labor resistance movement in Korea. The number of labor disputes that occurred until October 5th after the 6.29 Declaration (amending the constitution to provide for the direct election of the president) amounted to 3,479 cases(MOEL 2008, Kim, 2005). Labor disputes that occurred after the 6.29 Declaration are largely classified into three categories: wage increase, union establishment and retirement, and improvement of working conditions.

The first characteristic of disputes at this time is that they exceeded legitimate procedures or limitations. This reflects that path to resolution of conflicts by legal procedures was blocked. Second is that labor disputes are raised beyond the guidance and control of union organizations. In other words, it took the form of Wildcat Strike (a strike by some unionists against the union leadership) which indicates that a union was either unorganized or dysfunctional, even if it was organized. The third is that the struggle for solidarity by region, chaebol group and industry has become a major form of dispute. Forms of solidarity strike by region were demonstrated as transport workers' general strike in Ulsan, Gwangju, Busan, and Anyang. Solidarity strikes in the chaebol group including a strike at four regional workplaces of the Daewoo Heavy Industries & Construction, Ulsan Hyundai Group, especially the one through Hyundai Union Council became a new form of dispute in the Korean labor movement(MOEL 2006;2008, Kim, 2005).

The impacts of labor disputes on the characteristics of a labor movement in South Korea during this decade are as follows. First, South Korea established the ideological basis of the full-scale labor movement and changed the nature of the movement into a change-oriented one. Second, despite its progress in the late 1980s, Korea did not have a unified system in terms of organizational form and capacity; organizational capacity was neither stable nor widely gathered. In this sense, there was a limit to the organizational scope and capacity of the enterprise union; conflict between workers within the existing unions was part of the cause. Third, in terms of aspects and characteristics of disputes, it gradually shifted from the formerly spontaneous, isolated, and decentralized form to systematic and planned struggle; moreover, political struggles linked to the demand for democratization unfolded. These changes in the nature of labor movement can be seen as a result of increased consciousness and capacity of the labor movement. In this way, the labor movement in the first half of the 1980s can be regarded as a preparatory period for the qualitative transition and enhancement of the labor movement in the late 1980s.

Policies before the phase of 1987 had been pursuing changes in a comparatively small frame throughout industrialization. Prior to 1987, government policies placed priority on economic growth, while labor policies were largely governed by growth policies. In addition, a solution to labor disputes has been prepared in terms of national security and social stability, and thus has not provided a clear vision and policy framework for the balanced development of labor-management relations(MOEL 2006;2008).

A major change has taken place since 1987. The characteristics of labor relations and policies of the 6th Republic (1988-1992) can be explained by the distribution of the benefits of growth. The transition from industrialization process to information age has led to the start of new growth strategies and the establishment of democratic and autonomous labor-management relations. As the base of labor movement expanded and the forces organized and activated, conditions for equalization of labor-management relations were established. Inexperienced labor-management negotiations and immature problem-solving efforts at the beginning of this period became a stepping stone for enhanced labor-management relations.

In the labor market, the average unemployment rate is 2.4% (7.8% of the economic growth rate) and full employment. (1987-1997)(See Table 5-14)

Table 5-14 Trend of Economically Active Population (Unit: thousand persons,%)

Years	working age population	labor force	Employed	Unemployed
1987	28,955	16,873	16,354	519 (3.1%)
1997	34,851	21,782	21,214	568 (2.6%)

Source: MOEL, 2006.

Meanwhile, the Roh Tae Woo government pursued the revision and enactment of the Labor Relations Act and the flexible labor market policy, and this series of policy efforts were handed over to the Kim Young Sam government. Since the beginning of 1997, when large corporations have been bankrupt and the economic crisis deepened, the Kim Young Sam government applied for a bail-out to the IMF. As a result, the introduction of the restructuring and dismissal system took a turn for the worse, and the tripartite committee was established to discuss these labor market changes in the Kim Dae Jung administration(PRL).

1.3. After 1998: Period of Ordeal

In South Korea, various system reforms and revisions of Labor Relations Act were promoted in order to improve labor flexibility before and after the financial crisis in 1997(MOEL 2008, PRL).

The Kim Dae Jung administration has promoted strong policies for labor market flexibility from the beginning of the ruling period, despite the strong opposition from the labor union(PRL). In December 1997, restructuring of the entire industry was required under the IMF management system, in which flexibility of labor market and strengthening of employment insurance system were included. On January 15, 1998, the tripartite committee was established. On Feb. 6, 1998, layoffs and dispatching work systems were introduced in accordance with the '2. 6 Social Agreement', and the Social Pact to Overcome the foreign exchange Crisis was concluded in the next day. And the Labor Relations Act revised on February 20 as follow-up measures. Main contents are as follows: In the revision of the Labor Standards Act, employees are obliged to be dismissed when there is an urgent administrative necessity including transfer, merger, and takeover. In case of dismissal, 60 days before dismissal, the method and standard of dismissal are to be notified to the representative of the workers in advance. Employers' obligation to notify the Minister of Labor when dismissing a certain number of people or more, and duty of effort to recall redundant workers were introduced. In the case of labor union and labor relations adjustment laws, the period of notice for unilateral termination of collective agreement was extended from 3 months to 6. In addition, the Dispatched Worker Protection Act was enacted to legalize dispatched work so that the employer could operate the workforce more flexibly(MOEL 2006;2008, PRL).

There has also been a restructuring of personnel based on quantitative flexibility, with no exceptions in three areas: finance, business, and the public sector. This structural reform was carried out by active intervention of the government, not through a rational process by consensus and coordination between labor and management for searching alternatives. The restructuring of the financial and corporate sectors was led by the Financial Supervisory Commission, while public sector restructuring was achieved through the management innovation, budgeting guidelines, and the privatization of public enterprises by the Ministry of Planning and Budget.

The reform of the financial structure was the key to the restructuring of the financial institutions. During the first phase of the restructuring, numerous financial workers were dismissed and the vigorous resistance of financial workers ensued. Public sector restructuring has been promoted through organization and personnel restructuring of public enterprises and affiliated organizations. Like the banks, after restructuring the public corporations and the affiliated institutions, new employees were hired as non-regular workers. In the name of the management innovation plan for public corporations, the welfare system has been reduced; the performance-based pay system, the introduction of the annual salary and the contract system, and the abolition of the severance payment progress system(PRL).

The labor market situation during the foreign exchange crisis is shown as the number of employed persons and the number of economically active people '97. (Economic growth rate 4.4%)(See Table 5-15).

Table 5-15 Trend of Economically Active Population (Unit: thousand persons,%)

Years	working age population	labor force	Employed	Unemployed
1998	35,347	21,428	19,938	1,490 (7.0%)
2002	36,963	22,877	22,169	708 (3.1%)

Source: MOEL, 2006.

The Kim Dae Jung government's labor market softening policy fundamentally changed the labor market structure of Korea, which had been based on high growth and low unemployment. As the proportion of the long-term unemployed increased due to mass unemployment after the foreign exchange crisis, Korea's labor market structure has changed to a low-growth and high-unemployment structure.

Table 5-16 Labor Market Policy in South Korea

Division	Sprouting Period	Developing Period	Advancing Period	Period of Ordeal
	1961-1975	1976-1986	1987-1997	1998-
Government era	Park Chung Hee Government 1st stage: 1962-1971 2nd stage: 1971-1975	Transition period (1979-1980) Chun Doo Hwan Government (1980-1987)	Roh Tae Woo Government (1988-1993) Kim Young Sam Government (1993-1998)	Kim Dae Jung Government (1998-2002)
Labor Supply	Unlimited	Limited	Shortage	Shortage (due to low birthrate/aging)

Labor Demand	Sudden increase	Increase	Slow increase	Rapid decrease
Status of Labor Demand	High unemployment eased	Low unemployment	Manpower shortage Imbalance of supply and demand	High unemployment
Main Policy Tasks	• Solve excessive unemployment	• Train workforce for heavy and chemical industries	• Mobilize idle labor	• Overcome unemployment crisis, Ease youth unemployment • Protect non-regular workers
Main Policy Regulations	• Employment Security Law • Vocational Training Law	• Framework Act on Vocational Training • Vocational Training Promotion Fund Act	• Act on Equal Employment • Act on Employment Promotion for the Disabled • Act on Employment Promotion for the Aged • Employment Insurance Act • Framework Act on Employment Policy • Act on the Encouragement of Technical Skills	
Main Administrative Organizations	• Raise to the status of Employment and Labor Administration • Create Employment Security Bureau and Vocational Training Bureau	• Raise to the status of Ministry of Labor • Create Human Resources Development Service	• Enforce employment insurance • Create Employment Policy Office	• Change its name to Ministry of Employment and Labor

Source: MOEL 2006, Presidential Record Laboratories Labor Policies Outline of Labor Policies by President; http://www.pa.go.kr/research/contents/policy/index08.jsp

2. Current standing and discussions

2.1. Changes in labor policy

The Act on the Employment of Foreign Workers was enacted on Aug. 2003 since Roh Moo Hyun government was established(PRL). This was a plan to systematically introduce foreign workers and solve the manpower shortage of SMEs. In September 2003, the Labor Standards Act was amended to shorten legal working hours to 40 hours per week. The main amendment was to extend the flexible period of working hours within three months from the current one month to enable the flexible use of working hours. Employers have been able to grant leave in lieu of paying wages for overtime work, night work and holiday work, in agreement with the employee representative. Monthly paid vacation was abolished and the burden of employers was reduced by making the paid menstrual leave (a day per month) unpaid for the female workers(PRL).

On January 27, 2005, the provisions of the Article 34 of the existing Labor Standards Act were collected and the Employee Retirement Benefit Assurance Act was enacted and a new retirement pension system was introduced. As a result, retirement allowance system, operated mainly with lump sum payments, was converted into retirement pension system and the retirement benefit system was extended to workplaces with less than four regular employees. In addition, the Act on the Establishment and Operation of Labor Unions of Public Officials was enacted on January 28, 2006, stipulating matters related to the establishment and management of labor unions, collective bargaining and dispute settlement procedures(See Appendix Table 1).

In the amendment of the Labor Standards Act on March 31, 2005, the minimum age of employment was increased to the age at the end of compulsory education, and the protection of women workers was strengthened by adding maternity leave, childcare leave and so on. In the amendment of the Labor Standards Act on May 31, 2005, female workers who were or are pregnant, in case of miscarriage or stillbirth, obtained the right to take leave after 16 weeks of pregnancy upon her claims, the first 60 days of which shall be paid. If the state pays for post-maternity leave benefits in accordance with the Equal Employment Act, the employer shall not be liable for the payment of wages within the limits of such amount(See Appendix Table 1).

On December 30, 2006, the Labor Union and Labor Relations Adjustment Act was amended to abolish the arbitration system, which has been pointed out as limiting the right to dispute. Since January 2008, the mandatory maintenance system has been implemented. Accordingly, while it is possible to strike legitimately in essential public service projects, maintenance work should be maintained at a certain level during the strike period lest the public interest be seriously hindered.

The Labor Standards Act amended on January 26, 2007, removed criminal penalties for unfair dismissal, but imposed penalties for violating the Labor Relations Commission's mandate and the remedies ordered. It also shortened the notice period of dismissal from 60 days to 50 days. In addition, if new hires are recruited in the same business within three years, employers are legally required to hire the dismissed workers.

On December 21, 2006, the Act on the Protection of Temporary and Part-time Workers was enacted and the Labor-Management-Board Act was also amended. The Non-regular Worker Protection Act has banned unreasonable discriminatory treatment for non-regular workers such as fixed-term, short-term, dispatched workers and has introduced procedures for discrimination correction through the labor committee. In addition, if the employer continues to use the dispatched worker for more than two years, he / she is obliged to employ the dispatched worker directly(See Appendix Table 1).

The Roh administration proposed to strengthen the position of the Korea Tripartite Commission under the banner of "social unity of labor relations". The Fixed-term Employment Act has been introduced, according to which dispatch of workers were restricted to specific categories (i.e. the positive system) and the employers should hire employees directly when the dispatch period exceeds two years. However, inequalities such as the expansion of irregular employment and unemployment have spread to the labor market.

Table 5-17 Changes in Labor Policies by Period and Government After 1998

	1998-2002	2003-2007	2008-2012	2013-2017
Government era	Kim Dae Jung Government	Roh Moo Hyun Government	Lee Myung Bak Government	Park Geun Hye Government
Characteristics	Strong labor market flexibility	Strengthening the tripartite committee	Establishment of the rule of law on industrial relations	Introduction of temporary workers goal management system
Policy	• Financial, corporate, and public sectors: Quantitative flexibility based on personnel restructuring • Financial and corporate restructuring: led by the Financial Supervisory Commission • Public sector restructuring reform: Management	• The first measure by the government • Promoted the unified standardization of all Temporary workers the public sector • Declaration of the Indefinite Contract Work of usual and continuous work • Core / periphery of outsourcing business	• Increasing the flexibility of the labor market • Establishment of Labor Relations Law • Revision of laws related to plural unions and union full-Supplementing Temporary worker related systems to improve flexibility of fixed-term work and dispatch work • Improvement of advanced labor-	• Establish measures to stabilize employment and improve treatment of school accountants

	innovation / budgeting guidelines of the Ministry of Planning and Budget, privatization of public enterprises • Public institutions: performance-based pay system, annual salary system, employment contract system, severance pay		management relations system • Wages, working hours, employment flexibility • Reexamination of the labor regulation front is presented as concrete action plan.	
Status	• Early repayment of the IMF bailout in 2000 • Government-led comprehensive government unemployment measures (2 ~ 7 trillion annual input)			
Main Policy Tasks	• Discussion on improvement of labor standards system based on labor market changes • Development of wage claim guarantee system • Expanding system of employee welfare fund in enterprise • Activation of employee stock ownership plan • Expansion of support for prevention of industrial accidents at small and	• Enactment bill on Protection of fixed-term and short-term workers, etc. • Revision to the Act • Protection of Dispatched Workers, etc. • Amendment to the Labor Relations Commission Act	• Mobilize idle labor	• Establishment of employment contracts for Indefinite Contract Work • Promoting the introduction of duty-based contracts for Indefinite Contract Work

	medium-sized plants • Promotion of active unemployment measures and its problems • Enlargement of social safety net through substantiation of employment insurance			

Source: Presidential Record Laboratories, Labor Policies Outline of Labor Policies by President; http://www.pa.go.kr/research/contents/policy/index08.jsp

2.2. Characteristics of Public and Private Sector Policies

In order to overcome the economic crisis in the Kim Dae-jung administration, non-regular workers became widespread with the emergence of flexible employment policy. The Korean government has revised the Labor Laws several times in terms of labor management, and has enacted a law on the protection of short-term workers in 2007.

In the public sector - central administrative agencies, public institutions and enterprises, local governments, and educational institutions - irregular workers also appeared with the aim of providing jobs. The types of irregular workers in the public sector are diversified into direct employment and indirect employment (short-term, service, and dispatch).

Currently, the government is pursuing policies to transform irregular workers to regular ones to remedy for the vicious cycle of anxiety, discrimination, and low-wage work. The labor unions are working on organizational innovation and job creation policies in the crisis of organization.

Table 5-18 Characteristics of Public and Private Sector Policies

1998 ~ 2000	• Struggle against large-scale dismissal-based restructuring - Period of quantitative restructuring based on public sector restructuring after economic crisis - Began mass layoffs centering on lower and temporary workers - Struggle of Korea Telecom temporary workers Union
2001 ~ 2003	• Struggle against discrimination of temporary workers centered on budget control - Adoption of temporary jobs at all times by constant structural reform system - Various types of temporary workers appear - Damage to the wages and working conditions of temporary workers due to budgetary control - Struggle for temporary workers the Korea Labor Welfare Corporation
2004 ~ 2006	• Struggle over the direction of temporary measures in the public sector - In 2004, in the public sector temporary measures, some civil servants - The timing of the struggle against the systemization of the fixed-term system - Struggle for temporary workers the Human Resources Development Service of Korea (HRD Korea)
2007 ~ 2013	• Institutional provision of temporary workers the public sector - Total labor cost accounting for budget control Outsourcing and weapon contracting as public sector temporary measures - Free use of temporary worker through passing through period method - Mass production of new types of temporary jobs - Struggle for temporary workers the Korea Sports Promotion Foundation
2008 ~ 2017	• Employment Promotion Measures - 2008 Youth Employment Promotion Measures - Comprehensive measures to overcome economic difficulties - 2009 Work sharing plan - 2010 1-10 National Employment Strategy Conference - 2011 Young man making tomorrow 2nd project (1st 2010) - 2013 Young man tailored job measures - 2014 Step by step employment of youth employment measures Capacity-based society - 2015 Youth Employment Cliff Cutting Comprehensive Measures - Younger Overseas Employment Promotion Measures - 2016 Strengthening linkages between youth and women employment - 2017 Youth Employment Measures Supplement - 2017 job commitment - 2018 Youth Employment Measures

Source: As cited from PPIP 2014 and Ministry of Employment and Labor 2014

3. Labor Market Characteristics in South Korea

3.1 Characteristics of Labor Market: Labor Market Change and Labor Demand in 1980-90s

In the 1980s and 1990s, South Korea had a 2.4 percent annual unemployment rate and a 7.8 percent economic growth rate. This period was not only a time of full employment with three booms but also the beginning of structural problems such as a slowdown in population growth, a declining population growth rate, an aging population, an increase in the number of highly educated workforce, manufacturing employment shrinking, labor shortage in small business, and job insecurity of youth.

The labor supply and demand structure has also changed; in the 1980s, manufacturing led the increase in employment, while in the 1990s, social overhead capital and other services led the increase in employment.

In the 1980s, the number of employed workers in the manufacturing industry continued to increase at an average annual rate of 7.0%, but in the 1990s, the proportion of employee in the manufacturing sector dropped from 27.8% in 1989 to 23.6% in 1994(0.8% annual decrease).

In the 1980s, the number of workers in social overhead capital and other service industries increased by an average annual rate of 5.1%. The increase in the service demand in the 1990s increased to 6.2%, and as a result, the share of social overhead capital and other service increased from 47.0% to 62.3% in 1994.

Table 5-19 Annual Average Growth Rate of Employees and Employment Share

	growth rate of employees (Annual average)		employment share			
	1983-89	1990-'94	1983	1987	1991	1994
Total	3.3	2.5	100.0	100.0	100.0	100.0
Agriculture, forestry, and fishery	-3.7	-4.4	29.7	21.9	16.5	13.8
mining	6.8	-1.0	23.3	28.1	27.2	23.9
manufacturing	7.0	-0.8	22.5	27.0	26.8	23.6
SOC and others	5.1	6.2	47.0	50.0	56.3	62.3
Building	5.9	9.3	5.6	5.6	8.3	8.9

Source: Statistics Korea, Annual Report on Economically Active Population

Professional and clerical workers grew by an annual average of 6 ~ 7% due to the increase of highly educated manpower and growth of technology / information-intensive industries, while the average annual growth rate of production workers slowed to 1% from 6.7% of the 1980s.

Table 5-20 Changes in ratio of Employee by Occupation (%)

	1983	1987	1991	1994	Average annual increasing rate	
					1983-89	1990-94
Total	100.0	100.0	100.0	100.0	3.3	2.5
Professional, technical, and administrative position	6.1	7.5	9.2	10.3	8.7	7.7
clerical work	10.5	11.6	13.3	15.0	6.2	6.0
Service and sales	25.5	26.0	26.1	28.2	3.1	5.4
Agriculture, forestry, and fishery	29.5	23.4	16.4	14.6	-3.7	-4.7
Technician	28.4	31.6	35.0	31.9	6.7	1.0
Simple labor						

* *there was a time series discontinuity since 1994, because of the reorganization of the occupational classification*

Source: Statistics Korea, Annual Report on Economically Active Population

The employment rate by occupation status shows the annual average growth rate of employees has decreased from 6.4% in the 1980s to 3.4% in the 1990s due to the increase in wage burden and the contraction of the production base of light industry. Nevertheless, there was still a high rate of increase compared to other employees such as self-employed and unpaid family workers

Table 5-21 Changes in the share of Employees by Occupation Status (%)

	1983	1987	1991	1994	Annual growth rate	
					1983-89	1990-94
Total	100.0	100.0	100.0	100.0	3.3	2.5
self-employed	33.8	30.5	28.1	27.8	0.6	1.8
unpaid family worker	16.8	13.3	10.9	10.2	-2.2	-0.9
Employee	49.4	56.2	61.0	62.0	6.4	3.4
. permanent/temporary	41.4	46.9	51.2	53.1	6.3	4.0
. day laborer	8.0	9.3	9.8	8.9	7.0	0.5
Labor stability*	83.8	83.4	83.9	85.6	–	–

** (permanent and temporary workers)/(employees)x100*

Source: Statistics Korea, Annual Report on Economically Active Population

In terms of employment policy, the establishment of the minimum wage system('86), the Employment Promotion Act for the Disabled('90), the Employment Promotion Act for the Elderly('91), the Employment Policy Act ('93), the Employment Insurance Act ('95), and the Vocational Training Promotion Act('97) have founded the basis of active labor market policy.

3.2. Characteristics of Labor Market

Since the 1990s, as the labor market and management environment has changed drastically, the changes that take place in the production process of enterprises are promoting diversification of employment and working styles. Technological progress has led to an asymmetrical substitution of the labor demand of a firm according to its function and skill. The change speed of the labor market environment is so rapid that the contents of regular full-time employment relationships cannot keep up with it flexibly. Therefore, there is an increasing preference for outsourcing part of the production process, retaining only core employees with high skills and creative talent, and hiring non-regular workers who can easily adjust their employment.

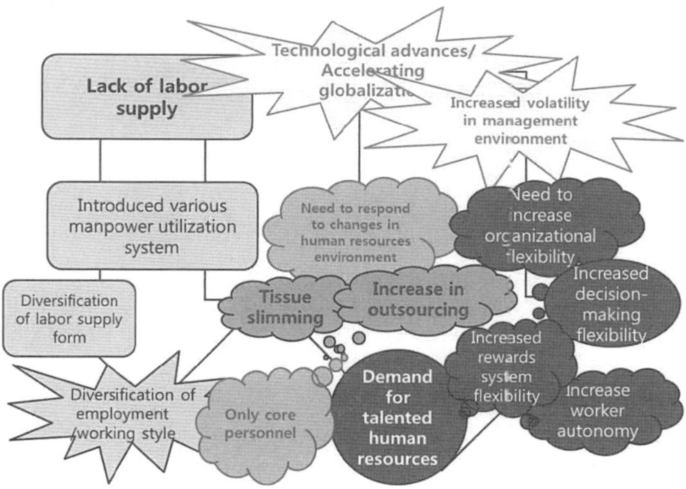

Figure 5-6 South Korea's Labor Flexibility: Employment Type Characteristics

Not only changes in the employment structure, but the work environment also transform to more flexible one. There are increasing cases of work and study at the same time, and the number of discretionary work that is difficult to distinguish between working and rest time is increasing, while working hours in offices and workplaces were significantly reduced. There is also a change in the compensation system, which is expanding contracts related to non-typical work and compensation. The establishment of an intra-company network using information and communication technologies gradually dismantled the existing vertical hierarchy and reduced the proportion of middle managers and general office workers, while the demand for executives, professionals or skilled technical workers who require high cognitive skills has increased. In reaction to this transformation, however, regular workers who hold jobs in occupations requiring high cognitive functions experienced job anxiety and increased autonomy, while workers who do simple repetitive tasks experienced job insecurity and relative wage decline at the same time.

In South Korea, the financial crisis at the end of 1997 prompted rapid and dramatic changes in the paradigm of corporate personnel management, which had gradually changed before, and spread the tendency of unemployment to the whole economy. Job insecurity and worsening income distribution have become the biggest bottlenecks in the labor market. In the process of restructuring, the demand for work with highly adaptability has increased significantly, while the low-skilled and labor intensive work has been dramatically dependent on outsourcing or irregular work.

3.3. Changes in labor structure and environment

Changes in Labor-Management Relations: South Korea experienced a slowdown in employment growth and worsening social distribution in the aftermath of the financial crisis in 1997, and unemployment growth in 2003 and 2009. The employment stability of the supplied jobs has been lower than in the past, and the number of jobs with increasing income has decreased with the increase of skill such as manufacturing technicians and skilled workers.

The employment of the large corporations was reduced by having only core manpower, and the wage gap between large enterprises and SMEs widened.

Changes in the economic environment have widened the dual structure between regular and public sector employees and SME workers. The problem of polarization between regular and non-regular workers is becoming serious; Wage gap between regular and irregular workers, and increased employment instability among temporary workers.

The deterioration of the employment status of youth due to the declining growth rate engaged with the employment problems of elderly groups and led to the problem of job conflicts among the generations.

This problem shifts the weight of labor-management relations to employment issues, and the importance of social safety nets such as job sharing, social insurance, and vocational training is increasing.

3.4. Characteristics of Labor-management Relations in South Korea

The existing labor-management relations are not only unstable but also have a developmental delay that does not respond flexibly to changes in the external environment.

Under the anarcho-syndicalist nature of Korean union movement, the mismatch between superior groups of labor unions who are obsessed with a just cause and enterprise unions who have a tendency to belligerence based on empiricism. Corporate unions tend to be dedicated to rigid negotiation strategies that only stick to wage and payroll increases or short-sighted job security. Employees seek to maximize short-term profits in the absence of social responsibility and to appease or weaken unions, which brings a tendency to accumulate mistrust. The government has contributed to the politics of justice by the higher-level labor unions due to the incentives that productive outcome should be achieved within the term of the administration, and it has also connived with decline of working conditions by regulating the secondary labor market asymmetrically.

Unlike large corporations and public sectors, which have internal regulations and bargaining power, SMEs and temporary workers are asymmetrically loosely regulated. Rigid labor-management relations and conflicts within the enterprise hamper the efficient utilization and deployment of internal labor force and hinder job creation.

Unions of large corporations and public corporations tend to collude with employers in the way of passing over their unfair trade, internal transactions and deterioration of working conditions for SMEs and non-regular workers when the unions can carry out their demands in the process of raising wages or distributing profits. Employers express their complaints about rigid labor relations through outsourcing, using irregular workers, and overseas transfer of production facilities. Therefore, the construction of high-performing workplaces in large corporations / public / financial industries where legal and institutional norms work is being delayed, and the tradition that lacks social solidarity keeps reproducing.

Employment- and welfare-friendly labor relations are necessary to secure a sustainable economy and create more and better jobs by raising the flexibility and safety of the labor market amid technological advances and the polarization of the economy due to globalization.

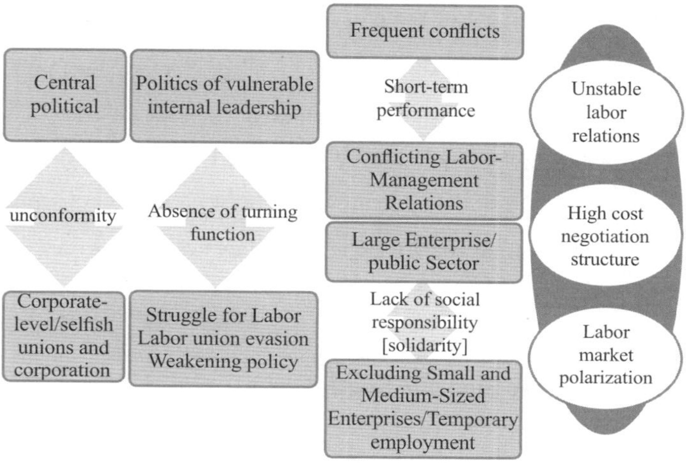

Figure 5-7 Characteristics of South Korean Industrial Relations

Employment- and welfare-friendly labor relations are necessary to secure a sustainable economy and create more and better jobs by raising the flexibility and safety of the labor market amid technological advances and the polarization of the economy due to globalization.

3.5. Characteristics and Problems of Industrial Relations in South Korea

The government plays a large role in the enforcement and improvement of the labor-management law system, and the nature of government roles is more like 'order holders' rather than 'coordinated mediators'. Whenever the regime changes, the government's labor relations policy has changed and the policy inconsistency has not been maintained, which hinders the development of industrial relations. In the process of intervention in the labor-management relationship, government conflicts with labor unions or business community.

Since the development of the universal welfare system was late in Korea, it depends mostly on company welfare. The tendency of corporate-oriented welfare and the introduction of the three major social insurance schemes came under governmental planning in the authoritarian regime, and the roles of labor and management were not significant along the way. In the consequence, the overall level of protection and coverage of welfare system in Korea is still low, despite the growth of formal welfare system.

3.6. Labor flexibility model in South Korea

Labor relations based on compromise and consultation did not appear in the past flexible stability model in Korea. In the process of seeking a model for the Korean version of the flexicurity model, however, the evolution of the tripartite structure from the current 'Flexibility-Safety-ALMP' to the future 'labor relations-welfare-employment.' It is emphasized in searching for the Korean model that the flexicurity can be established only when the changes in labor-management relations are accompanied. In the present and future model, a consensus among the roles of labor, management, and government is formed.

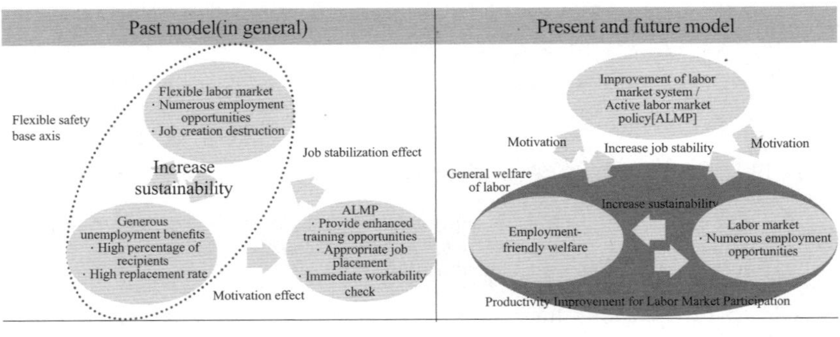

Figure 5-8 Korean Labor Flexibility Model

The Korean labor flexibility model improves the labor market dual structure and sets employment - welfare - friendly policy orientation.

- The government must provide an economic structure capable of creating high quality jobs such as establishment of start-up ecosystem in order to overcome the limit of the number of primary labor market jobs, and then pursue a policy to improve the quality of secondary labor market jobs.
- Labor and management are seeking cooperation not only within the enterprise but also in the dimension of entire labor market, for eliminating the dead zone of internal welfare and for finding solutions for internal training and child rearing.
- Labor and management cooperate in minimizing social exclusion, promoting the sustainability of work experience for workers, and supporting the manpower policy of SMEs.- Since the three elements – ALMP, employment and welfare - are not automatically consistent and do not guarantee flexicurity, it is necessary to improve the appropriate labor market system to pursue an practical combination of the elements.
- Through this, we should achieve high functional flexibility in the labor market, establish a welfare system compatible with work-family balance, and guarantee system improvement to reduce the blind spot of welfare.
- Economic growth rate is important for creating job and enhancing reliability, but it is not enough to improve the employment structure by increasing the growth rate alone. Therefore, improving the employment by modifying the structure and transaction practices of the product market and promoting the systemic reform related to vacation and working hour would be needed.
- The government should create an ecosystem where jobs are created and

destroyed actively by supporting the foundation and growth of start-ups and SMEs.

- The government should also ensure fair trade practices by cracking down on unfair trade and illicit internal transaction in the product market so that competitive SMEs' own efforts to expand their market would not be frustrated.

As shown in Figure 5-9, South Korea's past employment strategy has relied on economic growth. However, nowadays, Korean government is trying various policies to improve the labor market structure such as enhancing labor productivity, shifting workplaces for high-technology and high-performance, strengthening SME training, sharing jobs, as well as pursuing the sustainable development(See Figure 5-9).

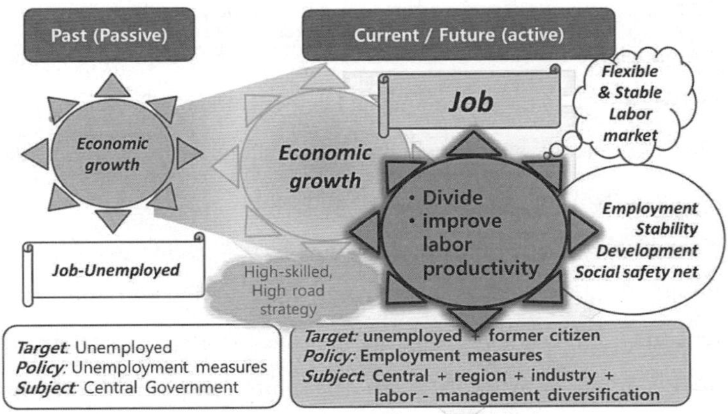

Figure 5-9 Korean Labor Flexibility Model Comparison (past and present)

3.7. Directions for Labor Flexibility

Considering changes in the environment, such as technological progress and global economic progress, the increasing welfare need, and the fact that employment is the best welfare, it is necessary to re-establish labor-management relations that aim for employment-friendly welfare to build a win-win relation between labor and management.

In order to create better jobs, it is necessary to correct dual structures, promote sustainability, and resolve labor-management conflicts through negotiations and broad consultations.

'Employment-friendly' labor-management relation refers to the relation that gives policy efforts to facilitate job transfer by adapting to changes in labor market or the relation that contributes to improving job ability and job potential.

※ It should be distinguished from the flexibility strategy of social conversation in the past as the primary goal of increasing quantity flexibility in the enterprise.

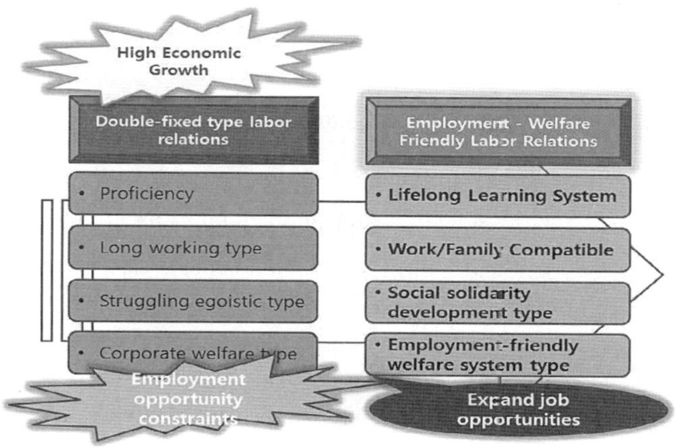

Figure 5-10 Direction for Labor Flexibility

V. Policy Recommendations

1. To-be: mid-term, long-term

1.1 Promote dialogue within and between enterprises, and in tripartite-plus structures

There is a need for an effective tripartite commission between the government, labor, and management to improve the labor relations policies necessary for crystalizing the legal system based on the Labor Standards Act, the Labor Union Act, the Labor Disputes Adjustment Act, and Labor Relations Commission Law. Dialogues in a trilateral consultation plays an important role in promoting socially responsible business and labor practices, and includes: (1) a dialogue between workers and employers (an intra-firm dialogue), (2) an industrial dialogue through an inter-firm dialogue (business-to-business); and (3) a dialogue within the extended tripartite structure (between industrial associations and the government).

(1) An intra-firm dialogue is related to employer-employee relationship.
(2) The goal of inter-firm dialogue is to promote a trust-based, committed, stable and long-term relationship among companies.
(3) The government and industrial associations can play an important role in the tripartite commission.

This tripartite commission functions significantly in establishing policies to maximize job creation by the three-way structure of workers, employers and government representatives.

1.2. Develop capacity of educational and training institutions

Improve the re-training policies such as the obligation of in-house vocational training.

It is necessary to change from the manpower supply policy that supports economic growth to the employment policy to promote disparity in supply and demand and job creation.

Vietnam seeks to improve the system of vocational training in preparation for the rapid change in the employment structure as the industrial structure moves from the labor-intensive industry to the capital-intensive industry.

1.3. Strengthen institutional capabilities

Preparing for the privatization of public enterprises, corporate restructuring and structural changes in the labor market, Vietnam should strengthen its administrative capacity in relation to the labor market flexibility policy.

Vietnam should also prepare for strengthening institutional capacities such as increasing minimum labor costs, improving working conditions, strengthening basic labor rights, and extending the coverage of social insurance.

1.4. Promote inter-ministerial policy coordination

Labor policy should take into account various factors such as economic growth, price stability, dispelling social unrest, and power relations between labor and management.

Labor policy has been changed and influenced by economic conditions, political situation, and terrain of labor relations by economic growth stage.

These influencing factors should be considered in policy cooperation between ministries.

1.5. Solutions for the financial deficit and realization of job policy: Taxing the Underground Economy

The underground economy of the advanced countries(the members of the OECD) is estimated to be around 13% of their GDP in 2007, but in the case of developing countries, about 26%.

An underground economy does not pay taxes and leads to a decrease in tax revenue. It also increases the burden on the public and deteriorates income distribution. In terms of securing welfare resources, improving tax equality, and countering corruption, legalization of the underground economy is a necessary policy task.

The reasons for the high proportion of underground economy are found in various aspects. First, the rate of self-employment in Vietnam is higher than the OECD average, and it is difficult to determine actual income of self-employed. Second, as the tax burden increases, the temptation to avoid tax increases as well. Third, high level of corruption is considered to be one of the main causes of underground economy. The corruption and opacity of each sector in the domestic society are factors that form illegal funds. Fourth, non-institutional labor market, such as day labor, is also the cause of underground economy.

Incorporation of workers and illegal foreign workers into the non-institutional labor market who have failed to find jobs in the official economy due to the economic downturn also leads to the formation of an underground economy. Increasing convenience transaction of real estate and expanding the financial market of the bond market also become a breeding ground of the underground economy.

In order to legalize the underground economy, it is necessary to prepare tailored countermeasures appropriate to domestic circumstances. Institutional incentives for securing tax revenue while minimizing the tax resistance of small scale self-employed persons and side effects towards people on low incomes.

1.6. Improve the labor structure(economic structure over 15 years old)

1. To improve the capacity of the existing Centers for Employment Services ("Trung tâm dịch vụ việc làm"); These centers would promote better skill training, and serve as bridge between business and labour.
2. To develop various forms of job market in provinces, which will facilitate information exchange among employers and employees, as well as to bridge the gap between labour supply and demand needs
3. To improve national database and surveys in labour markets to provide better information and employment trend;
4. To improve basic social services, especially in the housing and household permit system, for migration from rural to urban areas as well as labor movement among geographical areas.
5. To subsidize and focus on job creation for youth and special groups such as people with disability, minority ethnic groups
6. To create special fund for vulnerable group to participate in social insurance scheme

2. Long and Short Term Strategies

2.1. Long-term core vision

Long-term vision, goals, key tasks and strategies can be summarized as follows. Strategies: Building partnership with respect for labor and management; strengthening labor-management consultation function; consolidating a coordinative function between labor and management, Enhancing social dialogue Key tasks: Expanding opportunities for lifelong learning; policies on vacation and working hour for high productivity; reduction of blind spots for welfare and legal system application; establishment of fair trade order in product market; improvement of welfare delivery system; active policies for low-income bracket to help moving up the social ladder These key tasks can be progressed into a more specific extent depending on the agenda setting by the actors from labor and management.

- Promoting job stability through expansion of opportunities for lifelong education including mandatory training programs
- Promoting alternative work and functional flexibility related to the improvement of systems on training-vacation-worktime
- establishment of social insurance standards and sharing principles for workers with special conditions to strengthen the EITC and to reduce the blind spot of social insurance, withholding and return of insurance premiums
- Social consensus for priority consideration of second labor market participants in the process of delivering welfare such as childcare
- Establishing norms on labor supervision to reduce blind spots of law application

- Establishment of fair trade order in product market, correcting practices to impose monopolistic delivery
- Adopting active policy and building Korean model for unemployment assistance
- Labor-management participation and contribution to the improvement and monitoring process of the welfare delivery system

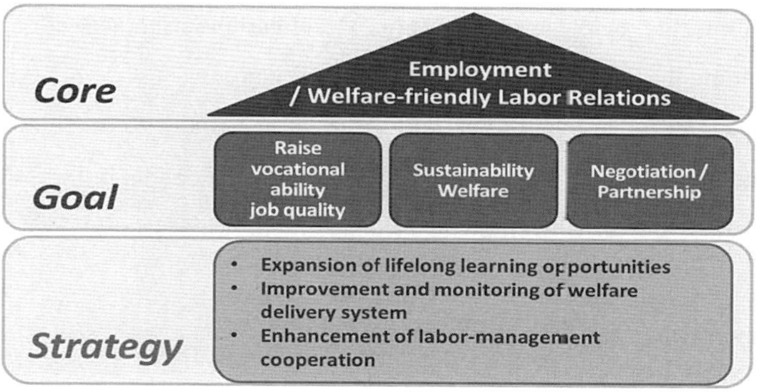

Figure 5-11 Long-term Vision

2.2. Short-term strategies based on employment status

In order to establish employment- and welfare-friendly relations, the labor and management work out the common principles of the Korea's flexible safety policy including the following factors.

Support for comprehensive lifelong learning: emphasizing the importance of lifelong learning by enhancing continuous work adjustment and employment possibility and by improving work skills through investing in human resources development of the enterprise, aiming at supplying learning program, at increasing participation and, by extension, at enhancing creative economy

Establishment of vacation and working hours system for balancing between work and family and between training and employment: labor time saving system, appropriate childcare support system, giving higher priority for childcare support to labor market participants.

Constructing modern social security system: building awareness of financial stability of unemployment benefits and pensions, appropriate pay period and substitution rate, health insurance, mutual obligation-based activation policy, and building the ladder of hope for lower-income group

Alleviation of the dual structure of the labor market: Reduction of blind spots, labor market policies that give priority to participants in the secondary labor market, and social welfare through sharing of social security principles.

2.3. Suggestions for Labor Flexibility Model

We propose the construction of labor flexibility model based on employment- and welfare-friendly labor relations.

Complete the tripartite composition of employment, welfare and labor relations in Vietnam through the implementation of actors' role in building labor-management relations and social corporatism based on consultation and mediation.

Contribute to the improvement of welfare system efficiency(ex. improvement of welfare service delivery) and welfare expansion based on evolved labor relations.

Changing the direction of enterprises' the personnel management standards to enhancing the job stability of labor market participants (activating of training and alternative work)

Expand the welfare system under the principle of increasing labor market participation and productivity, and adjust labor market norms and employment practices to enhance the sustainability of the welfare system.

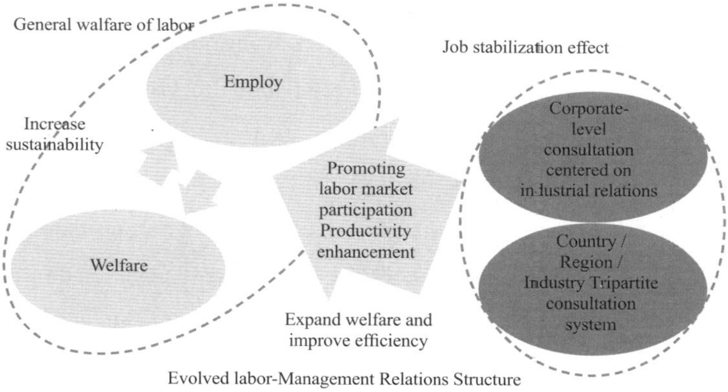

Figure 5-12 Future Model for Labor Flexibility

VI. Conclusion

The labor market environment in Vietnam is changing rapidly in recent years. In terms of the employment growth rate, the increase in foreign direct investment into Vietnam contributed significantly to Vietnamese economy than local businesses. The increased inward FDI has affected the labor market through various channels. The entry of foreign companies has also stimulated the total factor productivity growth of the local enterprises in Vietnam. Vietnamese workers, fueled by the trend of globalization and by increase in their average income since 2000, are now demanding the government to improve the labor-related systems. Several viable solutions are possible. Labor union related to the Vietnam General Confederation of Labor (VGCL) can prevent board members and managers from positions of major labor union. Simplification of governmental regulations to solve disputes related to industrial relations is also possible. As seen in the case of South Korea and many European countries, institutional reforms allowing the creation of workers council or joint labor-management council shall be considered as well. In the long term, Vietnam should consider fundamental institutional reforms of industrial relations system suitable for the demand of mature market economy.

When the Vietnamese government uses the labor policy recommendations, expected consequences or outcomes can be as follows. First, active labor policies for promoting employment- and welfare-friendly environment would be implemented, contrary to traditional passive ones to secure export competitiveness and attract foreign investment. Vietnam, which has achieved rapid economic growth since the 1990s and has the motivation to maintain it, recognizes the necessity of domestic market activation and real income increase as a feasible means for its sustainable development.

Second, labor-related laws and institutions would be restructured. In the course of a full-fledged transition to a market economy in the 1990s, the introduction of the labor laws and the modernization of the working environment have served as an opportunity to encourage changes in the labor sector. The Vietnamese government has established a set of legislation for labor unions and collective bargaining right, standards related to working hours including the youth, and work permit and visa systems. Workers' increased sense of entitlement in labor rights and populist activities of political parties could have positive effects on labor policy reconstruction. Although Vietnam's labor laws have not yet been subdivided as those of South Korea have, systematical and comprehensive revision of institutions is in need to make a smooth transition to a market economy system.

Finally, policy efforts would needed to bring up the underground economy. Considering fiscal deficit and government debt, it is necessary to legalize the underground economy such as family management and unofficial jobs, and to institutionalize policies to make taxation indices more transparent. Moreover, it is also necessary to provide productive opportunities through institutionalization, formalization and improvement of supply for alternative jobs, rather than mass production of unproductive jobs.

APPENDIX

APPENDIX

Appendix Table 1. Highlights of South Korea's financial deregulation since the early 1980s

This table shows the highlights of South Korea's financial deregulation since the early 1980s. Deregulations in italics are the ones that have been implemented in Vietnam.

Financial liberalization program	
Introduction of corporate paper	1981
Privatization of nationwide commercial banks	1981-83
Abolition of beneficial interest rates on policy loans	1982
Alleviation of government intervention in the internal operation of banks	1984
Introduction of negotiable CDs	1984
Introduction of a band for bank loan rates	1984
Indirect opening of the stock market through the Korea Fund	1984
Introduction of cash management accounts by short-term finance companies	1987
Introduction of bond management funds by securities companies	1987
Relaxation of entry barriers to financial industry, including banks, life insurance, lease, and investment trust	1988
Opening of the life insurance industry to foreign firms	1988
Announcement of phased deposit and loan rate deregulation	Dec. 1988
Opening of the securities industry to foreign firms	1991

Announcement of a four-step interest rate liberalization plan	1991
Conversion of some short-term finance companies to securities companies or Banks	1991
Opening of purchase of individual equity stocks on the Korea Stock Exchange to foreign investors	1992
Foreign exchange and capital account liberalization	
Switch to a basket-peg exchange rate system from a dollar-peg	1980
Foreign exchange forward transaction implemented	1981
Interest rate swap allowed	1984
Switch to a negative system in foreign direct investment policies	1984
Issuance of convertible bonds (CBs), warrant bonds (WBs), and depository receipts (DRs)	1985
Financial futures allowed	1987
Transaction to an IMF article VIII country	1988
Foreign exchange call market established	1989
Switch to the Market Average Exchange Rate System	1990
Switch to a negative system in foreign exchange management	1992

Source: (Park 1996) and updated by the authors.

Appendix Table 2. Third-stage blueprint for the liberalization and opening of the financial sector

This table shows the highlights of deregulation related to financial market liberalization. Deregulations in italics are the ones that have been implemented in Vietnam.

Schedule	Items
Phase I (1993)	*1. Liberalize all bank and nonbank lending rates (except for policy loans) and long-term deposits over two-year maturity.* 2. Issue Monetary Stabilization Bonds and government bonds of closeto market interest rates. 3. Operate M2 targets flexibly. 4. Liberalize call markets. 5. Widen the daily won-dollar trading margin from 0.8 to 1.0 percent. 6. Switch to the notification system for foreign direct investment into Korea.
Phase II (1994-95)	*1. Liberalize all lending rates and rates for short-term marketable instruments.* *2. Establish indirect monetary controls.* 3. Deregulate loans to large conglomerates. *4. Develop short-term financial markets.* 5. Further widen the daily won-dollar trading margin. 6. Further ease requirements for underlying documentation prior to foreign exchange transactions. 7. Expand limits on foreign investment in the stock market. 8. Allow foreign participation in primary markets for some bonds. 9. Ease requirements for opening branches of foreign securities companies.
Phase III (1996-97)	*1. Liberalize all deposit rates except for demand deposits (allow money market certificates and money market funds).* *2. Utilize open market operations as main monetary policy tool.* 3. Operate the Loans Management System as a prudential regulation. 4. Introduce free-floating exchange rate system. 5. Eliminate requirements for underlying documentation for the usual foreign exchange transactions. *6. Allow foreign borrowing through commercial loans.* *7. Allow foreign financial institutions to hold stock of domestic banks.*

Source: (Park 1996) and updated by the authors.

Appendix Table 3. Highlights of Vietnam's Financial Deregulation since the Late 1980s

Foreign Investment Law	1987
Two-tier banking system	1988
Two ordinances on banking operations were passed	1990
Reserve requirement was introduced	1990
Corporate law was passed and came into effected	1990
Credit ceiling	1991
Foreign exchange markets were formed	1991
Branch of foreign banks came Vietnam	1992
Positive interest rate policy	12/1992
VND inter- bank market	1993
Floor rate for deposit and ceiling for lending	10/1993
Foreign inter-bank market	1994
Corporate bonds	1994
The gap between lending and deposit rate was 0.35% was applied	10/1995
Introduction of treasury bills	1995
The State Securities Commission of Vietnam was established	1996
Law on State bank of Vietnam and law on credit institution was passed and came into effected	1997
The gap of 0.35% was removed, only ceiling for lending rates were applied	12/1997-1/1998
Credit ceiling was removed	1998
Forward exchange trading	1998
Domestic firms was allowed to invest abroad	1999
Open market operations	2000

The Ho Chi Minh central for securities trading (HOSTC) was established	2000
The first trading section with only two stocks	28/7/2000
Ceiling rate for foreign currencies lending was removed	2001
Foreign exchange swap	2001
Government and corporate bonds was allowed to trade in (HCMCS)	2001
Local government bond	2001
Foreign organizations and individuals shall only be permitted to transfer their investment capital abroad.	2002
Foreign organizations and individuals can transfer investment profits, dividends and bond interests abroad.	2002
Base interest rate was introduced and interest rate was liberalized	8/2002
Overdraft, overnight loans and electronic clearing	2002
The total number of shares that foreign investors can hold in a listed organization is increased from 20% to 30%	2003
Foreign organizations and individuals were allowed to buy and / or sell stocks on the Vietnam stock market	2003
FDI enterprises can be transform into joint-stock companies	2003
Government bond sold in international market	2005
Foreign investors may hold up to 49% of the total shares of the listed company in stock exchange market	2005
Vietnam Securities Depository was established	2005
Hanoi central for securities trading (HNX) was formed	2005
Convertible bonds	2005
The two first bank's stock was listed	2006
Law on Securities was passed in 23/6/2006 and came into effect in 2007	2006-2007

Ho Chi Minh Stock Exchange was operated	2007
Trading time expanded in HNX	2007
Government bond market was established	2008
Ceiling rate for lending was reapplied	8/2008
Hanoi Stock Exchange was formed	2009
Government bond in foreign currencies sold in domestic market	2009
Unlisted public company market was established	2009
Ceiling rate was removed and interest rate was liberalized again	2/2010
Vn30 index was introduced	2012
Shorten settlement time from T+4 to T+3	2012
Treasury bills was traded in HNX	2012
Trading time in HOSE was expanded to 3pm	2013
Trading time in HNX was expanded to 3pm	2013
Shorten settlement time from T+3 to T+2	2016
Derivatives stock market	2017

Appendix Table 4. TRENDS AND CONTENTS OF LABOR RELATIONS ACT

	Statute	year	Main Content
1	Employment Security Act (enacted)	1961	Provide everyone with the opportunity to work in a job that has adapted to their abilities
2	Minimum Wage Act (enacted)	1986	The minimum wage is defined and the minimum wage judging committee decides the low wage.
3	Labor Standard Act	1987	Wage bond repayment, abolition of flexible working hours system

4	Labor union law	1987	Allow union shop, shorten validity period of collective agreement from 3 years to 2 years, remove requirement for establishment of trade union
5	Gender Equality Employment Act	1987	Prohibit gender discrimination in recruitment, education, placement, promotion, retirement and dismissal, allow unpaid parental leave within one year
6	Enforcement Decree of the National Pension Act (enacted)	1987	registration for 10 or more workplace obligations
7	Labor Standard Act	1989	Expansion of application target, Labor Relief Ordinance System for unfair dismissal, Upward adjustment of vacation allowance, Reduction of legal working hours, Expansion of annual leave
8	Act on Employment Promotion of Disabled Persons Act (enacted)	1990	Employers with a certain number or more of the employees hire persons with disabilities in the range of 1-5%
9	In-house Work Welfare Fund Act (enacted)	1991	All employers establish an in-house welfare fund, and the proceeds of the fund are used to fund workers'
10	Employment Promotion Act for the Elderly	1991	Workplaces with a certain size or more are obliged to employ elderly people
11	Employment Insurance Act (enacted)	1993	The unemployment insurance premiums were applied to employers and workers in half
12	Basic Law on Employment Policy (enacted)	1993	The basis for more active employment policies, such as expanding the supply of available labor to less-skilled workers
13	Act on Improvement of Employment of Construction Workers	1996	Promoting employment improvement and welfare promotion of construction workers and development of construction industry
14	Labor Standard Act	1997	Introduction of time work system, adoption of flexible working time system, introduction of discretionary working time system

15	Vocational Education and Training Promotion Act (enacted)	1997	Linking vocational education and vocational training to establish new vocational education and training system
16	Labor union law	1997	Since 2002, we have introduced the doubles union. No wage payment for full-time union officials since 2002
17	Labor Committee Act	1997	Labor Relations Commission established for quick and fair execution of judgment and coordination in labor relations
18	Labor Standard Act	1998	Allow employment adjustment by management reasons, notify union within 60 days of employment adjustment, consultation
19	Act on the Protection of Dispatched Workers, etc. (enacted)	1998	Labor Market Flexibility Enhancement Act was enacted to protect workers from dispatched workers
20	Wage bond guarantee law (enacted)	1999	Wage bond guarantee fund introduced a system that allows a certain amount of unpaid wages to be paid
21	Act on the Establishment and Operation of Tripartite Commission (Established)	1999	Discuss ways to overcome the economic crisis and collaborate with labor and management to achieve a balanced development of the national economy.
22	Act on Establishment and Operation of Trade Unions of Teachers (Established)	1999	Legislative system, organization system, bargaining structure, collective bargaining matters, scope of guarantee of basic labor rights, bargaining window unification, union Membership qualification. Related to union full-time workers.
23	Employee Vocational Ability Development Act (enacted)	1999	To ensure that employers do not exceed 20 per cent of the total wage
24	Labor Standard Act	2003	Shortening working time shorten working hours within 40 hours a week and 2,000 hours a year, ②increase the number of holidays and vacation days that are reasonably adjusted for holidays and vacations, and ③ increase the number of vacation days. That

25	Act on the Employment, etc. of Foreign Workers (enacted)	2003	Effective employment management for foreign workers and protection of workers' interests
26	Employee Retirement Benefit Security Act (enacted)	2005	Extension of the retirement benefit system to contribute to population aging and the stable life of old people
27	Act on the Establishment and Operation of Labor Unions of Public Officials (Established)	2005	Allowing the establishment of the civil work council in the first stage and allowing the civil servant union in the second stage
28	Union law	2006	Abolition of the arbitration system (December 30, 2006 revision of the union law) Abolition of direct arbitration system for essential public service through revision of the union law
29	Introduction of legislation and non-discrimination system for irregular workers	2006	Introduction of legislation and non-discrimination system for non-regular workers (November 30, 2006) Non-regular worker discrimination prohibition method, limitation of reason for limited-time work and limited time method,
30	Labor Committee Act (enacted)	2006	Judge and adjust labor relations
31	Act on the Protection of Temporary Workers and Short-Time Workers (enacted)	2006	Non-regular workers such as fixed-term workers and short-time workers are rapidly increasing, protecting the working conditions of workers and promoting sound development of the labor market. Limit the period of use of fixed-term workers Limit of overtime work for short-time workers
32	Labor Standard Act	2007	Improvement of unfair dismissal system 'Unfair dismissal relief agencies and procedures, unfair dismissal relief methods, existence of criminal punishment rules, labor contracts and notification of dismissal, reorganization of dismissal dismissal, dismissal of corporations in bankruptcy proceedings, Improvement of shortening, change termination system '

33	Union law	2010 2011	Problems with union predecessors and multiple unions
34	Act on Support for Industrial Relations Development; Labor-Management Relations Development Act (enacted)	2010	Promoting the development of labor-management relations
35	Gender Equality Employment Act	2012	Establishment of systems for maternity protection and employment equality
36	Minimum wage law	2012	Strengthen protection of minimum wage payment such as simple work for fixed-term workers less than one year
37	Act on the Protection of Temporary Workers and Short-Time Workers	2014	For the deliberate or repetitive discrimination of the employer, the Labor Relations Commission shall, within three times the amount of damages incurred by the temporary and temporary employees
38	Act on Fairness of Recruitment Procedures	2014	Ensure fairness of job recruitment procedures and protect the rights of employers
39	Act on the Prohibition of Age Discrimination in Employment and Promotion of Employment of the Elderly	2016	Employment promotion for the elderly
40	Employment Insurance Act	2016	Support for training costs for employers conducting vocational ability development training for elderly and semi-elderly people Reconciliation of payroll
41	Special Act on Promotion of Youth Employment	2016	Extension of the mandatory requirement of employing 3% of the public institutions and local public enterprises as youth
42	Act on Support for Industrial Relations Development	2016	Act on Support for Industrial Relations Development And to clarify international cooperation projects related to the development of labor-management relations as a project of the Labor-Management Development Foundation.

43	Vocational Education and Training Promotion Act	2016	Protecting the safety and human rights of on-the-job practitioners such as vocational training and training time and improving environment
44	Employee Vocational Ability Development Act (enacted)	2016	In the process of vocational competency development training, abolition or relaxation of unnecessary or excessive regulation
45	Act on Improvement of Employment of Construction Workers	2016	Support for employment stability of construction workers', 'promotion of development and improvement of job ability', and 'promotion of welfare of construction workers'
46	Act on the Promotion of Economic Activities such as Women with Disrupted Careers	2017	Strengthen support to prevent career interruptions and promote economic activities
47	Employment Promotion for the Disabled and Vocational Rehabilitation Act	2017	Dispatch of Disabled Persons Competition Games and International Disabled Persons Olympics Competition and dispatch of athletes
48	Minimum wage law	2017	In the current situation, if you work for less than three months, you will need to pay minimum wage
49	Industrial Safety and Health Act	2017	Strengthen sanctions on cover-ups of industrial accidents at industrial sites
50	Act on collecting insurance premiums for employment insurance and industrial accident compensation insurance	2017	In case of accidents occurring during commute, it is recommended that the accident compensation system

Source: National Law Information Center (www.law.go.kr), Ministry of Employment and Labor Act (www.moel.go.kr/info/lawinfo)

REFERENCES

CHAPTER ONE:
Developmental Gap between Vietnam and Korea

Akamatsu, Kaname, "A Historical Pattern of Economic Growth in Developing Countries", Journal of Developing Economies, Vol. 1. No. 1, pp. 3-25 (1962).

Fei, John, Gustav Ranis, and Kazushi Ohkawa. "Economic Development in *Historical Perspective: Japan, Korea and Taiwan," in Japan and the Developing Countries*, Edited by Kazushi Ohkawa and Gustav Ranis, London: Basil Blackwell (1985)

Gerschenkron, Alexander, *Economic Backwardness in Historical Perspective,* Harvard University Press, Cambridge, Mass., 1962.

KDI, edited by Dong-Se Cha, Kwang Suk Kim, and Dwight H. Perkins, The Korean Economy 1945-1995: *Performance and Vision for the 21st Century,* KDI (1997).

KDI, *The Half-Century Korean Economy Policy Reports* (in Korean, 1995).

KDI, edited by Il Sakong Il and Youngsun Koh, *The Korean Economy Six Decades of Growth and Development,* KDI, 2010.

Lee, Doowon. "Privatization of Vietnam's Economy (in Korean)", *The Southeast Asian Review,* Vol. 10, The Korean Association of Southeast Asian Studies, pp. 29-65, 2000. 8.

Lee, Doowon, Ilgyu Han, "Can China Avoid the Middle-Income Trap?", *The*

Journal of Northeast Asian Economic Studies, Vol.26, No.2, pp.208-244 (June 2014)

Socialist Republic of Vietnam, *The Five Year Socio-Economic Development Plan* 2016-2020, Hanoi, 2016.

The World Bank, *Vietnam 2035: Toward Prosperity, Creativity, Equity, and Democracy,* 2015.

World Economic Forum, *Global Competitiveness Report 20*17-2018.

CHAPTER TWO:

Economic System for Vietnam: Social Welfare System

[National Basic Livelihood Security Act]

Ministry of Health and Welfare, "The 70 years history of Health and Welfare, Ministry of Health and Welfare," PDF file, 2017, http://prism.go.kr/homepage/theme/retrieveThemeDetail.do;jsessionid=FBC0DDB0661CCD4D3B4EEE9D98F82ACC.node02?cond_research_name=&cond_organ_id=&cond_research_year_start=&cond_research_year_end=&cond_brm_super_id=NB000120061201100031424&research_id=1351000-201400139&pageIndex=68&leftMenuLevel=110

e-Country Index, "The Recipients' Status of National Basic Living Security Program 2016," http://www.index.go.kr/potal/main/EachDtlPageDetail.do?idx_cd=2760, Accessed April 7, 2018.

National Archives of Korea, "Creation of Livelihood Protection Law," http://www.archives.go.kr/next/search/listSubjectDescription.do?id=000317,

Accessed April 7, 2018

National Legal Data Center, “Livelihood Protection Law,” http://www.law.go.kr/lsInfoP.do?lsiSeq=1061&ancYd=19611230&ancNo=00913&efYd=19620101&nwJoYnInfo=N&efGubun=Y&chrClsCd=010202#0000, Accessed April 7, 2018

[National Health Insurance]

National Health Insurance Service and Health Insurance Review Agency., National Health Insurance Corporation, “National Health Insurance Statistical YearBook 2016,” PDF file, 2017, https://www.hira.or.kr/bbsDummy.do?pgmid=HIRAA020045020000&brdScnBltNo=4&brdBltNo=2309&pageIndex

National Health Insurance Service and Health Insurance Review Agency., National Health Insurance Corporation, “National Health Insurance Statistical YearBook 2009,” PDF file, 2010, https://www.hira.or.kr/bbsDummy.do?pgmid=HIRAA020045020000&brdScnBltNo=4&brdBltNo=2302&pageIndex=1

National Health Insurance Service and Health Insurance Review Agency., “Health Insurance Review and Evaluation Statistical YearBook 2001,” PDF file, 2002, https://www.hira.or.kr/bbsDummy.do?pgmid=HIRAA020045010000&brdScnBltNo=4&brdBltNo=2202

National Health Insurance., “Health Insurance Review and Evaluation Statistical YearBook 2000,” PDF file, 2001, https://academic.naver.com/article.naver?doc_id=39555311

National Health Insurance Service, "Health Insurance Review and Evaluation Statistical YearBook 1998," PDF file, 1999, http://dl.kli.re.kr/search/detail/CATTOT000000008077

National Health Insurance Service, "The Outline of National Health Insurance Service," http://www.nhis.or.kr/menu/retriveMenuSet.xx?menuId=B2160, Accessed April 7, 2018

National Health Insurance Service, "Strengthening Measures for the Coverage of the National Health Insurance," http://medicare1.nhis.or.kr/hongbo/static/html/minisite/index.html, Accessed July 9, 2018

Health Insurance Review Agency., National Health Insurance Corporation, "National Health Insurance Statistical YearBook 2016," PDF file, 2017,https://www.hira.or.kr/bbsDummy.do?pgmid=HIRAA020045020000&brdScnBltNo=4&brdBltNo=2309&pageIndex=1

Health Insurance Review Agency., National Health Insurance Corporation, "National Health Insurance Statistical YearBook 2009," PDF file, 2010, https://www.hira.or.kr/bbsDummy.do?pgmid=HIRAA020045020000&brdScnBltNo=4&brdBltNo=2302&pageIndex=1 National Health Insurance Corporation, "Health Insurance Review and Evaluation Statistical YearBook 2000," PDF file, 2001, http://dl.nanet.go.kr/SearchDetailView.do?cn=MONO1200214664

[National Pension]

National Pension Service "National Pension Statistical YearkBook 2016," PDF file, 2017 http://www.nps.or.kr/jsppage/info/resources/info_resources_03_01.jsp?cmsId=statistics_year

National Pension Service, "National Pension Statistical YearkBook 2008," PDF file, 2009 http://www.nps.or.kr/jsppage/info/resources/info_resources_03_01.jsp?cmsId=statistics_year

National Pension Service, "National Pension Statistical YearkBook 2007," PDF file, 2008 http://www.nps.or.kr/jsppage/info/resources/info_resources_03_01.jsp?cmsId=statistics_year

National Pension Service, "National Pension Statistical YearkBook 2002," PDF file, 2003 http://www.nps.or.kr/jsppage/info/resources/info_resources_03_01.jsp?cmsId=statistics_year

National Pension Service, "National Pension Statistical YearkBook 1998," PDF file, 1999 http://www.nps.or.kr/jsppage/info/resources/info_resources_03_01.jsp?cmsId=statistics_year

[Occupational Health & Safety Insurance]

Korea Labor Welfare Corporation, "Korea Workers' Compensation and Welfare Service Statistical Yearbook 2015," PDF file, 2016 http://www.kcomwel.or.kr/Researchinstitute/lay1/program/S1T13C15/report_pg/view.do?total_search =&main_link=&division=&field=&published=&sdate=&edate=&rows=&cpage=&keyword=&condit ion=&seq=5706

Ministry of Employment and Labor, "Occupational Health and Safety Insurance Business YearBook 2015," PDF file, 2016 http://www.kcomwel.or.kr/Researchinstitute/lay1/program/S1T13C15/report_pg/view.do?total_search =&main_link=&division=&field=&published=&sdate=&edate=&rows=&cpage=&keyword=&condit ion=&seq=5705

Song, Y, A., "An Investigation of the Provision System of Workers' Compensation Insurance", Investigative Report, Korea Insurance Research Institute, 2010.

[Employment Insurance]

Employment Insurance, "The History of Employment Insurance," https://www.ei.go.kr/ei/eih/eg/ei/eiEminsr/retrieveEi0101Info.do

Korea Labor Welfare Corporation, "Korea Workers' Compensation and Welfare Service Statistical Yearbook 2015," PDF file, 2016 http://www.kcomwel.or.kr/Researchinstitute/lay1/program/S1T13C15/report_pg/view.do?total_search =&main_link=&division=&field=&published=&sdate=&edate=&rows=&cpage=&keyword=&condit ion=&seq=5706

Ministry of Employment and Labor, "The Employment Insurance White Paper 2015," PDF file, 2016 https://www.data.go.kr/dataset/15007435/fileData.do

[National Basic Livelihood Security Act]

e-Country Data, "Gross Domestic Product and Economic Growth Rate," http://www.index.go.kr/potal/main/EachDtlPageDetail.do?idx_cd=2736, Accessed April 7, 2018.

[National Basic Livelihood Security Act]

e-Country Data, "Gross Domestic Product and Economic Growth Rate," http://www.index.go.kr/potal/main/EachDtlPageDetail.do?idx_cd=2736,

Accessed April 7, 2018.

[Earned Income Tax Credit (EITC)]

National Tax Service, "Guidance on Earned Income Tax Credit and Child Tax Credit," https://www.hometax.go.kr/websquare/websquare.wq?w2xPath=/ui/pp/index_pp.xml&tmIdx=10&스 21Idx=1004000000&tabIndex=5, Accessed June29,2018 Song, H, J, and Shin, U, R, "The Effect of Expanding and Re-organizing EITC," Essay Contest of Korean Association of Public Finance, Vol. 2018, No. 1, Korean Association of Public Finance, 2018, pp. 1-25.

Birdsall, Nancy (2016), "Middle-class Heroes: the Best Guarantee of Good Governance." *Foreign Affairs*, March/April 2016 Issue.

Center for Excellence in Disaster Management & Humanitarian Assistance (2015), *Vietnam Disaster Management Reference Handbook*, Hawaii, USA

Chang, Jae-Hee and Phu Huynh (2016), *ASEAN in Transformation: the Future of jobs at risk of Automation,* International Labor Office, Bureau for Employers'Activities (ACT/EMP); ILO Regional Office for Asia and the Pacific, Working Paper No.9

Centre for Research on the Epidemiology of Disasters (2017), *The International disaster* database, accessed at: http://www.emdat.be/advanced_search/index.html.

Inter-Agency Standing Committee (IASC) and the European Commission (2017), *Index for risk management,* accessed at: http://www.inform-index.org/Countries/Country-profiles/iso3/VNM.

Oxford Poverty and Human Development Initiative (2017), *MPI Countries Briefing 2017.* [http://www.dataforall.org/dashboard/ophi/index.php/mpi/country_briefings]

UNDP (2017), *Human Development Indicator* (data released on 21/03/2017), [http://hdr.undp.org/en/countries/profiles/]

The World Bank (2017), *World Development Indicator 2017*, database 2017 https://data.worldbank.org/indicator/

Vietnam Academy of Social Science (2016), Policy Brief December 2016, Hanoi http://reliefweb.int/disaster/dr-2015-000180-vnm. http://www.unisdr.org/conferences/2017/globalplatform/en/programme/statements

CHAPTER THREE:
Indentifying and Promoting Sound Economic Policies for Growth and Financial Market Development

Bang, Vu. 2017. "Vietnamese stock market after 20 years of establishment: Prospect and development." ["Thị trường chứng khoán Việt Nam sau 20 năm thành lập: Triển vọng và phát triển."] *Journal of Economic and Forecast* No. 02 + 03/2017.

Barth, James, Gerard Caprio, and Ross Levine. 2001. "Banking Systems Around The Globe: Do Regulations And Ownership Affect Performance And Stability?" Pp. 31–96 in *Prudential Regulation and Supervision: What Works and What Doesn't,* edited by F. S. Mishkin.

Bhole, Bharat, and Sean Ogden. 2010. "Group lending and individual lending with strategic default." *Journal of development economics* 91(2): 348-363.

Blustein, Paul. 2003. *The Chastening: Inside The Crisis That Rocked The Global Financial System And Humbled The IMF.* PublicAffairs.

Boehmer, Ekkehart, Robert C. Nash, and Jeffry M. Netter. 2005. "Bank Privatization in Developing and Developed Countries: Cross-Sectional Evidence on the Impact of Economic and Political Factors." *Journal of Banking and Finance* 29(8–9 SPEC. ISS.):1981–2013.

Bonaccorsi di Patti, Emilia and Daniel C. Hardy. 2005. "Financial Sector Liberalization, Bank Privatization, and Efficiency: Evidence from Pakistan." *Journal of Banking and Finance* 29(8–9 SPEC. ISS.):2381–2406.

Boubakri, Narjess, Jean Claude Cosset, Klaus Fischer, and Omrane Guedhami. 2005. "Privatization and Bank Performance in Developing Countries." *Journal of Banking and Finance* 29(8–9 SPEC. ISS.):2015–41.

Calvo, Daniel, Juan Crisanto, Stefan Hohl, and Oscar Cutierrez. 2018. "Financial Supervisory Architecture: What Has Changed after the Crisis?" *BIS FSI Insights*.

Chen, Zhian, Donghui Li, and Fariborz Moshirian. 2005. "China's Financial Services Industry: The Intra-Industry Effects of Privatization of the Bank of China Hong Kong." *Journal of Banking and Finance* 29(8–9 SPEC. ISS.):2291–2324.

Cho, Hyekyung. 2010. "South Korea's Experience with Banking Sector Liberalization." *Center for Research on Multinational Corporations Research Report.*

Choi, Kiho and Boram Choi. 2014. "On the Effectiveness of Tax Exemption for Foreign Investment." *National Assembly Budget Office Research Report.*

Chu Khanh Lan. 2018. "Monetary policy and direction in 2018." Finance Journal. Retrieved from http://tapchitaichinh.vn/nghien-cuu--trao-doi/trao-doi-binh-luan/dieu-hanh-chinh-sach-tien-te-va-dinh-huong-trong-nam-2018-135403.html.

Chung, Kyuil and Seungwon Kim. 2014. "Capital Inflows and Policy Responses: Lessons from Korea's Experience." in *Volatile Capital Flows in Korea.* Palgrave Macmillan.

Clarke, George R. G. and Robert Cull. 1999. "Why Privatize? The Case of Argentina's Public Provincial Banks." *World Development* 27(5):865–86.

Clarke, George R. G. and Robert Cull. 2002. "Political and Economic Determinants of the Likelihood of Privatizing Argentine Public Banks." *The Journal of Law and Economics* 45(1):165–97.

Clarke, George R. G. G., Robert Cull, and Mary M. Shirley. 2005. "Bank Privatization in Developing Countries: A Summary of Lessons and Findings." *Journal of Banking and Finance* 29(8–9 SPEC. ISS.):1905–30.

Djankov, Simeon, Jan Jindra, and Leora F. Klapper. 2005. "Corporate Valuation and the Resolution of Bank Insolvency in East Asia." *Journal of Banking and Finance* 29(8–9 SPEC. ISS.):2095–2118.

Du, Huynh The, Nguyen Minh Kieu, and Do Thien Anh Tuan. 2013. "Vietnamese financial system." ["Hệ thống tài chính Việt Nam."], Economic teaching program, Fulbright University.

Duong, Pham Bao, and Yoichi Izumida. 2002. "Rural development finance in Vietnam: a microeconometric analysis of household surveys." *World Development* 30(2):319-335.

Economist. 2003. "'A Place for Capital Controls.'" May 3.

Eichengreen, Barry. 2002. *Financial Crises and What to Do About Them?* Oxford University Press, USA.

Eichengreen, Barry, Rachita Gullapalli, and Ugo Panizza. 2011. "Capital Account Liberalization, Financial Development and Industry Growth: A Synthetic View." *Journal of International Money and Finance* 30(6):1090–1106.

Epstein, Gerald, Ilene Grabel, and K. S. Jomo. 2008. "Capital Management Techniques in Developing Countries: Managing Capital Flows in Malayis, India, and China." in *Capital Market Liberalization and Development,* edited by J. A. Ocampo and J. E. Stiglitz. Oxford University Press.

Fischer, Stanely. 2002. "Financial Crises and Reform of the International Financial System." *NBER Working Paper 9297*.

Ha Thi Sau, and Vu Mai Chi. 2016. "Use of open market operations tools in the development of monetary market in Vietnam." *Banking Journal* 10.

Hiep, Le. Hong. 2017. "Vietnam's new wave of SOE equitization: Drivers and implications." *ISEAS Perspective*. Yusof Ishak Institute.

Hung, Nguyen Manh. 2016. "Vietnamese real estate market: reality and solutions." ["Thị trường bất động sản Việt Nam: Thực trạng và giải pháp."] Nam Can Tho University.

Hung, Duong Nhu, Nguyen Dinh Thien, and Nguyen Thanh Liem. 2017. "The impact of equitization on firm performance: The case of Vietnam.",

International Research Journal of Finance and Economics 164.

Huong, D. T. Minh. 2016. "Credit in rural areas in Vietnam." ["Tín dụng ở nông thôn Việt Nam."] *Journal of Social Sciences of Vietnam* 12(109).

IMF. 2000. *Annual Reports on Exchange Arrangements and Exchange Restrictions*. Washington, DC: International Monetary Fund.

IMF. 2012. *Global Financial Stability Report: The Quest for Lasting Stability.*

IMF. 2018. "Republic of Korea: Selected Issues." *IMF Country Report.*

Johnston, Barry, Salim Darbar, and Claudia Echeverria. 1997. "Sequencing Capital Account Liberalization: Lessons from the Experiences in Chile, Indonesia, Korea, and Thailand." *IMF Working Paper* 97/157.

Kim, Hakryul. 2014. *Financially Strong Nation*. Hakmin.

Kim, Shin-Haing. 2007. "Finance and Growth of the Korean Economy from 1960 to 2004." *Seoul Journal of Economics* 20(4).

Kose, Ayhan, Eswar Prasad, and Macro Terrones. 2006. "How Does Financial Globalization Affect Risk-Sharing? Patterns and Channels." *Paper Presented at the 7th Jacques Polak Annual Research Conference.*

Krugman, Paul. 1998. "Saving Asia: It's Time to Get Radical." *Fortune* 138(5).

Lee, Jaymin. 2017. *Foreign Currency Crises and The Korean Economy Afterwards*. Hanwool Academy.

Lee, Seungrae et al. 2015. "The Determinants of Greenfield and M&A Foreign Direct Investment." *KIEP Policy Analysis*.

Lim, Hyungjoon. 2011. "Effect of Currency Hedging Strategies on International Equity Investment Returns." *Korean Institute of Finance Research Paper.*

Megginson, William L. 2005. "The Economics of Bank Privatization." *Journal of Banking and Finance* 29(8–9 SPEC. ISS.):1931–80.

Ministry of Finance. 2017. *Annual Report 2017*.

National Finance Supervision Committee. 2017. "report on economic and financial status in 2017 and the outlook for 2018." ["Báo cáo tình hình kinh tế-tài chính năm 2017 và triển vọng năm 2018".] *Document for the government meeting*.

Nguyen Thi Kieu Nga. 2016. "Impact of interest rate channel on monetary policy of Vietnam." *Finance Journal*. Retrieved from http://tapchitaichinh.vn/kinh-te-vi-mo/tac-dong-cua-kenh-lai-suat-den-chinh-sach-tien-te-cua-viet-nam-99505.html.

Nguyen Thi Kim Thanh. 2010. "Interest Policy: Theory and Practice." *Banking Journal* 8.

Nguyen Thi Nhung, and Nguyen Van Luong. 2015. "The development of the financial market of Vietnam."

Ocampo, Jose Antonio, Shari Spiegel, and Joseph E. Stiglitz. 2008. "Capital Market Liberalization and Development." in *Capital Market Liberalization and Development*, edited by J. A. Ocampo and J. E. Stiglitz. Oxford University Press.

Otchere, Isaac and Janus Chan. 2003. "Intra-Industry Effects of Bank Privatization: A Clinical Analysis of the Privatization of the Commonwealth Bank of Australia." *Journal of Banking and Finance* 27(5):949–75.

Park, Ki Young. 2017. "The Wealthy Hand-to-Mouth Households in South

Korea." *Global Economic Review* 46(3).

Park, Ki Young and Soohyon Kim. 2018. "Dispersion of Household Debt and Its Macroeconomic Implications: A Case of South Korea." *Bank of Korea Economic Analysis* 24(1):2–22.

Park, Won-Am. 1996. "Financial Liberalization: The Korean Experience." in *Financial Deregulation and Integration in East Asia*, edited by T. Ito and A. Krueger. University of Chicago Press.

La Porta, Rafael, Florencio Lopez-De-Silanes, and Andrei Shleifer. 2002. "Government Ownership of Banks." *Journal of Finance* 57(1):265–301.

Le Quoc Ly. 2013. "Financial and Monetary Policy: Theory and Practice." National Political Publishing House, Hanoi.

Le Vinh Danh. 1996. "Money and Banking Activity." National Political Publishing House. Hanoi.

Schmukler, Sergio. 2008. "The Benefits and Risks of Financial Globalization." in *Capital Market Liberalization and Development*, edited by J. A. Ocampo and J. E. Stiglitz. Oxford University Press.

Shin, Inseok and Yunjon Wang. 2000. "How to Sequence Capital Market Liberalization: Lessons from the Korean Experience." *Korea Development Institute Working Paper.*

Single, L. .. and J. .. Kramer. 1996. "Tax Policy and the Location of Plants and Profits." *Journal of Accounting Literature* 15.

Sjöholm, F. 2006. "State owned enterprises and equitization in Vietnam." *Working paper*. Stockholm School Economics.

State Bank of Vietnam. *Annual Report 2008-2016*. Hanoi.

State Bank of Vietnam. 2010. "Law on State Bank of Vietnam and Credit Institutions." National Political Publishing House. Hanoi.

State Council. 1990. Ordinance No. 37-LCT/HĐNN8 on the State Bank.

State Council. 1990. Ordinance No. 38-LCT/HĐNN8 on Credit Institutions.

Stiglitz, Joseph E. 2000. "Capital Market Liberalization, Economic Growth, and Instability." *World Development* 28(6).

Stock investment. 2016. "The overview of Vietnamese stock market: 15 years of establishment and development." ["Tổng quan về thị trường chứng khoán Việt Nam: 15 năm thành lập và phát triển."] [URL: https://dautucophieu.net/tong-quan-ve-ttck-viet-nam-15-nam-hinh-thanh-va-phat-trien/].

Stock online. 2017. "The history and development of Vietnamese stock market." ["Lịch sử hình thành và phát triển của thị trường chứng khoán Việt Nam."] [URL: https://chungkhoanonline.vn/lich-su-hinh-thanh-va-phat-trien-cua-thi-truong-chung-khoan-viet-nam/].

Tarp, F. 2017. "Characteristics of the Vietnamese rural economy: Evidence from a 2016 rural household survey in 12 provinces of Vietnam." the United Nations University World Institute for Development Economic Research (UNU-WIDER).

To Kim Ngoc, Le Thi Tuan Nghia. 2012. "Exchange rate mechanism and inflation targeting policy." *Banking Journal* 21.

To Thi Anh Duong. 2014. *Monetary Policy in Vietnam*. Retrieved from www.ueb.edu.vn.

Tobin, James. 2000. "Financial Globalization." **World Development** 28(6).

Tran, T. B., Ong, B., Weldon, S.. 2015. "Vietnam Banking Industry Report." Duxton Asset Management.

Uthoff, Andras |. and Daniel Titelman. 1996. "The Relationship Between Foreign and National Savings Under Financial Liberalization." *Paper Presented at Workshop on Capital Flows and Investment Performance in Latin America.*

Vietnam Bank for Social Policy (VBSP). 2015. *Annual report.*

VP Bank Securities. 2014. "Vietnamese real estate market", *Industry report.*

VP Bank Securities. 2014. "Vietnamese banking industry", *Industry report.*

Wilson, Peter, Glenn Hubbard, and Joel Slemrod. 1993. "The Role of Taxes in Location and Sourcing Decisions." in *Studies in International Taxation.*

World Bank. 2014. *Review of Vietnam's economic development.*

World Bank. 2018. "Doing business", *Annual report.*

CHAPTER FOUR:
Enhancing the Industry Ecosystem in Vietnam

Nam, I. 2013. 2014 Modulization of Korea's Development Experience: Governance of SOEs and Public Institutions in Korea. Korea Development Institute (KDI).

Cho, C., Kim, K. & Kim, M. 2014. 2014 Modulization of Korea's Development Experience: Korea's Automotive Industry. Korea Development Institute (KDI).

Choi, S. 2008. The growth of big business and the relations between government and big business in historical perspective. History Review, 84(autumn): 100-128.

Eom, S. & Bae, K. 2014. The Governance System of Industrial Policy in the Era of Growth in Korea from the Perspective of State-Society Relations. *The Korean Journal of Policy Studies,* 29(3): 1-30.

Graham, E. M. 2003. Reforming Korea's Industrial Conglomerates. Institute for International Economics, Washington, DC.

Gregory, G., Harvie, C., & Lee, H. H. 2002. Korean SMEs in the 21st Century: Strategies, Constraints and Performance in a Global Economy. *Economic Papers: A journal of applied economics and policy*, 21(3): 64-79.

General Statistics Office of Vietnam (GSO) (2017), *Vietnamese Enterprises: 15 years of 21st Century (2000 – 2014)*, Statistical Publishing House, Hanoi.

GSO (2016), *Business results of Vietnamese Enterprises in the period 2010 – 2014*, Statistical Publishing House, Hanoi.

GSO (2013), *Development of Vietnam Enterprises in the period of 2006 – 2011*, Statistical Publishing House, Hanoi.

GSO (2007), *Vietnamese industry in 20 years of renovation and development,* Statistical Publishing House, Hanoi.

Hong, D. S. 2014. Competition Advocacy of the Korean Competition Authority. *Competition and the State*, Edited by Thomas K. Cheng, Ioannis Lianos, and D. Daniel Sokol, Stanford University Press.

Ishida, A. 2013. State enterprise groups in Vietnam following accession to the WTO, in Sakata, S. eds. Vietnam's economic entities in transition 2: 23-58.

Macmillan.

Jwa, S. 2001. A New Paradigm for Korea's Economic Development: from Government Control to Market Economy, Palgrave: NY.

Jones, L., & Sakong, I. 1980. *Government, Business, and Entrepreneurship in Economic Development: The Korean Case*. Korean Development Institute Press.

Kang, M. H. 1996. The Korean Business Conglomerate: Chaebol Then and Now. Institute of East Asian Studies, University of California, Berkeley.

Kim, P.S. & Kim, K. B. 2001. Appraising the New Institutional Arrangements for Privatization of Korean Sate-Owned Enterprises. *International Journal of Public Administration*, 24: 423-446.

Kim, G. M. 2007. *Making hidden winners. Future of Korean Economy and SMEs*. Special Contributions on Policy Direction for SMEs. The Presidential Commission on Small and Medium Enterprises, Republic of Korea.

Korea Development Institute (KDI). 2013. *Knowledge Sharing Program report*. Seoul: Korea Development Institute. (In Korean)

Lee, S., Kim, S., & Han, S. 1989. *Industrial Policy of Korea*, Seoul: Korea Institute for Industrial Economics and Trade. (in Korean)

Mah, J. S. 2007. Industrial Policy and Economic Development: Korea's Experience. *Journal of Economic Issues*, 41(1):77-92.

Nam, I. C., Oh, S. K. & Lee, I. M. 2003. A Study on the Ownership and Governance Structure of Privatized Public Firms. KDI school. (In Korean)

Nguyen Van Huy & Tran Van Nghia. 1996. Government Policies and State-owned Enterprise Reform, in Yuen, N. C., Freeman, N. J. & Huynh, F. H. eds. State-Owned Enterprise Reform in Vietnam: Lessons from Asia. 42-50. Singapore Institute of Southeast Asian Studies.

OECD. 2000. *Korea-The Role of Competition Policy in Regulatory Reform,* OECD Publishing, Paris.

OECD. 2013. *Structural Policy Challenges for Southeast Asian Countries,* OECD Publishing, Paris.

OECD. 2016. *State-owned enterprise in Asia: National Practices for Performance Evaluation and Management*, OECD Publishing, Paris.

OECD. 2017. *Disclosure and Transparency in the State-Owned Enterprise Sector in Asia: Stocktaking of National Practices*, OECD Publishing, Paris.

Painter, M. 2003. The Politics of Economic Restructuring in Vietnam: The Case of State-owned Enterprise "Reform". *Contemporary Southeast Asia*, 25(1): 20-43.

Park, J. S. & Park, S. H. 2011. Performance Evaluation and Future Task about Privatization of Public Enterprise. *Korea Institute of Public Finance report*. (In Korean)

Pham, A. 2006. The Development of Competition Law in Vietnam in the Face of Economic Reforms and Global Integration. *Northwestern Journal of International Law & Business*, 26.

Sakong, I. & Koh, Y. 2010. *The Korean Economy: Six Decades of Growth and Development*, Korea Development Institute, Seoul.

Sung, C. Y., Kim, K. C., & In, S. 2016. Small and medium-sized enterprises policy in Korea from the 1960s to the 2000s and beyond. *Small Enterprise*

Research, 23(3): 262-275.

Vu-Thanh, T. 2017. The Political Economy of Industrial Development in Viet Nam: Impact of State-Business Relationships on Industrial Performance, 1986–2013, in Page, J. & Tarp. F. eds. The Practice of Industrial Policy: Government—Business Coordination in Africa and East Asia. Oxford University Press, Oxford.

Wad, P. & Govindaraju, V.G.R.C. 2011. Automotive industry in Malaysia: an assessment of its development, *International Journal of Automotive Technology and Management*, 11(2), 152-171.

Yoo, J. 1989. The Government in Korean Economic Policy", KDI Working Paper no. 8904, Seoul: Korea Development Institute

CHAPTER FIVE:
Sustainable Welfare for Labor Market: Labor Flexibility and Employment Protection

---

Allegretto, S. A., A. Dube, and M. Reich. 2011. "Do Minimum Wages Really Reduce Teen Employment? Accounting for Heterogeneity and Selectivity in State Panel Data." *Industrial Relations*, 50(2), pp. 205-40.

Amable, Bruno and Donatella Gatti, 2004, "The Political Economy of Job Protection and Income Redistribution," IZA DP No. 1404.

Amable, Bruno, 2008. "Structural reforms in Europe and the (in) coherence of institutions," CEPREMAP Docweb No. 0809

ASEAN Secretariat, 2017. *ASEAN Statistical Yearbook* 2017. ASEAN

Bende-Nabende, A., Ford, J., and J. Slater, 2001. "FDI, Regional Economic Integration and Endogenous Growth: Some Evidence from Southeast Asia." *Pacific Economic Review*, 6(3), pp. 383-399.

BMI, 2016. Vietnam Country Report

Boeri, Tito, J. Conde-Ruiz and V. Galasso, 2003, "Protecting against Labour Market Risk: Employment Protection or Unemployment Benefits?," IZA DP No. 834.

Bonoli, Giuliano, 2003, "Social Policy through Labor Markets: Understanding National Differences in the Provision of Economic Security to Wage Earners," *Comparative Political Studies* 36(9).

Chung, Byeong-suk, 2010, *Evaluation of Korean Labour Market Policies and Suggestions for further Development: Applying Transitional Labour Market Theory*, Korea Labor Institute

Cunningham, 2017 *Vietnam future jobs,* Presentation in Hanoi

Dinh Ngoc Giang (2017) . "Công tác tuyển dụng, đào tạo cán bộ, công chức, viên chức hiện nay", *Lý luận chính trị số* 8-2016

General Statistical Office, 2017. *Báo cáo điều tra lao động việc làm* 2016 (Survey report on labor and employment 2016), Ha Noi.

General Statistical Office, 2017. *Báo cáo điều tra lao động việc làm Quý I-2017* (Survey report on labor and employment , The first quarter 2017), Ha Noi

Global Competitiveness Index 2017-2018

Jang, Jeeyeon et al., 2012. Employment Protection and Social Protection in OECD Countries, Labor Institute

Kim, Sang Joong, 2005. Labor policy in Korea, Korea Labor Institute.

Kim, Youn Sun, 2008. A Study on the Organization of Korean Trade Unions -Focusing on the analysis of the number of union members (organization rate), Korea Labor Institute.

Kwak, Sungil, Chan Kwon Bae, Jaewan Cheong, Jaeho Lee, Min Lee Shin, 2014. Study on Recent Change in Labor Market Environment in Southeast Asia and Korea's Strategies, Korea Institute for international economic policy (KIEP)

McCaig, Brian and Nina Pavcnik, 2013. "Moving Out of Agriculture: Structural Change in Vietnam." NBER Working Paper 19616. Cambridge, MA.

Ministry for Labour and Social Affairs (2017), *Report on Impact evaluation of the new Law on Social Security*, Hanoi.

Ministry of Employment and Labor, 2014, Achievements and Future Tasks of Measures for Non-regular Employees in the Public Sector.

Ministry of Employment and Labor, 2016, Assessment of Employment Improvement Measures for Non-regular Employees in the Public Sector,

MOEL, 2006. Changes in Korea's Employment Policy and Future Policy Tasks, Ministry of Employment and Labor.

MOEL, 2008. Labor Administration 2 (labor market policy), Ministry of Employment and Labor.

MOEL, 2018. Ministry of Employment and Labor 'Status of Labor Union.

Nguyen Ngoc Anh, Nguyen Than Thuong, Nguyen The Ha, Trinh Thi Thu Nga and Nguyen Van Thuy , 2015. *Labour market transitions of young women and men in Viet Nam*, ILO

Park, Jiyoung, Lee, DooWon, 2016. Research for the factors of economic development ASEAN countries and Korea with growth regression model, Journal of East and West Studies 28(2).

PPIP, 2014. 10-year evaluation and prospect of irregular labor movement in public sector, Public Policy Institute For People.

PRL, Labor Policies Outline of Labor Policies by President; http://www.pa.go.kr/research/contents/policy/index08.jsp

Schmillen, Achim, Daniel & Packard, Truman G., 2016. "Vietnam's labor market institutions, regulations, and interventions: helping people grasp work opportunities in a risky world," Policy Research Working Paper Series 7587, The World Bank.

World Economic Forum, 2017. Global Competitiveness Report (GCR)

Yang, Jae-jin, 2003. Labor Market Flexibility and the Korean Welfare State: Coping with the Mismatch between the Labor Market and the Social Welfare System, Korean Political Science Review 37(3), 2003.9, 403-428

http://www.molisa.gov.vn/vi/Pages/chitiettin.aspx?IDNews=25918 (accessed 2017.11.30.)

http://www.molisa.gov.vn/vi/Pages/chitiettin.aspx?IDNews=24744 (accessed 2017.12.10.)

http://www.molisa.gov.vn/vi/Pages/chitiettin.aspx?IDNews=27492 (accessed 2018.01.08.)

http://www.ovta.or.jp/info/asia/vietnam/07policy.html(accessed 2018. 1. 08).

Ministry of Employment and Labor .

http://www.moel.go.kr/policy/policydata/view.do?bbs_seq=1476236585978 (accessed:2018. 1. 08).

ASEAN Secretariat. http://www.asean.org/news/item/foreign-direct-investment- statistics, (Search date: 2018. 1. 07).

CEIC. http://webcdm.ceicdata.com/cdmWeb/dataManager.html?languageCode=en(Search date: 2017. 01. 05).

ILO Key Indicators of the Labour Market(KILM). (Search date: 2018. 1. 8).

ILO. NORMLEX. http://www.ilo.org/dyn/normlex/en/f?p=1000:12001:0::NO:::(Search date: 2018. 1. 7).

ILO. ILOSTAT Database. http://www.ilo.org/ilostat/faces/home/statisticaldata?locale=en%20&_afrLoop=400655678035956(Search date: 2017. 12. 16)

IMF International Financial Statistics. http://elibrary-data. imf.org/FindDataReports.aspx?d=33061&e=169393

Oxford Economics. http://www.oxfordeconomics.com/(Search date: 2017. 12. 15).

UN. http://esa.un.org/wpp/. World Population Prospects: The 2017 Revision(Search date: 2017. 10. 16).

UNESCAP. Online statistical database. www.unescap.org(Search date: 2017. 10. 24).

UNCTADSTAT. http://unctadstat.unctad.org/EN/Index.html(Search date: 2017. 11. 12).

World Bank's Entrepreneurship Survey and database. http://econ.worldbank.org/research/entrepreneurship(Search date: 2017. 11. 13).

World Bank. http://www.worldbank.org.

AUTHORS

Doowon Lee

Professor, School of Economics, Yonsei University

Vice President for International Affairs, Yonsei University

Former President, The Northeast Asia

Economic Association of Korea

Jin Park

Professor, KDI School of Public Policy and Management

President, National Assembly Futures Institute

Director, Administrative Reform Team,

Ministry of Planning and Budget

Associate fellow, Korea Development Institute

Ki Young Park

Associate Professor, School of Economics, Yonsei University

Former Assistant Professor, University

of Maryland Baltimore County

Former Economist, Bank of Korea

Yun Jeong Choi

Professor, School of Economics, Yonsei University
Member of the National Economic Advisory Council
Former Faculty, Faculty of Economics & Graduate
School of Public Policy, University of Tokyo

Ji Young Park

Instructor, School of Economics, Yonsei University
Former Research Professor, Yonsei Institute
of State Governance Studies